3 AF846106

Y LOAN

The Economics of Demand-led Growth

The Economics of Demand-led Growth

Challenging the Supply-side Vision of the Long Run

Edited by

Mark Setterfield

Associate Professor of Economics, Trinity College, Hartford, USA

Edward Elgar

Cheltenham, UK • Northampton, MA, USA

© Mark Setterfield, 2002

All rights reserved. No part of this publication may be reproduced, stored in a retrieval system or transmitted in any form or by any means, electronic, mechanical or photocopying, recording, or otherwise without the prior permission of the publisher.

Published by
Edward Elgar Publishing Limited
Glensanda House
Montpellier Parade
Cheltenham
Glos GL50 1UA
UK

Edward Elgar Publishing, Inc.
136 West Street
Suite 202
Northampton
Massachusetts 01060
USA

A catalogue record for this book
is available from the British Library

Library of Congress Cataloguing in Publication Data

The economics of demand-led growth: challenging the supply-side vision of the long run/edited by Mark Setterfield.
p.cm.
Includes bibliographical references and index.
1. Demand (Economic theory) 2. Supply-side economics. 3. Economics. 4. Economic policy. 5. Economic development. 6. United States – Economic policy. 7. United States – Economic conditions – 1945– I. Setterfield, Mark, 1967–

HB801.E28 2002
338.973 – dc21 2001051134

ISBN 1 84064 177 0

Typeset by Cambrian Typesetters, Frimley, Surrey
Printed and bound in Great Britain by Biddles Ltd, *www.biddles.co.uk*

LEEDS UNIVERSITY LIBRARY

Contents

List of figures

List of tables

List of contributors

George Argyrous	School of Social Science and Policy, University of New South Wales, Sydney, Australia
H. Sonmez Atesoglu	School of Business, Clarkson University, Potsdam, NY, USA
Robert A. Blecker	Department of Economics, American University, Washington, DC, USA
Mario Cassetti	Dipartimento di Scienze Economiche, Università Degli Studi di Brescia, Brescia, Italy
John Cornwall	Department of Economics, Dalhousie University, Halifax, NS, Canada
Joseph Halevi	Department of Economics, Université Pierre Mendès France, Grenoble, France and Political Economy, University of Sydney, Sydney, Australia
Marc Lavoie	Department of Economics, University of Ottawa, Ottawa, Canada
J.S.L. McCombie	Downing College, Cambridge University, Cambridge, England
Tracy Mott	Department of Economics, University of Denver, Denver, CO, USA
Edward J. Nell	Department of Economics, New School University, New York, NY, USA
Thomas I. Palley	Assistant Director of Public Policy, AFL/CIO, Washington, DC, USA
Pascal Petit	CEPREMAP, CNRS, Paris, France
Mark Roberts	New Hall College, Cambridge University, Cambridge, England

Mark Setterfield Department of Economics, Trinity College, Hartford, CT, USA

Luc Soete MERIT, University of Maastricht, Maastricht, The Netherlands

Réduane Taouil CEPSE, Université Pierre Mendès France, Grenoble, France

1. Introduction: a dissenter's view of the development of growth theory and the importance of demand-led growth

Mark Setterfield

Growth theory has enjoyed a somewhat chequered history in the development of economic thought, despite having been a defining feature of economic analysis during the century that followed the publication of Smith's *Wealth of Nations*. The works of Ricardo, Malthus, Mill and Marx – and even, as Nicholas Kaldor often pointed out, the early chapters of the *Wealth of Nations* itself – all attached central importance to issues of accumulation and growth. But in the wake of the late nineteenth-century marginalist revolution, with its emphasis on exchange, resource allocation and price determination, growth became a topic of secondary importance. The work of Harrod and Keynes in the 1930s revitalized interest in growth, and this interest remained central to the development of both neoclassical and Keynesian economic theory throughout the 1950s and 1960s. But growth theory is commonly believed to have lost its momentum once again thereafter. Indeed, it is now commonplace to refer to there recently having been a revival in growth theory, marked by the contributions of Romer (1986) and Lucas (1988) and the subsequent development, during the 1990s, of neoclassical endogenous growth (NEG) theory.

The alleged hiatus in growth theory during the 1970s and 1980s is, however, more apparent than real. The popularity of this idea is more representative of the overwhelming attention that has been paid to supply-side analyses of macroeconomic processes since the beginning of the classical counter-revolution, than of any genuine suspension of the development of growth theory after the late 1960s. In fact, the 1970s and 1980s witnessed some key contributions to the theory of demand-led growth – contributions on which many of the chapters in this volume seek to build. For example, Cornwall (1972) identified the reconciliation of the growth of demand with that of supply as one of the central issues in growth theory. In so doing, he rejected the neoclassical claim that demand adjusts passively to accommodate supply – so that the study of the supply side and the growth of potential output is all that is essential to growth theorists – in favour of a vision based on the Keynesian principle of effective demand.[1] For Cornwall, a central organizing principle of growth theory is 'Say's law in reverse', according to which the expansion of supply (and hence potential output) responds to the expansion of demand (and hence actual output). A central question then becomes the elasticity of this supply response with respect to the expansion of demand, upon the answer to which turns the prospects for stable growth without either ever-expanding excess capacity or excess demand.[2]

Meanwhile, Kaldor's (1970, 1972, 1981, 1985) championing of the Veblen–Myrdal notion of cumulative causation as the basis for a non-equilibrium growth theory resulted in his developing a theory of demand-determined growth in which the rate of growth of exports is the proximate determinant of income growth. The subsequent development of Kaldor's thinking (see, for example, Dixon and Thirlwall, 1975) inspired balance-of-payments-constraint growth (BPCG) theory (Thirlwall, 1979) from which Thirlwall's law – an empirically robust association between income growth, the income elasticity of demand for imports and the rate of growth of exports – emerges.[3]

The relationship between distribution and growth – central to the Kalecki-inspired Cambridge growth theory associated with, for example, Robinson (1956) – became an important constituent of the neo-Kaleckian growth models first developed during the 1970s and 1980s (see, for example, Harris, 1974, Asimakopulous, 1975, Rowthorn, 1982 and the various other contributions surveyed in Chapter 8). At the core of this literature is the question as to whether a redistribution of income away from wages and towards profits is capable of boosting growth, given the negative impact of a rising profit share of income on consumption spending, coupled with its positive impact on investment expenditures. Neo-Kaleckian models have explored the conditions necessary for growth to be either wage-led or profit-led, extending this analysis to incorporate open economy effects on growth, and to link growth dynamics with those of conflict-based inflation.[4]

During the 1970s and 1980s, demand-led growth theorists also developed a concern with the importance of the *composition* rather than simply the *amount* of demand as an influence on growth. Cornwall (1977) described growth as a process of movement through a commodity hierarchy, in which demand for the outputs of various sectors of the economy – agriculture, manufacturing and services – is characterized by a series of Engel curves which together form a 'hierarchy of commodities'.[5] The resulting transformation of the composition or structure of demand in the course of growth is shown to impact the rate of growth itself. The emergence of Transformational Growth theory (see, for example, Nell, 1992) helped to consolidate and extend these insights into the links between growth and structural change. Part of the purpose of Transformational Growth theory has been to provide a thorough account of the growth and development of demand itself in the course of capitalist history, from the earliest beginnings of the factory system through to the emergence of mass markets and the development of the modern state.[6]

It is thus possible to write a history of contemporary growth theory in which the 1970s and 1980s appear as part of a more-or-less continuous development of ideas first introduced in the 1930s by Harrod and Keynes. As intimated earlier, however, this is not how most contemporary histories of growth theory are, in fact, written. Moreover, having been overlooked in accounts of the recent development of growth theory, it is not surprising to find that contributions to demand-led growth theory have also been neglected in the period since the emergence of NEG theory. This is because NEG theory, like its neoclassical forebear the Solow model (Solow, 1956), provides a relentlessly supply-oriented account of the growth process, in which demand adjusts passively to accommodate the expansion of potential output. The most important difference between NEG theory and the Solow model is that, in the former, the marginal productivities of accumulable factors of production (such as physical capital, human capital, and new 'know-how' or technology) are bounded from below above zero. In other words, continual accumulation of these factors does not exhaust their contribution to production at the margin, so that it is possible to sustain growth through a steady process of accumulation. This is impossible in the Solow model, in which the marginal productivity of capital eventually diminishes to zero. This, in turn, rules out the possibility of sustaining growth through the continual accumulation of capital, something that is codified in one of the most famous results of the model, which suggests that changes in the propensity to save (and hence to accumulate, since saving is identical to investment in Solow) cannot affect the long-run growth rate. In NEG theory, however, anything that affects the savings rate will affect the long-run rate of growth, given the conventional neoclassical hypothesis that saving causes investment.

The essential difference between these first and second generation neoclassical growth theories, then, is the assumptions that they make about the technical properties of (accumulable) inputs into the production process. They are essentially similar, however, in their technocratic treatment of production, which pays no heed to Marx's argument that social as well as technical relations of production should always be at the forefront of any analysis of the conditions of supply. And more importantly for the purposes of this volume, the Solow model and NEG theories are similar in their treatment of growth as an essentially supply-side process. Since savings creates investment, effective demand failures are impossible, and autonomous changes in aggregate demand can only impact the utilization of resources in the short run as long as expectational errors or nominal rigidities – both of which are held to be transitory phenomena – interrupt the otherwise neutral (in terms of their impact on real variables) adjustment of prices. Meanwhile, the supply-determined potential output path of the economy – towards which the actual output path of the economy is attracted in the long run – is conventionally assumed to be independent of variations in demand and the transitory differences between actual and potential output to which these give rise. Demand is thus denied even an indirect influence on growth.[7]

The chapters in this volume rest on challenges to both of these propositions – that demand has only a transitory impact on the utilization of resources, and that the development of these resources (and hence of potential output) over time is independent of demand. In the first place, the role of demand in influencing the utilization of productive resources is understood to be chronic: there is no supply-determined equilibrium acting as a centre of gravity towards which the level of economic activity is inevitably and inexorably drawn. Instead, at *any* point in time, the utilization of existing productive resources is fundamentally demand-determined. What this, in turn, implies is that the actual output path of the economy, which describes its growth trajectory, is demand-determined. In other words, the sequence of short-run outcomes associated with the demand-determined utilization of productive resources traces out the economy's long-run growth trajectory, in a manner that is relatively autonomous of the conditions of supply defining the potential output path of the economy, which does not act as a strong attractor as in neoclassical growth theory.[8] This draws attention to an important methodological feature of demand-led growth theory, according to which the long run is understood to be an *ongoing process* (the result of which is the historical sequence of short-run outcomes alluded to above) rather than a *predefined position* towards which the economy inevitably 'tends'. This conception of the long run as a process is discussed further in Chapter 12, the focus of which is the principle of the traverse. However, it is equally obvious in the numerous chapters that make explicit use of equilibrium as an organizing concept in their discussions of long-run growth, and which either implicitly or explicitly acknowledge that what they are describing are positions of *conditional* or *provisional* equilibrium.[9] These are positions that do not possess the mechanical stability properties of conventional equilibria, and/or which may not be indefinitely reproduced over time as 'states of rest', even if the economy is able to 'get into' such a position initially (Setterfield, 1997a; Chick and Caserta, 1997).

Second, the very development of productive resources over time is influenced by demand. Supply conditions do not define the potential output path of the economy independently of the demand-determined actual output path. For example, the availability of labour is influenced by the realized level of economic activity, which can impact labour force participation rates, patterns of migration and the sectoral structure of employment (Cornwall, 1977). Capital accumulation is similarly influenced by realized output and hence demand, via accelerator effects.[10] And finally, technological change is demand-determined (and hence endogenous to the growth process), as was first recognized by Kaldor in his development of the technological progress function (Kaldor, 1957) and subsequent championing of the Verdoorn law.[11] Technical progress is induced by demand-led growth in part because of the fact that different vintages of capital embody different states of technology. Hence investment always contributes to aggregate demand, the available stock of capital *and* average productivity. Moreover, expansions of demand, by stimulating the amount of economic activity, can stimulate the amount of learning-by-doing in an economy, while the process of innovation is also influenced by demand (Schmookler, 1966; Brouwer and Kleinknecht, 1999).[12]

In sum, the natural rate of growth is ultimately endogenous to the demand-determined actual rate of growth. As discussed earlier, the natural rate is not an attractor in demand-led growth models – it does not constitute a centre of gravity towards which the economy automatically tends. Instead, by determining the potential output of the economy, the natural rate defines a ceiling to the level of economic activity at any given point in time. What we are now saying, however, is that this ceiling is not exogenously determined by supply-side forces. Rather, it is sensitive to the demand-determined actual rate of growth. The potential output path of the economy, which defines the maximum level of activity achievable at any point in time, cannot be exceeded by the actual output path. But the potential output path is elastic with respect to the actual output path, so that it is ultimately possible to speak of the former as well as the latter as being demand-led.

Note that this interaction between the actual and potential rates of growth also draws explicit attention to a second methodological feature of demand-led growth analysis, which is closely related to the first – the importance attached to the principle of path dependence. Just as any of the conditional or provisional growth equilibria described earlier may be influenced by the rate of growth actually achieved by the economy (see Chapter 12), so, too, may the potential rate of growth be influenced in the same way. From this point of view, the essence of macrodynamic analysis is to begin with the short run, and to understand the long run as a historical (path-dependent) sequence of these short-run outcomes. Whether viewed in terms of the actual rate of growth achieved or the maximum rate of growth achievable, the point is that 'the long-run trend is . . . a slowly changing component of a chain of short-period situations' (Kalecki, 1971, p. 165) rather than a preordained trajectory.

The remainder of this volume is organized into five sections. The resulting division of chapters is somewhat false, not least because the issues that are confronted in each section – such as the impact of distribution on growth, the reconciliation of the growth of demand and supply in the long run, the importance of international factors and so on – frequently overlap. Nevertheless, the division is retained because it does serve a useful organizational purpose, by grouping together chapters that are concerned with a particular facet of or approach to analysing demand-led growth.

The first section addresses Fundamental Issues in the Theory of Demand-led Growth and, in particular, the contrast between demand- and supply-led visions of the growth process, the importance of the separation of investment and saving and the empirical significance of demand-led growth. Thomas Palley examines the compatibility of short-period Keynesian analysis with long-run growth theory, arguing that central to this compatibility is the idea of an endogenous natural rate of growth that is sensitive to the evolution of aggregate demand. Palley begins by describing the Solow model, which he takes to be paradigmatic of 'old' growth theory. It is shown that this model is consistent with both new classical macroeconomics and neoclassical-synthesis Keynesianism. Each of these theories postulates that the economy progresses along a supply-determined, full employment, steady-state growth path in the absence of shocks, the occurrence of which causes transitory departures from (but has no effect on the intrinsic nature of) the trend rate of advance. However, the Solow model is not compatible with 'fundamentalist' Keynesianism, according to which the economy advances along a realized output path characterized by a sequence of demand-constrained equilibria, displaying no automatic tendency to gravitate towards a supply-determined, steady-state growth trajectory consistent with full employment.

Palley then introduces the notion of endogenous growth, according to which the long-run rate of growth is influenced by the process of accumulation. It is shown that both new classical macroeconomics and neoclassical-synthesis Keynesianism can be reconciled with endogenous growth theory. More importantly for Palley, so, too, can fundamentalist Keynesianism. This is perhaps not surprising, as Kaldor's (1957) technical progress function is identified as the progenitor of endogenous growth theory, and Kaldor's cumulative causation models (based on the recursive and self-reinforcing interaction of demand and productivity growth) anticipate NEG theory by two decades. To demonstrate his point, Palley develops a model of endogenous growth in which both the level and the rate of growth of demand enter into the determination of the long-run equilibrium growth rate. The chapter ends with a critical examination of two other models that seek to integrate demand into the analysis of long-run growth – the model of unbalanced growth developed by Cornwall and Cornwall (1994) and the BPCG model due originally to Thirwall (1979).

Joseph Halevi and Réduane Taouil identify the principle of effective demand as developed by Keynes and Kalecki as *the* major conceptual distinction between Keynesian economics on one hand, and both neoclassical and classical economics on the other. Both Keynes and Kalecki conceive capitalism as an open system, in which the level of economic activity – and its growth and fluctuations over time – are essentially indeterminate. The leading element in the analyses of both Keynes and Kalecki is investment spending, the relative autonomy of which is the proximate source of openness in their models of economic activity.

Halevi and Taouil first describe a Marxian model of accumulation, demonstrating how its results are radically altered by the introduction of effective demand considerations. The latter arise from the separation of investment and savings decisions, and the inability of increases in saving to automatically generate more investment spending. In other words, investment spending is established as an independent variable, rather than a dependent variable (dependent, specifically, upon savings) as in the Marxian model. They then discuss the treatment of investment as the determinant of the level and distribution of income in Kalecki, and as the determinant of the level of income in Keynes. In both cases, it is shown that the level of investment spending is essentially indeterminate – so that while it can be stated that there exists a causal relationship between changes in investment and changes in income, this causal relationship is not reducible to a mechanical 'law of motion' from which the evolution of income can be deduced and predicted. More specifically, fluctuations in investment cannot be reduced to foreclosed explanation in terms of supply-side variables, which would permit deterministic explanation of variations in demand and total income in terms of changes emanating from the supply side. Instead, the long run is conceived as an inter-temporal sequence of short runs, in each of which autonomous, demand-side forces are the essential determinants of the level of economic activity. Capitalism as viewed through the lens of the principle of effective demand is, therefore, an open system, in which fluctuations in and the growth of output over time are indeterminate, historical processes.

Motivated by neoclassical claims that the long-run growth of output is driven by real factors on the supply side of the economy, Sonmez Atesoglu investigates the roles of money and autonomous expenditures (including investment, government spending and exports) in determining the path of real output. Using quarterly data for the US economy from 1960–97, he first establishes that real gross domestic product (GDP), investment, government spending, exports and the M2 money supply are all integrated of order one. Atesoglu then shows that real output is cointegrated with investment, government spending, exports and the money supply, that there is bidirectional causality among real output, investment and the money supply and that there is unidirectional causality from government spending and exports to real output. In other words, there exist long-run relationships between real output and precisely the monetary and demand-side variables that are routinely overlooked in neoclassical growth theory. Moreover, there are feedback effects from real output to both investment and the money supply. These are precisely the relationships that post-Keynesian macroeconomic analysis, with its emphasis on the non-neutrality of money and the importance of aggregate demand (even in the long run), would predict. Atesoglu concludes by remarking upon the policy implication of his results, which is that demand-management can have potent effects on real output in both the short and long run.

The second section contains chapters on various Kaldorian Models of Demand-led Growth. Kaldor's development of the Veblen–Myrdal concept of cumulative causation has inspired a subsequent generation of growth theorists to consider the two-way or joint interaction between the growth of demand and supply, while his focus within the same analysis on the importance of interregional trade ultimately gave rise to contemporary BPCG theory. The chapters in this second section reflect these different facets of contemporary Kaldorian growth analysis. Mark Setterfield and John Cornwall develop a neo-Kaldorian model of growth, which is used to explain changes in the rates of growth of output and productivity in the advanced capitalist economies since the Second World War. The basic theoretical insight is that the parameters of a standard Kaldorian model of cumulative causation can be treated as being institutionally determined. Different parameter values, corresponding to different, relatively enduring 'institutional regimes' in capitalist history, can then be used to characterize different episodes of capitalist growth performance. Three such episodes are identified: the Golden Age (1945–73), the Age of Decline (1973–89) and a new growth episode in the USA during the 1990s. In each case, historically specific institutions are shown to give rise to different demand and productivity regimes, whose cumulative interaction explains differences in the growth performance of capitalist economies between different growth episodes.

The focus of the chapter by John McCombie and Mark Roberts is the importance that attaches to the growth of exports in the determination of economic growth, not just because of the direct contribution of increasing export demand to demand-led growth, but because export growth provides a basis for faster expansion of domestic demand (and hence more 'homespun' growth) without the latter resulting in balance-of-payments difficulties.[13] This result is, of course, encapsulated in Thirlwall's law, which equates the long-run rate of growth with the product of export growth and a dynamical version of the foreign trade multiplier.

McCombie and Roberts demonstrate that financial flows – which have become an increasingly significant feature of the international environment in recent decades – cannot significantly relax the BPCG rate. The claim that BPCG theory is flawed owing to a fallacy of composition is rebutted, and the criticism that Thirlwall's law is a traditional equilibrium theory of growth that does not accord with Kaldor's vision of growth as a historical process is addressed. As regards the latter, it is shown that by endogenizing the income elasticities of demand for exports and imports, the dynamics of the BPCG model can be made chaotic. This renders its growth outcomes path dependent in the sense of being highly sensitive to initial conditions. Finally, McCombie and Roberts survey recent empirical investigations of Thirlwall's law, with a particular emphasis on the ability of this law to explain the rapid rates of growth experienced in East Asia since the mid-1960s.

In a chapter that picks up from the contributions of Cornwall (1972) discussed earlier, Thomas Palley argues that an important agenda for demand-led growth theory is to model not just the rate of growth of demand, but also the rate of growth of supply and (crucially) the interaction between the two.[14] This helps render explicit the 'Say's law in reverse' property of demand-led growth models, and also draws attention to the need for the rates of growth of supply and demand to be reconciled if a growth path is to be sustainable in the long run. Palley demonstrates the importance of this latter point in the context of a BPCG model. This model is shown to be overdetermined, giving rise to two rates of growth (a rate of growth of demand and a rate of growth of supply) whose equivalence is a special case. Palley then proposes various resolutions to this problem, based on demand- or supply-side adjustments to changes in the rate of capacity utilization. For example, it is postulated that the income elasticity of demand for imports may be a negative function of excess capacity. This is because as excess capacity falls, bottlenecks in domestic industry become more prevalent, and these supply constraints increase the proportion of incremental income that is spent on imports. As a result, the rate of growth of demand that is consistent with a given rate of growth of world income (as determined by Thirlwall's law) adjusts towards the rate of growth of demand consistent with supply growth (as determined by the rate of growth of the labour force and Verdoorn's law).

The third section of the book, entitled Kaleckian Models of Demand-led Growth, builds on the Kalecki–Robinson tradition in Cambridge growth theory, according to which the rates of accumulation and profit are determined by a two-sided relationship between investment and profits. On one hand, investment determines profits through a Keynesian income-generating mechanism. On the other, profits determine investment, both by fuelling expectations of the future profitability of investment, and by influencing firms' access to finance. An important theme in this literature is the impact of changes in the distribution of income on the rates of capacity utilization and growth, a comprehensive account of which is found in the chapter by Robert Blecker. Blecker begins by developing a traditional Kaleckian growth model, which is stagnationist and exhibits wage-led growth. In other words, an increase in the profit share of income reduces capacity utilization and the rate of growth. The remainder of the chapter then shows how various extensions to and modifications of this basic model can render other results more likely. For example, Blecker shows that the possibilities of exhilarationism (an increase in the profit share raises the rate of capacity utilization) and profit-led growth (an increase in the profit share raises the rate of growth) are enhanced by modifications to the investment function which place greater emphasis on the importance of the profit share in the determination of investment plans; allowance for savings out of wages and the effects of taxation (both of which reduce the 'consumption dividend' associated with a rise in the wage share of income); and open economy effects, which render either trade flows sensitive to changes in relative prices, or capital flows sensitive to profit rate differentials across national borders. Blecker's conclusion is that while capitalist economies can be either stagnationist or exhilarationist and exhibit either wage-led or profit-led growth in principle, recent changes in fiscal policy, workers' saving behaviour and the globalization of trade and capital flows may have made exhilarationist and/or profit-led growth outcomes more likely in contemporary capitalism. One way of thinking about this result is in terms of the importance of the institutional structure of capitalism (including its policy norms) in determining the influence of distribution on growth.

A common misconception in macroeconomics is that Keynesian economics is centred on imperfections (such as wage and/or price rigidities, or expectational errors) that create demand-constrained outcomes in the short run, whereas in the long run, adjustments take place (in expectations or prices/wages) that automatically restore the economy to a position of supply-determined equilibrium. Tracy Mott addresses this misconception by using a Kaleckian model of the short run to study the impact on macroeconomic outcomes over time of changes in longer-run factors, such as the quantity and type of capital used in production, and the conditions of competition between firms. The point is to explore the possible evolution of an economy from a position of short-run equilibrium when these longer-run factors are allowed to change – the point being that the conventional conception of automatic convergence towards a supply-determined equilibrium defined independently of demand conditions is simplistic and inaccurate. Instead, Mott uses the longer-run forces named above to help explain historical developments in twentieth-century US capitalism in the context of a modified Steindl model of secular stagnation. Instead of being the temporary result of various self-correcting aberrations, then, the Keynes–Kalecki short run is revealed as being the point of departure for study of the forces that determine accumulation and growth in a capitalist economy.

The chapters by Marc Lavoie and Mario Cassetti draw attention to the potential interplay of the conflict theory of inflation and Kaleckian growth theory. Lavoie develops a mechanism, based on the conflict theory of inflation, which reconciles the actual and target rates of return in a Kaleckian growth model.[15] A standard Kaleckian growth model is first developed, exhibiting both the paradox of thrift (an increase in the propensity to save reduces the rates of profit and growth) and the paradox of costs (an increase in real wages increases the rates of profit and growth). One problem with this model is that the actual and target rates of return (and hence the actual and normal rates of capacity utilization) need not be equal in the long run. When a mechanism that causes the target rate of return to adjust towards the actual rate is introduced, this problem is solved – but at a cost. The paradox of costs disappears.

Lavoie then introduces the conflict theory of inflation, in which inflation is a function of inconsistencies in the income aspirations of workers and firms. He shows that when this model of inflation is combined with the standard Kaleckian growth model, the latter exhibits the paradox of thrift. Moreover, when a mechanism that causes the target rate of return to adjust towards the actual rate is introduced, not only are these rates of return equalized in the long run, but the rate of capacity utilization remains endogenous. This ensures that the model also exhibits the paradox of costs.

Mario Cassetti further develops this marriage of conflict inflation and Kaleckian growth theories by considering a two-way interaction between the rates of capacity utilization and growth on one hand, and the distribution of income on the other. This is done by first integrating a conflict inflation model into a Kaleckian growth model, as in the previous chapter. In the resulting model, changes in distribution can affect capacity utilization and growth, as in the standard Kaleckian model. But these changes in capacity utilization and growth are then allowed to have feedback effects on the dynamics of wage- and price-setting behaviour and hence the distribution of income, operating via their influence on the bargaining power of workers and firms.

Cassetti shows that either a positive or negative relationship between capacity utilization and the profit share can emerge, depending on whether increases in the utilization rate enhance the bargaining power of firms relative to that of workers, or vice versa. As a result, a variety of equilibrium positions can emerge, which differ according to the profit shares of income and the rates of growth and capacity utilization associated with them, depending on (among other things) whether it is the relative bargaining power of firms or workers that is enhanced by increases in the rate of capacity utilization. An extension of the model to an open economy setting reveals that the equilibrium rate of capacity utilization in a closed economy may not be sustainable in an international environment, if the resulting rate of inflation exceeds that of the rest of the world. Ruling out the possibility of continuous exchange rate depreciation, the economy is confronted with two choices: deflate, or use an incomes policy to reconcile the competing income claims of workers and firms with the constraint imposed by external inflation. Once again, the analysis recalls the potential importance of the institutional environment in conditioning the outcomes of growth dynamics.

According to Kriesler (1999, p. 401) 'the traverse is at the same time one of the most important concepts in economic theory, and also one of the most neglected'. Mark Setterfield takes up this theme in the section on Traverse Analysis and Demand-led Growth, arguing that, despite being one of few Hicksian concepts to have languished in obscurity, the principle of the traverse is suggestive of a general method suitable for all macrodynamic analysis. He applies this idea to Kaldorian growth theory, reinterpreting Kaldor's cumulative growth schema as a traverse towards a steady state. The conditions and hence position of the latter are, however, shown to be sensitive to the traverse path itself. What emerges is a model of long-run growth that nests medium-term episodes of cumulative causation within growth 'regimes', the structure of which is endogenous to the economy's past growth performance. The way in which this endogeneity – and hence the economy's path dependence – is modelled involves systemic openness and novelty, giving rise to what is described as evolutionary hysteresis. Ultimately, the model both extends Kaldorian growth analysis by allowing for endogenous changes in relative growth rates, and suggests an analytical framework that, because of its faithfulness to Kaldor's emphasis on historical process, may be conducive to the further development of Kaldorian growth theory.

Each of the chapters in the final section on Structural Change and Demand-led Growth draws attention to the fact that growth involves not just the expansion of demand and productive capacity in the aggregate, but also changes in what is produced, how it is produced and for whom. These changes in the composition or structure of economic activity are, at once, influences on and influenced by the rate of growth in the aggregate, with which most growth analysis is, of course, solely preoccupied. George Argyrous notes that, although demand is a lead element in the growth process according to some economists, little attention has been devoted to theorizing the historical evolution of aggregate demand itself. Transformational growth theory, however, provides just such a historically based account of the evolution of demand, and the primary purpose of Argyrous's chapter is to outline this account.

Three key processes are identified as having been instrumental in the emergence and subsequent growth and development of mass markets in contemporary capitalism: the initial creation of a wage-labour (and hence non-self-sufficient) class; the productivity-enhancing (and therefore cost- and price-reducing) effects of industrial mass production; and changes in the composition of demand as personal incomes have grown. These developments in the market for *consumer* goods are then shown to stimulate the growth of demand for *investment* goods, as production itself is transformed in response to the transformational growth of consumer demand. This, in turn, further enhances the development of the mass market for consumer goods, the result being a cumulatively self-reinforcing process of growth in the demand for consumer and investment goods. Argyrous notes, however, that although industrial production and mass consumer markets have been subject to a virtuous circle of self-reinforcing growth in the past, their further growth and development is not inevitable. Instead, endogenously generated obstacles to growth – such as short-run limits to production in the capital goods sector, distributional effects or the increasing tertiarisation of the economy – may ultimately inhibit the growth process.

The chapter by Edward Nell returns to Argyrous's theme that theorizing the growth of demand is an important but underdeveloped pursuit in economics. Despite the fact that firms require an expansion of demand if they are to realize profits from the production of additional goods and services, most long-run macroeconomic theory simply assumes that demand responds passively to supply, so that the expansion of the latter is all that is of interest to growth theorists. Meanwhile, Nell argues that even theories that purport to take demand seriously in the long run – such as the Harrod–Domar and Cambridge growth models – are deficient in their treatment of demand.

Based on a critique of Lancaster's (1966) 'characteristics' theory of consumption, Nell develops a theory of the transformational growth of demand in which social pressures result in a demand for self-improvement which is, in turn, associated with both the growth of productivity and consumer demand. Particular attention is paid to the relationship between self-improvement and the emergence of new markets (especially for services such as education and communications), which is identified as the *sine qua non* of sustained growth. A model of this process is used to shed light on the incentive to introduce new technology that is labour saving but capital using – a tendency that has been an enduring feature of capitalist economies. Furthermore, education and communications are identified as *collective goods* – goods that are not consumed individually (like ice-creams or sweaters) but by networks of users, thus creating interdependencies between consumers. Nell argues that the need to coordinate consumers of collective goods and to capture the network externalities associated with them enhances the role of the state, so that as an economy develops and the importance of collective goods increases, there is a tendency for government spending to increase as a proportion of total income. This expansion of the government sector further contributes to the expansion of markets set in motion by the quest for self-improvement, thus itself contributing to the processes by which growth in developed economies is sustained.

The interplay between patterns of consumer demand, productivity and the importance of networked activities brought to light in Nell's chapter provides the central focus of the final chapter in this volume, by Pascal Petit and Luc

Soete. Petit and Soete begin by identifying three stylized facts associated with the current growth episode in capitalist economies – an increase in income inequality, skill-biased technological change in the workplace and polarization in the consumption of quality improvements in consumer goods – positing that these stylized facts are causally linked in a self-reinforcing process of cumulative causation. It is recognized that transitions between growth episodes are lengthy, so that the trends described above may be transitory effects of the slow diffusion of new information and communication technologies (ICTs) embodied in producer and consumer goods. But Petit and Soete argue that the potential exists for these trends to interact cumulatively and thereby influence long-run growth outcomes. In this scenario, a group of sophisticated consumers use their high incomes, human capital and access to intermediation services to create markets for 'high-tech', high-value-added output, in the production of which their skills and abilities to use intermediation services are also essential. Their consumption and production activities are thus mutually self-reinforcing – as are those of a group of less sophisticated, lower-income consumer/workers, who are simultaneously engaged in less technologically intensive and less remunerative production and consumption activities. This threatens to create a segmented or dualistic society that is less socially cohesive than the more economically unified Fordist growth regime, associated with the postwar (1945–73) Golden Age of capitalist growth. Moreover, the segmentation or dualism in patterns of consumption and production, by limiting the diffusion of and positive externalities associated with ICTs on both the demand and supply sides, threatens to inhibit the growth-enhancing potential of current technological change. Petit and Soete end with a review of the debates on skill-biased technological change and the mismeasurement of the consumer price index, designed to highlight some of the most significant connections between technology, learning and patterns of production and consumption.

NOTES

1. See also Chapters 2 and 3.
2. These issues are taken up in Chapter 7.
3. See McCombie and Thirlwall (1994) and Chapters 5–7 and 12 for further discussion of these various strands of Kaldorian growth theory.
4. Chapters 8–11 are illustrative of these developments.
5. See also Pasinetti (1981) and Petit (1986) for discussions of the importance for growth of economic structure, and Cornwall and Cornwall (1994) for a more recent exposition of the ideas described above.
6. Chapters 13–15 discuss the relationship between demand-led growth and economic structure, including the structure of demand itself.
7. In fairness, it should be noted that some neoclassical analyses do entertain the possibility that short-run variations in aggregate demand can affect the economy's potential output path

and hence long-run rate of growth (see, for example, Blackburn 1999). But this hypothesis is strictly peripheral to the core of neoclassical growth theory, which claims that long-run growth is determined by factors on the supply side of the economy. There is certainly no truth to the suggestion that aggregate demand is viewed as a necessary constituent of growth analysis in neoclassical theory. This is, however, precisely the view held by advocates of demand-led growth theory.

8. It may be objected that, by defining the economy's potential output at any point in time, the conditions of supply define a 'ceiling' below which the actual output path described above must lie. But this ceiling concept merely serves to draw attention to the general importance of effective demand failures in demand-led growth theory, as a result of which the economy is normally expected to suffer a shortage of demand relative to potential supply. Moreover, the potential output path of the economy is not independent of its actual output path, as will become clear below.
9. See, for example, the chapters by Setterfield and Cornwall, Blecker, Mott, Lavoie and Cassetti.
10. See the chapter by Blecker in this volume for a survey of different investment functions embodying this principle.
11. Chapters 2, 5, 7 and 12 all make use of Kaldor's notion of endogenous technical progress. See also McCombie and Thirlwall (1994, p. 464) for a demonstration of the relationship between Kaldor's technical progress function and the Verdoorn law.
12. See Boyer and Petit (1991) and Setterfield (1997b, pp. 48–50) for further discussion of the sources of demand-led technical change.
13. McCombie and Robert's chapter is based on their 'Demand and economic growth from a Kaldorian perspective', *Review of Political Economy*, 15, forthcoming (http://www.tandf.co.uk).
14. Palley's chapter is reprinted from the *Review of Political Economy*, 15, forthcoming (http://www.tandf.co.uk).
15. Lavoie's chapter is based on his 'Kaleckian effective demand and Sraffian normal prices: towards a reconciliation', *Review of Political Economy*, 15, forthcoming (http://www.tandf.co.uk).

REFERENCES

Asimakopulous, A. (1975) 'A Kaleckian theory of income distribution', *Canadian Journal of Economics*, 8, 313–33.

Blackburn, K. (1999) 'Can stabilisation policy reduce long-run growth?' *Economic Journal*, 109, 67–77.

Boyer, R. and P. Petit (1991) 'Kaldor's growth theories: past, present and prospects for the future', in E.J. Nell and W. Semmeler (eds) *Nicholas Kaldor and Mainstream Economics*, New York, St. Martin's Press, 485–517.

Brouwer, E. and A. Kleinknecht (1999) 'Keynes-plus? Effective demand and changes in firm-level R&D: an empirical note', *Cambridge Journal of Economics*, 23, 385–99 .

Chick, V. and M. Caserta (1997) 'Provisional equilibrium in macroeconomic theory', in P. Arestis, G. Palma and M. Sawyer (eds) *Markets, Unemployment and Economic Policy: Essays in Honour of Geoff Harcourt*, Vol. II, London, Routledge pp. 223–47.

Cornwall, J. (1972) *Growth and Stability in a Mature Economy*, London, Martin Robertson.

Cornwall. J. (1977) *Modern Capitalism: Its Growth and Transformation*, London, Martin Robertson.

Cornwall, J. and W. Cornwall (1994) 'Growth theory and economic structure', *Economica*, 61, 237–51.
Dixon, R. and A.P. Thirlwall (1975) 'A model of regional growth rate differences along Kaldorian lines', *Oxford Economic Papers*, 27, 201–14.
Harris, D. (1974) 'The price policy of firms, the level of employment and distribution of income in the short run', *Australian Economic Papers*, 13, 144–51.
Kaldor, N. (1957) 'A model of economic growth', *Economic Journal*, 67, 591–624.
Kaldor, N. (1970) 'The case for regional policies', *Scottish Journal of Political Economy*, 18, 337–48.
Kaldor, N. (1972) 'The irrelevance of equilibrium economics', *The Economic Journal*, 82, 1237–55.
Kaldor, N. (1981) 'The role of increasing returns, technical progress and cumulative causation in the theory of international trade and growth', *Économie Appliquée*, 34, 593–617.
Kaldor, N. (1985) *Economics Without Equilibrium*, Cardiff, University College Cardiff Press.
Kalecki, M. (1971) 'Trend and the business cycle', in *Selected Essays on the Dynamics of a Capitalist Economy, 1933–1970*, Cambridge, Cambridge University Press.
Kriesler, P. (1999) 'Harcourt, Hicks and Lowe: incompatible bedfellows?' in C. Sardoni and P. Kriesler (eds) *Themes in Political Economy: Essays in Honour of Geoff Harcourt*, London, Routledge, pp. 400–417.
Lancaster, K. (1966) 'A new approach to consumer theory', *Journal of Political Economy*, 74, 132–57.
Lucas, R.E. (1988) 'On the mechanics of economic development', *Journal of Monetary Economics*, 22, 3–42.
McCombie, J.S.L. and A.P. Thirlwall (1994) *Economic Growth and the Balance of Payments Constraint*, London, Macmillan.
Nell, E.J. (1992) *Transformational Growth and Effective Demand*, London, Macmillan.
Pasinetti, L. (1981) *Structural Change and Economic Growth: A Theoretical Essay on the Dynamics of the Wealth of Nations*, Cambridge, Cambridge University Press.
Petit, P. (1986) *Slow Growth and the Service Economy*, New York, St. Martin's Press.
Robinson, J. (1956) *The Accumulation of Capital*, London, Macmillan.
Romer, P. (1986) 'Increasing returns and long-run growth', *Journal of Political Economy*, 94, 1002–37.
Rowthorn, R.E. (1982) 'Demand, real wages and economic growth', *Studi Economici*, 18, 3–53.
Schmookler, J. (1966) *Innovation and Economic Growth*, Cambridge, MA, Harvard University Press.
Setterfield, M. (1997a) 'Should economists dispense with the notion of equilibrium?' *Journal of Post Keynesian Economics*, 20, 47–76.
Setterfield, M. (1997b) *Rapid Growth and Relative Decline: Modelling Macroeconomic Dynamics with Hysteresis*, London, Macmillan.
Solow, R. (1956) 'A contribution to the theory of economic growth', *Quarterly Journal of Economics*, 70, 65–94.
Thirlwall, A.P. (1979) 'The balance of payments constraint as an explanation of international growth rate differences', *Banca Nazionale Del Lavoro Quarterly Review*, 128, 45–53.

PART ONE

Fundamental Issues in the Theory of Demand-led Growth

2. Keynesian macroeconomics and the theory of economic growth: putting aggregate demand back in the picture

Thomas I. Palley

INTRODUCTION

Keynesian macroeconomics, which dominated the economics profession from World War II through to the mid-1970s, emphasized the significance of the level of aggregate demand for the determination of the level of economic activity. Yet, when it came to constructing a theory of growth, the effect of aggregate demand was visibly absent. This absence created a significant internal inconsistency that likely contributed to the decline of the Keynesian paradigm. In stark contrast, new classical macroeconomics, which came to supersede Keynesian macroeconomics as the dominant paradigm in the mid-1970s, was consistent with growth theory. This consistency promoted its rise.

Over the last decade, there has emerged a new 'endogenous' growth theory that breaks with the earlier 'old' growth theory by making the steady-state growth rate endogenous to the system. This chapter uses a simple analytical framework predicated on the familiar distinction between potential and actual output to frame the relation between growth theory and macroeconomics. The framework is then used to explore the relation between growth theory, new classical macroeconomics, neo-Keynesian macroeconomics and Keynesian macroeconomics. Whereas old growth theory was deeply inconsistent with Keynesian macroeconomics and its emphasis on aggregate demand, new endogenous growth theory is not. Growth theory can therefore now be rendered consistent with Keynesian macroeconomics. This is a significant advance in the reconstruction of a consistent Keynesian paradigm.

OLD GROWTH THEORY

The Solow (1956) neoclassical growth model represents the paradigmatic model of old growth theory. The most important feature of the model is that the steady-state growth rate depends exclusively on the rates of population growth and labour augmenting technical technical progress, and as long as these variables are exogenous, steady-state growth is also exogenous.

Figure 2.1 illustrates the path of potential gross domestic product (PGDP) as described by the Solow growth model.[1] The vertical axis plots the natural logarithm of output, while the horizontal axis plots time. The slope of the PGDP line represents the rate of growth of potential output, and is given by:

$$g_y = n + a \qquad [2.1]$$

where g_y is the rate of growth of output, n is the rate of population growth and a is the rate of labour-augmenting technical progress. Within this model, the level of potential output can be raised by increasing the rate of capital accumulation (that is, the savings rate), but the steady-state rate of output growth remains unchanged. This is illustrated in Figure 2.1 by the shifting-up of the PGDP line at time t_0. The increase in the capital stock per worker, caused by

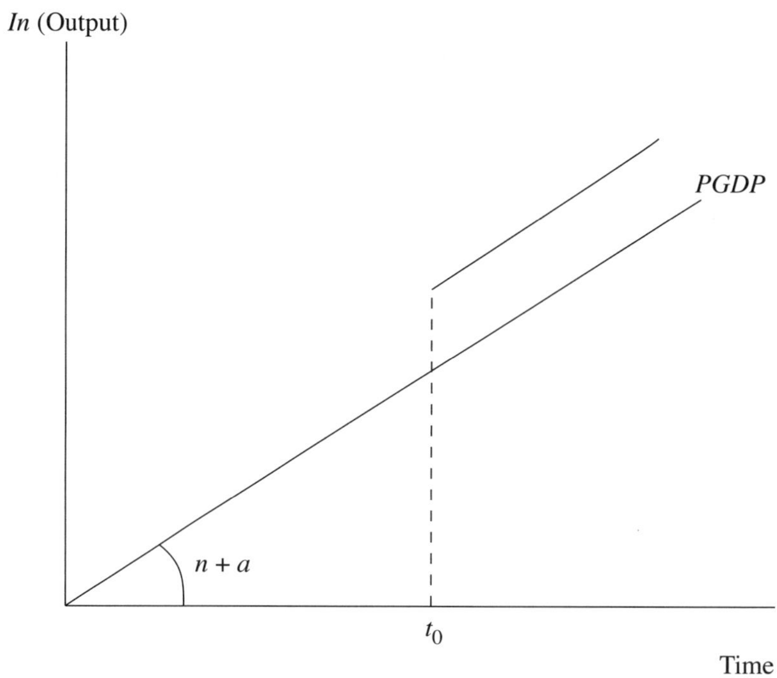

Figure 2.1 The evolution of potential output, and the effect of an increase in the capital–labour ratio in the Solow growth model

PGDP - Potential GDP.

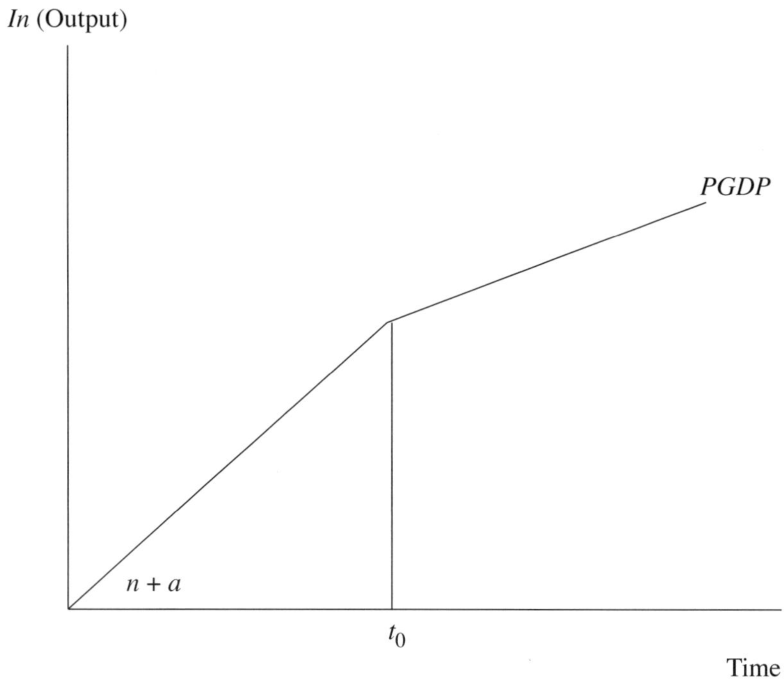

Figure 2.2 The effect on the evolution of potential output of an exogenous change in the rate of labour augmenting technical progress

increased saving, increases the level of PGDP. However, the growth rate, which is given by the slope of the PGDP line, remains unchanged.

The effect of a change in the trend rate of growth is illustrated in Figure 2.2, in which the PGDP line is kinked at time t_0. In this instance, the trend rate of growth is shown as falling, since the slope of the PGDP line falls. This is how the Solow model would represent the productivity growth slowdown which afflicted the USA in the 25-year period after 1973. The slowdown is seen as the product of an exogenous decrease in the rate of labour-augmenting technical progress. Those who argue that the USA has become characterized by a 'new economy' in the 1990s would argue that the productivity growth slowdown has reversed itself, and the slope of the PGDP line has steepened and reverted to its earlier slope.

The rate of potential output growth can also be made to exhibit variability by adding a random error term to equation [2.1], which becomes:

$$g_{yt} = n + a + e_t \qquad [2.1']$$

where e_t represents white noise. The expected rate of potential output growth is exogenous, given by:

$$E_t[g_y] = n + a \qquad [2.2]$$

In terms of Figure 2.1, the PGDP line now represents the expected PGDP line, and its slope is the expected rate of potential output growth. Actual potential GDP randomly fluctuates around the expected PGDP line.

The Solow growth model embodies the core features of the neoclassical paradigm. However, it lacks any concern with monetary factors, and the real interest rate is determined exclusively by real factors, being equal to the marginal product of capital. Tobin (1965) expanded the scope of the model by incorporating money and portfolio considerations. The motivation behind this step was to show how the inclusion of money and portfolio choices affected the steady-state interest rate and capital–labour ratio. In making this change, Tobin incorporated the Keynesian liquidity preference theory of interest rates into neoclassical growth theory, thereby making Keynesian monetary theory relevant for long-run economics.[2]

However, though incorporating monetary factors, Tobin's amendments to the Solow model do not endogenize steady-state growth, and nor do they change the exclusively supply-determined nature of growth. Thus, in the Tobin model, growth is still determined by the exogenously given rates of population growth and technical progress, and the growth path (potential and actual) remains as in Figure 2.1. Increases in the rate of nominal money supply growth have an affect akin to an increase in the saving rate in the Solow model. They therefore cause the PGDP line to shift up, but do not alter its slope. The logic is that faster money supply growth causes higher steady-state inflation, and this causes a portfolio shift away from money holdings towards holdings of real capital, thereby raising the steady-state capital–labour ratio and raising PGDP.

Moreover, as in the Solow model, capital accumulation continues to be driven by household savings behaviour rather than firms' investment spending, so that saving drives investment. In these regards, Tobin's monetary growth model remains similar to the Solow model, and both models are severely non-Keynesian, owing to their neglect of demand-side influences on growth.

OLD GROWTH THEORY AND NEW CLASSICAL MACROECONOMICS

The analytical framework above can be used to illustrate the relationship between short-run macroeconomics and growth theory. Neoclassical growth

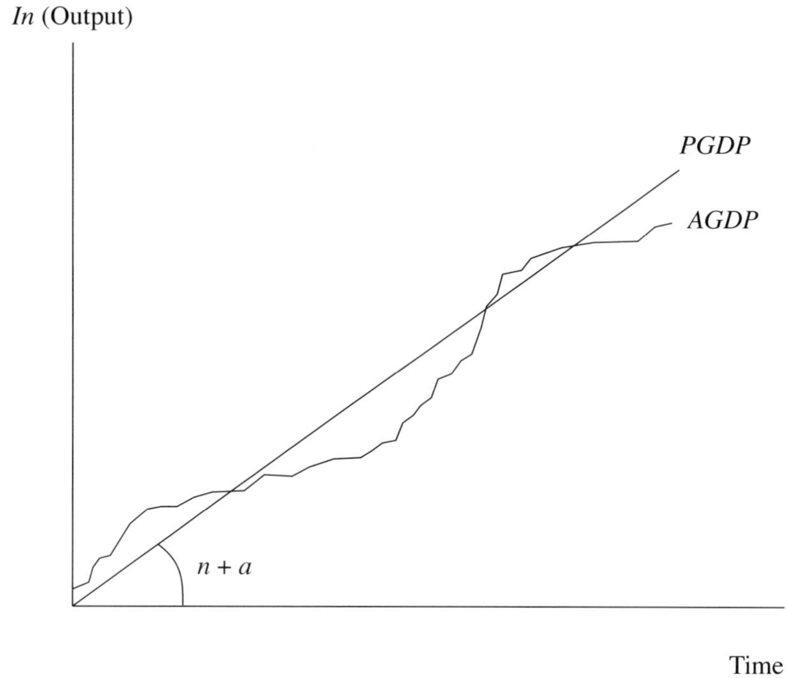

Figure 2.3 The relationship between potential and actual output

theory is fully consistent with new classical equilibrium business cycle models, such as those developed by Lucas (1975) and Long and Plosser (1983). In both cases, actual output (AGDP) fluctuates around the PGDP line as shown in Figure 2.3. In the Lucas (1975) model, these fluctuations are due to monetary surprises, and the speed of return of AGDP to PGDP depends on the degree of persistence of the shocks. Such persistence derives from capital stock effects. Positive monetary surprises induce overinvestment, which then keeps AGDP above PGDP until the excess capital has been depreciated away. The reverse holds for negative monetary surprises. The size of AGDP fluctuations around PGDP depends on the size of monetary surprises. The noisier monetary policy is, the noisier the path of AGDP around PGDP. Figure 2.3 also captures Long and Plosser's (1983) real business cycle model, only now the fluctuations in AGDP are due to temporary technology shocks that impact the aggregate production function.

The underlying consistency between new classical macroeconomics and neoclassical growth theory derives from the fact that both adopt a competitive equilibrium approach to economics. Growth in the Solow model takes place along a full employment path, factor markets clear and factors are paid their marginal products. The same considerations apply to new classical macroeconomics, only now there is room for temporary departures from equilibrium owing either to monetary surprises which confound expectations, or to technology shocks that work their way through the system gradually, owing to convex costs of adjustments.

OLD GROWTH THEORY AND KEYNESIAN MACROECONOMICS

Whereas the theoretical relationship between new classical macroeconomics and old growth theory is clear, the relationship between old growth theory and Keynesian macroeconomics is less so. Here, there is a need to distinguish between 'fundamentalist' Keynesian macroeconomics and neo-Keynesian macroeconomics. Whereas the latter is consistent with old growth theory, the former is not.

From a neo-Keynesian perspective, the PGDP line in Figure 2.3 represents potential output, and its slope corresponds to the natural rate of output growth. The PGDP line describes the long-run evolution of output, and is constructed on the basis of the neoclassical growth model. The evolution of output continues to be represented by AGDP, which wanders around PGDP, but now the level of AGDP is determined according to the principles of neo-Keynesian macroeconomics as reflected in models such as the IS–LM framework. Thus, negative shocks to the level of aggregate demand decrease the level of AGDP, with the gap between PGDP and AGDP corresponding to the 'Okun gap'.

What is the relationship between AGDP and PGDP? Neo-Keynesian macroeconomics interprets the path of AGDP in terms of a disequilibrium process. This interpretation dates back to Modigliani's (1944) extension of the IS–LM model to include a labour market, in which nominal wage rigidity blocks off the Keynes and Pigou effects, thereby preventing an instantaneous return to full employment. This disequilibrium approach was rigorously formalized in the general disequilibrium literature associated with Clower (1965), Barro and Grossman (1971) and Malinvaud (1977). According to the neo-Keynesian disequilibrium perspective, frictions in the process of price and nominal wage adjustment mean that economies can temporarily get stuck below potential output. However, over time, prices and nominal wages are flexible, and this allows AGDP to gradually drift back to PGDP.

Within the neo-Keynesian framework, the PGDP line therefore represents a centre of gravitation and actual output eventually converges back to potential. The role of monetary and fiscal stabilization policy is to stabilize the path of actual output around potential output by minimizing fluctuations in aggregate demand. If actual output is subject to a large negative demand shock, monetary and fiscal policy can speed up the process of adjustment.

New Keynesian macroeconomics elaborates on this interpretation, and seeks to provide a microeconomic justification for the neo-Keynesian assumption of downward stickiness of prices and nominal wages. Mankiw (1985) explains such stickiness in terms of menu costs. An alternative explanation relies on the kinked nature of firms' demand curves, and emphasizes informational and strategic considerations that provide firms with an incentive not to change prices (Woglom, 1982).[3]

Another question concerns whether recessions have permanent effects on either the level or growth of potential output. Within the neo-Keynesian framework, the answer is no. Recessions (large Okun gaps) are characterized by reductions in the level of investment spending, and this lowers the rate of growth of the capital stock. If the reduction in investment spending were permanent, the economy would shift to an output trajectory with a lower equilibrium capital–labour ratio. However, once it had reached the new equilibrium, output would continue to grow at the exogenously given natural rate. This follows from the logic of the Solow growth model.

The microeconomics of marginal productivity theory, which underpin both the neo-classical growth model and the neo-Keynesian macro model, also dictate that there is a unique capital–labour ratio that is jointly determined by the rate of time preference and the natural rate of growth (Sidrauski, 1967). Thus, investment spending must ultimately recover all the ground lost in the recession, such that the steady-state equilibrium interest rate is:

$$r = f_k - d = n + a + s \qquad [2.3]$$

where r denotes the real interest rate, f_k is the marginal product of capital, d is the rate of depreciation and s the rate of time preference. This means that the steady-state capital–labour ratio and the level of potential output are both unchanged by recessions.

In sum, within the neo-Keynesian construction of the macro-growth bridge, the effects of recessions are temporary. Though recessions are costly, in that they cause a 'flow' loss of output that is never recovered, they leave behind no permanent mark in the form of a permanently lower capital stock per worker, a permanently lower potential output per worker or a permanently changed rate of potential output growth.

Whereas neo-Keynesian economics can be rendered consistent with old growth theory, the same is not true of fundamentalist Keynesian macroeconomics. Keynes (1936) argued that economies can get stuck at equilibria with less than full employment because of a persistent shortage of aggregate demand. A fundamentalist Keynesian perspective therefore has economies characterized by a continuum of possible 'demand-determined' equilibria. This contrasts with the neoclassical 'supply-constrained' conception of equilibrium, according to which there exists a unique full employment level of output that is determined by constraints on the supply side of the economy.[4] The important implication is that from a fundamentalist Keynesian perspective, the AGDP line in Figure 2.3 itself represents an equilibrium outcome, and the PGDP line is not a centre of gravity.

Fundamentalist Keynesian macroeconomics also challenges the sticky-price construction of macroeconomics, on the grounds that price adjustments may be destabilizing. One line of argument emphasizes the Fisher (1933) debt effect. The logic of this effect is that if debtors have a higher marginal propensity to consume than creditors do, reductions in the price level can reduce aggregate demand owing to the existence of inside debt. This is because lower prices raise the burden of debt, and make creditors wealthier at the expense of debtors. Consequently, the resultant decrease in spending by debtors exceeds the increase in spending by creditors. A second line of argument is the Mundell (1963)–Tobin (1965) effect, whereby price deflation makes monetary assets relatively more attractive. This promotes a portfolio shift into money which raises real interest rates, thereby reducing investment spending and aggregate demand. These arguments challenge the claim that price adjustment can restore full employment.

From a growth theoretic perspective, this fundamentalist Keynesian critique raises a number of issues. First, if points on the AGDP line can be points of steady-state equilibrium, what determines the steady-state growth rate (that is, the slope of the AGDP line)? Second, the possibility that the AGDP growth rate may differ from the PGDP growth rate implies that the scale of the Okun gap (the amount of excess capacity) may matter for the growth rate. Keynes, of course, had nothing to say about these issues in *The General Theory*, which was a tract on the determination of the *level* of output rather than the *rate of growth*.

NEW ENDOGENOUS GROWTH THEORY

Whereas the steady-state rate of growth is exogenously determined in the 'old' Solow growth model, new endogenous growth theory introduces a range of mechanisms that render steady-state growth subject to endogenous variation. These mechanisms involve respecifying the process generating technical change so as to allow it to depend on the decisions of economic agents.

Within endogenous growth models the rate of growth is given by:

$$g_y = n + a(x) \qquad a' > 0 \tag{2.4}$$

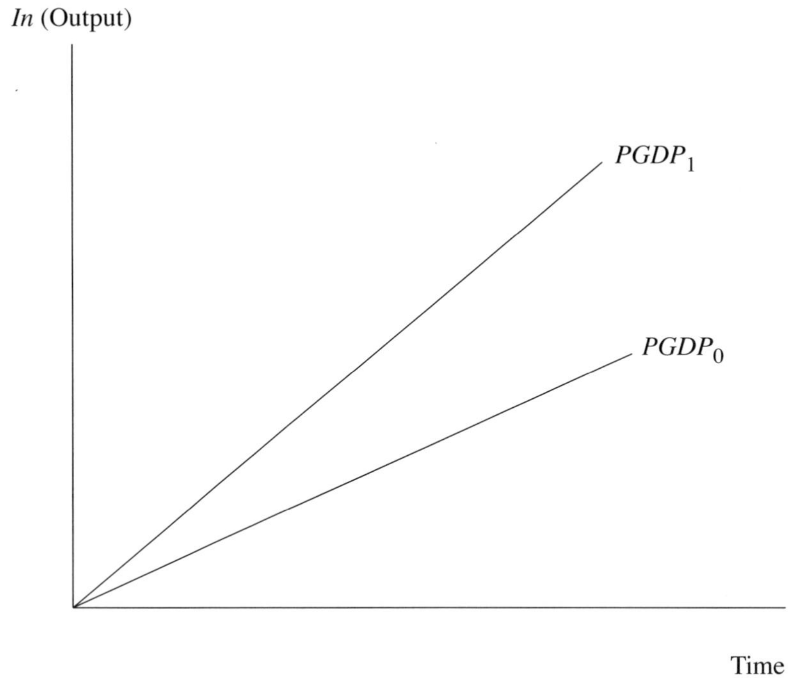

Figure 2.4 Alternative paths of potential output in an endogenous growth model

where x is a vector of choice variables positively affecting the rate of labour-augmenting technical progress. The endogenous growth approach is illustrated in Figure 2.4, in which the line denoted PDGP_0 corresponds to $x = x_0$, and the line PGDP_1 corresponds to $x = x_1$. There are now a continuum of possible growth paths, each of which is contingent on the particular selection of x.

Within the USA, endogenous growth theory has emphasized knowledge and human capital formation, and the steady-state rate of growth is therefore affected by choices, policies and institutions affecting knowledge and human capital acquisition. Endogenous growth emerges when the aggregate stock of human capital is allowed to have an external effect on the rate of technical change, as in Romer (1990). Human capital is therefore identified as the 'x' variable.

The British variant of endogenous growth emphasizes investment in physical capital. Drawing on a line of reasoning pioneered by Kaldor (1957) and Kaldor and Mirrlees (1961/2), Scott (1989) suggests that endogenous growth operates through the effects of investment spending on the flow rate of technological innovation.[5] Technical progress is therefore both 'revealed' and 'realized' through investment, so that investment serves simultaneously as the means of expanding the capital stock, feeding technical innovations into the production process and uncovering further possibilities for innovation. Expanding the capital stock is the traditional 'old growth' interpretation of investment. Feeding innovations into the capital stock is the 'vintage' approach to investment. Uncovering new possibilities for further technical advances is the endogenous growth interpretation of investment.

The notion of endogenous growth can be captured through the following specification of the technical progress function (Palley, 1996b):

$$a = Ak^{b}I^{c} \qquad A > 0 \qquad [2.5]$$

Equation [2.5] determines the rate of labour-augmenting technical progress, which is a positive function of the capital–labour ratio and the level of investment spending per worker. Nested within [2.5] is the standard case of exogenous technical progress, which occurs if $b = c = 0$. If $b = 0$, then only the 'flow' of investment spending per worker affects the rate of technical advance. If $c = 0$, only the current 'stock' of capital per worker has an effect.[6]

Equation [2.5] is a reduced form specification. The microeconomics of why investment spending affects the rate of technical advance are detailed in Scott (1989). From a policy standpoint, the important implication is that the rate of technical progress can be influenced by policies that affect either the capital stock per worker, or the flow of investment per worker.

Exactly the same considerations apply for representative agent, choice theoretic endogenous growth models that rely on knowledge and R&D expenditures (for example, Romer, 1990). In these models, research and development (R&D) spending affects the growth rate, and policies or institutional arrangements that affect R&D spending therefore affect the equilibrium growth rate. Such models implicitly embody a Kaldorian technical progress function in which the symbols k and I are replaced by the stock and flow of R&D. This reveals Kaldor (1957) to be the progenitor of endogenous growth theory.

Equation [2.5] also sheds light on the issues of cumulative causation and the cross-country convergence of growth rates. If the rate of technical progress is positively affected by the capital stock and the level of investment spending per worker, then countries with larger capital stocks and greater investment spending per worker will have faster growth rates. Both channels promote cumulative causation, since the flow of investment spending tends to be positively related to the capital stock. Accumulation of capital therefore accelerates the growth process, and this explains why capital-abundant countries have had historically rising growth rates. It can also help explain why cross-country growth rates have diverged, with the gap between capital-abundant and capital-scarce countries growing over time.

The divergence in growth rates between capital-abundant (developed) and capital-scarce (undeveloped) countries would be further compounded if there are positive externalities in firms' production functions. This could occur if the productivity of firms' private capital stocks is positively impacted by the aggregate capital stock. The effect would be to promote de-industrialization in capital-scarce countries, as firms would have an incentive to locate in capital-abundant countries where the private marginal product of capital is higher owing to the positive externality. In this fashion, the technological progress function in [2.5] can help explain a range of puzzles regarding the pattern of cross-country growth and development.

MACROECONOMIC IMPLICATIONS OF ENDOGENOUS GROWTH THEORY

Rendering the rate of labour-augmenting technical progress endogenous makes the rate of potential output growth endogenous. This is a development that can be readily incorporated into old neoclassical growth models (Palley, 1996b). In the earlier old growth models (Tobin, 1965), monetary and fiscal policies could be used to affect the flow of investment spending and the steady-state capital–labour ratio, but the steady-state growth rate was unaffected. Now, these same instruments also affect the growth rate.

New Classical Macroeconomics and New Growth Theory

New classical macroeconomics was always consistent with old growth theory, and it is also consistent with new endogenous growth theory. The latter continues to use a competitive equilibrium framework to determine the steady-state growth path, and new classical macroeconomics shares this approach. Thus, a Lucas (1975) monetary surprise mechanism can be included by making the level of investment spending a positive function of the gap between the actual and expected money supply. This would then generate a monetary surprise business cycle, in which AGDP fluctuates around the endogenously determined path of PGDP. Similarly, real business cycle effects can be introduced by having temporary technology shocks that impact the production function. The only difference from the earlier synthesis between old growth theory and new classical macroeconomics is that business cycle fluctuations will now take place around the particular growth path that the economy is locked into as a result of choice of the vector of factors (x) affecting the growth rate.

The new growth framework also introduces a distinction between short-run macroeconomic policy and long-run growth policy. The conduct of optimal short-run macroeconomic policy remains unchanged, and policy should be directed to minimizing the extent of fluctuations around the given growth path by keeping monetary surprises to a minimum. Long-run growth policy should be directed to ensuring that the economy is placed on a Pareto optimal growth path. If the growth process depends positively on externalities generated by the stock of capital (be it physical, human or intellectual), *laissez-faire* is suboptimal, since private agents do not internalize these externalities. This opens a role for government subsidies to encourage private acquisition of capital.

Fundamentalist Keynesian Macroeconomics and New Growth Theory

Whereas old growth theory was deeply inconsistent with fundamentalist Keynesian macroeconomics, new endogenous growth theory offers the prospect of reconciliation. In equation [2.5], growth depends on the flow of investment spending. This dependence, in turn, provides a channel whereby demand considerations can enter the growth process. This is illustrated in Figure 2.5. Demand conditions affect investment spending, which, in turn, affects the rate of labour-augmenting technical progress. This then affects the rate of output growth, which feeds back on demand growth. Traditional Keynesian policy interventions can therefore affect the growth process either by directly impacting investment spending, or by impacting demand conditions.

The Keynesian framework for growth suggested above is captured in the following model, taken from Palley (1996c):

$$I = z(g^d, E) \qquad z_{gd} > 0 \; z_E > 0 \tag{2.6.1}$$

$$\dot{k} = I - [d + n + a]k \tag{2.6.2}$$

$$g_y = n + a + s_k \dot{k}/k \tag{2.6.3}$$

$$a = a(k, I) \qquad a_k > 0, \; a_{gd} > 0, \; a_E > 0 \tag{2.6.4}$$

$$\dot{g}^d = G(g_y / g^d) \qquad G' > 0 \tag{2.6.5}$$

$$E = D/Y \tag{2.6.6}$$

$$\dot{E} = g^d - g_y \tag{2.6.7}$$

where I is gross investment per worker, g^d is the growth of demand, k denotes the capital–labour ratio, d is the rate of depreciation, n is the population growth

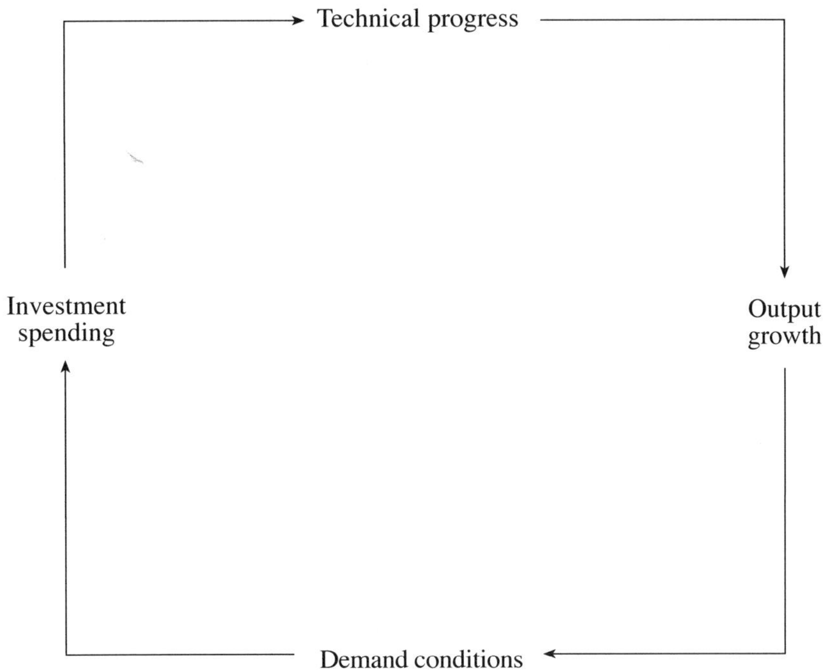

Figure 2.5 The link between demand conditions and output growth in a fundamentalist Keynesian model with endogenous growth

rate, g_y denotes the rate of growth of output, E is the level of excess capacity utilization, D is the level of demand, Y is potential capacity, a is the rate of labour-augmenting technical progress and s_k is the elasticity of output with respect to capital in a Cobb–Douglas production function.

Equation [2.6.1] is the investment function. Investment spending is positively related to the growth of aggregate demand, with firms expanding capacity to meet growing demand. This represents a form of the accelerator model. Investment is also a positive function of the level of excess capacity, E, reflecting the impact of excess demand on the incentive to expand capacity. Equation [2.6.2] determines the evolution of the capital–labour ratio (capital deepening). Equation [2.6.3] determines the rate of output growth, while equation [2.6.4] (the technical progress function) is the mechanism of endogenous growth, in which both the capital stock per worker and the flow of investment per worker positively affect the rate of technical progress.

Equation [2.6.5] determines the evolution of the rate of aggregate demand growth, which responds positively to the rate of output growth. For an equilibrium to exist, demand growth must ultimately equal output growth, or else the economy would be characterized by ever-expanding excess demands or supplies. In the current formulation, aggregate demand growth is assumed to respond positively to output growth. This represents what may be termed the case of 'optimistic Keynesian dynamics' (Palley, 1997), and involves faster supply growth drawing forth faster demand growth. An alternative case of 'pessimistic Keynesian dynamics' is when aggregate demand growth responds negatively to output growth, and in this case demand growth slows when supply growth accelerates. Finally, equation [2.6.6] defines the level of excess capacity, while [2.6.7] defines its rate of change.

Substituting [2.6.1] into [2.6.4] yields:

$$a = a(k, z(E, g^d)) = a(k, g^d, E) \qquad [2.6.4']$$

and differentiating with respect to E yields:

$$da/dE = a_I z_E > 0$$

The effect of excess demand on the rate of technical progress is therefore positive, reflecting the effect of excess demand on investment spending and extensive growth. Consequently, the size of the Okun gap now matters for the rate of growth.[7]

By a process of substitution, the system of equations above can be reduced to the dynamic, three-equation system:

$$\dot{k} = z(E, g^d) - [n + a(k, g^d, E) + d]k \qquad [2.7.1]$$

$$\dot{g^d} = G\left(\left\{n[1 - s_k] + a(k, g^d, E)[1 - s_k] + s_k z(E, g^d)/k\right\}/g^d\right) \qquad [2.7.2]$$

$$\dot{E} = g^d - n[1 - s_k] - a(k, g^d, E)[1 - s_k] - s_k z(E, g^d)/k \qquad [2.7.3]$$

This system can be linearized around a local equilibrium. As a three-dimensional system, the stability conditions are complicated expressions that may or may not be satisfied.

The logic of potential instability is readily understandable, and rests on the interaction between the process of capital deepening and demand growth. Thus, a positive shock to the rate of demand growth could accelerate the process of capital deepening, thereby accelerating the pace of technical advance and output growth. Thanks to equation [2.6.5], this would then accelerate demand growth, giving rise to the potential for a cumulatively unstable process.

Such instability can be viewed as the dynamic analogue of multiplier instability in the static income–expenditure model. In the latter, stability requires

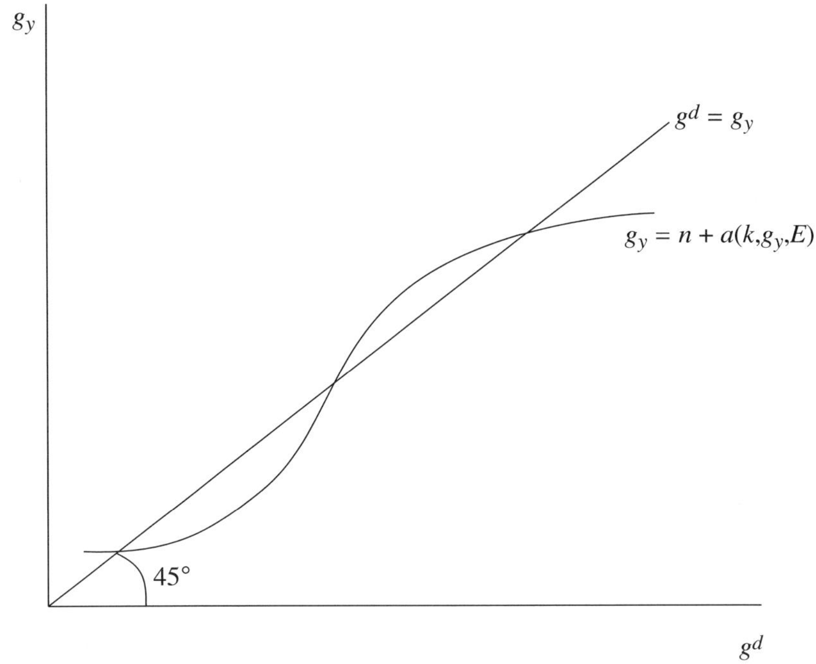

Figure 2.6 Determination of the equilibrium rate of growth in a fundamentalist Keynesian growth model in which the growth of demand affects investment spending and technical progress

that induced increases in the level of demand be less than the initial increase in income. In a Keynesian growth model, stability requires that the induced increase in demand growth be less than the initial increase in output growth.

Figure 2.6 illustrates the possibility of multiple equilibria, with the outer equilibria being stable and the inner equilibrium being unstable. The interesting feature of the model is the fact that the Okun gap affects equilibrium growth. This means that traditional Keynesian aggregate demand management, which directly affects the size of the Okun gap, can be used to influence steady-state growth.

In equilibrium, the level of excess demand, the capital–labour ratio, and the rate of demand growth are all constant. Setting $\dot{E} = \dot{k} = 0$ and $g^d = g_y$ implies that:

$$z(E, g^d) - [n + a(k, g^d, E) + d]k = 0 \qquad [2.8.1]$$

and:

$$n + a(k, g^d, E) - g^d = 0 \qquad [2.8.2]$$

Totally differentiating equations [2.8.1] and [2.8.2] with respect to k, g^d, E and n, and arranging in matrix form, yields:

$$\begin{bmatrix} z_{gd} - a_{gd}k & -a_k k - n - a - d \\ a_{gd}k - 1 & a_k \end{bmatrix} \begin{bmatrix} dg^d \\ dk \end{bmatrix} = \begin{bmatrix} -z_E + a_E k & k \\ -a_E & -1 \end{bmatrix} \begin{bmatrix} dE \\ dn \end{bmatrix}$$

The Jacobian is given by $|J| = a_k[z_{gd} - a_{gd}k] + [a_{gd} - 1][a_k k + n + a + d]$. Assuming the Jacobian to be negative, the effect of an increase in the rate of population growth is:

$$dg^d/dn = -[n + a + d]/|J| > 0$$

The effect of a change in the level of excess demand on the steady-state rate of growth of output is given by:

$$dg^d/dE = \{a_k[a_E k - z_E] - a_E[a_k k + n + a + d]\}/|J| > 0$$

This outcome is illustrated in Figure 2.7, which shows the determination of equilibrium between the rate of growth of demand and output. Figure 2.7 is analogous to a growth theoretic income–expenditure diagram. An increase in excess demand initially shifts the output growth function upwards. At this stage, output growth exceeds demand growth and excess demand starts to decline, which pulls the output growth function down. This process continues until a new equilibrium, given by the intersection of the broken line and the 45° line, is reached. This equilibrium is characterized by higher steady-state output growth.

The above construction of economic growth fits with a fundamentalist Keynesian view of macroeconomics. For instance, attempts to use downward nominal wage and price adjustment to restore the economy to full employment may actually increase unemployment and lower growth. This is because such measures can reduce aggregate demand and create excess supply owing to the Fisher (1933) debt effect and the Mundell (1963)–Tobin (1965) deflation effect.[8] In terms of Figure 2.7, nominal wage deflation pulls the output growth function down. Aggregate demand shocks now impact growth through their influence on the level of excess demand.

Finally, the fact that the equilibrium rate of growth depends on the state of excess demand means that it will be stochastic and hysteretic in character. The logic is as follows. Stochastic disturbances to the level of macroeconomic activity affect the equilibrium level of excess demand, and this then affects the

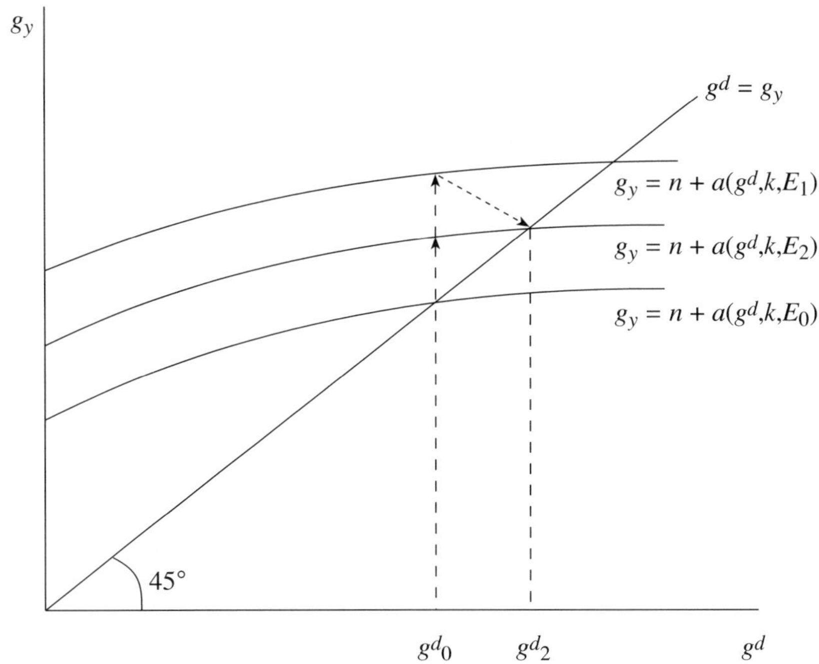

Figure 2.7 The effect of an increase in the level of demand on the equilibrium rate of growth in a fundamentalist Keynesian endogenous growth model

growth rate and renders it stochastic. To the extent that these shocks impact investment spending and change the capital–labour ratio, they will then impact the steady-state growth rate, which can then exhibit hysteresis.

SOME LOOSE ENDS: SECTORAL AND BALANCE-OF-PAYMENTS GROWTH MODELS

The above construction of the growth process explicitly introduces aggregate demand into the theory of economic growth, thereby linking growth theory with static Keynesian macroeconomics. By way of closing, it is worth contrasting this approach with two other approaches that emphasize sectoral influences and the balance of payments, respectively. Doing so serves to illuminate the comprehensive and novel nature of the above construction.

Cornwall and Cornwall (1994) present a model of endogenous growth in which the equilibrium rate of growth changes over the course of development because of the changing composition of output. This compositional change occurs because of changing income elasticities of demand that result from movement along Engel income–expansion curves. As a result, the rate of growth exhibits a time-varying, hysteretic path, with demand factors mattering through their influence on the composition of output.

However, a closer examination of the Cornwall model shows that it continues in the tradition of old exogenous growth theory, and the influence of demand is neoclassical rather than Keynesian. The model consists of three sectors – agriculture, manufacturing and services. Within each sector, the rate of growth is exogenous. Manufacturing has the highest rate of growth. The economy-wide growth rate is a weighted average of the sectoral rates of growth, the weights determined by sectoral output shares. The model can be summarized as follows:

$$g_y = s_{\text{agr}}a_{\text{agr}} + s_{\text{man}}a_{\text{man}} + s_{\text{ser}}a_{\text{ser}} \qquad a_{\text{man}} > a_{\text{agr}},\ a_{\text{ser}} > 0 \qquad [2.9.1]$$

$$s_{\text{agr}} + s_{\text{man}} + s_{\text{ser}} = 1 \qquad [2.9.2]$$

$$1 > s_{\text{agr}} = s_{\text{agr}}(y) > 0 \qquad s'_{\text{agr}} < 0 \qquad [2.9.3]$$

$$1 > s_{\text{man}} = s_{\text{man}}(y) > 0 \qquad s'_{\text{man}} > 0 \text{ initially, then } s'_{\text{man}} < 0 \qquad [2.9.4]$$

$$1 > s_{\text{ser}} = s_{\text{ser}}(y) > 0 \qquad s'_{\text{ser}} > 0 \qquad [2.9.5]$$

where a denotes the exogenous rate of growth in the jth sector (j = agr, man, ser), s is the output share of the jth sector and y is the level of output per capita. The agricultural share of output declines with income, as spending shifts towards spending on manufactures and services. Initially, manufactured goods have an income elasticity greater than one, and spending shifts towards manufacturing. However, once a certain level of income is reached, spending on manufacturing declines as a share of income. Services are strong normal goods, and the share of spending on services rises throughout the process of development.

This elegant model is capable of producing a rich pattern of growth. The growth rate initially accelerates as economic activity shifts from the agricultural sector into the manufacturing sector. However, at some stage the output share of the manufacturing sectors peaks, and the growth rate then declines as activity shifts into the service sector.

The aggregate growth rate is endogenous because of the changing expenditure shares. However, at the sectoral level, growth rates are exogenous, and in this sense the model remains in the spirit of old growth theory. Demand factors affect growth by changing the composition of spending. This is a neoclassical treatment and not Keynesian, in the sense that the level of aggregate demand does not matter. Instead, it is preferences that matter. Moreover, the economy is also always at full employment along the growth path. For these reasons, the model remains un-Keynesian.

A second branch of growth theory that emphasizes demand is balance-of-payments-constrained growth (BPCG) theory (Thirlwall, 1979; McCombie and Thirlwall, 1994). In these models, the rate of export growth acts as a constraint on growth, because countries are unable to grow with ever-increasing current account deficits measured as a share of output.

Such models are clearly intended to be Keynesian in spirit, with export growth serving as the engine of demand growth. However, though Keynesian in intent and though elevating conventional Keynesian demand factors to the fore, the BPCG model suffers from two distinct weaknesses. First, the world economy is ultimately a closed system, so that export growth cannot be the engine of growth for the world economy as a whole. At best, the BPCG model may apply to small open economies, but this then calls for a separate theory of growth for the large industrialized economies.[9] Second, and even more troubling, is the lack of attention given to the supply side and the need to balance supply growth and demand growth. In particular, if the rate of productivity growth exceeds the rate of demand growth (as determined by the rate of export demand growth), then there will be ever-increasing excess potential supply and unemployment. The reverse holds if demand growth exceeds supply growth.

This problem can be seen from the following simple statement of the BPCG growth model:

$$x = a_0 g^* \quad [2.10.1]$$

$$m = b_0 g \quad [2.10.2]$$

$$x = m \quad [2.10.3]$$

$$l = c_0 + c_1 g \quad [2.10.4]$$

$$g^s = l + n \quad [2.10.5]$$

where x represents the rate of export growth, g^* is the rate of foreign income growth, m denotes the rate of import growth, g is the rate of domestic income growth, l is the rate of labour productivity growth, g^s is the rate of output growth and n is the rate of population growth. Equation [2.10.1] is the export demand growth equation. Equation [2.10.2] is the import demand equation. Equation [2.10.3] is the balance-of-payments constraint, which requires equality between

LEEDS UNIVERSITY LIBRARY

the long-run rates of import and export growth to prevent a growing current account deficit or surplus. Equation [2.10.4] is the Verdoorn law, which endogenizes productivity growth by linking it to domestic output growth. Finally, equation [2.10.5] determines the rate of potential output growth.

Solutions for the equilibrium rates of actual and potential output growth are given by:

$$g = a_0 g^* / b_0 \tag{2.11.1}$$

and:

$$g^s = c_0 + c_1 a_0 g^* / b_0 + n \tag{2.11.2}$$

The model is overdetermined, and it is only by chance that actual output growth will equal potential output growth. The necessary condition is:

$$g^* = [c_0 + n]/[a_0/b_0 - c_1]$$

If this condition is not satisfied, there will be growing imbalance between actual and potential output. If $g^* > [c_0 + n]/[a_0/b_0 - c_1]$, there will be growing excess demand. If $g^* < [c_0 + n]/[a_0/b_0 - c_1]$, there will be growing excess supply.

The above inconsistency is fundamental to Keynesian models that seek to extrapolate short-run supply conditions to the long run. In the short run, a small increase in the 'level' of demand can change the equilibrium level of output because idle capacity exists. In the long run, demand and supply capacity must grow together, and this imposes an additional equilibrium condition because of the technical relations implied by production conditions.[10]

CONCLUSION

Keynesian macroeconomics and growth theory have tended to exist as separate branches of economics. This chapter has explored the consistency between different branches of macroeconomics and growth theory. Whereas Keynesian macroeconomics was inconsistent with old growth theory, it is compatible with new endogenous growth theory. At the heart of this compatibility lies the Kaldorian concept of an endogenous technical progress function, which allows demand-side influences to feed back and impact the supply side. The reconciliation of growth theory and Keynesian macroeconomics is an important development in the construction of a unified theory of Keynesian economics.

NOTES

1. In the Solow growth model, the PGDP path is also the realized GDP path.
2. Tobin's (1965) approach to money and growth was macroeconomic in character, in that it assumed the existence of a well-defined money demand function. Sidrauski (1967) adopted a microeconomic approach that sought to provide a microeconomic foundation for money based on the presence of money in either households' utility functions or firms' production functions.
3. Viewed in this light, we can see the commonalities and differences between the neo-Keynesian and Friedman (1968)–Lucas (1975) research paradigms. Both emphasize disturbances that push AGDP away from PGDP. Neo-Keynesians emphasize demand disturbances originating within the macro-economy. Friedman and Lucas emphasize disturbances attributable to the monetary authority. A big difference is that neo-Keynesians believe the economy only drifts back to PGDP slowly, and this calls for policy interventions to speed up the adjustment process. Friedman and Lucas believe that adjustment is fairly rapid, and that policy cannot do anything to systematically speed up the process (the rational expectations hypothesis). New Keynesians aim to provide a justification for the neo-Keynesian claim of slow adjustment to equilibrium, and thereby open a way for systematic policy to affect economic activity.
4. The differences between the Keynesian and classical approaches to macroeconomic equilibrium are fully explored in Palley (1996a).
5. Another dimension to Scott's (1989) work is the issue of growth accounting, and measurement of capital. This latter issue is not addressed in the current chapter.
6. Stock effects may be important because they introduce increasing returns to the growth process, and this can explain the non-convergence of cross-country growth rates. A possible microeconomic rationale of their effect is that more capital per worker yields more opportunities for seeing where innovations are possible.
7. Palley (1996c) allows excess demand to directly affect the rate of technical progress through its effect on the incentive to innovate. In this case, the sign of the effect of excess demand on technical progress can be ambiguous.
8. These effects are discussed extensively in Palley (1996a, chapter 5).
9. For further discussion of this issue, see Chapter 6 by McCombie and Roberts.
10. See Chapter 7 for a suggested resolution of this problem in the context of the BPCG model.

REFERENCES

Barro, R. and H. Grossman (1971) 'A general disequilibrium model of income and employment,' *American Economic Review*, 61, 82–93.

Clower, R.W. (1965) 'The Keynesian revolution: a theoretical appraisal,' in F.H. Hahn and F. Brechling (eds) *The Theory of Interest Rates*, London, Macmillan, 103–25.

Cornwall, J. and W. Cornwall (1994) 'Growth theory and economic structure,' *Economica*, 61, 237–51.

Fisher, I. (1933) 'The debt-deflation theory of great depressions,' *Econometrica*, 1, 337–57.

Friedman, M. (1968) 'The role of monetary policy,' *American Economic Review*, 58, 1–17.

Kaldor, N. (1957) 'A model of economic growth,' *Economic Journal*, 67, 591–624.

Kaldor, N. and J.A. Mirrlees (1961/2) 'A new model of economic growth,' *Review of Economic Studies*, 29, 174–90.

Keynes, J.M. (1936) *The General Theory of Employment, Interest and Money*, London, Macmillan.

Long, J.B. and C. Plosser (1983) 'Real business cycles,' *Journal of Political Economy*, 91, 39–69.
Lucas, R.E. Jr. (1975) 'An equilibrium model of the business cycle,' *Journal of Political Economy*, 83, 1113–44.
Malinvaud, E. (1977) *The Theory of Unemployment Reconsidered*, New York, Halstead Press.
Mankiw, G. (1985) 'Small menu costs and large business cycles: a macroeconomic model of monopoly,' *Quarterly Journal of Economics*, 100, 529–39.
McCombie, J.S.L. and A.P. Thirlwall (1994) *Economic Growth and the Balance of Payments Constraint*, London, Macmillan.
Modigliani, F. (1944) 'Liquidity preference and the theory of interest and money,' *Econometrica*, 12, 45–88.
Mundell, R. (1963) 'Inflation and real interest,' *Journal of Political Economy*, 59, 280–83.
Palley, T.I. (1996a) *Post Keynesian Macroeconomics: Debt, Distribution and the Macroeconomy*, London, Macmillan.
Palley, T.I. (1996b) 'Old wine for new bottles: putting old growth theory back into the new,' *Australian Economic Papers*, 35, 250–62.
Palley, T.I. (1996c) 'Growth theory in a Keynesian mode: some Keynesian foundations for the theory of economic growth,' *Journal of Post Keynesian Economics*, 19, 113–35.
Palley, T.I. (1997) 'Aggregate demand and endogenous growth: a generalized Keynes–Kaldor model of economic growth,' *Metroeconomica*, 48, 161–76.
Romer, P.M. (1990) 'Endogenous technical change,' *Journal of Political Economy*, 98, S71–102.
Scott, M.F.G. (1989) *A New View of Economic Growth*, Oxford, Clarendon Press.
Sidrauski, M. (1967) 'Rational choice and patterns of growth in a monetary economy,' *American Economic Review*, 57, 534–44.
Solow, R.M. (1956) 'A contribution to the theory of economic growth,' *Quarterly Journal of Economics*, 70, 65–94.
Thirlwall, A.P. (1979) 'The balance of payments constraint as an explanation of international growth rate differences,' *Banca Nazionale Del Lavoro Quarterly Review*, 128, 45–53.
Tobin, J. (1965) 'Money and economic growth,' *Econometrica*, 33, 671–84.
Woglom, G. (1982) 'Underemployment equilibria with rational expectations,' *Quarterly Journal of Economics*, 97, 89–108.

3. The exogeneity of investment: from systemic laws of accumulation and growth to effective demand conditions

Joseph Halevi and Réduane Taouil

INTRODUCTION

This chapter argues that the concept of effective demand constitutes a major conceptual break not just with marginalist economics, but also with classical political economy. The nature of the break lies in the treatment of investment as an exogenous variable. Classical economics can be considered as the most coherent form of endogenous growth theory. This is especially true for Marx's theory of cyclical growth.

As shown in the next section, Marx explained cyclical fluctuations in terms of changes in the reserve army of labour. Investment is, in this context, an endogenous variable, determined by the rate of profit. By giving primacy to capitalists' expenditure, Kalecki distanced himself from Marx in a twofold manner. On one hand, he considered investment as a causal variable determining the level of profits; on the other, he viewed investment as being determined independently from savings.

The third section discusses the way in which Kalecki treats investment as an exogenous variable. Firstly, we analyse Kalecki's approach to the trade cycle by pointing out the crucial distinction between output as determined by productive capacity and output as determined by the level of investment. Secondly, we study Kalecki's use of Marx's schemes of reproduction and argue that, unlike Marx's, they are never closed in terms of the allocation of investment goods. The absence of closure is not accidental: it reflects the view that there is no internal mechanism establishing how many investment goods will be produced and in what proportion they will be distributed to the capital and consumption goods sectors of the economy. The existence of such a mechanism would amount to the formulation of an endogenous investment function. It is then pointed out that when writing about a socialist planned economy, Kalecki was perfectly capable of closing his growth model through the decision rule of the planning authority.

Finally, Keynes' approach to the problem of investment decisions is discussed. It is argued that the author of the *General Theory* put forward two interpretations of investment: one based on the comparison between the rate of interest and the position on the marginal efficiency of investment schedule, and one centred on the state of long-run expectations. We contend that the latter interpretation has the upper hand and that investment is fundamentally a variable which cannot be determined through some kind of functional relation.

MARX'S CYCLE AND THE ABSENCE OF EFFECTIVE DEMAND

A simple model will suffice to highlight the main points of Marx's theory, wherein the rate of profit drives the rate of accumulation and growth. Let X be the level of output of a one-sector corn economy, K its corn capital stock, d its rate of depreciation, β the output per unit of capital, n the number of workers per unit of corn capital, W the wage bill and w the corn wage rate. We then have the following accounting expression for the level of profits:

$$P = X - W - dK \qquad [3.1]$$

With $d = 1$, all capital is circulating capital.

Expressing X and W in terms of K we have:

$$X = \beta K \qquad [3.2]$$

$$nK = E \qquad [3.3]$$

where E is employment, and:

$$W = wE \qquad [3.4]$$

Substituting equations [3.4], [3.3] and [3.2] into [3.1] and dividing by K, we obtain the following expression for the rate of profit:

$$r = \beta - wn - d \qquad [3.5]$$

The rate of profit is thus proportional to the output-capital ratio β, and varies inversely to the wage rate and to the number of workers per machine. Neglecting the extremely special case of a falling rate of profit in the long run, caused by a fall in β not offset by a still greater fall in n, Marx's theory of the trade cycle is fully captured by equation [3.5].

Under the pressure of competitive tendencies, capitalists ought to invest the bulk of their surplus, so that:

$$sP = I = gK \tag{3.6}$$

where s is the propensity to save out of profits (which is assumed to be very near unity) and g is the discrete growth rate of capital. By dividing [3.6] by K we get:

$$g = sr \tag{3.7}$$

Substitution of [3.5] into [3.7] yields:

$$g = s(\beta - wn - d) \tag{3.7a}$$

The expression in brackets in equation [3.7a] is the *full capacity rate of profit*.

Equation [3.7] is the familiar Kaldor–Pasinetti expression for long-run growth. As pointed out at the end of this chapter, the Kaldor–Pasinetti condition does not prescribe a 'law' of accumulation but only establishes the prerequisites for the capitalist system to function. In a Marxian context, r varies in accordance with the reserve army mechanism, so that the expression in brackets in [3.7a] varies systematically with the unemployment cycle. Thus, in a Marxian framework, [3.7a] defines the cyclical *law* of capitalist accumulation.

In Marx, the accumulation of capital is not constrained by the growth of the active population. Starting from an initial situation of abundant labour supply, the acceleration of the rate of accumulation generates a dwindling reserve army of labour. The ensuing increase in the wage rate will, as prescribed by equation [3.5], reduce the rate of profit and with it the rate of accumulation (Marx, 1967, 1968; Sylos-Labini, 1984). This process is at the root of Marx's theory of technical change. The rise in the wage rate (fall in the profit rate) leads to the adoption of more mechanized methods of production. The emergence of technological unemployment and the reduced intake of workers into the system caused by the profit squeeze replenishes the reserve army of labour. This factor sets the stage for a new upturn in profitability and growth as prescribed by equation [3.7].

The Marxian cycle combines variations in the rate of profit with movements in the industrial reserve army in a precise manner. Investment varies in relation to the rate of profit which, in turn, varies in relation to the reserve army. Investment appears, therefore, as an endogenous variable. In this framework, cyclical changes in the rate of profit and in the distribution of income form, along with the tendency of the rate of profit to fall in the long run, the *general law* of the accumulation of capital.

In effect, Marx's *law*, far from being general, finds its application only in a monosectoral competitive classical economy. The *law* assumes away the influence that variations in the size of the reserve army may have on the effective demand for wage goods. The introduction of effective demand implies the abandonment of the hypothesis of a tendency towards a long-period position in favour of a short-period temporal framework. Indeed, as soon as we consider a two-sector economy and we introduce the concept of effective demand, the results turn out to be different from Marx's.

The growth of the reserve army cannot possibly take place without also affecting the level of aggregate demand. The fall in the wage rate coming in the wake of the expansion of the reserve army will negatively affect the demand for consumption goods. Thus unused capacity is likely to emerge in the consumption goods industries, thereby creating an additional layer of unemployment but, this time, of a Keynesian nature. The Keynesian component of unemployment will lead, in the absence of wage fixing by trade unions, to a further downward pressure on the wages of employed workers. The cumulative effects of both reserve army and Keynesian unemployment are likely to engender a persistent underutilization of equipment in the consumption goods sector. Such an occurrence will negatively affect the degree of utilization of equipment in the capital goods sector via the reduced demand for capital goods emanating from the consumption goods sector.

As a consequence, in contrast to Maxian cyclical growth theory, the economy will not experience a new upswing but will enter, instead, a state of chronic depression and stagnation. It follows that the formation of the reserve army does not generate the renewal of the growth process, as much as competition does not ensure the viability of progressive accumulation. Hence, through the introduction of the concept of effective demand, the time horizon of the economy logically becomes that of the short period.

The Conceptual Break

The emergence – via the mechanism of effective demand – of unused productive capacity as a structural tendency in the economy no longer allows for a clear-cut inverse relation between the rate of profit and the wage rate. If u denotes the rate of capacity utilization, the actual profit rate, σ, becomes:

$$\sigma = u(\beta - wn - d) \qquad [3.8]$$

where $d < 1$ because $u < 1$.

Neglecting, for simplicity, changes in the rate of depreciation stemming from changes in the rate of capacity utilization, an increase in the rate of profit is compatible with an increase in the wage rate when the differential of σ in relation to u and w yields:

$$(\beta - wn - d)u' > unw' \qquad [3.9]$$

Since the expression in brackets (call it h) represents net output per machine at full capacity – or the full capacity profit rate – equation [3.9] can be restated as:

$$[u'/w'] > [u/h]n \qquad [3.10]$$

Equation [3.10] states the conditions necessary for a rise in the rate of profit when the wage rate also increases.

With unused capacity as a persistent phenomenon in the system, both the wage rate and the rate of profit can rise (Halevi and Kriesler, 1991). In non-depressionary situations, a rise in the wage rate is likely to induce an increase in the degree of capacity utilization due to the multiplier effect, as well as a further set of increases due to accelerator effects. Thus it may be concluded that, barring the extreme cases of $u = 1$ and of u approximating very low values, the inverse link between the rate of profit and the wage rate is not a general case. The existence of unused capacity cannot be considered a temporary phenomenon, since it is inherent in the workings of a decentralized economy. It results from the separation between investment and saving.

When a fall in wages leads to unused capacity in the consumption goods sector, society has performed an act of saving. Yet there is nothing in this action that will instruct capitalists to increase investment and production in the capital goods sector. It must be noted that this outcome is possible because of the very existence of money that allows savers not to spend at least part of their income on goods and services. In a two-sector model, the monetary separation between saving and investment is consistent with the assumption that all profits and no wages are saved. Indeed if, because of the emergence of a reserve army, money wages fall with consumption goods prices remaining the same or declining by a lesser amount, money profits in the consumption goods sector will also fall by the amount of the reduced wage bill in the capital goods sector. Hence the savings and investment of the capitalists in the consumption goods sector will have declined. It is the capital goods sector that will end up with greater savings, but in the form of unused capacity.

From the foregoing analysis it may be concluded that investment ceases to be an endogenous variable since, whenever consumption demand falls in the wake of a rise in unemployment, no automatic increase in investment will occur. Profits, while remaining the objective of capitalists' activities, do not *lead* accumulation but instead *depend* on the externally given level of investment, as argued by Kalecki. Hence the crucial multiplier in Kalecki is the profit multiplier (Kalecki, 1971, p. 2). Thus:

$$P = [1/(1 - s)](A + B) \qquad [3.11]$$

where B is capitalists' autonomous expenditure and A gross accumulation (gross investment), both appearing as exogenous variables. Here, the multiplier is $1/(1 - s)$ with the multiplicand being the sum of gross accumulation and capitalists' autonomous consumption.

THE EXOGENEITY OF INVESTMENT: KALECKI

In the *Theory of Economic Dynamics*, Kalecki maintained that the profit multiplier relation – equation [3.11] – is the *differentia specifica* between the actual behaviour of a capitalist economy and the way in which a planned economy ought to function (Kalecki, 1954, 1971). This view was reiterated in two papers quite critical of steady-state growth theories (Kalecki, 1968a).

In Kalecki (1962), the distribution of income is explicitly included. Hence:

$$Y = P/q \qquad [3.12]$$

where Y is aggregate output and q is the share of profits. The level of profits, P, is deemed to be a function of the level of investment, I, so that equation [3.11] becomes:

$$P = zI \qquad [3.13]$$

where $z > 1$.

It follows that profits are determined by the level of investment and that, *given* q, investment determines the level of income. However, if q were not fixed, then Y could increase even with a stable level of P for any fall in q. According to Kalecki, the latter case ought to be the norm in a planned economy where output is determined by the level of productive capacity and not by the link between investment and profits via the fixity of the distributive factor, q. To summarize a long quotation from Kalecki (1954, 1971, p. 97),[1] a fall in investment, under conditions of an invariant distribution of income, will lead to a fall in profits and in national income causing unused capacity in both the capital goods and the consumption goods sectors. By contrast, if q were downwardly flexible – a situation which Kalecki ascribed to a centrally planned economy[2] – full capacity could be maintained in both sectors. A lower level of (net) investment would, in this context, imply an increase in the share of the consumption goods sector's output in national income. In other words, wages would have to be increased relatively to prices.

The important point to retain from the above discussion is that nowhere does Kalecki gauge the dynamics of profits and of national income in terms of the endogenous capacity to accumulate. Attempts to introduce internal elements in the determination of investment decisions were made in the paper published subsequently in 1968, a sequel to the 1962 essay. Yet the conclusions reached by the author are extremely negative. In particular, for reasonable initial values of the capital stock and profit share of income, the economy may display chronic unused capacity – even under significant technical progress which, in general, accelerates the obsolescence of capital equipment (Kalecki, 1968a; Halevi, 1992).

These results prompted Kalecki to leave the factors influencing investment decisions mostly outside the model and to express the conviction – outlined in a paper delivered at the 1968 UNESCO Conference on the centenary of *Das Kapital* – that capitalism, if left to its own devices without strong external impulses of an institutional and political nature, may well settle into a state of simple reproduction (Kalecki, 1968b).

The UNESCO paper is one of the most lucid characterizations of the question of effective demand from a Marxian perspective. Using a three-sector model (capital goods, wage goods and luxury goods), Kalecki shows that there is no reason to assume that realized profits will lead to a corresponding level of capital accumulation. By contrast, when Marx goes on to study the mechanism of expanded reproduction, the intersectoral equilibrium condition also specifies the part of surplus value invested in the expansion of constant capital in the department producing the means of consumption, as well as the additional variable capital accruing to the department producing the means of production. In other words, in order to generate growth Marx had to specify, regardless of the problem of effective demand, the way in which the surplus is invested.

Such is not the case in Kalecki's approach, where the schemes of reproduction are open on the demand side. The level of profits in the wage goods sector, P_w, is given by the spending out of wages in the capital and luxury goods sector. The size of P_w may well be above the level of replacement requirements, i.e., above simple reproduction. Yet we do not know how the realized profits P_w will be spent. This will depend on the degree of capacity utilization in all three sectors and on capitalists' expectations of future demand. The passive nature of P_w, relative to what investment might be, arises from the fact that the determinants of changes in wage bill of the capital goods sector are capitalists' autonomous investment decisions. Kalecki cannot be accused of not knowing how to close a two-sector Marxian model. Indeed, elsewhere he closed it in his writings on the economic growth of a socialist economy (Kalecki, 1972). In the first case, he developed a Feldman-type model, in which the structure of investment – i.e., the proportion of investment allocated to the capital goods sector – is determined by the planned rate of growth (Kalecki, 1972, chapter 11; Halevi, 1981; Kriesler, 1995).

By comparing and contrasting the ways in which Kalecki used the Marxian schemes of reproduction and sectoral growth models in capitalist and planned economies, we cannot but help observe that the crucial difference lies in the absence of a closure in the capitalist case. This confirms that investment is not viewed as an endogenous variable.

KEYNES: EXPECTATIONS AND THE EXOGENEITY OF INVESTMENT

In Kaleckian theory, the exogeneity of investment (and thus of the main engine of accumulation and growth) emerges in a straightforward manner. Keynes, however, presented two interpretations of the factors governing the level of investment. One was centred on the motives leading to investment decisions by means of a calculation based on comparing a downward-sloping marginal efficiency schedule with the interest rate, while the other was based on the state of confidence of entrepreneurs. The view that it may not be possible to determine the level of investment in the long run through a causal relation is embedded in this second interpretation.

The relationship between the level of investment and the rate of interest, via the downward-sloping marginal efficiency of investment curve, appears in the second chapter of the *General Theory* and does not sit well with the principle of effective demand. The determination of the marginal efficiency of investment is similar to the determination of the internal rate of return, which equalizes the cost of and future returns to an investment project. Future returns are determined by the difference between the expected values of sales and the cost of production stemming from a given investment project. Thus, if C is the cost of the project and R_t is the value of expected sales proceeds, while V_t is the cost of the production flow generated by the investment project during its life span, we have:

$$C = \sum_{t=0}^{n} \frac{R_t - V_t}{(1+e)'} \qquad [3.14]$$

or, multiplying both sides of [3.14] by $(1 + e)'$, we obtain:

$$C(1+e)^n = \sum_{t=0}^{n} (R_t - V_t)(1+e)^{n-t} \qquad [3.15]$$

The stream of future returns is given by:

$$R_0 - V_0, \; \frac{R_1 - V_1}{1+e}, \ldots, \frac{R_n - V_n}{(1+e)^n} \qquad [3.16]$$

Future returns are therefore identical to the returns that a given amount of capital would generate if it were financially invested at an annual rate of return e. Now, the left-hand side of equation [3.15] is the value of capital at period t growing at the compound interest rate e per year. The right-hand side of the expression is nothing but the net returns earned by an investment project made in period t calculated over $n - t$ periods at the rate e. Over the lifespan of the project, net proceeds are thereby equalized to the proceeds associated to the interest capitalization of an investment fund. This equalization must imply that profits, or net proceeds, must always be invested at a rate of return e. Such a calculation is based on the presupposition that the entrepreneur knows the lifespan of a capital good, as well as the distribution over time of proceeds, costs and profits.

In this context, we cannot but conclude that the marginal efficiency of investment approach to the determination of the level of investment is in contrast with the existence of uncertainty. The very reinvestment of profits is uncertain for reasons that Keynes himself explained in chapters 12 and 16 of the *General Theory*. Whenever decisions are taken in a framework of uncertainty, in which the future is unknown and unknowable, the determination of investment requires the integration of subjective elements, such as the state of business confidence. Thus, for any given rate of interest, the level of investment depends upon the state of expectations and the state of confidence. If firms are optimistic, the level of investment at any given rate of interest will be higher than otherwise. However, if we ascribe to investment decisions an eminently subjective dimension, the amount of investment cannot be ascertained by means of a function which depends upon the calculation of future returns. The marginal efficiency-based investment function is not compatible with Keynes's notion of uncertainty and if we wish to keep the latter, the hypothesis of an exogenously determined level of investment becomes necessary.

The hypothesis of diminishing returns must also be treated with caution, since it conflates long with short-period phenomena. The hypothesis is, in Keynes, based on decreasing returns due to the growth in the size of the stock of capital (a long-period phenomenon) and on the rise in the price of capital resulting from the increase in investment. The latter falls unambiguously within the realm of short-period analysis. In this context, the investment function developed by Keynes in chapter 11 starts from an arbitrary choice, as it takes into account only the impact of investment on prices. The calculations based on a compound interest rate imply both stable expectations and the absence of any realization problem, whereas the hypothesis of diminishing returns leads to the elimination of uncertainty because returns are evaluated on the basis of the whole lifespan of capital goods.

At any rate, the short and the long run cannot be projected on the same plane since, as Sylos-Labini has pointed out, their treatment is asymmetrical (Sylos-Labini, 1984). In relation to the short period, Keynes calculates profits as the excess of the value of production relative to users' costs. In the long run, returns are determined by the marginal efficiency of investment. The distinction between the two periods has a twofold consequence. In the short run, entrepreneurial decisions do not stem from the comparison between current returns and interest rates. In the long run, investment decisions depend precisely on such a comparison. Furthermore, long-term returns are tied to capital goods, whereas in the short run, with a given stock of capital, returns depend entirely on the expansion of employment levels.

The hypotheses of diminishing returns and of the systematic reinvestment of profits turns out to be inconsistent with each other. The former implies a decline in the rate of return so as to discourage investment, whereas the latter requires a continuous growth of investment. Under these circumstances, the curve defining the marginal efficiency of investment is indeterminate. It is therefore impossible to aggregate all the demand curves for capital goods in order to construct a downward-sloping macroeconomic demand curve for capital.

Chapter 12 of the *General Theory* demonstrates the impossibility of fixing the determinants of investment in the same manner as consumption and savings. Long-term expectations are crucially influenced by subjective factors which, in Keynes's terminology, are referred to as the 'state of confidence'. These expectations are, in their turn, fashioned by evaluations concerning the future, as well as by the trust bestowed on them by entrepreneurs themselves. In other words, expectations depend on the degree to which entrepreneurs believe in what they are thinking. It follows that – unlike the ironclad mechanics of classical accumulation – the state of long-run expectations rests on too fragile a basis to allow for the formulation of a stable functional expression of the factors governing investment decisions.

Keynes's approach to the trade cycle is a good example of the importance assigned to the state of confidence. The analysis carried out in chapter 22 of the *General Theory*, while listing a series of objective factors, stresses the role played by the way in which entrepreneurs conceive and perceive their own environment. On the basis of the collective psychology approach, the trade cycle is split into three phases. During the *phase of illusion*, entrepreneurs overestimate future returns, although neither the expected nor the current interest rate would justify such optimism. Investment decisions are, in this case, the outcome of a cumulative race despite the rising costs of capital. The *phase of disillusion* signals a sudden reversal in expectations due to the rising gap between actual and expected returns. This phase brings to the fore the precarious nature of the evaluations forming the basis of expectations, thereby leading to a decline in the level of investment that heralds the *phase of depression*. The fall in investment generates conditions for mutually reinforcing tendencies that bring about a decline in the volume of production and in the level of employment.

It is in the treatment of the trade cycle that Keynes's philosophical differences *vis-à-vis* Marx regarding the dynamics of capitalism emerge in a remarkably clear-cut way. In the Marxian theory of cyclical accumulation, there is strict symmetry between the upward and the downward phases. When the rate of profit falls as the result of previous accumulation, the downswing begins because very little *corn* profits are left for investment. The ensuing slackening in the growth rate, coupled with technological transformations (Sylos-Labini, 1984), regenerates the reserve army of the unemployed. Workers, by competing against each other, drive down the real wage. The rate of profit, the share of profits and the share of investment will rise anew, rekindling the dynamics of accumulation. A permanent crisis, Marx stressed quite wrongly, cannot exist. The crisis is, for the author of *Capital*, part and parcel of the self-renewal process of capital accumulation. Unused capacity is just an occurrence during the crisis as it does not hinder in any fundamental way the transition from recession to recovery (Halevi, 1985).

For Keynes, by contrast, the upward and downward phases of the cycle are asymmetrical. In chapter 22 Keynes argued that while the recovery, once started, tends to feed on itself, in the downward phase – with large amounts of unused capacity in the economy – 'the schedule of the marginal efficiency of capital may fall so low that it can scarcely be corrected, so as to secure a satisfactory rate of new investment by any practicable reduction in the rate of interest' (Keynes, 1936, pp. 219–20). It follows that there is no natural and endogenous way out from a recessionary state. This means that, as far as the determination of investment is concerned, Keynes's model has no closure, just like that of Kalecki. Given the instability of the state of long-run expectations, the forces pulling the system out of a situation of unemployment and idle capacity lie in the institutional and political spheres.

The conceptual implications of the volatile nature of investment which, as a consequence, makes the formulation of an endogenous investment decision function a virtually insurmountable task, are summarized by Keynes in the following passage:

> The theory can be summed up by saying that, given the psychology of the public, the level of output and employment as a whole depends on the amount of investment. I put it in this way, not because this is the only factor on which aggregate

> output depends, but because it is usual in a complex system to regard as the *causa causans* that factor which is most prone to sudden fluctuations. More comprehensively, aggregate output depends on the propensity to hoard, on the policy of the monetary authority as it affects the quantity of money, on the state of confidence concerning the perspective yield of capital assets, propensity to spend and on the social factors which influence the level of the money-wage. But of these several factors it is those which determine the rate of investment which are most unreliable, since it is they which are influenced by our views of the future about which we know so little (Keynes, 1937, p. 221).

CONCLUSION

Jean-Pierre Dupuy vividly summarizes the behaviour of the Keynesian entrepreneur as follows: 'Without illusions who would ever dare invest in the long run?' (Dupuy, 1992, p. 186. Authors' translation from French). Such a statement contains a major implication: investment depends on incalculable elements which are, necessarily, exogenous when the stimulus to invest is tied to uncertain expectations. By taking investment as the exogenous variable, Kalecki constructed his version of the principle of effective demand on a recursive model in which capitalists' expenditure – the prime mover of the system – is outside the static logic in which expectations are given and stable.

We can find the same conception of economic activity in Keynes once we separate his analysis of the relationship between marginal efficiency of capital and the rate of interest from that of the state of long-run expectations. In this context, the principle of effective demand is *anti-classical*. It militates against the role assigned to the relationship between savings and investment by the classical economists, including Marx, whose theory of accumulation is radically different from that of Kalecki. The theory of effective demand does not require that investment be expressed by means of a determinate relation indicating the direction of growth. Instead, the only meaningful relation describing investment is that given by the inequality set out in an approximate way by Kaldor and made robust by Pasinetti (1974). The importance of the Kaldor–Pasinetti inequality lies in that it defines the essential conditions for the existence of a capitalist economy. Hence, as Kaldor (1996, p. 28) correctly noted, if total investment were not larger than saving out of wages 'the sales proceeds of entrepreneurs as a class would fall short of their outlays and the capitalist system couldn't function'. It follows that the share of investment in national income has to be smaller than the percentage of profits saved and greater than the percentage of wages saved. The Kaldor–Pasinetti inequality, therefore, while essential for understanding the *raison d'être* of capitalism, avoids the trap of foretelling history by constructing a scientific *law of motion*.

NOTES

1. The full quotation is as follows:

> When investment reaches its top level during the boom the following situation arises. Profits and national income, whose changes are directly related to those of investment, ceases to grow as well, but capital equipment continues to expand because net investment is positive. The increase in productive capacity is thus not matched by the rise in effective demand. As a result, investment declines and this causes in turn a fall in profit and national income. To put the causation of the downswing into proper perspective it is useful to inquire what would have happened in a similar situation in a socialist economy. (...) the changes in national income would not be tied to those in investment but would follow the changes in productive capacity. If investment remained constant while the stock of fixed capital expanded, prices would be reduced or wages raised. In this way the demand for consumption goods would increase in accordance with the expansion of the stock of capital (Kalecki, 1962, pp. 139–40).

2. For Kalecki, a socialist economy should be characterized by central planning but not by investment priority in the capital goods sector. To this effect, he criticized both the practice dominating in the USSR and Eastern Europe, as well as Dobbs's preference for capital-intensive techniques of production (Kalecki, 1972).

REFERENCES

Dupuy, J.P. (1992) *Introduction aux sciences sociales*, Paris, Ellipses.

Halevi, J. (1981) 'The composition of investment under conditions of non-uniform growth,' *Banca Nazionale del Lavoro Quarterly Review*, 137, 213–32.

Halevi, J. (1985) 'The contemporary significance of Baran and Sweezy's notion of monopolistic capitalism,' in M. Jarsulic (ed.) *Money and Macro-policy*, Boston and Dotrecht, Kluwer Nijhoff, pp. 109–33.

Halevi, J. (1992) 'Kalecki and modern capitalism,' *Monthly Review*, 44, 42–52.

Halevi, J. and P. Kriesler (1991) 'Kalecki and the surplus approach,' *Review of Political Economy*, 3, 79–92.

Kaldor, N. (1996) *Causes of Growth and Stagnation in the World Economy*, Cambridge, Cambridge University Press.

Kalecki, M. (1954) *The Theory of Economic Dynamics*, London, Allen and Unwin.

Kalecki, M. (1962) 'Observations on the theory of growth,' *Economic Journal*, 72, pp. 134–53. Reprinted in M. Kalecki (1991), *op. cit.*, pp. 411–34.

Kalecki, M. (1968a) 'Trend and business cycle reconsidered,' *Economic Journal*, 78, pp. 263–76. Reprinted in M. Kalecki (1991), *op. cit.*, pp. 65–83.

Kalecki, M. (1968b) 'The Marxian equations of reproduction and modern economics,' *Social Science Information*. Reprinted in Kalecki (1991) *op cit.*, pp. 459–66.

Kalecki, M. (1971) *Selected Essays on the Dynamics of the Capitalist Economy 1933–1970*, Cambridge, Cambridge University Press.

Kalecki, M. (1972) *Selected Essays on the Economic Growth of the Socialist and the Mixed Economy*, Cambridge, Cambridge University Press.

Kalecki, M. (1991) *Collected Works of Michal Kalecki*, Vol. II. *Capitalism: Economic dynamics*, ed. Jerzy Osiatynski, trans. Chester Adam Kisiel, Oxford, Clarendon Press.

Keynes, J.M. (1936) *The General Theory of Employment, Interest and Money*, London, Macmillan.
Keynes, J.M. (1937) 'The General Theory of Employment,' *Quarterly Journal of Economics*, 51, pp. 209–23. Reprinted in G.K. Shaw (ed.) (1988) *The Keynesian Heritage*, Vol. 1, Aldershot, Edward Elgar 7–21.
Kriesler, P. (1995) 'Feldman's structural model of economic growth,' in P. Groenewegen and B. Mcfarlane (eds) *Socialist Thought in the Post Cold War Era*, Manila, Journal of Contemporary Asia Publishers in conjunction with the Centre for the Study of the History of Economic Thought at the University of Sydney, pp. 27–38.
Marx, K.H. (1967) *Capital*, vols I, II, III, Moscow, Progress Publishers.
Marx, K.H. (1968) *Wage, Price and Profit*, Moscow, Progress Publishers.
Pasinetti, L. (1974) *Essays on Growth and Income Distribution*, Cambridge, Cambridge University Press.
Sylos-Labini, P. (1984) *The Forces of Economic Growth and Decline*, Cambridge, MA, MIT Press.

4. Growth and fluctuations in the USA: a demand-oriented explanation

H. Sonmez Atesoglu[1]

INTRODUCTION

This chapter provides a demand-oriented explanation of growth and fluctuations in aggregate output in the USA. Empirical cointegration and vector error correction models are developed using quarterly data. Findings reveal that investment, government spending, exports and the money supply determine the time path of output. These results suggest that there is bidirectional causality among output, investment and the money supply, and unidirectional causality running from government spending and exports to output, investment and the money supply.

In recent years, there has been a growing emphasis on the role of supply-side factors, such as technology shocks, in accounting for growth and fluctuations in aggregate output. In neoclassical macroeconomic theory, the possibility that aggregate demand and the money supply have long-term effects on output is generally ignored. Indeed, in some versions of the neoclassical approach, such as the new classical rational expectations models, not even short-term aggregate demand effects on output are allowed for.[2]

The neoclassical 'endogenous growth' theory recognizes, in addition to technological change, the crucial role of investment in explaining economic growth (see for example, Romer, 1986). The simpler neoclassical growth models of the Feder (1983) type allow exports and government spending a crucial role in determining economic growth.[3] But in these neoclassical growth models, there is no room for either aggregate demand or (and in particular) the money supply in determining economic growth.

The empirical evidence reported below in favour of the demand-oriented explanation of output, which allows the money supply to interact with investment, government spending and exports in explaining growth and fluctuations, raises doubts about the relevance of the neoclassical approach while lending support to the Keynesian/post-Keynesian alternative.

ANALYSIS OF THE DATA

The time paths of the macroeconomic variables examined below are depicted in Figures 4.1–4.4. Here, QL represents real GDP, IL is real investment (gross private domestic investment), GL is real government spending (government consumption expenditures and gross investment), XL is real exports (exports of goods and services) and M2L is the real M2 money supply (M2 deflated by a chained price index).[4] All of these variables are stated in natural logarithms. Observe that, in general, investment, government spending, exports and the money supply all move together over time with output, suggesting that these variables are likely to be cointegrated. The main exception to this observation is government spending in the late 1960s and late 1980s. The information conveyed in Figures 4.1–4.4 supports the demand-driven explanation of growth and fluctuations in output, which emphasizes the role of investment, government spending, exports and the money supply in providing an account of movements in the macro-economy.

A more rigorous confirmation of the demand-oriented explanation of growth and fluctations requires a formal empirical demonstration that the above variables are integrated of order one, and that their first differences are stationary. In addition, a quantitative cointegrating relation must be

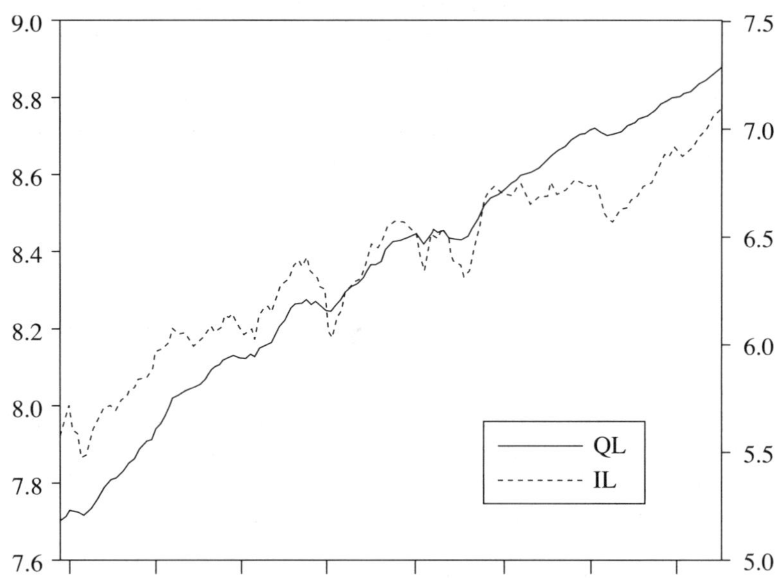

Figure 4.1 Real GDP and real investment

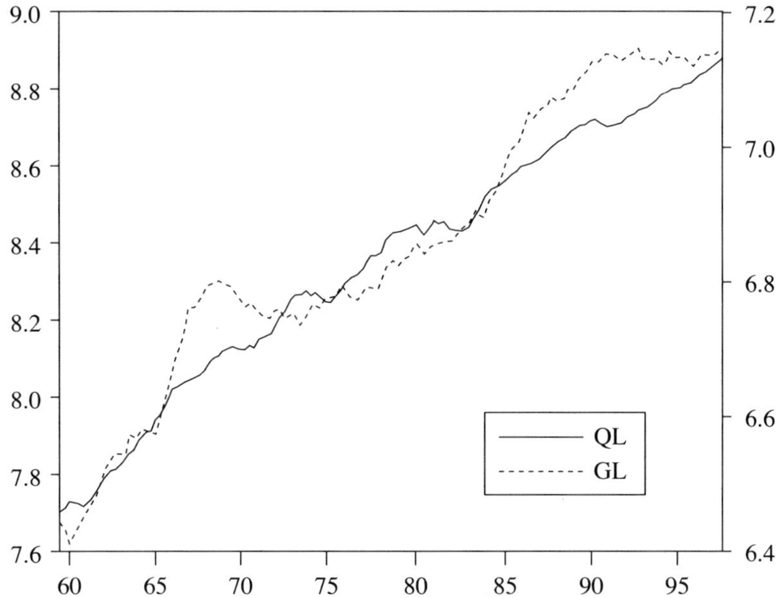

Figure 4.2 *Real GDP and real government spending*

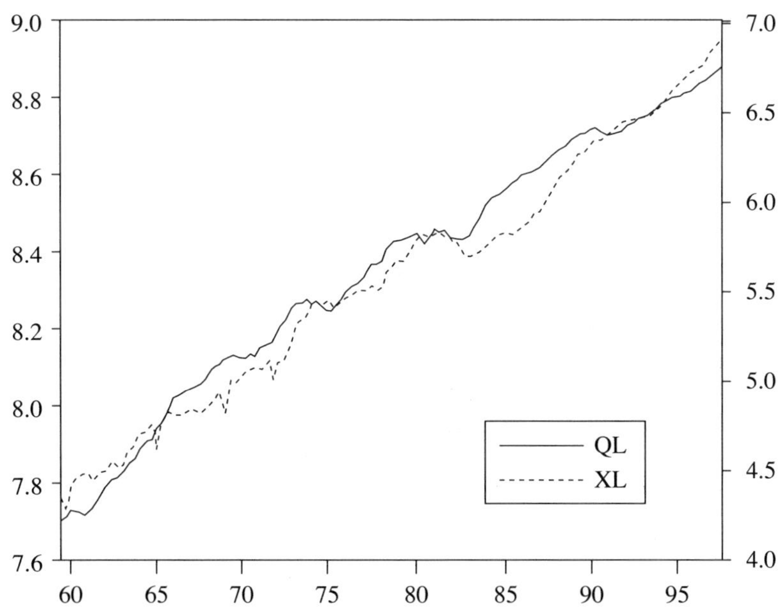

Figure 4.3 *Real GDP and real exports*

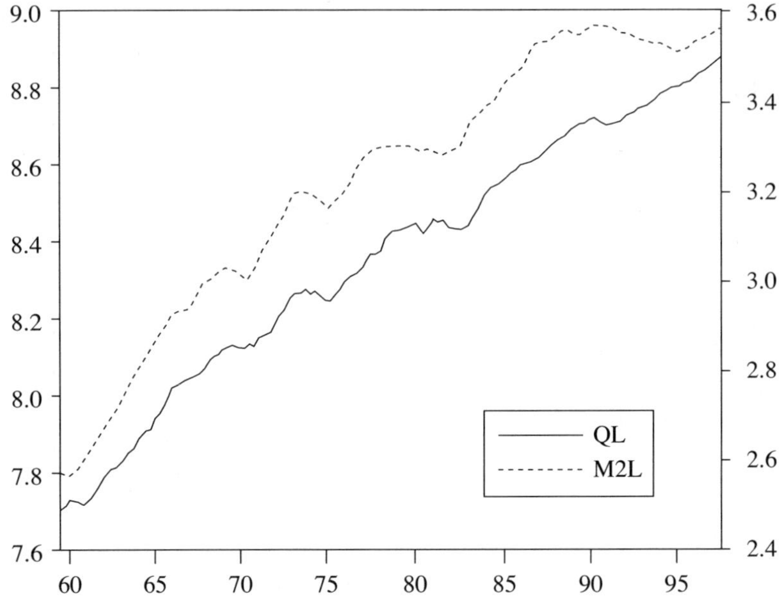

Figure 4.4 Real GDP and real M2 money supply

demonstrated, with the functional signs required by a Keynesian, demand-driven aggregate output equation.

In Table 4.1, Augmented Dickey-Fuller (ADF) test results are reported. These results indicate that QL, IL, GL, XL and M2L are integrated of order one, and that their first differences are stationary.

A DEMAND-ORIENTED EXPLANATION

The aggregate output equation was estimated by employing the Johansen procedure and the EViews program (Version 2.0, Quantitative Micro Software). The Johansen procedure is considered to be superior to other cointegration procedures (see Gonzalo, 1994). However, there is an important consideration in employing the Johansen method – the selection of the lag length to be employed. Recently, Granger (1997) has emphasized this practical difficulty while recognizing the advantages of the Johansen cointegration procedure.

Since the results of the Johansen procedure and their interpretation can differ with the lag lengths employed, in this study, following the suggestion by Charemza and Deadman (1997, chapter 6, pp. 200–1), the lag length was

Table 4.1 Tests of stationarity

Variable	Sample (adjusted)	Levels	Differences
		ADF test statistic	
QL	1960:4–1997:3	−1.782	
	1961:1–1997:3		−5.382*
IL	1960:4–1997:3	−1.168	
	1961:1–1997:3		−6.949*
GL	1960:4–1997:3	−1.814	
	1961:1–1997:3		−3.210*
XL	1960:4–1997:3	0.629	
	1961:1–1997:3		−5.573*
M2L	1960:4–1997:3	−2.557	
	1961:1–1997:3		−3.058*

Notes: Rejection of the unit root hypothesis according to McKinnon's critical value at 5 per cent is indicated with an asterisk. In the test equation, an intercept and four lagged differences are included.

selected by first estimating the cointegration equation starting with a relatively long lag length (12 quarters). The lag length was then systematically reduced to 8 and then to 6 quarters, while observing that there were no notable changes in the estimates and the cointegration test results. Since at the lag length of 4 quarters the results changed, the appropriate lag length was taken to be 6 quarters. A lag length of 6 quarters is also close to the lag length of 4 quarters that is most commonly employed with quarterly data.

The estimated empirical aggregate output model is given by the following long-run cointegration equation:

$$\underset{}{QL} = 3.446 + \underset{(0.018)}{0.255IL} + \underset{(0.023)}{0.213GL} + \underset{(0.011)}{0.128XL} + \underset{(0.024)}{0.346\,M2L} \qquad [4.1]$$

Sample: 1959:3–1997:3, number of observations = 146,
eigenvalue = 0.280, likelihood ratio = 82.896 and 5 per cent
critical value = 68.52, lag interval = 1 to 6.
A linear deterministic trend is assumed in the data.

The parameter estimates in equation [4.1] are normalized long-term cointegration coefficients. Values in parentheses are the standard errors of normalized cointegration coefficients. The likelihood ratio (Trace) test indicates one cointegrating equation at the 5 per cent critical level.

The results in equation [4.1] reveal a significant and positive long-run cointegrating relationship between output and investment, government spending, exports and the money supply. This important empirical finding, which lends strong support to the demand-oriented explanation of changes in aggregate output, is also supported by the results from an estimation of equation [4.1] using the OLSQ method:

$$\underset{}{QL} = 0.683 + \underset{(0.010)}{0.173IL} + \underset{(0.018)}{0.215GL} + \underset{(0.005)}{0.180XL} + \underset{(0.016)}{0.342\,M2L} \quad [4.2]$$

Sample: 1959:3–1997:3, number of observations = 153,
R-squared = 0.999, S.E. = 0.011, DW = 0.474.
Values in parentheses are standard errors.

Note that the parameter estimates in equation [4.2] have the same signs as and similar values to those reported in equation [4.1]. The results in equation [4.2] are consistent with and complementary to those of the Johansen procedure, and raise confidence in the conclusion that there is a positive long-run cointegrating relationship between output and investment, government spending, exports and the money supply.[5]

In Table 4.2, results from the vector error correction model estimated by the Johansen procedure are reported. Each of the five equations of the vector error correction model can be thought of as short-run explanations of changes in output, investment, government spending, exports and the money supply, respectively.

The error correction term in each equation of the vector error correction model indicates whether or not the dependent variable adjusts in response to

Table 4.2 Results from estimation of vector error correction model

	Error correction equation, dependent variable				
	ΔQL	ΔIL	ΔGL	ΔXL	ΔM2L
Error correction term	0.189	1.942	–0.103	0.026	0.112
(t-statistic)	(2.315)	(5.111)	–1.032	(0.070)	(1.791)
[s.e]	[0.082]	[0.380]	[0.100]	[0.367]	[0.063]
R-squared	0.421	0.518	0.303	0.326	0.655
S.E. (equation)	0.008	0.037	0.010	0.035	0.006

Notes: Sample (adjusted): 1961:2–1997:3, number of observations = 146 (after adjusting end points), lag interval = 1 to 6. Standard errors are reported in brackets and t-statistics in parentheses. In each error correction equation, in addition to the error correction term and an intercept, lagged values of ΔQL, ΔIL, ΔGL, ΔXL and ΔM2L were included as explanatory variables.

disequilibrium between the dependent variable and the explanatory variables of the error correction equation (see Enders, 1995). It can be seen that the error correction term is a significant determinant of output, investment and the money supply. However, the error correction term is not a significant determinant of government spending and exports.

The above findings and cointegration results from equation [4.1] suggest that there is bidirectional causality among output, investment and the money supply, and unidirectional causality running from government spending and exports to output, investment and the money supply. These causal relations are consistent with Keynesian and post-Keynesian macroeconomic theory, in which government spending and exports determine output, while investment and the money supply both affect output and are, themselves, influenced by developments in the macro-economy.

CONCLUSION

The findings discussed above provide rigorous empirical support for demand-oriented explanations of growth and fluctuations. The empirical models estimated indicate that investment, government spending, exports and the money supply play a crucial role in determining the time path of aggregate output. These macroeconomic variables typically occupy a central place in Keynesian and post-Keynesian macroeconomic theory (see for example Kaldor, 1981; Weintraub, 1981–2; Davidson, 1994; Cornwall and Cornwall, 1997). An important feature of post-Keynesian macroeconomic thought is the idea that the real and monetary sectors of the economy are interdependent. The positive cointegrating relationship reported above between the money supply and other (real) variables confirms this Keynesian view.

The strong empirical support that the demand-oriented approach to growth and fluctuations receives from USA data corroborates the favourable empirical evidence from other industrialized countries (see Atesoglu, 1996; Cornwall and Cornwall, 1997).[6] The findings reported in this study also help to defuse the aggregate demand management pessimism (which claims that Keynesian demand management policies are neither effective nor required)[7] that has been embraced by neoclassical macroeconomists in recent years, and which seems to hold great sway among policy makers.

NOTES

1. An earlier version of this chapter was presented at the Eastern Economic Association, 25th Annual Conference, March, 1999. I would like to thank the session participants for their comments.

2. Gordon (1993) and Mankiw (1997) discuss the varieties of neoclassical macroeconomics. For a critique of the neoclassical approach to economic growth, see McCombie and Thirlwall (1994, 1997) and McCombie (1999).
3. In addition to Feder (1983), see also Ram (1986).
4. The source of this data is the 'Fred' database of the Federal Reserve Bank of St. Louis, as of 21 December 1997.
5. Granger (1997) recommends comparing and complementing results from the Johansen procedure with OLSQ-based results, despite Gonzalo's (1994) demonstration that the Johansen procedure is the best available for estimating cointegration relations.
6. Favourable results for the demand-oriented Keynesian theory also corroborate those findings supportive of the demand-driven, balance-of-payments-constrained growth model of Thirlwall (see Atesoglu, 1997), and the post-Keynesian explanation of employment in the USA by Atesoglu (1999).
7. Cunningham and Vilasuso (1994–5) and Davidson (1996) discuss this demand management pessimism.

REFERENCES

Atesoglu, H.S. (1996) 'A demand-oriented explanation of economic growth in Germany,' *Journal of Post Keynesian Economics*, 19, 101–11.

Atesoglu, H.S. (1997) 'Balance-of-payments-constrained growth: evidence for the U.S. economy,' *Journal of Post Keynesian Economics*, 19, 327–53.

Atesoglu, H.S. (1999) 'A Post Keynesian explanation of employment in the United States,' *Journal of Post Keynesian Economics*, 21, 603–610.

Charemza, W.W. and D.F. Deadman (1997) *New Directions in Econometric Practice*, Aldershot, Edward Elgar.

Cornwall, J. and W. Cornwall (1997) 'The unemployment problem and legacy of Keynes,' *Journal of Post Keynesian Economics*, 19, 525–42.

Cunningham, S.R. and J. Vilasuso (1994–5) 'Is Keynesian demand management policy still viable?' *Journal of Post Keynesian Economics*, 17, 187–210.

Davidson, P. (1994) *Post Keynesian Macroeconomic Theory*, Aldershot, Edward Elgar.

Davidson, P. (1996) 'The viability of Keynesian demand management in an open economy context,' *International Review of Applied Economics*, 10, 91–105.

Enders, W. (1995) *Applied Econometric Time Series*, New York, John Wiley and Sons

Feder, G. (1983) 'On exports and economic growth,' *Journal of Development Economics*, 12, 59–73.

Gonzalo, J. (1994) 'Five alternative methods of estimating long-run equilibrium relationships,' *Journal of Econometrics*, 60, 203–33.

Gordon, R.J. (1993) *Macroeconomics*, New York, Harper Collins.

Granger, C.W.J. (1997) 'On modelling the long run in applied economics,' *Economic Journal*, 107, 169–77.

Kaldor, N. (1981) *Origins of the New Monetarism*, Cardiff, University College Cardiff Press.

Mankiw, N.G. (1997) *Macroeconomics*, New York, Worth Publishers.

McCombie, J.S.L. (1999) 'A problem with the empirical neoclassical analysis of multisector growth,' in M. Setterfield (ed.) *Growth, Employment and Inflation: Essays in Honour of John Cornwall*, London, Macmillan, 127–48.

McCombie, J.S.L. and A.P. Thirlwall (1994) *Economic Growth and the Balance of Payments Constraint*, New York, St. Martin's Press.

McCombie, J.S.L. and A.P. Thirlwall (1997) 'The dynamic Harrod foreign trade multiplier and the demand-oriented approach to economic growth: an evaluation,' *International Review of Applied Economics*, 11, 5–26.
Ram, R. (1986) 'Government size and economic growth: a new framework and some evidence from cross-section and time-series data,' *American Economic Review*, 76, 191–203.
Romer, P.M. (1986) 'Increasing returns and long-run growth,' *Journal of Political Economy*, 94, 1002–37.
Weintraub, S. (1981–2) 'Keynesian demand serendipity in supply-side economics,' *Journal of Post Keynesian Economics*, 4, 101–11.

PART TWO

Kaldorian Models of Demand-led Growth

5. A neo-Kaldorian perspective on the rise and decline of the Golden Age

Mark Setterfield and John Cornwall

INTRODUCTION

The focus of this chapter is the generalized slowdown in output and productivity growth rates in the advanced capitalist economies since 1973. Our purpose is to construct a neo-Kaldorian model capable of explaining this growth slowdown.

Our approach rests on the notion that capitalism is not self-regulating, because it does not automatically create either sufficient demand or the institutional structures necessary for rapid – much less full employment – growth. The model posits that capitalistic growth occurs in discrete episodes, and that each episode can be characterized in terms of a historically specific *Macroeconomic Regime* (MR). These MRs comprise a process of income generation embedded within a historically specific institutional framework, which together give rise to the conditional steady-state output and productivity growth outcomes characteristic of a growth episode.[1] The conditionality of these steady states arises from the fact that institutions, although relatively inert and enduring, are not immutable – they can and do change over time. Any equilibrium is thus *conditional* on the reproduction over time of a specific institutional structure.

The resulting model is neo-Kaldorian in the sense that it modifies a traditional Kaldorian growth schema, based on cumulative causation, by introducing institutional considerations. These are modelled as discrete parameter changes, thereby allowing us to characterize the *episodic* nature of capitalist growth. Our ultimate aim is to apply the model in order to explain the Golden Age (1945–73) and Age of Decline (post-1973) as distinct and relatively enduring growth episodes.[2] This is a task to which mainstream (neoclassical) growth theory is particularly unsuited. Its 'once and for all' characterization of growth dynamics makes no systematic effort to distinguish between structurally different episodes in capitalist growth and the marked differences in growth performance with which they can be associated.

The rest of the chapter is organized as follows. The next section outlines some stylized facts of modern capitalism and the essential features of our neo-Kaldorian conception of growth. The third section then constructs models of the Golden Age (GA) and Age of Decline (AoD), showing how differences in the institutional structures of these growth episodes have resulted in the generalized slowdown in growth since 1973. A fourth section offers some conjectures about the 1990s and the prospects for a new, neoliberal growth episode and the final section concludes.

STYLIZED FACTS, GROWTH EPISODES AND A NEO-KALDORIAN CONCEPTION OF GROWTH

Some Stylized Facts about Modern Capitalism

It is well known that the post-war Golden Age of capitalism (1945–73) was characterized by low rates of unemployment and inflation, rapid rates of output and productivity growth, high rates of investment, stable international trade and payments systems coupled with a rapid rate of growth of world trade and a 'value sharing' norm of distributive justice that resulted in a high and stable wage share of income and growing real wages.[3] By contrast, the era since 1973 has witnessed high rates of unemployment and inflation, a generalized output and productivity growth slowdown, lower rates of investment, volatile international trade and payments systems coupled with a reduction in the rate of growth of world trade and the emergence of a 'winner take all' norm of distributive justice, associated with an increase in the profit share of income and the stagnation of real wages.

The stylized facts reported above suggest that the GA and AoD constitute two distinct *episodes* in modern capitalism, distinguished by differences in both their structure and macroeconomic performance. The *stylized facts of performance* indicate that the GA was a high-(productivity and output) growth episode, whereas the AoD is a low-growth episode. Meanwhile, the GA and AoD can also be distinguished in terms of two important sets of *structural stylized facts*, pertaining to norms of distribution on one hand, and the institutional structure of international trade and finance on the other.

The GA was characterized by a 'value sharing' norm of distributive justice. Central to this norm were social bargains between capital, labour and the state that reconciled the competing claims on total income of the social classes (Cornwall, 1990, 1994; Cornwall and Cornwall, 2001).[4] Under the terms of these social bargains, capital retained the 'right to manage' the workplace, in return for a commitment to a high and stable wage share of income and annual growth in real wages. By reconciling distributional conflict, social bargains prevented the emergence of an inflationary constraint on macroeconomic performance during the GA.[5] This facilitated a second important aspect of the GA norm of distributive justice – the state's commitment to and active pursuit of conditions of full employment.

By way of contrast, the AoD is characterized by a 'winner take all' norm of distributive justice. This emerged from the collapse of the GA social bargains (see Cornwall, 1990, 1994) and the subsequent emergence of a 'market power' approach to industrial relations by capital, labour and the state. Initially (that is, during the late 1960s/early 1970s), the market power approach manifested itself in a challenge to capital's control of the workplace and pressure on the profit share of income – the latter accompanied by the unleashing of inflationary pressures. However, this provoked reactions by both capital and the state, the results of which have become the hallmark of the AoD norm of distributive justice: changes in corporate organization, changes in labour law and the abandonment of the full employment goal, the latter part of a deliberate strategy to raise unemployment, disempower workers and subdue inflationary pressures (Cornwall, 1990, 1994; Palley, 1998; Osterman, 1999).

A second set of structural stylized facts that distinguish the GA from the AoD concerns the institutions of international trade and finance. During the GA, international trade and payments were governed by the Bretton Woods system. A particularly important feature of this system was its use of capital controls to protect fixed exchange rates and, at the same time, liberate macroeconomic policy to pursue domestic goals. By contrast, the AoD has been characterized by the collapse of the Bretton Woods system and increasing deregulation of international financial markets. The increased prominence and mobility of financial capital in this new regime has encouraged the use of deflationary domestic macroeconomic policies designed to placate the inflation- and currency-depreciation-averse international financial community (Cornwall and Cornwall, 2001; Palley, 1998).[6]

The question that now confronts us is how, if at all, these structural stylized facts can be related to the stylized facts of performance discussed earlier? In other words, can we relate the institutional differences between the GA and AoD to their different growth performances?

It was suggested earlier that growth episodes can be understood as being the result of an income-generating process embedded within an institutional framework. The structural stylized facts discussed above describe key aspects of the institutional frameworks of the GA and AoD growth episodes. In order to relate these institutional frameworks to growth outcomes, then, we need to articulate the income-generating processes embedded within them. It is to this task that we now turn.

A Neo-Kaldorian View of Growth

The income-generating process characteristic of both the GA and the AoD rests on what we identify as two 'fundamentals' of a capitalist economy. By a fundamental, we mean a causal proposition that we take as basic to the functioning of capitalism, regardless of the precise growth episode that we are dealing with. These fundamentals are, of course, necessary but not sufficient for the analysis of capitalist economies; they must be supplemented by historically specific institutional features of the system if we are to understand actual economic outcomes. Our fundamentals reduce to the following propositions:

a. the actual rate of growth is demand determined. Because there is no inherent tendency for the value of demand to equate with the value of what is produced, neither the level of economic activity at a point in time nor its growth over time can be analysed exclusively in supply-side terms. Rather, explicit account must be taken of the propensity for relatively autonomous demand forces to determine both the utilization rate of existing resources (capital and labour) at any point in time, and changes in this utilization rate over time.

b. the division of labour depends on the extent of the market or, more generally, the potential (or Harrodian natural) rate of growth is influenced by demand. Demand affects not just the utilization of productive resources at any point in time, then, but also the very development of these resources over time, through induced technological progress and innovation, and the influence of demand on labour force participation and the allocation of labour across different sectors of the economy (see, for example, Cornwall, 1977, chapters 6 and 7). It should be noted that the influence of demand on supply as postulated here is accompanied by feedbacks from supply to demand, as will become clear in the formal model developed below. Ultimately, then, there exists a recursive, joint interaction between supply and demand in our growth schema. However, supply cannot automatically create its own demand, whereas we can (although need not) observe 'Say's law in reverse' (demand creating its own supply). Demand, therefore, occupies a privileged position in this recursive interaction, from which our emphasis on demand and the nomenclature 'demand-led growth' emerge straightforwardly.

The fundamentals identified above, together with the notion of an institutional framework within which they are embedded, permit us to identify three 'regimes' on which the analysis of capitalistic growth can be based. These are the Demand Regime (DR), the Productivity Regime (PR) and the Institutional Regime (IR).[7] A DR describes demand formation or, more precisely, the determination of the rate of growth of aggregate demand, and the relationship in which the latter stands to the growth of output (of which it is the proximate determinant). Beyond this fundamental relationship, the precise form of the DR is influenced by the dominant theoretical and policy visions regarding the role of aggregate demand in the economy, and hence the extent to which aggregate demand is or is not purposively managed in the pursuit of utilizing and encouraging the development of productive resources.

A PR, meanwhile, describes the determination of the rate of productivity growth. It is based on the fundamental proposition that the division of labour depends on the size of the market – that is, that the determinants of the natural rate of growth are, themselves, demand-determined. Beyond this fundamental relationship, the precise form of the PR depends on those institutions that impinge upon the organization of the production process, as reflected in the size of the elasticity of productivity with respect to output, or the Verdoorn coefficient.

Finally, an IR is a relatively enduring macro-institutional structure within which economic behaviour takes place. It constitutes the 'operating system' that provides the social infrastructure necessary, in an environment of uncertainty and conflict, to create stability, undergird the state of long-run expectations, reconcile competing distributional demands and hence facilitate economic activity among decentralized decision makers.

As demonstrated below, the idea of an income-generating mechanism based on a DR, a PR and their joint interaction can be derived from Kaldor's (1985) model of cumulative causation. Essentially, then, our neo-Kaldorian model proposes that capitalistic growth can be understood as a series of growth episodes, each characterized by a Kaldorian cumulative growth schema embedded in a historically specific IR (the latter evidenced by the different structural stylized facts of each episode). The DR, PR and IR thus combine to form the *Macroeconomic Regime* (MR) on which the growth episode is based. This, in turn, yields the conditional steady-state outcomes from which an episode's stylized facts of performance can be derived.[8] By employing a Kaldorian growth schema in tandem with the structural stylized facts described earlier, then, we can model the GA and AoD growth episodes, and explain the growth slowdown characteristic of the latter episode. It is to this task that we now turn.

MODELLING THE GA AND THE AOD: THE ANATOMY OF THE GROWTH SLOWDOWN

A Traditional Kaldorian Growth Schema

Our basic model of the income-generating process is a traditional Kaldorian model of cumulative causation (see, for example, McCombie and Thirlwall,

1994). The model, which provides a stylized description of a 'representative' advanced capitalist economy, can be stated as follows:

$$q = r + \alpha y \qquad [5.1]$$

$$p = w - q + \tau \qquad [5.2]$$

$$x = \beta(p_w - p) + \gamma y_w \qquad [5.3]$$

$$y = \lambda(\omega_X x + \omega_A a) \qquad [5.4]$$

where q denotes productivity growth, y is the rate of growth of output, p is the rate of inflation, w denotes nominal wage inflation, τ is the rate of growth of the gross mark-up,[9] x is the rate of growth of exports and a is the rate of growth of autonomous expenditures other than exports. Meanwhile, the parameter r represents exogenous determinants of q, α is the elasticity of productivity with respect to output or Verdoorn coefficient, β is the price elasticity of demand for exports, γ is the income elasticity of demand for exports, λ is an expenditure multiplier and ω_X and ω_A denote, respectively, the shares of exports and other autonomous expenditures in real income. The subscript w denotes the value of a variable in the rest of the world.[10]

Notice that this model does more than capture the fundamentals of growth described earlier. First, implicit in the structure of the second and third equations are features of an IR – namely, the convention of cost-based (rather than non-price) competition. Specifically, international competition is described as working through the impact of the growth of unit labour costs on inflation (equation [5.2]) which, in turn, has an inverse effect on export growth via its effects on the relative prices of tradables (equation [5.3]).[11] Second, the value of key parameters (such as r, α, a and y_w) will be affected by the IR, as will become clearer in what follows. For now, note that the model can be written in reduced form as:

$$q = r + \alpha y \qquad [5.1]$$

$$y = \Omega + \lambda\omega_X\beta q \qquad [5.5]$$

where $\Omega = \lambda(\omega_A a - \omega_X\beta r + \omega_X(\gamma - \alpha_w\beta)y_w)$. Equation [5.1] represents the PR, and [5.5] is the DR. Assuming that $\Omega > 0 > -r/\alpha$ and that $1/\alpha > \lambda\omega_X\beta \Rightarrow \lambda\omega_X\alpha\beta < 1$,[12] the PR and DR described above can be represented as in Figure 5.1, in which the PR intersects with the DR from below, giving rise to the conditional steady-state rates of output and productivity growth y_G and q_G. Suppose, however, that y and q are below their conditional equilibrium values

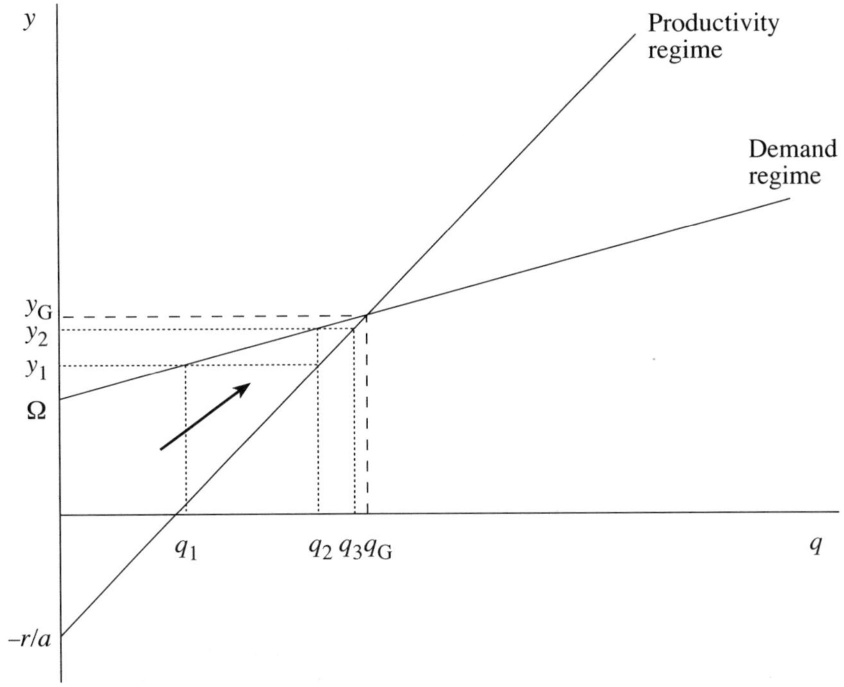

Figure 5.1 The Golden Age growth episode

to begin with. At q_1, for example, the economy will initially experience the demand-determined rate of output growth y_1. But this rate of output growth will cause an increase in productivity growth to q_2, thanks to the Verdoorn effects captured in the PR (equation [5.1]). The increase in productivity growth so described will then stimulate an increase in the rate of output growth to y_2. This occurs as the increased rate of productivity growth lowers domestic inflation (equation [5.2]) which spurs export growth (equation [5.3]) and hence the growth of demand (equation [5.4]) – a sequence of events that is summarized by the DR in equation [5.5]. The new, higher rate of output growth y_2 will cause a further increase in productivity growth to q_3, and so on. In fact, productivity and output growth will continue to increase in this fashion (as indicated by the arrow in Figure 5.1) until they reach their conditional steady-state values.[13]

Modelling the GA and AoD

Now suppose that the model above represents the GA – in other words, that the parameters of [5.1] and [5.5] reflect the two structural stylized facts about the GA described earlier, so that q_G and y_G in Figure 5.1 represent, respectively, the conditional steady-state rates of productivity and output growth during the GA. Suppose further that the AoD can be represented by the following PR and DR, again derived from an income-generating process similar to that described in equations [5.1]–[5.4], but this time reflecting the structural stylized facts of the AoD:

$$q = r' + \alpha' y \qquad [5.6]$$

$$y = \Omega' + \lambda\omega_x\beta q \qquad [5.7]$$

where $\Omega' = \lambda(\omega_A\alpha' - \omega_X\beta r' + \omega_X(\gamma - \alpha_w\beta)y'_w)$. Equation [5.6] captures the PR of the AoD, and equation [5.7] the DR of this episode.

It is clear by inspection of equations [5.1], [5.5], [5.6] and [5.7] that any differences between the growth performances of the GA and AoD must stem from differences between the parameters r and r', and α and α' and Ω and Ω' – or, in other words, differences between the GA and AoD IRs, and the impact of these IRs on the PR and DR of the Kaldorian income-generating mechanism outlined above. The question that now confronts us, then, is what is the relative size of these parameters?

Changes in the institutional structure of postwar capitalism since the end of the GA have adversely affected both its DR and PR, and hence its growth performance. Consider first the DR. The GA IR was conducive to both reflationary macroeconomic policies and high rates of accumulation.[14] As noted earlier, both the social bargains of the norm of distributive justice and the institutions of international trade and finance relieved macroeconomic policy constraints (inflation problems and the need to placate international financial capital, respectively), while the commitment to full employment embodied in the social bargains ensured that macroeconomic policy was reflationary in its orientation. Meanwhile, high rates of accumulation can be explained by the relative absence of distributional conflict and uncertainty as to the profit share of income, together with the accelerator-type effect of high and rising aggregate demand (and hence conditions of full employment) – both of which were products of the GA IR.

However, the demise of the GA IR resulted in the advent of both deflationary macroeconomic policies (Epstein and Schor, 1990, pp. 143–9) and a decreased rate of accumulation (Glyn et al., 1990, p. 87). The former, which was coordinated across individual capitalist economies, constituted a deliberate effort to increase labour market discipline in response to inflationary pressures. The latter can be understood as having initially been the consequence of increased conflict and uncertainty as the GA IR unravelled, and subsequently, of new policy norms embedded in the AoD IR, which included abandonment of the state's commitment to the maintenance of high and rising aggregate demand in the pursuit of full employment. These changes in the orientation of macroeconomic policy and the rate of investment amount to declines in the rates of growth of domestic autonomous demand and (owing to the synchronization of deflationary policies and reduced accumulation among capitalist economies) world income. In terms of equations [5.5] and [5.7], they can be captured by the inequalities $a' < a$ and $y'_w < y_w$, so that *ceteris paribus*, $\Omega' < \Omega$.[15]

Meanwhile, the demise of the GA IR adversely affected the PR of capitalist economies in two ways. First, since investment is necessary for the realization of technical progress embodied in physical capital, the decline in the rate of accumulation noted above had a negative impact on productivity growth.[16] Second, the demise of the GA social bargains had a direct, negative effect on productivity growth. This is because the 'effective effort' of labour (i.e., both exertion and cooperation) is necessary for the realization of productivity gains associated with technological and organizational change (Buchele and Christiansen, 1999). But the labour market discipline effects of slower growth and high unemployment – a necessary accompaniment of the market power AoD IR – are not an effective substitute for the explicit conciliation and cooperation of a social bargain in eliciting effective effort from workers (Weisskopf, 1987). In terms of equations [5.1] and [5.6], these developments can be captured by a reduction in the Verdoorn coefficient, so that we have $\alpha' < \alpha$.

Finally, there is one important structural change unrelated to institutions that has nevertheless had an important effect on the PRs of capitalist economies during the postwar era. Specifically, the ongoing transformation of capitalism associated with the increasing prominence of the service sector has had an adverse effect on productivity growth during the postwar years (Cornwall and Cornwall, 2001). In terms of equations [5.1] and [5.6], this can be captured by a decline in the autonomous trend rate of productivity growth, so that we have $r' < r$.

Comparative Growth Performance during the GA and AoD

Based on the considerations in the previous section, we can now restate our neo-Kaldorian models of postwar growth as:

$$q = r + \alpha y \qquad [5.1]$$

$$y = \Omega + \lambda\omega_X\beta q \qquad [5.5]$$

for the GA, and:

$$q = r' + \alpha' y \qquad [5.6]$$

$$y = \Omega' + \lambda\omega_X \beta q \qquad [5.7]$$

for the AoD, where $r' < r$, $\alpha' < \alpha$ and $\Omega' < \Omega$. Assuming that $\Omega' > 0 > -r'/\alpha'$ and that $1/\alpha' > \lambda\omega_X\beta \Rightarrow \lambda\omega_X\alpha'\beta < 1$,[17] the PRs and DRs of the GA and AoD – and hence their comparative growth outcomes – can be represented by Figure 5.2.

In Figure 5.2, y_A and q_A denote, respectively, the conditional steady-state rates of growth of output and productivity during the AoD. This figure clearly depicts the decline in output and productivity growth that has occurred since the end of the GA. The declines in these growth rates can be associated with changes in both the PR and DR over the post-war period, changes that can, in turn, be traced to differences between the IRs of the GA and AoD. The result of these structural differences – as depicted in Figure 5.2 – has been a generalized slowdown in output and productivity growth in capitalist economies during the post-1973 period.

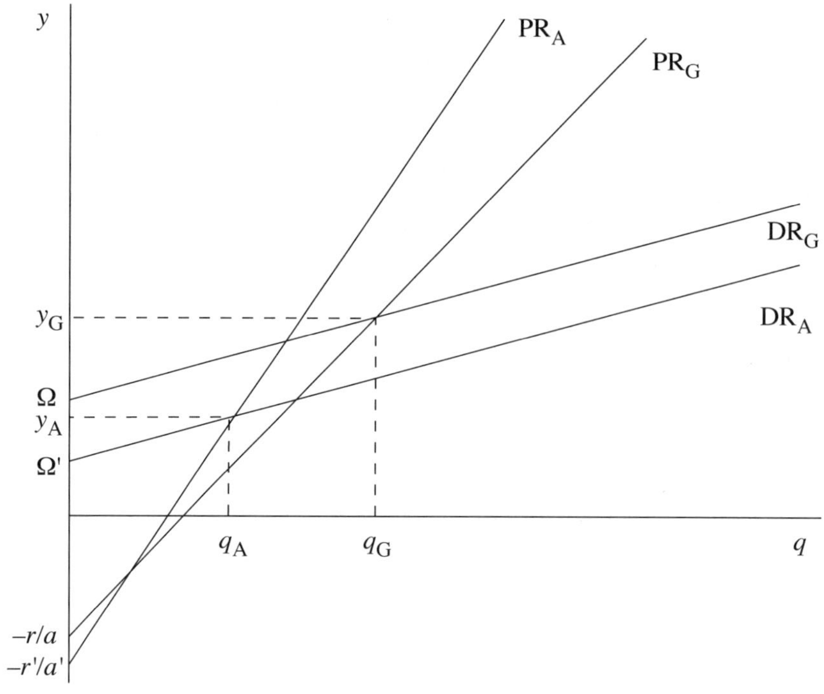

Figure 5.2 The golden age and age of decline growth episodes compared

What all this demonstrates is that by taking a Kaldorian growth schema to represent the 'fundamentals' of the income-generating mechanism of capitalism, structural changes that are primarily institutional in nature, and which alter the social environment or 'operating system' within which the fundamentals of income generation are embedded, can be used to explain the marked differences in growth performance between the GA and the AoD.

CONJECTURES ON THE 1990S: A NEW, NEOLIBERAL GROWTH EPISODE IN THE MAKING?

During 1990s, the macroeconomic performance of the US economy has markedly improved, relative to its own performance during the 1970s and 1980s, and that of other capitalist economies. In particular, a long boom has resulted in the reduction of unemployment to levels last seen at the end of the GA, without the accompaniment of significant inflation. More recently, there has also been an improvement in productivity growth. The purpose of this section is to suggest that these developments can be explained in terms of our neo-Kaldorian model, by taking into account the institutional characteristics of the 1990s' boom in the USA, and their impact on the PR and DR of the US economy.

A key development in the US economy in recent decades has been the institutionalization of the discipline necessary to relieve pressure on the profit share/rate of inflation in a market power industrial relations system. This has been brought about by anti-labour law in the 1980s and its impact on trade unions, changes in the structure of the labour market (in particular, the growth of part-time and contingent work), and increased capital mobility, which has resulted in the ability of US producers to 'import' the disciplinary effects of unemployment from other capitalist economies (and from high unemployment regions within its own borders) by threatening to relocate production (Setterfield, 2000). Finally, there has been a deflation of worker aspirations – a change in the norms advising worker demands, resulting in the emergence of a new convention of expecting less in an environment characterized by the 'natural order' of 'free markets'. In sum, both constraints and (lack of) aspirations have resulted in institutionalized worker compliance.

These changes suggest that, at the present point in time, the USA does not need to use deflationary policies designed to maintain high unemployment in order to discipline workers and thus contain inflation. A reflation of the US DR has thus been permitted, led by a relaxation of monetary policy and a debt-financed consumption boom (Godley, 1999, pp. 8–10). Fiscal policy has remained restrictive, however, and although the rate of growth of investment has increased significantly relative to its rate during the AoD (see Table 5.1),

Table 5.1 Average annual rates of growth of real non-residential investment in the USA, selected periods, 1960–99

Period	Rate of growth of investment (%)
1960–67	7.73
1967–73	5.83
1973–79	5.20
1979–89	3.17
1989–99	7.16

Source: Bureau of Economic Analysis (2000).

it has done so only since the mid-1990s, as a result of a surge in investment in information technology.[18] The US DR during the 1990s can thus be written as:

$$y = \Omega'' + \lambda\omega_X\beta q \quad [5.8]$$

where $\Omega' < \Omega'' < \Omega$.

As regards its PR, the USA can now rely on an increased supply of 'effective effort' by workers (and its concomitant positive effects on the Verdoorn coefficient) because of a mixture of non-unemployment-based discipline effects coupled with aspiration deflation (see Osterman, 1999).[19] There remains controversy, however, as to whether or not coercing workers in this fashion is as successful in eliciting effective effort as GA-style social bargain methods, based on the 'carrots' of participation and value sharing (Buchele and Christiansen, 1999).

A second controversy surrounding the US PR concerns the impact of information and communications technologies (ICTs), and the extent to which there is now a 'new economy' in the USA in which investment in ICTs has raised the trend rate of productivity growth. As noted above, there has been a boom in investment in ICTs in the USA since 1995. At the same time, labour productivity has grown at about 2.5 per cent per annum 1995–99, a full percentage point higher than its rate of growth during the previous four years. According to Oliner and Sichel (2000), this is no coincidence: ICTs account for two-thirds of the increase in the rate of labour productivity growth in the USA since 1995. Gordon (2000), however, is doubtful as to whether this constitutes a 'new economy' in the sense described above.[20] First, he notes that a significant portion (as much as 0.5 percentage points) of the increase in productivity growth is attributable to cyclical effects. Second, he finds that while the trend rate of multi-factor productivity growth has increased in the durable manufacturing sector, there has been a *decrease* in the trend rate of multi-factor productivity growth in the remaining 88 per cent of the US economy, despite large-scale investments in ICTs outside the durable manufacturing sector.[21] According to Gordon, then, there still exists a Solow paradox – the idea that computers can be found everywhere except in the productivity statistics – in most of the US economy.

Finally, it is worth noting that the rate of accumulation during the 1990s still falls marginally short of its rate during the similarly long boom of the 1960s (see Table 5.1),[22] and that there has been no change in the trend towards increasing service sector dominance of US employment. Combining the various elements of the foregoing discussion, the US PR during the 1990s can be written as:

$$q = r' + \alpha'' y \qquad [5.14]$$

where $\alpha' < \alpha'' < \alpha$.

The US DR and PR during the 1990s (DR_{90s} and PR_{90s}, respectively) and their implications for q and y (denoted as q_{90s} and y_{90s}, respectively) are shown in Figure 5.3, which also contains the GA and AoD PRs and DRs for the purpose of contrast.

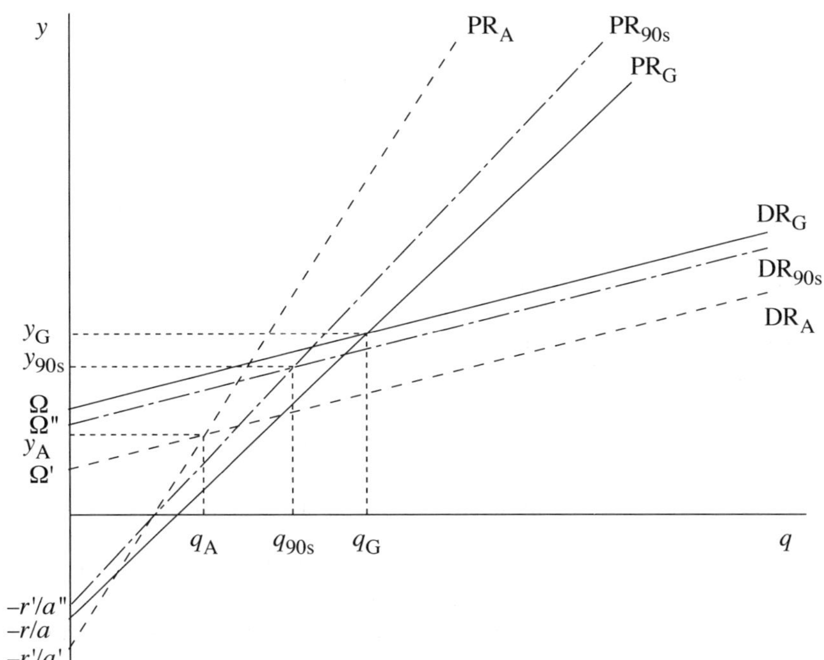

Figure 5.3 The 90s boom – the start of a neoliberal growth episode?

Table 5.2 Average annual rates of growth of non-farm real output, labour productivity and employment in the USA, selected periods, 1960–98

Period	Output growth (%)	Productivity growth (%)	Employment growth (%)
1960–67	5.1	3.4	1.7
1967–73	4.3	2.6	1.7
1973–79	3.3	1.3	2.0
1979–89	3.2	1.4	1.8
1989–98	3.4	1.9	1.5
1960–73	4.7	3.0	1.7
1973–89	3.2	1.4	1.9
1989–98	3.4	1.9	1.5
1989–98[1]	3.4	2.2	1.2

Notes: 1. Productivity and output growth are calculated here using the accounting proportions of the 1960–73 period – i.e., each one percentage point of real output growth is associated with 0.72 percentage points of productivity growth and 0.28 percentage points of employment growth.

Source: *Economic Report of the President*, 2000, p. 363.

Figure 5.3 shows increases in y and q in the USA during the 1990s relative to the AoD; neither recovers to rates comparable with the GA. Furthermore, Figure 5.3 shows that regardless of the inferiority of PR_{90s} relative to PR_{GA}, it is still possible for the USA to raise both y and q by reflating the DR (confirming the views of Howes, 1999), but that any given rate of output growth is now associated with lower productivity growth. This is confirmed in Table 5.2, in which the final row shows what the 1990s' boom would have looked like had the reflation of the US DR during this decade been accompanied by a PR akin to that of the GA.

A final question that confronts the analysis in this section is whether or not recent US performance is sustainable. The USA may now have a new MR, if the institutional features of the 1990s' boom described above are enduring. But the resulting neoliberal growth episode will feature lower per capita income growth ($q_{90s} < q_{GA}$) and both higher inequality and the potential for greater social strife than during the GA, owing to the corporate-dominated market power IR on which US growth is currently based.

Alternatively, it is possible that the current US market power IR will not prove sustainable, if growth and lower unemployment rapidly lead to the reflation of worker aspirations and/or increasing challenges to the structural constraints on labour embedded in this IR. In this case, US performance during the 1990s represents a long boom in GDP, and not the start of a new long-run growth episode.

CONCLUSIONS

This chapter has argued that modern capitalism can be subdivided into discrete growth episodes, characterized by different stylized facts of performance and different structural stylized facts. Moreover, given certain 'fundamental' properties of the income-generating process common to advanced capitalist economies, it has been shown that differences in the stylized facts of performance as between the GA and the AoD growth episodes can be explained by differences in the structures – and in particular, the institutional frameworks – of these growth episodes, within which the fundamentals of income generation are embedded. Structural and especially institutional differences, as captured by the structural stylized facts of the GA and AoD episodes, can therefore explain the generalized slowdown in output and productivity growth since 1973.

The chapter also claims that the same neo-Kaldorian model of growth can be used to understand improvements in the relative macroeconomic performance of the US economy during the 1990s. Again, structural and in particular institutional changes in the US economy provide an explanation of why US growth rates have improved, although not to rates comparable with those of the GA. Whether the recent improvement in US performance is a long trade-cycle boom or the start of a new long-run growth episode is an open question, the answer to which depends, according to this analysis, on the durability of the market power IR that has been established in the USA over the past two decades.

APPENDIX 5.A

Equation [5.4] is derived from the expression:

$$Y = cY + X - mY + A$$

where $A \equiv I + G$, i.e., investment plus government deficit spending. This can be written as:

$$Y = \lambda(X + A)$$

where $\lambda = 1/(1 - c + m)$

$$\Rightarrow y = \lambda(\omega_X x + \omega_A a)$$

where $\omega_X = X/Y$ and $\omega_A = A/Y$.

Equation [5.5] is derived by substituting equations [5.2] and [5.3] into equation [5.4], which yields:

$$y = \lambda(\omega_X[\beta(p_w - w + q - \tau) + \gamma y_w] + \omega_A a)$$

Assuming that $q_w = r + \alpha_w y_w$ and $p_w = w_w - q_w + \tau$, we can write:

$$y = \lambda(\omega_X[\beta(w_w - r - \alpha_w y_w + \tau - w + q - \tau) + \gamma y_w] + \omega_A a)$$

and given that $w_w = w$ (the Kaldorian stylized fact of constant wage relativities), we get:

$$y = \Omega + \lambda\omega_X\beta q \qquad [5.5]$$

The values y_G and q_G shown in Figure 5.1 are derived as follows. Substituting [5.1] into [5.5], we get:

$$y = \lambda\omega_A a - \lambda\omega_X\beta r + \lambda\omega_X(\gamma - \alpha_w\beta)y_w + \lambda\omega_X\beta r + \lambda\omega_X\alpha\beta y$$

$$\Rightarrow y_G = \frac{\lambda(\omega_A a + \omega_X[\gamma - \alpha_w\beta]y_w)}{1 - \lambda\omega_X\alpha\beta}$$

Substituting [5.5] into [5.1], we get:

$$q = r + \alpha\lambda\omega_A a - \alpha\lambda\omega_X\beta r + \alpha\lambda\omega_X(\gamma - \alpha - w\beta)y_w + \alpha\lambda\omega_X\beta q$$

$$\Rightarrow (1 - \alpha\lambda\omega_X\beta)q = (1 - \alpha\lambda\omega_X\beta)r + \alpha\lambda(\omega_A a + \omega_X[\gamma - \alpha_w\beta]y_w)$$

$$\Rightarrow q_G = r + \frac{\alpha\lambda(\omega_A a + \omega_X[\gamma - \alpha_w\beta]y_w)}{1 - \alpha\lambda\omega_X\beta}$$

The conditional steady-state values q_A and y_A, and q_{90s} and y_{90s}, in Figures 5.2 and 5.3 are similarly derived, taking into account relevant changes in parameter values.

NOTES

1. Note that there may be feedbacks from growth outcomes to the institutional framework of which they are, in part, a product. In this case, MRs will both determine and, in turn, be influenced by the rate of growth, resulting in a two-way or joint interaction between growth outcomes and the MRs of which they are a product. This would give rise to a path-dependent growth model, in which a MR creates growth outcomes that feed back onto the structure of the MR itself, giving rise to structural change in the MR and hence a new growth episode.
2. The Golden Age is sometimes described as having begun in 1948 or 1950, given that several of the advanced capitalist economies were under reconstruction (both physically and in terms of their institutions) immediately after the Second World War. However, the precise dating of the GA growth episode does not affect the broad, comparative conclusions about capitalist growth episodes that are drawn below.
3. See Glyn et al. (1990) for further discussion of the stylized facts described above.
4. This social bargain strategy was not pursued uniformly among capitalist economies. It was most clearly in evidence in the northern European and Japanese economies, and much less well developed in the Anglo-Saxon economies. In the USA, for example, the GA was characterized by a limited 'capital–labour accord' (Bowles et al., 1990), but retained features of what is described below as a 'market power' approach to industrial relations. This lack of uniformity in the pursuit of social bargains helps to account for differences in macroeconomic performance among the advanced capitalist economies during the GA (see Cornwall, 1990, 1994).
5. See Cornwall (1990, 1994) and Cornwall and Cornwall (2001) on the inflationary bias in capitalism, and the chapters by Lavoie and Cassetti in this volume on the relationship between distributional conflict and inflation.
6. The trend towards greater central bank independence can be understood as both a reaction and contributory factor to these new constraints on macroeconomic policy. See, for example, Epstein and Schor (1990) on the relationship between central bank independence and macroeconomic policy.
7. Note that this trichotomy is somewhat false, since both the DR and PR are embedded in (in other words, partially constituted by) the IR. Because they derive some of their features from the IR, it is thus impossible to fully specify the nature of the DR and PR independently of the IR.
8. As intimated earlier, the conditionality of the steady state stems from the fact that it is contingent on the reproduction of the structure of the MR over time. See Setterfield (1997) on the notion of conditional equilibria, and Chick and Caserta (1997) on the related notion of provisional equilibria.
9. The gross mark-up is given by $(1 + \varphi)$ in the mark-up pricing equation:

$$P = (1 + \varphi)\frac{WN}{Q}$$

   where P is the price level, $0 < \varphi < 1$ is the percentage mark-up of prices over average prime costs, W is the nominal wage, N is the level of employment and Q is the level of output. Note that the wage share of income varies inversely with $(1 + \varphi)$, so that $\tau \neq 0$ will affect the distribution of income. In what follows, we overlook the implications for the DR of redistribution for the sake of simplicity – but see the chapters by Blecker, Mott, Lavoie and Cassetti in this volume on how redistribution can affect demand-led growth.
10. Whichever growth episode is being characterized, it is assumed that the MR in the rest of the world is identical to that of the individual economy under discussion.

    See Appendix 5.A for notes on the form of equation [5.4], and also on the derivation of the results that follow.
11. The model does not preclude non-price competition, which can be thought of as affecting export growth via its impact on the income elasticity of demand for exports, γ, in [5.3].

However, the cost-based competition described above is central to the two-way interaction between q and y in the system of equations [5.1]–[5.4].

McCombie and Thirlwall (1994) argue that non-price factors are now of overwhelming importance in international trade. Carlin et al. (2001), however, while not disputing the importance of non-price competitiveness, do find that unit labour costs have a significant impact on export performance. Hence the emphasis on cost-based competition in the two-way interaction between q and y above can be regarded as an incomplete but not entirely inappropriate description of international competition.

12. These conditions are sufficient to ensure that a positive and stable conditional steady-state growth rate exists. The stability of the conditional steady state is demonstrated intuitively below.
13. Similarly, any initial rates of output and productivity growth higher than y_G and q_G will result in successive reductions in y and q until conditional equilibrium is regained – again, assuming that the structure of the MR is invariant with respect to this process of traverse.
14. From 1950–73, the average annual rate of growth of the non-residential, fixed capital stock was 5.5 per cent. This was more than three times greater than its rate of growth from 1913–50, and constituted 'an investment boom of historically unprecedented length and vigour' (Glyn et al., 1990, p. 42).
15. Note that $\partial\Omega/\partial a = \lambda\omega_A > 0$, while $\partial\Omega/\partial y_w = \lambda\omega_X(\gamma - \alpha_w\beta) > 0$ if $\gamma > \alpha_w\beta$. This latter condition is plausible, given the importance of non-price relative to price competition (suggesting $\gamma > \beta$ – see McCombie and Thirlwall, 1994) and the likelihood of $\alpha_w < 1$ (i.e., a less-than-unit elasticity of productivity with respect to output).

    Note that even with $a' < a$ and $y'_w < y_w$, it does not automatically follow that $\Omega' < \Omega$, because $\partial\Omega/\partial r = -\lambda\omega_X\beta < 0$ and, as will be argued below, $r' < r$. However, it is plausible to argue that $(\partial\Omega/\partial a)da + (\partial\Omega/\partial y_w)dy_w + (\partial\Omega/\partial r)dr = d\Omega < 0$ nevertheless, on the basis of some simple stylized facts.

    First, according to Cornwall and Cornwall (2001, chapter 11), some 42.6 per cent of the 2.28 percentage-point decline in productivity growth after 1973 is accounted for by factors unrelated to the pressure of demand on output, suggesting that $dr \approx 0.97$ percentage points. But the rate of growth of investment alone fell by 1.1 percentage points in the six years after 1973, before falling further thereafter (Glyn et al., 1990, pp. 42, 86–7). Given that this was accompanied by a move towards contractionary macroeconomic policies that would have caused further reductions in the rate of growth of autonomous expenditures, it would appear that $|da| > |dr|$ in the transition from the GA to the AoD.

    Meanwhile, the average value of ω_A from 1965–85 (calculated as the share of government consumption plus gross fixed capital formation and net additions to stocks) was approximately 41 per cent, whereas that of ω_X was closer to 17 per cent (using OECD figures as reported in OECD Historical Statistics). Given the importance of non-price relative to price competition as mentioned above, it is highly unlikely that $\beta > 2.5$. On this basis, it is possible to conclude that $\lambda\omega_A > \lambda\omega_X\beta$.

    In sum, what these stylized facts suggest that, even neglecting the role of $(\partial\Omega/\partial y_w)dy_w < 0$, we have $(\partial\Omega/\partial a)da + (\partial\Omega/\partial r)dr < 0$ and hence $d\Omega < 0$ in the transition from the GA to the AoD.
16. Cornwall and Cornwall (2001, chapter 11) estimate that the declining rate of growth of investment accounted for over 13 per cent of the decline in productivity growth in the advanced capitalist economies after 1973.
17. Again, these conditions are sufficient to ensure that a positive and stable conditional steady-state growth rate exists for the AoD model.
18. Beginning from a low base in the early 1990s, real investment in computers and peripheral equipment grew at an annual average rate of 18.71 per cent up to 1995, since when its rate of growth has more than doubled to 46.88 per cent per annum (*Economic Report of the President*, 2000, p. 327).
19. The US economy was always ripe for this outcome. Unlike other capitalist economies, discipline was capable of raising productivity in the USA even during the early phases of the AoD (Weisskopf, 1987).

20. Both Oliner and Sichel's and Gordon's findings are based on a neoclassical growth accounting framework, in which long-run productivity growth is conceived as a technical, supply-side phenomenon. The demand-side and socio-institutional influences on long-run productivity growth emphasized in the model developed in this chapter are overlooked, although Gordon does allow for a short-run impact of demand on productivity growth over the course of the cycle. Moreover, as Gundlach (2001) points out, the rate of growth of total factor productivity, which is calculated as a residual and is crucial to the sustainability of increased productivity growth in these growth-accounting exercises, is sensitive to assumptions about whether technological progress is capital or labour augmenting, or both. Hence growth accounting provides no means of specifying the exact size of any increase in the trend rate of productivity growth it purports to identify.
21. Over 76 per cent of all computers are used in the wholesale and retail trades, finance, insurance, real estate and other services (Gordon, 2000, p. 57).
22. This may be, in part, because 'zapping labour' does not just institutionalize discipline, but also, by relieving wage pressures on employers, influences the choice of technique. Instead of going 'high tech' to avoid costly labour, then, some US industries can now afford to adopt labour-intensive production techniques. The result is an adverse effect on the Verdoorn coefficient – productivity becomes less elastic with respect to output than it was during higher wage pressure eras prior to the 1990s.

REFERENCES

Bowles, S., D. Gordon and T. Weisskopf (1990) *After the Waste Land*, Armonk, NY, M.E. Sharpe.

Buchele, R. and J. Christiansen (1999) 'Labor relations and productivity growth in advanced capitalist economies,' *Review of Radical Political Economics*, 31, 87–110.

Bureau of Economic Analysis (2000), *Survey of Current Business*, www.bea.doc.gov/bea/pubs.htm.

Carlin, W., A. Glyn and J. Van Reenen (2001) 'Export market performance of OECD countries: an empirical examination of the role of cost competitiveness,' *Economic Journal*, 111, 128–62.

Cassetti, M. (2000) 'Conflict, inflation, distribution and terms of trade in the Kaleckian model,' *this volume*.

Chick, V. and M. Caserta (1997) 'Provisional equilibrium and macroeconomic theory,' in P. Arestis, G. Palma and M. Sawyer (eds) *Markets, Unemployment and Economic Policy: Essays in Honour of Geoff Harcourt*, vol. 2, London, Routledge, 223–47.

Cornwall. J. (1977) *Modern Capitalism: Its Growth and Transformation*, London, Martin Robertson.

Cornwall, J. (1990) *The Theory of Economic Breakdown*, Oxford, Basil Blackwell.

Cornwall, J. (1994) *Economic Breakdown and Recovery*, Armonk, NY, M.E. Sharpe.

Cornwall, J. and W. Cornwall (2001) *Capitalist Development in the Twentieth Century: An Evolutionary- Keynesian Analysis*, Cambridge, Cambridge University Press.

Economic Report of the President (2000), Washington DC, US Government Printing Office.

Epstein, G. and J. Schor (1990) 'Macropolicy in the rise and fall of the Golden Age,' in S.A. Marglin and J.B. Schor (eds) *op. cit.*, 126–52.

Glyn, A., A. Hughes, A. Lipietz and A. Singh (1990) 'The rise and fall of the Golden Age,' in S.A. Marglin and J.B. Schor (eds) *op. cit.*, 39–125.

Godley, W. (1999) 'Seven unsustainable processes: medium-term prospects and policies for the United States and the world,' Special Report of The Jerome Levy Economics Institute at Bard College.

Gordon, R.J. (2000) 'Does the "new economy" measure up to the great inventions of the past?' *Journal of Economic Perspectives*, 14, 49–74.

Gundlach, E. (2001) 'Interpreting productivity growth in the new economy: some agnostic notes,' Kiel Institute of World Economics, Working Paper no. 1020.

Howes, C. (1999) 'Must U.S. per capita income growth be constrained by slow productivity growth in services?' *Review of Radical Political Economics*, 31, 30–9.

Kaldor, N. (1985) *Economics Without Equilibrium*, Cardiff, University College Cardiff Press.

Lavoie, M. (2000) 'The Kaleckian growth model with target return pricing and conflict inflation', *this volume*.

Marglin, S.A. and J.B. Schor (eds) (1990) *The Golden Age of Capitalism: Reinterpreting the Post War Experience*, Oxford, Oxford University Press.

McCombie, J.S.L. and A.P. Thirlwall (1994) *Economic Growth and the Balance-of-Payments Constraint*, London, Macmillan.

Oliner, S.D. and D.E. Sichel (2000) 'The resurgence of growth in the late 1990s: is information technology the story?' *Journal of Economic Perspectives*, 14, 3–22.

Osterman, P. (1999) *Securing Prosperity: The American Labor Market: How It Has Changed and What to Do about It*, Princeton, Princeton University Press.

Palley, T.I. (1998) *Plenty of Nothing: The Downsizing of the American Dream and the Case for Structural Keynesianism*, Princeton, Princeton University Press.

Setterfield, M. (1997) 'Should economists dispense with the notion of equilibrium?' *Journal of Post Keynesian Economics*, 20, 47–76.

Setterfield, M. (2000) 'Is recent US economic performance replicable? Some remarks on the "logic" of neo-liberalism,'mimeo, Trinity College.

Weisskopf, T.E. (1987) 'The effect of unemployment on labor productivity: an international comparative analysis,' *International Review of Applied Economics*, 1, 127–51.

6. The role of the balance of payments in economic growth

J.S.L. McCombie and M. Roberts

INTRODUCTION

Kaldor's long insistence on the importance of both static and dynamic increasing returns to scale (broadly defined to include induced technical progress) in understanding the growth process has been largely vindicated by recent developments in neoclassical 'endogenous' growth theory. This theory assumes that there are no diminishing returns to capital (see Kaldor, 1977, where he is one of the first to make this assumption). Kaldor's argument that it is equally (or even more) important to consider the role of demand, as opposed to the supply side, in economic growth has, however, been largely ignored by the orthodoxy. The purpose of this chapter is to present an interpretative survey of some of the work that has taken forward the Kaldorian view. In particular, the role of the balance of payments in limiting economic growth below the maximum potential determined by supply-side considerations is discussed. This was implicit in Kaldor's earlier writings (see Thirlwall, 1987, pp. 284–5). It was the influential paper by Thirlwall (1979) that both formalized and popularized this approach (see Thirlwall, 1997), and it was endorsed by Kaldor (1981).

Kaldor's views on the importance of the growth of demand did not originate fully developed, but evolved over the years. Nevertheless, it is possible in his writings to distinguish between two categories of demand that play different roles in the economic growth process. The first, which applies to a largely closed economy, is the role of the growth of demand emanating from the agricultural sector in determining the overall pace of economic growth. The second, in an open economy, is the crucial role that the growth of demand originating from exports plays. In both cases it is necessary, of course, for Say's law not to hold, even in the long run. In other words, as Kaldor was fond of pointing out, Ricardo was fundamentally wrong when he asserted that 'there is no amount of capital which may not be employed in a country because demand is only limited by production'.

In the first case, it is not possible to understand growth without explicitly considering the complementary roles played by the agricultural sector, which is subject to diminishing returns and surplus labour, and the more advanced industrial sector. Kaldor (1975, 1977, 1996) demonstrated that there may not be any set of relative prices that enables markets in both sectors to clear simultaneously ensuring the full utilization of resources, and that the growth of the industrial sector may be constrained by the lack of the growth of agricultural purchasing power and (to a certain extent) vice versa.

With economic development, the relative importance of the agricultural sector in the economy clearly declines. Nevertheless, Kaldor argued that even for the advanced countries, the growth of exogenous demand is still the key to understanding relative growth performances (see Kaldor, 1981). While the less developed countries can hardly be considered to be resource-constrained, according to Kaldor, it is difficult to argue persuasively that the growth of even advanced countries is determined by the exogenously given growth of effective employment (see Cornwall, 1977). Countries differ in their growth rates because of variations in the growth of demand for their exports. That is to say, overall economic growth is ultimately constrained by the rate of growth of exports, and it is not something that can be remedied by merely pump-priming the economy in Keynesian fashion and by boosting the growth of aggregate demand. It is not investment, as Keynes argued, that is the key element of exogenous demand, but, in an open economy, the growth of demand for a country's exports. A common theme in both the closed and the open economy Kaldorian models is the importance of the role of the (dynamic) Harrod foreign trade multiplier and the Hicks super-multiplier (Harrod, 1933; Hicks, 1950).

We first consider the question as to why other forms of demand, such as investment, cease to be the key exogenous factors that determine the rate of economic growth – a question which goes back to the North–Tiebout debate of 1956.[1] The argument that changes in the exchange rate have little effect on the growth of trade flows, and that the growth of capital flows has little effect on the balance-of-payments equilibrium growth rate is then elaborated and assessed. An extension of the balance-of-payments equilibrium growth model in which growth becomes path dependent is then outlined. Finally, we consider the degree to which this approach can explain the rapid growth of the East and Southeast Asian economies. We conclude by discussing an export-led growth strategy and the fallacy of composition.

EXPORT-LED GROWTH AND THE BALANCE-OF-PAYMENTS CONSTRAINT

Kaldor was by no means the first to stress the importance of the export sector as a determinant of the overall rate of economic growth. One of the earliest was North (1955), who used it to explain the growth of the Pacific Northwest of the USA, in the process of developing one of the earliest cumulative causation models. North was also aware of the importance of the foreign trade multiplier – 'since residentiary industry depends entirely on demand within the region, it has been historically dependent upon the fate of the export base'. Tiebout (1956), however, raised two potentially damaging criticisms of export-led growth models, although, as we shall see, these turn out not to be serious.

First, 'there is no reason to assume that exports are the sole, *or even the most important*, autonomous variable determining regional income' (Tiebout, 1956, emphasis added). From the national income accounting identity and the consumption, investment, government expenditure and import demand functions, the growth of demand may be expressed as $y^d = \alpha a + \beta x$ where a is the growth of autonomous domestic expenditure and x is the growth of exports. The coefficients α and β denote the dynamic domestic and foreign trade multipliers (McCombie, 1993). The question is 'what is so important about the growth of exports compared with any other autonomous increase in demand?'.[2]

Second, the theory is spatially scale-dependent, which Tiebout saw as a disconcerting feature. At one extreme, an individual is normally wholly dependent upon exporting labour services. At the other extreme, 'obviously, for the world as a whole, there are no exports' (Tiebout, 1956).

Tiebout came to the conclusion that the export-base theory may be a useful explanation of the *short-run* growth of a region; but it is not the complete story, especially in a long-term context. In particular, he notes that 'since a region must optimize the use of factors and residential outputs, a decline in export activity may even be accompanied by rising regional income'.

North's (1956) reply is not particularly convincing, merely asserting that the exogenous growth rates of categories such as investment have only a short-term effect. The most effective rebuttal to Tiebout, which North does not make, is that there is a major difference between the growth of exports and other components of autonomous demand, in that only the former automatically generates foreign earnings to pay for imports. Once this is taken into account, the growth of exports is revealed as the crucial exogenous component of demand growth (although there may be some feedback from the growth of output to that of exports. In this sense, the growth of exports is weakly exogenous). An increase in the growth rate of exports has two effects on the growth of income. First, it increases the growth rate of income through the dynamic Harrod foreign trade multiplier. Second, by relaxing the balance-of-payments constraint, it permits the growth of other 'autonomous' components of demand. That is to say, the growth of other supposedly autonomous expenditures is actually endogenous to export growth. The combination of these effects represents a working of the Hicks 'super-multiplier' (McCombie, 1985; McCombie and Thirlwall, 1994, chapter 6). This answers not only Tiebout's first but also his second criticism. Even though the value of exports may be small in comparison to total income, the balance-of-payments constraint and the super-multiplier mean that export growth is still the determining factor of total growth. Of course, Tiebout is perfectly correct to say that, for the world as a whole, growth cannot be export-led. Likewise, all countries cannot be simultaneously balance-of-payments-constrained. However, all that is required is for one trading bloc to be 'policy-constrained' (the deliberate restriction of growth due, for example, to the fear of inflation) or 'supply-constrained' (there may be a limit to the rate at which labour can be transferred between sectors or capacity can be increased). This, through the operation of the balance-of-payments constraint, will limit the growth rates that other countries can achieve, even though domestic conditions could sustain a faster growth rate (see McCombie, 1993).

The implications of this are far-reaching, as Kaldor has noted:

> This doctrine [of the foreign trade multiplier and the super-multiplier] asserts the very opposite of Say's law: the level of production will *not* be confined by the availability of capital and labour; on the contrary, the amount of capital accumulated, and the amount of labour effectively employed at any one time, will be the resultant of the growth of external demand over a long series of past periods which permitted the capital accumulation to take place that was required for enabling the amount of labour to be employed and the level of output to be reached which was (or could be) attained in the current period (Kaldor, 1977).

Following the seminal work of Thirlwall (1979), what may be termed the 'standard' balance-of-payments-constrained growth model consists of the following equations (where all variables are expressed as growth rates):[3]

$$\text{Export demand equation: } x = \varepsilon z + \eta(p_d - p_f - er) \quad [6.1]$$

$$\text{Import demand equation: } m = \pi y - \psi(p_d - p_f - er) \quad [6.2]$$

$$\text{Balance-of-payments identity: } \omega x + (1 - \omega)f \equiv m + p_f + er - p_d \quad [6.3]$$

where x, m, y and z are the growth rates of exports, imports, domestic income and the income of the rest of the world, respectively, f is the growth of real capital flows expressed in terms of the domestic currency and er is the growth of the nominal exchange rate ($er > 0$ representing a continuous appreciation of the currency). The subscripts d and f denote 'domestic' and 'foreign', respectively. The parameters ε and π are the income elasticities of demand for exports and imports, while ω is the share of exports in total foreign exchange

Thirlwall → growth is demand-determined

receipts. The parameters $\eta\,(< 0)$ and $\psi\,(< 0)$ are the price elasticities of demand for exports and imports (for ease of exposition, the own and cross-price elasticities are assumed to have the same absolute values).

One of the key differences between the Thirlwall model and the Solow neoclassical model of growth is the former's emphasis on the importance, especially in highly oligopolistic markets, of non-price competition, such as quality improvements, product innovation, etc.[4] This is (imperfectly) captured by the differences between countries in the values of their income elasticities of demand for imports, as well as international differences in the income elasticities of demand for exports.[5] We are not in a world where trade flows respond rapidly to small changes in relative prices. This allows the development of a simple model, which gives some illuminating insights into the growth process, but clearly further work (such as that of Greenhalgh, 1990) is needed to model more explicitly the non-price factors that determine the growth of demand for imports and exports. The other difference between the Thirlwall and Solow models is that growth in the former is essentially demand-determined.[6]

Underlying this model is a theory of the firm where prices are determined by a constant mark-up over unit costs. The firm sets the price and is prepared to meet demand at this price. An element of excess capacity is maintained to meet short-term increases in demand and a generally Keynesian approach is adopted in that investment is determined by the rate of growth of expected future sales. (See Blecker, 1998, for an elaboration of the possible microfoundations underlying this approach.)

Substituting equations [6.1] and [6.2] into [6.3], we obtain an equation for what might be termed the 'extended' balance-of-payments equilibrium growth rate of the country under consideration:[7]

$$y_{B1} = \frac{\omega\varepsilon z + (1 + \omega\eta + \psi)(p_d - p_f - er) + (1 - \omega)f}{\pi} \qquad [6.4]$$

If changes in relative prices have no effect on the growth of income and the weighted growth rate of capital flows is relatively insignificant (both of which are generally the case, as we see below), the balance-of-payments equilibrium growth rate becomes $\varepsilon z/\pi = x/\pi$, which has come to be known as 'Thirlwall's law' (Thirlwall, 1979). (We denote this growth rate simply by y_B). If the growth of productive potential (y_P) exceeds the balance-of-payments equilibrium growth rate, the actual growth rate (y_A) will be equal to the latter. It is the growth of income that adjusts to make $y_A = y_B < y_P$. The neoclassical approach, however, has the rate of change in relative prices relaxing the balance-of-payments constraint, allowing y_B to increase until it reaches y_P.[8,9]

PRICE AND NON-PRICE COMPETITION IN INTERNATIONAL TRADE

As we have noted, a central tenet of this approach is that the rate of change in relative prices does not have a significant impact on increasing the balance-of-payments equilibrium growth rate, and hence the growth rate is given by Thirlwall's law. This is not to say that exchange rate adjustments have no effect on the current account at a *given* growth rate.[10] What the empirical evidence does suggest is that it is implausible that a devaluation can affect the long-run growth rates of exports and imports and thereby remove the balance-of-payments constraint. Relative prices are unimportant in spite of the fact that they may change in the short run, either because these changes do not translate into sustained real exchange rate movements or, even if they do, they have little impact on trade flows. The reason for the former, especially in the short run, may be pricing to market and, in the longer term, the effect of real wage resistance.[11] Knoester (1995) provides evidence of real wage resistance for the advanced countries, which goes a long way to answering the criticism that this is an *ad hoc* assumption of the model. Even if there are changes in the real exchange rate (and this has been the case post-1972, although often in response to capital rather than trade flows), these have little impact because of the importance of non-price competitiveness and the fact that the price elasticities of demand for imports and exports are low. (The ineffectiveness of floating exchange rates after the breakdown of Bretton Woods soon became apparent. A floating exchange rate did not prevent the UK's sterling crisis of 1976, which resulted in the International Monetary Fund (IMF) being called in and subsequent deflationary policies being imposed. Nor did floating exchange rates prevent balance-of-payments crises in, for example, Italy in 1980–1 and France in 1982.)[12]

Moreover, changes in the real exchange rate are often reversed in the medium to long term. The success of a country in world markets is due to product innovation, namely, developing products for which world demand will rapidly grow. It is unlikely that merely reducing the prices of existing products by squeezing costs and real wages will be a successful long-term strategy. In other words, in the context of the long run, outward shifts of a product's demand curve are more important than shifts down the demand curve.

There are now numerous studies estimating import and export demand functions as part of a test of Thirlwall's law, and these generally report estimated price elasticities that are either statistically insignificant, low or have *a priori* unexpected signs (see the discussion in McCombie and Thirlwall, 1994, chapter 3). For example, Alonso and Garcimartin (1998–9) estimated import and export demand functions for ten advanced countries using a disequilibrium approach. They found that although the individual price elasticities were statistically significant in many cases, the sums of the absolute values of these price elasticities were not large, ranging from 1.41 (Canada) to 0.57 (Sweden) (excluding Japan, which had an exceptional value of 2.43). The Marshall–Lerner condition was satisfied in only 4 out of 10 cases. Moreover, with traditional multiplicative import and export demand functions, an increase in the balance-of-payments equilibrium growth rate requires a sustained rate of change of relative prices. For example, if $\omega = 1$, $\pi = 1.5$ and $|\eta + \psi| = 1.2$, relative prices must fall by 7.5 per cent per annum to bring about a permanent increase in the rate of output growth of one percentage point. (This is the same order of magnitude that was found for the UK using the National Institute of Economic and Social Research forecasting model – see McCombie and Thirlwall, 1994, chapter 10.) For the advanced countries at least, the rate of change in relative prices necessary to raise the equilibrium growth rate by one or two percentage points is likely to be much too large to be plausible.

There is also a good deal of other evidence that suggests that price competition is relatively unimportant. Kravis and Lipsey (1971), for example, found that few firms in Germany or the USA attributed their success in exporting to their price competitiveness. McCombie and Thirlwall (1994, chapter 4) discuss this and other evidence on the importance of non-price competitiveness in more detail.

The price elasticities of homogeneous products are likely to be significantly higher than for goods characterized by significant product differentiation. There is some evidence that a devaluation, by encouraging the production of more homogeneous goods, may actually switch production away from the more sophisticated products for which the world income elasticity of demand is high (Brech and Stout, 1981). Thus, paradoxically, a devaluation may harm the prospects for future export growth.

THE IMPACT OF THE GROWTH OF CAPITAL FLOWS

With increasing liberalization of international financial flows over the last couple of decades, it is important to see to what extent this has relaxed the balance-of-payments constraint. The answer, as we shall see, is not to any great degree.

International financial markets become increasingly nervous if the net foreign debt to income ratio approaches a certain critical maximum, although this value is likely to vary between countries. In the international debt crisis that began in 1982, the debt to GDP ratio of the 'Baker 15' less developed countries reached 46.6 per cent in 1984 (see Toye, 1992, Table 1.4, p. 27). We may therefore infer that any figure over about 40 per cent is likely to present

Table 6.1 The relationship between the growth of income, the maximum net debt to income ratio and the maximum current account deficit to income ratio

Growth of income (% per annum)	Current Account Deficit to Income Ratio (%)		
	(40)	(50)	(60)
1	0.4	0.5	0.6
2	0.8	1.0	1.2
3	1.2	1.5	1.8
4	1.6	2.0	2.4
5	2.0	2.5	3.0
6	2.4	3.0	3.6

Notes: Figures in parentheses are the net foreign debt to income ratios (percentage).

a less developed country (and some advanced countries) with serious financial problems. Let this maximum debt to income ratio be denoted by $D/Y = \theta_{max}$, where D and Y are the stock of real net foreign debt and the level of real income. Differentiating D/Y with respect to time gives $d(D/Y)/dt = \mu - y(D/Y)$ where μ denotes the current account deficit expressed as a proportion of income. Setting $d(D/Y)/dt = 0$ it follows that $\mu_{max} = y\theta_{max}$. In other words, for any given y, θ_{max} implies that there is a maximum sustainable ratio of the current account deficit to income, and vice versa (see McCombie and Thirlwall, 1997b and Moreno-Brid, 1998–9 for an alternative derivation of this relationship). Table 6.1 reports the values of μ_{max} and θ_{max} for given growth rates of income.

What is interesting is that the balance-of-payments equilibrium growth rate need not necessarily imply that the current account should exactly balance, if financial markets are prepared to tolerate a certain persistent net debt to income ratio. Moreover, the faster the growth of income (and exports), the larger is the current account deficit that will be sustainable for any given debt to income ratio. Nevertheless, after an allowance is made for this, the effect on the balance-of-payments equilibrium growth rate is negligible.

To see this, first assume that there is no growth in real capital flows. From equation [6.4] (assuming that the weighted changes in relative prices are unimportant), the expression for the balance-of-payments equilibrium growth rate becomes $y_{B2} = \omega x/\pi$. For a relatively open economy where the ratio of exports to income is, say, 30 per cent and the initial current account deficit is, for example, 2 per cent of income, $\omega = 0.94$. In other words, if we assume that $\pi = 1.5$, the balance-of-payments equilibrium growth rate will be given by

$y_{B2} = 0.63x$ instead of by $y_B = 0.67x$.[13] Thus, for any given growth rate of exports, an initial balance-of-payments deficit on current account reduces the equilibrium growth rate. Or to put it another way, for any given growth rate of income, the growth rate of exports has to be commensurately higher if there is an initial current account deficit. But the differences are negligible. If $x = 4$ per cent per annum, y_B equals 2.67 per cent per annum when the current account is in equilibrium. If, however, the current account deficit equals 2 per cent of income, y_B is reduced slightly as $y_{B2} = 2.50$ per cent per annum.

What happens if we instead assume that the ratio of the current account deficit to income does not alter? Again assuming no changes in relative prices, the equation for the balance-of-payments equilibrium growth rate when $f = y$ becomes:

$$y_{B3} = \omega x/(\pi - 1 + \omega) \qquad [6.5]$$

It can be seen that this growth of capital flows is unlikely to substantially affect the balance-of-payments equilibrium growth rate.[14] If π is greater than unity, as is generally the case, the balance-of-payments equilibrium growth rate will be reduced. It will be unaffected if $\pi = 1$. For illustrative purposes, consider again our economy where exports are 30 per cent of income, $\pi = 1.5$, and the foreign exchange markets consider that a current account deficit of 2 per cent of income is sustainable. It follows that the equilibrium growth rate is given by $y_{B3} = 0.65x$, whereas if there is no growth in capital flows and the current account is in equilibrium, $y_B = 0.67x$. This result proves insensitive to the exact share of exports in income. If the figure is 10 per cent instead of 30 per cent, for a current account deficit equal to 2 per cent of GDP, $y_{B3} = 0.63x$ and if the share of exports in income is 50 per cent, y_{B3} only increases to $0.66x$.

A small complication is that, as may be seen from Table 6.1, a current account deficit of 2 per cent of income will lead to a stabilization of the debt to income ratio at different values, depending on the growth rate. If financial markets set a maximum debt to income ratio, then the maximum current account deficit as a proportion of income will vary according to the growth rate. But once again, this does not significantly alter the balance-of-payments equilibrium growth rate. Suppose that $\theta_{max} = 50$ per cent. Then assuming exports account for 30 per cent of income, the growth of exports necessary for income growth of 2 per cent per annum is 3.1 per cent per annum, instead of 3 per cent when the current account balances.[15] If the growth rate of income rises to 6 per cent per annum (which, as may be seen from Table 6.1, will lead to a sustainable current account deficit to an income ratio of 3 per cent), the necessary growth rate of exports is 9.3 per cent per annum (compared with 9 per cent per annum when the current account is balanced). Again, this result proves relatively insensitive to the degree of openness of the economy. The overall picture is clear – even if there is a sustainable current account deficit, the quantitative impact on the equilibrium growth rate is so small that $y = x/\pi = \varepsilon z/\pi$, i.e. Thirlwall's law, will give a very good approximation to the balance-of-payments-constrained growth rate.

However, this is not to say that a rapid inflow of capital such as some less developed countries have experienced, even though unsustainable in the long run, may not temporarily enable the growth rate to exceed that predicted by Thirlwall's law (see Thirlwall and Hussain, 1982). This may be illustrated by a final numerical example. Suppose we have a less developed country with exports equal to 30 per cent of income, $\pi = 1.5$, its current account in balance and its net foreign debt equal to zero. Its exports are growing at a rapid rate of 8 per cent per annum and so y_B equals 5.33 per cent per annum. Let us further suppose that in year 1, there are capital inflows equivalent to 4 per cent of income and these grow at twice the rate of exports for the next ten years. The growth of income will increase by nearly one percentage point to 6.26 per cent per annum. However, by year 10, the debt to income ratio will have risen to 66 per cent and the ratio of the current account deficit to income will have increased to just over 10 per cent, which is likely to be unsustainable.

RECENT TESTS OF THE BALANCE-OF-PAYMENTS-CONSTRAINED EQUILIBRIUM GROWTH MODEL

Since the publication of Thirlwall's (1979) seminal article, there have been numerous attempts to test the balance-of-payments-constrained growth model. In this section, we briefly consider some of the studies that have been undertaken since those surveyed in McCombie and Thirlwall (1994), although no claim is made for completeness. The more recent studies use modern time-series analysis, such as testing for stationarity and cointegration, but these results have largely confirmed the results of earlier studies. For example, Andersen (1993) took a sample of 16 OECD countries and using pooled data for 1960–73, 1973–80 and 1980–90 concluded that having estimated the values of ε and π using an error correction model, there was a close relationship between y and y_B 'merely' in the long run. But, of course, it is precisely in the long run when the law is expected to hold.

In the spring edition of the 1997 *Journal of Post Keynesian Economics*, there was a mini symposium on Thirlwall's Law. Hieke (1997) showed that the model performed well for the USA over the period 1950–90, even though it has been able to run current account deficits for long periods. However, in the light of the discussion on capital flows above, and the fact that the current account deficit did not increase as a percentage of GDP, this is not particularly surprising. During the period 1967–90, there was a substantial slowdown in the growth rate of the US economy, resulting from an increase in the income elasticity of demand for imports, which reduced y_B. This result was also found by Atesoglu (1995). Atesoglu (1997) showed that the USA's exports and income were cointegrated over the period 1924–94.[16] This relationship broke down in the post-Bretton Woods era, but only due to increased capital flows that made it easier to finance current account deficits, rather than any relaxation of the balance-of-payments constraint resulting from the increased flexibility of nominal exchange rates.

McCombie (1997) surveyed the various methods for testing Thirlwall's law and revisited the law for the USA, Japan and the UK, explicitly allowing for structural breaks in the estimation of the import demand function. Japan has always been treated as an outlier, with y_A significantly below y_B. This has been accompanied by the accumulation of large trade surpluses. However, it was found that when the import demand function was estimated using first differences of the logarithms of the levels of variables, rather than the log levels themselves, the possibility that Japan was growing at its balance-of-payments-constrained growth rate could not be ruled out. Turner (1999) found that the post-1973 slowdown in the growth of the G7 countries could be explained in terms of the fall in the growth rate of world trade, together with the growing internationalization of the world economy.

Bairam (1997) found that for a small sample of less developed countries (LDCs), ε is negatively related to the level of per capita income while π showed no correlation (the latter is not surprising, given the prevalence of various forms of import controls in the LDCs). On the face of it, this would suggest that the less developed a country is, the less likely it is to be balance-of-payments-constrained. While the possibility of a relationship between the income elasticities of demand and the level of development is worth pursuing, Thirlwall (1997) suggests that Bairam's sample is too small for any firm conclusions to be drawn.

Hussain (1995) has examined the relevance of Thirlwall's law for the developing countries and suggests that the balance-of-payments constraint is more severe for the low-income African countries than for the more developed Southeast Asian countries. However, in many cases the estimates of the import demand functions are implausible, which is no doubt due to the existence of serious errors in the measurement of income for these countries arising from their large informal economies and their rudimentary collection of national income statistics. This indicates that care must be taken when testing Thirlwall's law for countries that are in the very early stages of development.

León-Ledesma (1999) tested Thirlwall's law for the Spanish economy over the period 1965–93. Having estimated the import demand function and obtained a value of π, he used this together with mean decennial growth rates of exports in overlapping periods to calculate y_B. A close correspondence between y_A and y_B for most years was found and where there was a divergence, this was the result of a sudden change in capital flows (which were not incorporated into the formal model). León-Ledesma concludes that 'although for the periods that cover the two energy crises, the movement of relative prices and long-run capital flows could have been expected to have played a role, the long run regularity shows that the adjustment to balance-of-payments equilibrium came via income'.

Moreno-Brid and Perez (1999) and Perez and Moreno-Brid (1999) considered the applicability of the model to the long-term growths of countries in Central America (Costa Rica, El Salvador, Guatemala, Honduras, Nicaragua, Panama and two Caribbean countries, namely the Dominican Republic and Haiti) over the period 1950–97. These countries have had a turbulent post-war experience, including stagnation during the 1980s (coincident with the debt crisis), and periods of political instability and repression. Both studies found that growth conformed to Thirlwall's law, with the exception of Haiti, where other factors had led to a growth rate below the balance-of-payments equilibrium growth rate. 'Its [Thirlwall's law's] empirical adequacy may be grounded on these developing countries' key dependence on imported machinery, equipment and other inputs from abroad so that the availability of foreign exchange puts a ceiling on the rate of domestic production'. A significant long-term relationship between the growth of exports and that of GDP is found, with no evidence of any significant effect of changes in the terms of trade on growth. Moreno-Brid (1999) also considered the degree to which Mexico's growth could be explained in terms of the balance-of-payments-constrained growth model. The results confirmed a positive and statistically significant cointegrating relationship between real GDP and exports over the period 1950–96. Interestingly, Mexico experienced sustained and rapid growth until the debt crisis of 1982 and a subsequent period of slow growth punctuated by balance-of-payments crises. The latter period was not accompanied by any marked slowdown in the growth rate of exports (their growth rate actually increased). Instead, there was a marked increase in the income elasticity of demand for imports from 1.04 over the period 1950–81 to 2.47 for 1982–96. This reduced the balance-of-payments equilibrium growth rate and is attributed by Moreno-Brid to the end of import substitution policies in Mexico and the liberalization of trade.

These studies suggest that, at the very least, explanations of long-run growth that ignore the role of demand and economic openness are likely to be incomplete.

CUMULATIVE CAUSATION, THE BALANCE-OF-PAYMENTS EQUILIBRIUM GROWTH RATE AND STRUCTURAL CHANGE

A major theme in Kaldor's later writings is that growth is a historical, rather than an equilibrium, process. It is to be understood not by reference to unexplained, exogenously determined data as in, say, the Solow model, but by reference to the growth path that has previously been traversed. Probably the clearest statement of this is Kaldor (1972) and, although this emphasis is usually contrasted with his attempts to model the growth process prior to his 1966 inaugural lecture, Setterfield (1998) has persuasively argued that the origins of Kaldor's interest in path dependency may be traced back much further, in particular, to one of his earliest papers, 'A classificatory note on the determinateness of equilibrium', published in 1934.

However, despite this, the 'standard' cumulative causation model of Dixon and Thirlwall (1975) that is often taken as providing a formal representation of Kaldor's post-1966 views on the growth process is essentially a model of equilibrium growth.[17] This is equally true of Thirlwall's law.

These models are not, therefore, completely in accord with Kaldor's views of the growth process. Setterfield (1997) has suggested that perhaps the transitional dynamics of the Dixon–Thirlwall model are so slow that, in fact, all we generally observe is disequilibrium growth. If this were so, it would mitigate the seriousness of the problem, although not entirely remove it. This is because during the disequilibrium phase of growth in the standard cumulative causation model, an economy's growth rate is a function of its assumed initial growth rate. However, as has been shown by Roberts (2001a), for reasonable parameter and exogenous variable values, the model's transitional dynamics operate extremely rapidly – indeed, much more quickly than in standard neoclassical growth models.

More interestingly, Setterfield (1997) has suggested that an alternative approach to overcoming the inconsistency is to acknowledge that the exogenous parameters of the standard cumulative causation model are, in reality, 'deeply endogenous'.[18] That is to say, they are not data that are fixed independently of an economy's past growth performance. Rather, there is a feedback from an economy's past growth performance to the values of the model's parameters, thereby rendering them dependent on its historical growth path. Thus, for example, Setterfield suggests that the income elasticity of demand for an economy's exports is a function of its past growth rates of output: that is, $\varepsilon_t = f(y_0, y_1, \ldots, y_i, \ldots, y_{t-1})$ where $\partial f / \partial y_i \neq 0$.[19] In particular, he argues that, at least for mature economies, previous fast growth rates of output are likely to have a negative effect on the income elasticity of demand for an economy's exports. This is because, if a country is to succeed in international markets, it must, over time, keep up with the movement of international consumer demand through a commodity hierarchy. However, to do so requires a continual adaptation of the structure of production. Fast growth rates in previous periods might make this difficult because they tend to encourage the lock-in of a production structure that subsequently becomes outmoded.[20]

One problem, formally speaking, is that specifying the income elasticity of demand for exports to be a negative function of previous growth rates is not a sufficient condition for removing the equilibrium properties of the standard cumulative causation model. Indeed, such a specification actually makes the equilibrium of the standard model more stable. This implicitly follows from Roberts's (2001a) demonstration that specifying the income elasticity of demand for exports to be a positive function of the previous period's growth rate slows down the transitional dynamics of the standard model. What is needed to transform the standard model into a truly historical model of growth is not only to specify the income elasticity of demand as a function of past growth rates, but as a *strongly non-linear* function of past growth rates (see Roberts, 2001b). In particular, while high values of previous growth rates may be allowed to have the negative impact on the income elasticity postulated by Setterfield, low values of previous growth rates must have a positive impact. This can be justified on the grounds that while high values of previous growth rates may be expected to give rise to the forces for lock-in that Setterfield describes, low values cannot. Rather, one would expect poor previous growth performance to give rise to a sense of dissatisfaction and thus to pressure for reform of an economy's production structure. This dissatisfaction can be expected to arise at two levels. The first is at the political level as the electorate becomes dissatisfied with poor growth rates, and the high levels of unemployment and low rates of real wage growth that inevitably accompany such a poor performance. The second is at the level of production itself, as shareholders become dissatisfied with the rates of return being earned on their investments.

However, our concern in this study is not with the standard cumulative causation model, but with the balance-of-payments-constrained growth model. Yet, identical considerations to those discussed above apply here. In this model, an economy's growth rate is traditionally specified as independent of its past growth performance. This is because the income elasticities of demand for imports and exports have been assumed to be exogenous. However, the income elasticities of demand do in fact change, albeit generally slowly, as relative non-price competitiveness changes. It therefore follows that while the model captures the Kaldor–Thirlwall idea that the balance-of-payments acts as a constraint on growth, it is inconsistent with Kaldor's wider views concerning the historical nature of the long-run growth process. Furthermore, it follows that one can overcome this problem by respecifying the exogenous parameters in this model as deeply endogenous functions of previous growth rates, with the functional forms being assumed to be strongly non-linear. In particular, for expositional purposes assume that:

$$(\varepsilon/\pi)_t = \gamma_1 + \gamma_2(\phi - y_{t-1})y_{t-1} \qquad \gamma_1 > 0, \quad \gamma_2 > 0 \qquad [6.6]$$

Where γ_1, γ_2 and ϕ are constants, equation [6.6] specifies that the current ratio of the income elasticity of demand for an economy's exports to its income elasticity of demand for imports is a strongly non-linear function of its past growth performance, as represented by the growth rate of income in the previous period, y_{t-1}. It should be noted that the non-linearity is such that the ratio of ε to π is increasing with y_{t-1} at low levels of y_{t-1}, but decreasing with y_{t-1} at high levels of y_{t-1}. This reflects the intuition outlined above that poor previous growth rates can be expected to give rise to pressure for reform, while high previous growth rates can be expected to encourage lock-in. Also, note that it has been assumed that it is the *ratio* of ε to π rather than just ε that is deeply endogenous here. This is plausible because, given that they both reflect an economy's non-price competitiveness, ε and π tend to be jointly determined. Thus, reform of an economy's production structure can be expected to not only increase its value of ε, but also reduce its value of π. Conversely, lock-in of a production structure that subsequently becomes outmoded can be expected not only to reduce its value of ε, but also increase its value of π.

Upon substituting equation [6.6] into Thirlwall's law, growth emerges as a historical process for plausible parameter and exogenous variable values. For example, assume $\gamma_1 = 0.70$, $\gamma_2 = 746.123$, $\phi = 0.10$ and that the growth rate of world income is constant at 4 per cent per annum. These values imply that ε/π is bounded from above by the value 2.565 and from below by the value 0.50 – values that are very similar to those experienced by Japan and the UK, respectively, during the period 1955–65 (see Houthakker and Magee, 1969; McCombie and Thirwall, 1994; Krugman, 1989). The emergence of growth as a historical process in the model is depicted in Figure 6.1, which illustrates a growth path that commences from point A.

Examining Figure 6.1, it makes more sense to think of the periods t not as calendar years, but as growth eras. The figure shows the model economy evolving through a seemingly random series of growth eras, each growth era giving rise to the forces that bring about eventually, for better or for worse, its own demise. The seeming randomness of the growth era changes reflects the fact that the depicted dynamics are chaotic in nature, and it is this that makes the model a truly historical one of the growth process. This is because the chaotic dynamics rule out the existence of a determinate equilibrium growth rate at which the economy will settle down. Furthermore, they mean that it is not possible to predict an economy's future pattern of growth era changes without knowing its

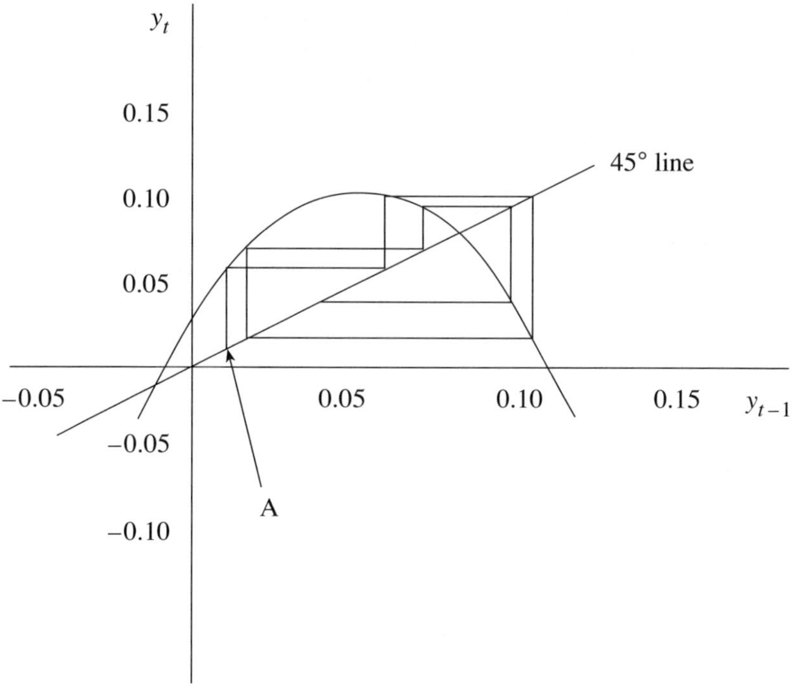

Figure 6.1 The balance-of-payments equilibrium growth rate when ε/π changes endogenously

growth rate during the current era with infinite precision, something that measurement and sample errors in data collection make impossible. This, in turn implies that the behaviour of the economy is strongly path dependent.

This approach is suggestive of the way future research may go, rather than being a definitive method. But it certainly accords with Kaldor's views on growth, according to which the state of the economy 'cannot be predicted except as a result of [perfect knowledge of] the sequence of events in previous periods [eras] which led up to it' (Kaldor, 1972).[21]

THE EAST ASIAN MIRACLE AND THIRLWALL'S LAW

We now briefly consider the implications of Thirlwall's law for economic development. We do not undertake any new statistical testing but show that the balance-of-payments-constrained growth approach can be a useful one for understanding development strategies.

The term 'economic miracle' has been justifiably used in the case of a number of East Asian countries that have achieved unprecedented high rates of both total and per capita output growth over the last three decades. The most notable successes are what have come to be known as the four 'Asian Tigers' (Hong Kong, South Korea, Singapore and Taiwan). Over the period 1965–96, the Tigers averaged growth rates of output per capita in excess of 6 per cent per annum. This is truly remarkable, given that these growth rates were sustained for more than 30 years. The Southeast Asian economies (Indonesia, Malaysia, the Philippines and Thailand) also grew rapidly on the coat-tails of the Tigers. Over the same 30-year period their average per capita growth rates were around 4 per cent per annum.[22]

The causes of the rapid growth of the East Asian Tigers are still unresolved, but there are two main explanations. The first, stemming from the detailed growth accounting approach of Young (1992, 1995), and popularized by Krugman (1994), suggests that growth was largely the result of the rapid increase of factor inputs. On the other hand, the 'assimilationists' stress the role of the diffusion of innovations from the more advanced countries (see Nelson and Pack, 1999, for a recent discussion of these views and one which tends to support the latter interpretation). There is not space here to discuss these competing explanations: suffice it to say that most of the evidence seems to be that growth was export-led, resulting in high rates of capital accumulation. There has also been a debate about whether growth was, in Wade's (1990) terms, based on the 'free market', the 'simulated free market' (where governments intervened to correct distortions and hence attempted to simulate the free market) or the 'governed market' (where there was active government intervention). Wade's careful analysis of the somewhat conflicting evidence suggests that the governed market was the rule rather than the exception. It is also noticeable that in much of neoclassical growth theory, there is virtually no mention of international trade or the growth of exports except where it is to discuss technological externalities or spillovers. Yet discussions of the Asian miracle, whether from a neoclassical or any other viewpoint, are often centred on the role of exports, although there is controversy over the direction of causation.

There has been a plethora of cross-country regression studies using various samples of advanced countries and LDCs that have attempted to explain the determinants of growth. Of particular interest in this context is the study of Thirlwall and Sanna (1998). Surveying the literature, they note that when a trade variable is included 'it is invariably insignificant or loses its significance when combined with other variables'. But in many studies this is because the effect of trade appears to work through investment. 'If this is the case, it is an interesting and significant conclusion, because it means that many of the studies would support the Keynesian/post-Keynesian position that it is not saving that drives investment, but trade and the growth of output itself'. Their own empirical work suggests that export growth (as opposed to static measures of the degree of openness such as the ratio of exports to GDP) is a significant determinant of economic performance and that the debt-service ratio is also an important constraint on economic growth in developing countries.

In the East Asian countries, it was deliberate government policy (at least initially) to encourage the development of those exports for which world demand was either growing, or was likely to grow fast. The export structure in East Asia has, in the words of the World Bank (1998), 'become characterized by (a) early exit from low-skill labour-intensive exports; (b) specialization in high-technology exports, and (c) strong inter-regional links'. In terms of the balance-of-payments-constrained growth model, this led to high income elasticities of demand for the region's exports that enabled a fast growth of demand through the dynamic Harrod trade multiplier and the Hicks super-multiplier.[23]

Although their sample period is now somewhat dated, Bairam and Dempster (1991) have provided some estimates of balance-of-payments equilibrium growth rates for four of the East Asian countries, namely, Singapore, Indonesia, the Philippines and Thailand. Their results are presented in Table 6.2.

It can be seen that both specifications of Thirlwall's law give a good approximation to the observed growth rates of the East Asian countries. A corollary is that capital flows and the rate of change of relative prices had little impact on the equilibrium growth rate (it should be remembered that this period was before financial liberalization led to a rapid increase in short-term capital flows). In all cases but one, the estimated price elasticities of demand were not statistically different from zero, and in the one case where a price elasticity was significant (the price elasticity of demand for exports for Indonesia), it took the wrong sign. The key to the fast growth rates of these countries was thus the especially high income elasticities of demand for their exports.

Table 6.2 Balance-of-payments equilibrium growth rates in selected Asian economies

Country	Period	ε	π	$y_B = \varepsilon z/\pi$	$y_B = x/\pi$	y
Singapore	1973–80	7.9	3.6	7.5	9.2	8.2
Indonesia	1966–85	3.5	2.7	4.8	7.9	6.5
Philippines	1961–85	2.6	2.4	4.1	4.1	4.4
Thailand	1961–85	3.4	1.9	6.8	7.0	6.9

Source: Bairam and Dempster (1991).

More recently, Ansari, et al. (2000) have undertaken a further analysis of the applicability of Thirlwall's law to Indonesia, Malaysia, the Philippines, and Thailand over the period 1970–96. The terminal date was chosen to exclude the period of the East Asian financial crisis. They calculated the average balance-of-payments-constrained growth rate (excluding any allowances for the growth of capital flows) for these four countries to be 5.41 per cent per annum, while their actual average growth rate was 6.40 per cent per annum. The difference between the actual growth rate, y and y_B was only statistically significant in the case of Thailand, where $y > y_B$. Ansari et al. attribute this to the marked deterioration in Thailand's trade deficit as a percentage of GDP after 1983, which resulted from the decline in export earnings of tin, sugar and tapioca. The imposition of quota restrictions further exacerbated the situation. It is interesting to note that this explanation is couched in terms of the relative failure of export performance, rather than in terms of physical supply constraints. It is also instructive to note that while the price term took the *a priori* expected sign in Ansari et al.'s regressions, it was only statistically significant in the case of the Philippines. In the cases of Indonesia, Malaysia and the Philippines, Ansari et al. conclude that 'Thirlwall's proposition cannot be rejected . . . The main policy implication is that these countries should continue to follow the outward-looking growth strategy with emphasis on export performance for a continued high rate of economic growth'.

As we have seen above, the achievement of a high income elasticity of demand for exports is not the result of a once-and-for-all effort. Over time, with technical change and product innovation, world tastes and sectoral demand are continually changing, and to maintain a growth rate above the world average requires a continual process of rapid structural change. Based on his work on what constitutes a successful development strategy, Wade (1990, p. 362), following some sceptical comments on the effectiveness of devaluation, emphasized the importance of non-price competitiveness, broadly defined:

> Where, nevertheless, heavy reliance is to be placed on trade, the government must recognise that successful exporting of manufactured goods to richer countries is not just a matter of getting the exchange rate right and keeping labour cheap, in the absence of protection. This is because many kinds of manufactured exports to richer countries are only saleable as complete packages meeting all buyer specifications, including packaging, labelling, colors, raw materials, finishes and technical specifications. Costs rule out the option of importing an incomplete or defective package and correcting the defects in a subsequent stage of manufacturing. Thus, marketing, transmission of information and quality control turn out to be the key activities for export success. Buyers can supply some of these services; but especially because of externalities the government also has an important role. The government can arrange for information about foreign markets and about domestic suppliers to be easily and freely available; it can directly help the promotion of some products (e.g.

through trade fairs); and it can help to curb the tendency of firms without brand names to compete by producing shoddy goods, spoiling the country's reputation for other producers. Very importantly, the government can also inspire producers to seek out export markets as a normal part of their operations.

Nevertheless, there are limits to a strategy of export-led growth, and we now turn to a consideration of this.

EXPORT-LED GROWTH STRATEGIES AND THE FALLACY OF COMPOSITION

One potential criticism that needs to be examined is that the export-led growth strategy is flawed as it is subject to a fallacy of composition. As already mentioned, Tiebout (1956) correctly pointed out that, for the world as a whole, growth cannot be export-led. Moreover, there are problems for individual countries, especially the LDCs, in trying to promote export-led growth, especially if they concentrate on similar industries. A particular country will inevitably face fierce competition from other countries in the same position, and may find that a successful growth strategy can only be achieved at the expense of another country. But ironically, while this could be treated as a weakness of the balance-of-payments-constrained growth model, precisely the opposite is the case. The fact that *all* countries are unlikely to be able to generate fast rates of growth of exports that will enable them to raise their rate of growth to that of their productive potential shows the importance of the external constraint. There is the danger of confusion here between the export-led growth theory and the balance-of-payments-constrained growth theory. The early export-led growth theories did not incorporate a balance-of-payments constraint (see, for example, Beckerman, 1962). To argue that an export-led growth strategy for a particular country is necessary for rapid growth not to be hindered by balance-of-payments crises is not the same as implying that all countries can simultaneously achieve any growth rate of exports they desire. It has been argued that, in the long run, the only effective strategy is to encourage production of those goods for which there is a high world income elasticity of demand.[24] But if a number of countries are simultaneously trying to follow such a policy and, especially if they are concentrating on the same group of export industries, the end result may be that only a few of the countries will, *ex post*, achieve a marked increase in ε. The others may simply have been running fast to stay still, and concomitantly, excess capacity may develop.[25] In fact, one could argue that if the simple export-led growth theory did not suffer from a fallacy of composition, there could be no such thing as balance-of-payments-constrained growth in the long run.

The problem is that by generating a rapid domestic expansion, countries experience a rapid increase in imports from other countries. If they cannot increase their growth of exports *pari passu*, then they are likely to encounter a balance-of-payments crisis. This problem may be compounded by the fact that the additional imports need not be supplied by the countries to which the economies in our example are trying to export. There may be a geographical mismatch in the composition of the growth of demand, which would need to be analysed in a three-country model. The problem is also exacerbated by some countries (such as Japan) running substantial trade surpluses. An implication is that persuading these countries to open their markets may be one way to increase the growth rates of balance-of-payments-constrained economies, although this will be a one-off effect. Far more damaging to the growth of, for example, the Asian countries for which Japan provides the major export market has been the substantial decline in Japan's growth rate since the mid-1970s.

Kaldor (1981) was fully aware of all this, and summarized the situation as follows. The newly industrializing countries (NICs) will generate increased export penetration in the advanced countries. The resulting increase in the growth of income in the NICs will, in turn, stimulate the growth of demand for the industrial countries' exports. But as Kaldor remarks:

> there is no guarantee that if we take any arbitrarily chosen pair of countries, or even a group of 'developed' or developing countries . . . that these two changes – reduced export share of the older industrialized countries and the increase in total world demand – will fully offset one another. Taking any individual manufacturing exporter, the tendency to such an offset (which is the same as the tendency for a country to gravitate to a state of equilibrium in its external balance of payments) may well be brought about through variations in growth rates.

If we were in a neoclassical world where countries faced an infinitely elastic price elasticity of demand for their exports, there could be no such thing as a balance-of-payments constraint. The foreign exchange revenue required to fund the growth in imports would be generated through an increased growth in exports resulting from an infinitesimal rate of change of relative prices. Likewise, if through industrial policies countries could actually increase the income elasticities of demand for their exports irrespective of the actions of competitor countries, then, in the long run, the balance-of-payments constraint would no longer exist. But it should be remembered that if a group of countries are following this strategy in a related product area, *ex post*, none of them might find that their income elasticity of demand for a particular type of export has risen to any large extent. There are limits to the rate of growth of exports on a global scale, which in fact imposes a constraint on the growth rates of individual countries, and which constrains their rate of economic growth below its potential. This does not mean, however, that there is necessarily any more efficient method of increasing the rate of growth. It would be erroneous to interpret Thirlwall's law as implying all countries could, by pursuing export-led growth strategies, simultaneously achieve any desired rate of growth of output.

CONCLUSIONS

This chapter has discussed one major aspect of the Kaldorian approach to economic growth, namely the importance of the growth of autonomous demand. In particular, it has been shown that, in open economies, the key to understanding a country's economic growth is to be found in the performance of its exports, or rather in the ratio of the income elasticities of demand for exports and imports together with the growth rate of the rest of the world – as encapsulated in Thirlwall's law. A corollary of this is that changes in relative prices do not affect the growth rates of exports and imports, at least in the long run, and that the growth of capital flows does not significantly raise the balance-of-payments-constrained growth rate in the long run. It has been shown that recent tests of Thirlwall's law have confirmed the results of earlier studies that support the law. Estimates of balance-of-payments-constrained growth rates generally closely approximate actual growth rates.

As Davidson (1990–1) has noted, problems will arise for LDCs if they concentrate on exporting raw materials and other basic commodities for which Engel's law suggests the advanced countries have low income elasticities of demand. This is the case even though the static comparative advantage of LDCs lies in these goods. Furthermore, if these countries also have a high income elasticity of demand for the manufactured products of the advanced countries, then their balance-of-payments-constrained growth rates will be commensurately lower than those of the advanced countries. This suggests that 'if economic development and balance of payments equilibrium is left to the free market then [Thirlwall's law] indicates that the LDCs are condemned to relative poverty, and the global inequality of income will become larger over time' (Davidson, 1990–1). Convergence in productivity levels and per capita income is by no means assured by the operation of market forces.

NOTES

1. For a discussion of Kaldor's agriculture/industry two-sector model and a more detailed treatment of some of the issues raised in this paper, see McCombie and Roberts (2000). Kaldor's emphasis on the role of increasing returns in economic growth is considered by McCombie (2002).

2. The growth of autonomous demand could also be the growth of agricultural demand. The transition between agricultural-led and export-led growth is not satisfactorily modelled at present and awaits the attention of future researchers. Thirlwall (1986) makes some suggestions as to how this may be accomplished.
3. Thirlwall (1997) provides an interesting discussion of the derivation of this approach and the relationship of his work to that on similar lines by Kaldor. Although Kaldor never devised a formal model, he intuitively saw many of its conclusions. In 1977, two UK government economists questioned whether the UK had a balance-of-payments problem since, while imports as a proportion of GDP had grown markedly over the postwar period, so too had exports. But as Kaldor pointed out, any *autonomous* increase in the share of imports in national income reduces demand for domestic goods and investment 'until a sufficient contraction occurs in the gross domestic product relative to exports to make the spontaneous rise in one ratio to be matched by an induced increase in the other'. Kaldor (1981) presents an analysis using Thirlwall's balance-of-payments-constrained growth model to explain growth rate differences.
4. More recent neoclassical trade and endogenous growth models are, however, beginning to consider these factors.
5. Note that it is the relative differences, not the absolute values, of the income elasticities that matter. Although the average values of ε and π may fall in the long run, this will not prevent some countries still being balance-of-payments-constrained.
6. The earlier 'standard' model of cumulative causation of Dixon and Thirlwall (1975), which did not include a balance-of-payments equilibrium constraint, had the Verdoorn law as an integral part. (The Verdoorn law is the empirical relationship which shows that a faster growth of output induces a faster growth of productivity. See McCombie and Thirlwall, 1994, chapter 2.) Starting from an initial position, an increase in the growth rate will, via the Verdoorn law, give rise to a positive feedback through an improvement in relative prices. However, given plausible parameter values, the growth rates in the model will converge to an equilibrium rate. It is a straightforward matter to include the Verdoorn law in the model above. However, given the fact that relative prices play an unimportant role in the model, the Verdoorn law instead leads to a faster-growing country having a faster growth of real wages (assuming rates of exogenous productivity growth are the same for all countries). It, therefore, does not affect the balance-of-payments equilibrium growth rate. Thus, for expositional ease, we have not incorporated it into the balance-of-payments-constrained model.
7. While this incorporates the balance-of-payments identity, equation [6.4] is not itself an identity. There is no reason, *a priori*, why the two income elasticities of demand should be statistically significant. Indeed, under the neoclassical approach where changes in relative prices equilibrate the balance of payments, there is no theoretical reason why this should be the case.
8. The balance-of-payments-constrained growth model has not been without its critics. For a discussion of the more important objections that have been raised concerning this approach together with a rebuttal, see McCombie and Thirlwall (1997a).
9. See McCombie (1993) for a generalization to a two-country model and one that also explicitly includes the domestic determinants of economic growth.
10. Thus the approach does not simply *assume* that changes in relative prices have *no* effect at all on trade flows, as is sometimes erroneously asserted.
11. Real wage resistance implies that *relative* purchasing power parity holds. This should not be confused with the neoclassical theory of *absolute* purchasing power parity.
12. Kaldor, who had originally been an advocate of floating exchange rates, soon changed his mind in the light of this experience.
13. Note that as exports are growing faster than income and imports, both ω and the current account deficit will decrease slowly over time. If exports grow at 8 per cent per annum over a ten-year period, the average value of ω is 0.95. However, we shall ignore this minor complication here.
14. It is assumed that $(\pi - 1 + \omega) > 0$, which implies $(1 - \omega)/\pi < 1$. To see what happens if this is not the case, let us assume that $f_t = y_{t-1}$ (where we have dropped the subscript *B*3 for notational ease) and $x_t = x_{t-1} = x$. If $(1 - \omega)/\pi > 1$, the solution to the difference equation

$y_t = \omega x/\pi + (1 - \omega)y_{t-1}/\pi$ is explosive and there is no balance-of-payments equilibrium growth rate. It should also be noted that unless $\pi = 1$, ω will change slowly over time. The intuition is that ω will only be constant if both x and f are equal to the growth of total foreign exchange receipts and thus imports. Given that y is a weighted average of x and f this can only occur if $m = y$. However, $m = y$ will only hold, and hence ω will only be constant, if $\pi = 1$. If $\pi > 1$, which is empirically likely to be the case, there will be global stability with ω converging to 1, thus yielding Thirlwall's law ($y_B = x/\pi$). If $\pi < 1$, then there is only saddle-path stability and, in general, ω will tend to explode (Barbosa-Filho, 2001). In the latter case, the government will have to use exchange rate adjustment or, as this is likely to be ineffective, alter the growth rate by domestic demand management policies to take the economy on to the stable manifold. The discussion in the text assumes that the length of the period is such that ω is approximately constant.

15. If $\theta_{max} = 50$ per cent, then if y is 2.0 per cent per annum, the maximum sustainable current account deficit to income ratio is 1 per cent (see Table 6.1). Thus, from $y_{B3} = \omega x/(\pi - 1 + \omega)$, it follows that $y_{B3} = 2.0 = 0.645x$ per cent per annum, or $x = 3.1$ per cent per annum.
16. See also the chapter by Atesoglu in this volume.
17. Dixon and Thirlwall (1975) argued that 'it also serves some purpose to give a not (unrealistic) specification which suggests on empirical grounds that divergence is not very likely, if only to induce those who adhere to the cumulative causation model to specify more precisely the model they have in mind and to show the conditions under which regional growth rates would diverge through time'. They argue that the most likely extension would be that 'the price and income elasticities could change in the course of time as the structure of production changed'. We show below how this may be accomplished in the context of the balance-of-payments-constrained growth model.
18. See also the chapter by Setterfield in this volume.
19. He gives another example of this mechanism as affecting the value of the Verdoorn coefficient.
20. Conversely, it is possible that a more rapid rate of growth, through generating a faster rate of capital accumulation, may induce enterprise (rather than defensive) investment – to use Lamfalussy's term – together with a faster increase in R&D expenditure and product innovation. This may actually lead to higher values for the world income elasticities of demand for a particular country's exports.
21. Figure 6.1 indicates that the rationale required to justify the non-linear functional form specified for ε/π is slightly more subtle than is indicated in the main text. This is because to the left of the intersection between the curve depicting the function and the 45° line, the gap separating the two at first increases before proceeding to decline. The implication is that the pressure for reform must have a positive (absolute) impact on ε/π that at first increases with y_{t-1} before then declining. This can be justified by arguing that reform of an economy's production structure is a costly business. At low levels of y_{t-1}, a marginally higher y_{t-1} is then associated with greater positive reform because the higher y_{t-1} provides more revenue to both government and firms to finance reform measures. However, at higher levels, a marginally higher y_{t-1} is associated with less positive reform because the pressure for change has diminished to a level where revenue to finance what is demanded is no longer a problem.
22. 1997 saw the onset of the East Asian financial crisis which caused a collapse in growth rates in the region. It is beyond the scope of this study to consider the causes of this save to note that, currently, there has been some recovery in East Asian economic performance. For a survey of the issues involved, see Nixson and Walters (1999).
23. It should not be forgotten that a vibrant export sector is important for other reasons, especially in LDCs. The more open an economy, the greater the degree of competition and the faster the rate of diffusion of innovations. A faster growth of exports also means that foreign exchange earnings grow more rapidly, allowing a greater growth of imports of advanced technological capital equipment. Trade also allows greater specialization in production and hence enhanced possibilities of benefiting from economies of scale (see Edwards, 1993, for a survey).
24. Hence an industrial strategy (infant industry protection, export subsidies, etc.) may be necessary to improve the rate of growth of exports.

25. An implication is that to increase the success of an export-led growth strategy, countries, especially the LDCs, should not concentrate on the same broad product areas.

REFERENCES

Alonso, J.E. and C. Garcimartin (1998–9) 'A new approach to the balance-of-payments constraint: some empirical evidence,' *Journal of Post Keynesian Economics*, 21, 259–82.

Anderson, P.S. (1993) 'The 45°-rule revisited,' *Applied Economics*, 25, 1279–84.

Ansari, M., N. Hashemzadeh and Y. Xi (2000) 'The chronicle of economic growth in Southeast Asian countries: does Thirlwall's law provide an adequate explanation?' *Journal of Post Keynesian Economics*, 22, 573–88.

Atesoglu, H.S. (1995) 'An explanation of the slowdown in U.S. economic growth,' *Applied Economics Letters*, 2, 91–94.

Atesoglu, H.S. (1997) 'Balance-of-payments-constrained growth model and its implications for the United States,' *Journal of Post Keynesian Economics*, 19, 327–35.

Bairam, E.I. (1997) 'Levels of economic development and appropriate specification of the Harrod foreign-trade multiplier,' *Journal of Post Keynesian Economics*, 19, 337–44.

Bairam, E.I. and G.J. Dempster (1991) 'The Harrod foreign trade multiplier and economic growth in Asian countries,' *Applied Economics*, 23, 1719–24.

Barbosa-Filho, N.H. (2001) 'The balance-of-payments constraint: from balanced trade to debt sustainability,' paper presented to the 2001 meeting of the *Eastern Economic Association*, New York.

Beckerman, W. (1962) 'Projecting Europe's growth,' *Economic Journal*, 72, 912–25.

Blecker, R.A. (1998) 'International competitiveness, relative wages, and the balance-of-payments constraint,' *Journal of Post Keynesian Economics*, 20, 495–526.

Brech, M.J. and D. Stout (1981) 'The rate of exchange and non-price competitiveness: a provisional study within UK manufactured exports,' *Oxford Economic Papers*, 33, 268–81.

Cornwall, J. (1977) *Modern Capitalism: Its Growth and Transformation*, London, Martin Robertson.

Davidson, P. (1990–1) 'A Post Keynesian contribution to 'theory',' *Journal of Post Keynesian Economics*, 13, 298–303.

Dixon, R.J. and A.P. Thirlwall (1975) 'A model of regional growth-rate differences on Kaldorian lines,' *Oxford Economic Papers*, 27, 201–14.

Edwards, S. (1993) 'Openness, trade liberalization and growth in developing countries,' *Journal of Economic Literature*, 31, 1358–93.

Greenhalgh, C. (1990) 'Innovation and the trade performance in the United Kingdom,' *Economic Journal*, 100, 105–18.

Harrod, R.F. (1933) *International Economics*, Cambridge, Cambridge University Press

Hicks, J.R. (1950) *A Contribution to the Theory of the Trade Cycle*, Oxford, Oxford University Press.

Hieke, H. (1997) 'Balance-of-payments-constrained growth: a reconsideration of the evidence for the U.S. economy,' *Journal of Post Keynesian Economics*, 19, 313–25.

Houthakker, H. and S. Magee (1969) 'Income and price elasticities in world trade,' *Review of Income and Statistics*, 60, 111–25.

Hussain, M. (1995) 'The balance of payments and growth,' *African Development Report* (African Development Bank).

Kaldor, N. (1934) 'A classificatory note on the determinateness of equilibrium,' *Review of Economic Studies*, 1, 122–36.
Kaldor, N. (1972) 'The irrelevance of equilibrium economics.' *Economic Journal*, 82, 1237–55.
Kaldor, N. (1975) 'What is wrong with economic theory.' *Quarterly Journal of Economics*,' 99, 347–57.
Kaldor, N. (1977) 'Equilibrium theory and growth theory,' in M. Boskin (ed.) *Economics and Human Welfare: Essays in Honour of Tibor Scitovsky*, New York, Academic Press, 273–291.
Kaldor, N. (1981) 'The role of increasing returns, technical progress and cumulative causation in the theory of international trade and economic growth,' *Économie Appliquée*, 34, 593–617.
Kaldor, N. (1996) *Causes of Growth and Stagnation in the World Economy*, Cambridge, Cambridge University Press.
Knoester, A. (1995) *Why a Depreciating Currency does not Improve the Current Balance*, Erasmus University, Rotterdam, Research Memorandum no. 9506.
Kravis, I.B. and R.E. Lipsey (1971) *Price Competitiveness in World Trade*, New York, National Bureau of Economic Research.
Krugman, P. (1989) 'Differences in income elasticities and trends in real exchange rates,' *European Economic Review*, 33, 1001–46.
Krugman, P. (1994) 'The myth of Asia's miracle,' *Foreign Affairs*, November/December, 62–78.
León-Ledesma, M.A. (1999) 'An application of Thirlwall's law to the Spanish economy,' *Journal of Post Keynesian Economics*, 21, 431–39.
McCombie, J.S.L. (1985) 'Economic growth, the Harrod foreign trade multiplier and the Hicks super-multiplier,' *Applied Economics*, 17, 55–72.
McCombie, J.S.L. (1993) 'Economic growth, trade interlinkages, and the balance-of-payments constraint,' *Journal of Post Keynesian Economics*, 15, 345–505.
McCombie, J.S.L. (1997) 'The empirics of balance-of-payments constrained growth,' *Journal of Post Keynesian Economics*, 19, 345–75.
McCombie, J.S.L. (2002) 'Increasing returns and economic growth from a Kaldorian perspective,' in J.S.L. McCombie, M. Pugno and B. Soro (eds) *Productivity, Growth and Economic Performance: Essays on Verdoorn's Law*, Basingstoke, Palgrave (forthcoming).
McCombie, J.S.L. and M. Roberts (2000) 'Demand and economic growth from a Kaldorian viewpoint,' mimeo, Downing College and New Hall, Cambridge.
McCombie, J.S.L. and A.P. Thirlwall (1994) *Economic Growth and the Balance-of-Payments Constraint*, London, Macmillan.
McCombie, J.S.L. and A.P. Thirlwall (1997a) 'The dynamic Harrod foreign trade multiplier and the demand-orientated approach to economic growth: an evaluation,' *International Review of Applied Economics*, 11, 5–26.
McCombie, J.S.L. and A.P. Thirlwall (1997b) 'Economic growth and the balance-of-payments constraint revisited,' in P. Arestis, G. Palma and M. Sawyer (eds) *Markets, Unemployment and Economic Policy: Essays in Honour of Geoff Harcourt, Volume Two*, London, Routledge, 498–511.
Moreno-Brid, J.C. (1998–9) 'On capital flows and the balance-of-payments constrained growth model,' *Journal of Post Keynesian Economics*, 21, 283–89.
Moreno-Brid, J.C. (1999) 'Mexico's economic growth and the balance of payments constraint: a cointegration analysis,' *International Review of Applied Economics*, 13, 149–59.

Moreno-Brid, J.C. and E. Pérez (1999) 'Balance-of-payments-constrained growth in Central America: 1950–1996,' *Journal of Post Keynesian Economics*, 22, 131–47.

Nelson, R.R. and H. Pack (1999) 'The Asian growth miracle and modern growth theory,' *Economic Journal*, 109, 416–36.

Nixson, F.I. and B. Walters (1999) 'The Asian crisis: causes and consequences,' *Manchester School of Economics and Social Studies*, 67, 496–523.

North, D.C. (1955) 'Location theory and regional economic growth,' *Journal of Political Economy*, 63, 243–58.

North, D.C. (1956) 'Reply,' *Journal of Political Economy*, 64, 165–68.

Pérez, E. and J.C. Moreno-Brid (1999) 'Terms of trade, exports and economic growth in Central America: a long-term view,' *Banca Nazionale del Lavoro Quarterly Review*, 211, 431–49.

Pugno, M. (1998) 'The stability of Thirlwall's model of economic growth and the balance-of-payments constraint,' *Journal of Post Keynesian Economics*, 20, 559–81.

Roberts, M. (2001a) *Essays in Cumulative Causation*, Department of Land Economy, University of Cambridge, unpublished Ph.D dissertation.

Roberts, M. (2001b) 'Endogenous structural change,' *Zagreb International Review of Economics and Business*, 4, 1–22. University of Cambridge.

Setterfield, M.A. (1997) '"History versus equilibrium" and the theory of economic growth,' *Cambridge Journal of Economics*, 21, 365–78.

Setterfield, M.A. (1998) 'History versus equilibrium: Nicholas Kaldor on historical time and economic theory,' *Cambridge Journal of Economics*, 22, 521–37.

Thirlwall, A.P. (1979) 'The balance of payments constraint as an explanation of international growth rate differences,' *Banca Nazionale Del Lavoro Quarterly Review*, 128, 45–53.

Thirlwall, A.P. (1986) 'A general model of growth and development on Kaldorian lines,' *Oxford Economic Papers*, 38, 199–219.

Thirlwall, A.P. (1987) *Nicholas Kaldor*, Brighton, Wheatsheaf.

Thirlwall, A.P. (1997) 'Reflections on the concept of balance-of-payments-constrained growth,' *Journal of Post Keynesian Economics*, 19, 375–85.

Thirlwall, A.P. and M.N. Hussain (1982) 'The balance of payments constraint, capital flows and growth rate differences between developing countries,' *Oxford Economic Papers*, 34, 498–570.

Thirlwall, A.P. and G. Sanna (1998) 'The macro determinants of growth and "New" Growth Theory: an evaluation and further evidence,' in R. Arestis (ed.), *Employment, Economic Growth and the Tyranny of the Market: Essays in Honour of Paul Davidson*, Aldershot, Edward Elgar, 131–56.

Tiebout, C.M. (1956) 'Exports and regional economic growth,' *Journal of Political Economy*, 64, 160–64.

Toye, J. (1992) 'Britain, the United States and the world debt crisis,' in J. Michie (ed.), *The Economic Legacy, 1979–1992*, London, Academic Press, 11–33.

Turner, P. (1999) 'The balance of payments constraint and the post 1973 slowdown of economic growth in the G7 economies,' *International Review of Applied Economics*, 13, 41–53.

Wade, R. (1990) *Governing the Market: Economic Theory and the Role of Government in East Asian Industrialization*, Princeton, Princeton University Press.

World Bank (1998) *East Asia: The Road to Recovery*, Washington, DC, The World Bank.

Young, A. (1992) 'A tale of two cities: factor accumulation and technical change in Hong Kong and Singapore,' *National Bureau of Economic Research, Macroeconomics Annual*, 13–54.

Young, A. (1995) 'The tyranny of numbers: confronting the statistical realities of the East Asian growth experience,' *Quarterly Journal of Economics*, 110, 641–80.

7. Pitfalls in the theory of growth: an application to the balance-of-payments-constrained growth model

Thomas I. Palley

INTRODUCTION

Over the last decade, under the banner of new endogenous growth theory, there has been a revival of interest in the theory of economic growth. Though endogenizing steady-state growth, the new theory persists with the claim that growth is a purely supply-side phenomenon. This is at odds with Keynesian economics that emphasizes the demand-side dimension of the growth process. However, the Keynesian paradigm has, itself, fallen into the pitfall of failing to properly account for the supply side. In the long run, there is a requirement that the rates of demand and supply growth be equal. Absent this, there will either be growing excess capacity or excess demand. If potential output growth is subject to influences other than those acting on the demand side, or if it does not respond one-for-one to changes in the rate of demand growth, this requires mechanisms that equilibrate the two.

This study presents a short treatment of the demand- and supply-growth problem, and then applies it to balance-of-payments-constrained (BOPC) growth theory (Thirlwall, 1979). In its simplest form, the BOPC model is a pure demand-constrained model of growth. A Verdoorn law equation can be added to describe the supply side, but this introduces problems of reconciling supply growth with the BOPC rate of demand growth. Building on Palley (1996), the study suggests how this inconsistency can be reconciled.

THE PROBLEM OF BALANCING DEMAND AND SUPPLY GROWTH

Neoclassical growth theory (Solow, 1956) claims that steady-state growth is determined by supply-side forces. Thus, in steady state the equilibrium growth rate is determined by:

$$g^s = g(S) \qquad [7.1]$$

$$g = g^s \qquad [7.2]$$

where g is the steady-state growth rate, g^s is the growth of potential output and S is a vector of supply-side forces. In the Solow model, the supply-side forces are the rate of population growth and the rate of technological advance, both of which are taken to be exogenous. Equation [7.2] implicitly assumes a 'dynamic' version of Say's law, whereby the growth of supply creates a matching growth of demand.

New endogenous growth theory retains this overarching framework, except that the steady-state growth rate is now subject to influence by the choices of government and agents (Romer, 1993, 1994). Thus, equation [7.1] becomes:

$$g^s = g(S, t) \qquad [7.1a]$$

where t is a vector of choice variables subject to control by government and private sector agents. These choice variables include public research and development (R&D) spending, the stock of public capital, public investment, the stock of human capital and investment in human capital. The central implication is that the steady-state growth rate is subject to endogenous variation despite an exogenously given vector of other supply side forces, S.

This neoclassical perspective contrasts with a Keynesian perspective, which emphasizes demand-side factors. In the Keynesian paradigm, growth is given by:

$$g^d = g(D) \qquad [7.3]$$

$$g = g^d \qquad [7.4]$$

where g^d is the growth of demand, and D is a vector of demand-side forces, which can be both exogenous and endogenous. Equation [7.4] implicitly assumes that the growth of supply adjusts to the growth of demand.

However, if there is a separate supply side (i.e. a production side of the economy), this requires that the following condition hold:

$$g = g^s = g^d \qquad [7.5]$$

Absent the satisfaction of this condition, there will either be growing excess capacity or growing excess demand – neither of which are observed in modern capitalist economies in the long run. The imposition of this growth equilibrium condition in turn raises questions as to how equilibrium is achieved. In an endogenous growth framework, variation in the choices of individuals and governments could enable equilibration of demand and supply growth, but this raises questions as to what are the market mechanisms and signals that give agents an incentive to change their choices?[1]

The implications of requiring steady-state balance between demand and supply growth are illustrated by the following Keynesian model (Palley, 1997):

$$g^s = g(S, g^d) \tag{7.6}$$

$$g^d = g(D) \tag{7.7}$$

$$g = g^s = g^d \tag{7.8}$$

The model is Keynesian in that demand growth influences the rate of potential output growth, and the rate of demand growth is influenced by choice of *D*. Thus, government policy can influence the rate of demand growth, and in so doing it can influence the rate of potential output growth. Yet despite this, the set of growth equilibria may be very limited, and there may even be only a single equilibrium point. This is illustrated in Figure 7.1, in which the rate of

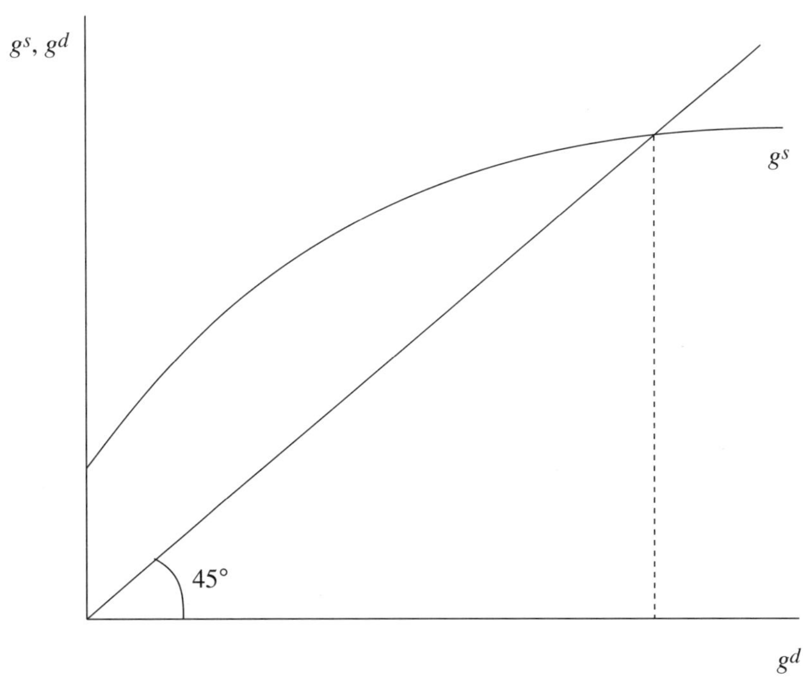

Figure 7.1 Equilibrium growth with a strictly concave supply growth function

supply growth is a strictly concave function of the rate of demand growth. In this dynamized income–expenditure model, there is only on equilibrium point. Figure 7.2 illustrates an alternative representation, in which supply growth is a quasi-concave function of demand growth and there are three equilibria.[2] Though increased in number, the set of equilibria is still very restricted. The model here is also very different from static Keynesian models of the equilibrium 'level' of income, which are marked by a continuum of equilibria. In these static models, policy makers can continuously vary the equilibrium level of income by changing the level of demand. In the above dynamic model, they can only cause jumps between equilibria, and even this requires that the supply growth function be shaped in a particular way. These differences illustrate the critical importance of properly accounting for demand and supply growth, as well as the pitfalls of failing to do so.

Finally, in connection with the above distinction between static and dynamic Keynesian models, the work of Cornwall (1972) provides a possible intermediate position. Cornwall recognizes the importance of the distinction between the growth of supply and the growth of demand, and also recognizes

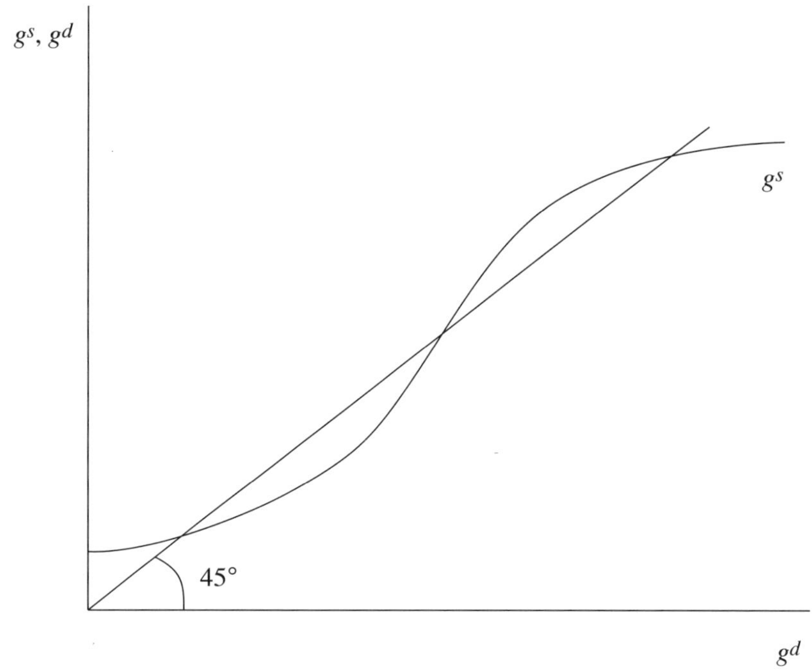

Figure 7.2 Equilibrium growth with a quasi-concave supply growth function

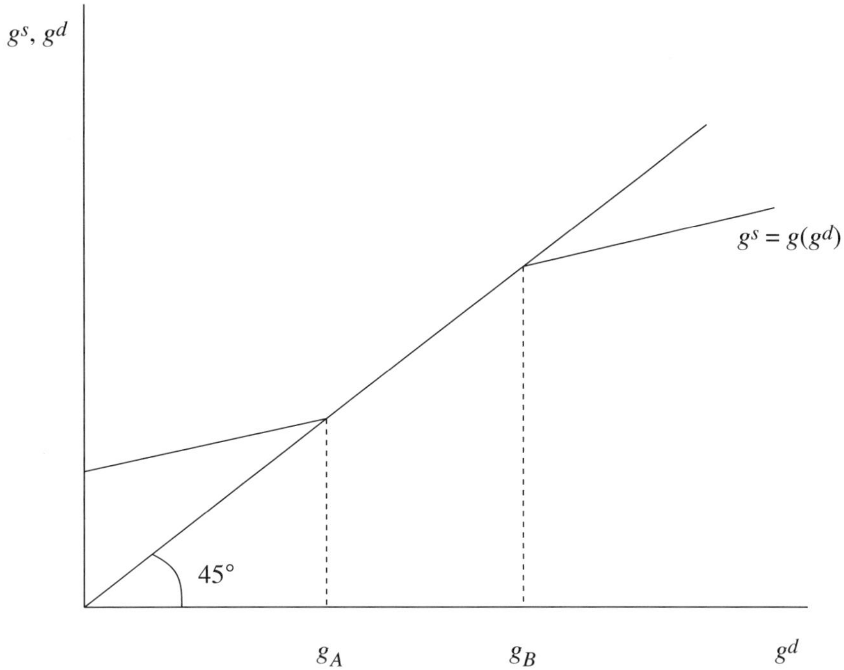

Figure 7.3 The Cornwall (1972) model, with a region of correspondence between supply and demand growth

that the two must be equal in equilibrium. He then postulates that there may be a range of demand growth where the two coincide. This is illustrated in Figure 7.3, in which the growth of supply and demand correspond over the region $g_A - g_B$.

AN ILLUSTRATION: THE BOPC GROWTH MODEL

The BOPC growth model introduced by Thirlwall (1979) has become a work-horse of post-Keynesian growth theory. The BOP growth model is intended to show how country growth rates are ultimately constrained by the rate of growth of demand, thereby making for a Keynesian theory of growth. In this regard, the growth of exogenous demand provided by exports is especially important. The logic is that the current account provides an ultimate constraint on growth, because countries cannot continuously increase their foreign debt to gross domestic product (GDP) ratios. Consequently, if domestic income and import demand are growing in excess of export demand, at some stage the rising foreign debt to GDP ratio implied by a growing current account deficit will force a slowdown that restores current account balance.

However, the BOPC model embodies an internal inconsistency owing to its failure to consistently incorporate the supply side of the economy. In the long run, not only is growth constrained by the requirement of dynamic current account balance, but there is also a requirement that the rate of growth of output equal the rate of growth of potential output. This leads to the potential for inconsistency between the dual requirements of capacity balance and current account balance. The problem can be seen from the following simple statement of the BOPC growth model:

$$x = a_0 g^* \tag{7.9}$$

$$m = b_0 g^d \tag{7.10}$$

$$x = m \tag{7.11}$$

$$\lambda = c_0 + c_1 g^d \tag{7.12}$$

$$g^s = \lambda + n \tag{7.13}$$

where x is the rate of export growth, g^* is the rate of foreign income growth, m is the rate of import growth, g^d is the rate of domestic income growth, λ is the rate of labour productivity growth, g^s is the rate of potential output growth and n is the rate of labour force growth. Equations [7.9] and [7.10] are, respectively, export and import growth equations. Equation [7.11] is the balance-of-payments constraint, which requires equality between the long-run rates of import and export growth to prevent a growing current account deficit or surplus. Equation [7.12] is the Verdoorn law equation which endogenizes productivity growth by linking it to domestic output growth. Lastly, equation [7.13] determines the rate of potential output growth.

Solutions for the equilibrium rates of actual and potential output growth are given by:

$$g^d = a_0 g^* / b_0 \tag{7.14}$$

and:

$$g^s = c_0 + c_1 a_0 g^* / b_0 + n \tag{7.15}$$

The model is overdetermined, and it is only by chance that the BOPC rate of output growth will equal potential output growth. The necessary condition is:

$$g^* = [c_0 + n]/[a_0/b_0 - c_1] \qquad [7.16]$$

If this condition is not satisfied, there will be growing imbalance between actual and potential output. If $g^* > [c_0 + n]/[a_0/b_0 - c_1]$, there will be growing excess demand. If $g^* < [c_0 + n]/[a_0/b_0 - c_1]$, there will be growing excess supply.

A SUGGESTION FOR RECONCILING THE INCONSISTENCY IN THE BOP MODEL

The theoretical good sense of the BOP model and its ability to make empirical sense of many countries' growth experience (McCombie, 1997; Bairam and Dempster, 1991) suggest that the model is a worthwhile one. That said, reconciling the inconsistency between the current account and the capacity balance constraints is an important matter.

A possible means of reconciliation is suggested by Palley (1996), who shows how steady-state excess supply conditions can impact the steady-state rate of growth. This allows for growth without full employment. Such a suggestion can be incorporated into the BOP growth model by making the income elasticity of demand for imports a negative function of the state of excess capacity, *E*. One rationale for this is that imports are driven by bottlenecks. As excess capacity and unemployment decrease, bottlenecks become more prevalent and the share of increments in income spent on imports increases. Thirlwall and White (1974) and Thirlwall and Hughes (1979) provide some empirical evidence for this hypothesis, showing that the elasticity of demand for imports increases in conditions of excess demand.

In steady-state equilibrium excess capacity is constant, indicating that demand and supply are growing at the same rate. Given this, the model becomes:

$$x = a_0 g^* \qquad [7.9]$$

$$m = b_0(E) g^d \qquad [7.10a]$$

$$x = m \qquad [7.11]$$

$$\lambda = c_0 + c_1 g^d \qquad [7.12]$$

$$g^s = \lambda + n \qquad [7.13]$$

$$g^d = g^s \qquad [7.17]$$

where E is the ratio of current output to normal capacity output.[3] The changes from the earlier model concern the specification of [7.10a] and the addition of a capacity balance condition given by [7.17].

The workings of the model can be understood as follows. The existence of a balance-of-payments constraint requires that export growth equal import growth in the steady state. This imposes the condition:[4]

$$g^d = a_0 g^* / b_0(E) \qquad [7.18]$$

Simultaneously, the requirement that demand growth equal supply growth imposes the condition:[5]

$$g^d = [c_0 + n]/[1 - c_1] \qquad [7.19]$$

The potential inconsistency is illustrated in Figure 7.4. The ray from the origin shows the rates of demand growth consistent with foreign income growth, while the horizontal line determines the rate of demand growth consistent with

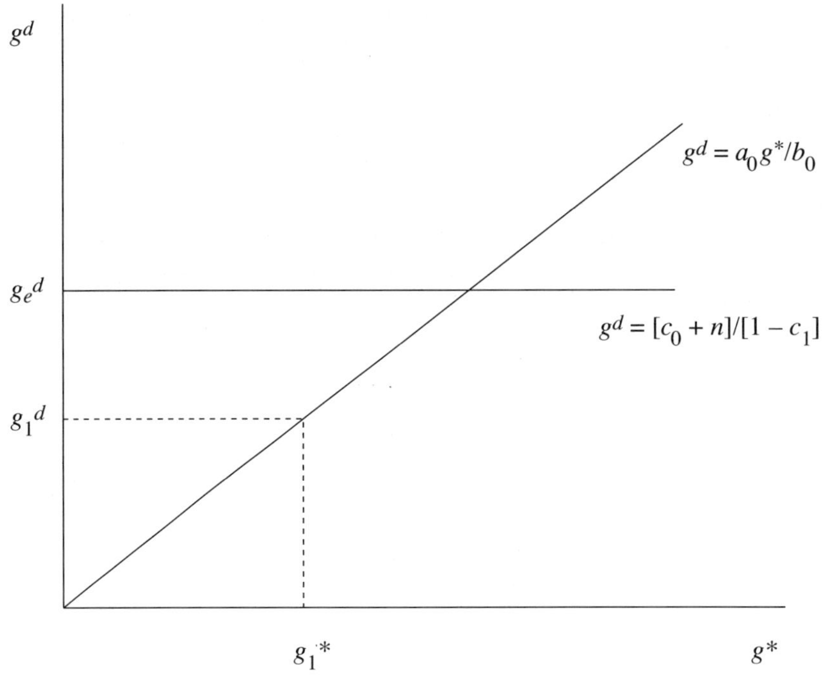

Figure 7.4 The inconsistency between the BOP-constrained growth rate and the capacity balance growth rate

supply growth (as determined by Verdoorn's law). Given an exogenously determined rate of foreign income growth, g^*_1, demand is constrained to grow at g^d_1. However, this is below the rate of demand growth consistent with supply growth (g^d_e), and as a result there is growing excess capacity.

The adjustment to steady-state equilibrium occurs as follows. The increase in excess capacity pulls down the elasticity of demand for imports, b_0, thereby relaxing the external constraint on growth. This, in turn, allows for faster aggregate demand growth consistent with BOPC equilibrium. The adjustment process so described will continue until the BOPC growth rate has been raised to a level consistent with the underlying supply growth process. In terms of Figure 7.4, the increase in excess capacity causes the ray from the origin (the BOPC growth) to gradually rotate upward, and this continues until the BOPC growth rate equals the capacity balance growth rate. From equations [7.18] and [7.19], this is satisfied when:

$$a_0 g^* / b_0(E) = [c_0 + n]/[1 - c_1] \qquad [7.20]$$

The implicit function theorem then implies that the equilibrium level of excess capacity associated with steady-state growth is:

$$E = b_0^{-1}(a_0 g^*[1 - c_1]/[c_0 + n]) \qquad [7.21]$$

Lastly, when the supply–demand growth problem is resolved in this fashion, the steady-state growth rate again becomes uniquely determined on the supply side by Verdoorn's law (equations [7.12] and [7.13]). However, the degree of excess capacity along the growth path is impacted by the demand side, operating though the BOP constraint (equation [7.9]).

OTHER POSSIBLE WAYS OF RECONCILING THE INCONSISTENCY IN THE BOP MODEL

Adjustment of the elasticity of import demand represents a demand-side mechanism for ensuring consistency between the balance-of-payments constraint and the rate of growth of supply. However, there also exist supply-side mechanisms for ensuring consistency, but here it is necessary to distinguish between medium-run mechanisms and long-run mechanisms. The former can ensure consistency between the balance of payments and the rate of output growth for prolonged periods of time, but they cannot sustain a steady state. The latter, however, can.

These supply-side mechanisms can be seen by respecifying equation [7.13], which describes the rate of output growth, as follows:

$$g^s = \lambda + h + s + p \qquad [7.13a]$$

where h is the rate of growth of hours worked, s denotes the rate of growth of labour force participation and p is the rate of population growth. According to [7.13a], the growth of labour input can result from longer hours, greater labour force participation or a growing population. In the event that a country is growth-constrained by its balance of payments, the rate of growth of supply can adjust down to a consistent level. This can be achieved by falling hours, falling participation rates or falling population growth. However, falling hours and participation rates represent medium-term adjustment mechanisms, because these variables are ultimately bounded. Both are bounded from below by zero, while hours are bounded from above by 24, and participation rates are bounded from above by 100. Hours and participation rate adjustment must ultimately exhaust themselves, then, and at this stage the only sustainable long-run adjustment mechanism is the rate of population growth. For instance, the rate of population growth may ultimately fall in response to persistent excess supply growth that generates rising unemployment (as happened in industrialized countries during the Great Depression), thereby reducing the rate of supply growth. Such an adjustment mechanism would support a steady-state equilibrium.

CONCLUSION

Growth models have tended to assume away the problem of reconciling demand and supply growth. Neoclassical models assume away the demand side, while Keynesian models tend to assume away the supply side. This chapter presents a brief treatment of the demand and supply growth problematic, and illustrates this problematic with an application to the BOPC growth model. It then suggests a resolution of the problem that has the steady-state growth rate being uniquely determined by supply-side factors. Demand constraints then impact the degree of excess capacity along the growth path, which in turns affects demand growth until the latter is reconciled with the growth of supply.

NOTES

1. The adoption of marginal productivity theory to explain income distribution introduces additional complications, since it requires that the steady-state capital–labour ratio be constant, which then further restricts the set of possible equilibria. In a marginal productivity framework, a constant capital – labour ratio is needed to prevent capital deepening from driving the interest rate to zero.

2. Which of the three are stable depends on the details of the dynamic adjustment mechanism. See Palley (1997).
3. The rate of change of excess capacity is given by $dE/E = g^d - g^s$. Thus, $dE/E = 0$ when $g^d = g^s$. In the background of the current model is a multi-sector model with the stochastic demand distribution, such as is described in Tobin (1972) and Palley (1994). In such an economy, random shifts in demand mean that some sectors have excess capacity while others are at full capacity (bottleneck sectors). If the trend rate of aggregate demand growth exceeds the trend rate of aggregate supply growth, there will be a steady increase in the proportion of sectors subject to bottlenecks. The reverse holds if the rate of supply growth exceeds the rate of demand growth.
4. This condition is derived using equation [7.9], [7.10a] and [7.11].
5. This condition is derived using equation [7.12], [7.13] and [7.17].

REFERENCES

Bairam, E.I. and G. Dempster (1991) 'The Harrod trade multiplier and economic growth in Asian countries,' *Applied Economics*, 23, 1719–24.

Cornwall, J. (1972) *Growth and Stability in a Mature Economy*, London, Martin Robertson.

McCombie, J.S.L. (1997) 'The empirics of balance of payments constrained growth,' *Journal of Post Keynesian Economics*, 19, 345–75.

Palley, T.I. (1994) 'Escalators and elevators: a Phillips curve for Keynesians,' *Scandinavian Journal of Economics*, 96, 117–23.

Palley, T.I. (1996) 'Growth theory in a Keynesian mode,' *Journal of Post Keynesian Economics*, 19, 113–35.

Palley, T.I. (1997) 'Aggregate demand and endogenous growth: a generalized Keynes–Kaldor model of economic growth,' *Metroeconomica*, 48, 161–76.

Romer, P.M. (1993) 'Endogenous technical change,' *Journal of Political Economy*, 98, S71–S102.

Romer, P.M. (1994) 'The origins of endogenous growth,' *Journal of Economic Perspectives*, 8, 3–22.

Thirlwall, A.P. (1979) 'The balance of payments constraint as an explanation of international growth rate differences,' *Banca Nazionale Del Lavoro Quarterly Review*, 128, 45–53.

Thirlwall, A.P. and J.J. Hughes (1979) 'Imports and labour market bottlenecks: a disaggregated study for the UK.' *Applied Economics*, 11, 77–94.

Thirlwall, A.P. and H. White (1974) 'US merchandise imports and the dispersion of market demand,' *Applied Economics*, 6, 275–92.

Tobin, J. (1972) 'Inflation and unemployment,' *American Economic Review*, 62, 1–26.

PART THREE

Kaleckian Models of Demand-led Growth

8. Distribution, demand and growth in neo-Kaleckian macro-models

Robert A. Blecker[1]

In economic theories that allow for aggregate demand to influence long-run growth, a crucial and unresolved question is how the distribution of income between wages and profits affects aggregate demand and the growth rate. A long tradition of 'underconsumptionist' thinking dating back to the early nineteenth century (surveyed by Bleaney, 1976) asserted that low wages (and high profits) would lead to chronically depressed consumer demand, which in turn would tend to cause overall economic stagnation unless offset by some other factors. However, another strand of thinking dating back to Ricardo and Marx recognizes that a high rate of profit can be a stimulus to capital accumulation or, in more modern terms, demand for investment. These alternative views have led to different perspectives about whether demand-determined growth is more likely to be wage-led or profit-led, and thus whether there is a conflict between growth and equity objectives in the formulation of economic policy.

This chapter analyses the problem of distributional effects on aggregate demand and economic growth through the lens of macroeconomic models in the neo-Kaleckian tradition. Michał Kalecki was the first economist to construct formal models in which workers had a higher marginal propensity to consume than capitalists, and he often assumed for simplicity that workers spent all of their wages on consumption.[2] He also analysed investment functions in which the rate of investment depended positively on retained profits, which he justified by the idea that internal funds could relieve the financial constraints on investment implied by his principle of 'increasing risk' (Kalecki, 1937, 1954). Thus, Kalecki's analysis incorporated the two-sided effects of income distribution on consumption and investment demand. Kalecki also made two other key analytical contributions to macroeconomic modelling. First, he grounded his theory of factor shares in a model of oligopolistic mark-up pricing in manufacturing industries. Second, he constructed models of economies with excess capacity, in which aggregate demand determined the equilibrium levels of realized profits and national income.

This chapter utilizes macroeconomic models in the tradition of Kalecki to analyse how the distribution of income between wages and profits affects the level of aggregate demand and the rate of economic growth. These effects (that is, on demand and growth) do not always go in the same direction, and can vary depending on both the source of a distributional shift and the structure of the economy involved. While there is thus no simple answer to the question of whether demand-driven economies are more likely to be wage-led or profit-led, it is possible to construct a fairly complete analysis of the conditions under which one or the other result will obtain for any given objective (e.g., employment or growth). This chapter attempts to provide such a comprehensive treatment within a neo-Kaleckian modelling framework.

A SURVEY OF NEO-KALECKIAN MACRO-MODELS

In the aftermath of the Great Depression and World War II, the early literature that built on Kalecki's work tended to emphasize the implication of a tendency towards secular economic stagnation. Especially, Steindl (1952) argued that there was a strong tendency in capitalism for industries to concentrate, leading to the emergence of oligopolistic competition with increasing profit margins. Since rising profit margins imply an increasing share of profits in national income, overall consumer demand would stagnate.[3] Steindl also believed that the emergence of oligopoly would dampen investment demand because large, concentrated firms would want to avoid installing undesired excess capacity. Hence, a 'mature' economy would tend towards a state of chronic stagnation in the absence of expansionary government policies or foreign trade surpluses.

The next generation of neo-Kaleckian macro-models generally reinforced the 'stagnationist' view promoted by Steindl for economies with oligopolistic firms and excess capacity. Harris (1974) and Asimakopulos (1975) developed static neo-Kaleckian macro-models in which an increase in the profit mark-up rate causes a contraction of output and employment. These authors took investment as exogenously given, however, while emphasizing other issues such as the role of overhead labour costs and the determination of the profit share. Krugman and Taylor (1978) developed a stagnationist model for a developing country, in which a currency devaluation has a contractionary effect on domestic output because it redistributes income towards profits (an idea originally due to Díaz-Alejandro, 1963). They also took investment as exogenous.

Del Monte (1975), Rowthorn (1982), Dutt (1982, 1984, 1987), Taylor (1983, 1985) and Amadeo (1986) then made the breakthough of building neo-Kaleckian models in which investment demand was endogenous.[4] Most of these authors assumed that investment was an increasing function of both the profit rate and capacity utilization, and that all saving came out of profits.[5]

These models generally preserved the strong stagnationist result than an increase in the profit share (or a reduction in the real wage) necessarily depresses both capacity utilization[6] and economic growth in an economy characterized by excess capacity, although each of these authors also considered a variety of other, related issues.[7]

Later, several economists showed that stagnationism is not a necessary outcome in more general neo-Kaleckian models, even assuming oligopolistic firms with mark-up pricing and excess capacity. Bhaduri and Marglin (1990) and Marglin and Bhaduri (1990) coined the term 'exhilarationism' to describe the opposite case, in which a higher profit mark-up (or profit share) stimulates aggregate demand and raises capacity utilization.[8] Exhilarationism occurs in their models if there is a strongly positive response of investment demand to increases in the profit share. Taylor (1990) showed that allowing for positive saving out of wages also creates the possibility of an exhilarationist outcome, since it reduces the consumption-stimulating effects of redistributing income towards labour – a result also demonstrated by Mott and Slattery (1994b). Blecker (1989) and Bhaduri and Marglin (1990) argued that exhilarationism could result from international price competition, because a wage cut that redistributes income towards profits also improves external competitiveness. If the resulting positive effect on the trade balance is large enough, aggregate demand and economic growth may increase even if domestic expenditures are depressed.[9]

While both stagnationist and exhilarationist cases have thus been presented in the literature, there has not yet been a synthetic treatment that unifies the various cases and reveals the overall conditions required for distributional effects on demand and growth to go in one direction or the other.[10] The rest of this chapter attempts to provide such a unifying framework and, thereby, to illuminate the key question of whether (or under what conditions) it is possible to promote higher employment and faster growth with a more equitable distribution of income. In order to focus sharply on the determinants of aggregate demand, all the models in this chapter take distributional relations and supply-side conditions (for example, productivity) as exogenously given. Thus, these are not models of fully adjusted, long-run equilibrium positions. Although the models in this chapter may be considered as merely 'short-run', static analyses, it is also possible to view them as models of 'medium-run' or 'provisional' equilibria in the sense of Chick and Caserta (1997). In addition, the models in this chapter are 'real' models that largely ignore monetary and expectational factors. The intention is to provide a comprehensive framework for analysing the effects of income distribution on aggregate demand and its components, which can be incorporated into models with more explicit dynamic feedbacks from growth and employment to distributive shares, and with more explicit treatment of finance and expectations.[11]

A SIMPLE STAGNATIONIST MODEL

Consider the following very simple macro-model of a one-sector, closed economy with no government and no workers' saving.[12] Prices are set by a mark-up on what Kalecki called 'prime costs', or what are now called average variable costs (labour and raw materials). Abstracting from raw materials and overhead costs for simplicity, and assuming that labour costs are constant, the pricing equation for the representative firm is

$$P = \varphi a W \qquad [8.1]$$

where $\varphi > 1$ is the profit mark-up factor or price-cost margin (one plus the mark-up rate), a is the labour coefficient (hours/unit of output), W is the money wage rate and aW is unit labour cost (both a and W are exogenously given). The profit margin φ is assumed to reflect Kalecki's 'degree of monopoly' and is also taken as exogenously given in a closed economy.[13]

Abstracting from raw materials, price equals value added, and therefore the profit share of value added is $\pi = (P - aW)/P$. Substituting [8.1] into this expression and simplifying yields:

$$\pi = (\varphi - 1)/\varphi \qquad [8.2]$$

where $\partial\pi/\partial\varphi > 0$. Furthermore, from the definition of the profit rate r,

$$r = (P - aW)Y/PK = [(\varphi - 1)/\varphi]u = \pi u \qquad [8.3]$$

where Y is real output, K is the capital stock, and $u = Y/K$ is the output-capital ratio used as a proxy for the rate of capacity utilization.[14] Defining the rate of accumulation made possible by realized saving as $g^s = S/K$, and assuming that all saving comes out of profits at the constant rate s_r ($0 < s_r < 1$), the saving function (expressed as a proportion of the capital stock) is

$$g^s = s_r r \qquad [8.4]$$

To complete the model, we need to specify an investment demand or 'desired accumulation' function. Following Rowthorn (1982), Dutt (1984, 1987) and Taylor (1983, 1991), investment is assumed to depend positively on the profit rate and the utilization rate. Writing the function in linear form for convenience,[15] we have

$$g^i = f_0 + f_1 r + f_2 u, \qquad f_j > 0 \ (j = 0, 1, 2) \qquad [8.5]$$

where $g^i = I/K$ is investment demand in proportion to the capital stock (ignoring depreciation for simplicity). The intercept term $f_0 > 0$ reflects Keynesian 'animal spirits' of entrepreneurs, or the state of business confidence. The positive effect of r can be justified either by reference to the use of corporate retained profits for relieving financial constraints on investment, or else by thinking of r as the expected rate of return on new investment (assuming that expected profits equal actual profits for simplicity). The positive effect of u is the static equivalent of the accelerator effect, i.e., the effect of output growth on the demand for new capital equipment, which is proxied here by the effect of capacity utilization as reflected in the output-capital ratio.[16]

The goods market equilibrium condition is $g^s = g^i$ (saving equals investment). Substituting [8.3] into [8.4] and [8.5] and setting the resulting equations equal, the equation for a neo-Kaleckian 'IS curve' can be written as:

$$s_r \pi u = f_0 + f_1 \pi u + f_2 u \qquad [8.6]$$

which, since it is linear, yields an explicit solution for the equilibrium level of the output-capital ratio (utilization):

$$u = f_0/[(s_r - f_1)\pi - f_2]. \qquad [8.7]$$

In order for the goods market to be stable, the induced increase in investment as u rises must be less than the induced increase in saving, which requires that the denominator of [8.7] be positive.

From this the stagnationist result follows directly. Suppose that firms increase their monopoly power and thereby raise their mark-ups φ. This will raise the profit share π by [8.2], and differentiating [8.7] with respect to π yields

$$du/d\pi = -(s_r - f_1)f_0/[(s_r - f_1)\pi - f_2]^2 < 0 \qquad [8.8]$$

The assumption that the denominator of [8.7] is positive for stability ensures that $s_r - f_1 > f_2/\pi$. Given the assumption that $f_2 > 0$, it follows that $s_r - f_1 > 0$ and therefore $du/d\pi < 0$. This result also implies a positive relationship between the real wage and capacity utilization, since $W/P = 1/a\varphi = (1-\pi)/a$, and thus a decrease in φ (or π) implies increases in both W/P and u. Since employment ($N = auK$) is also positively related to utilization, we have the remarkable result that raising the real wage leads to increased employment – although workers can only get a higher real wage in this model if they can induce firms to accept lower mark-ups.

Furthermore, not only is u negatively affected by a rise in π, but also the equilibrium profit rate r and growth rate g (that is, the rate at which $g^s = g^i$) are both negative functions of the profit share in this model. Differentiating $r = \pi u$ with respect to π and substituting [8.8] for $du/d\pi$ yields

$$du/d\pi = -f_2 f_0/[(s_r - f_1)\pi - f_2]^2 < 0 \quad [8.9a]$$

and, using [8.4] with the chain rule,

$$dg/d\pi = -s_r f_2 f_0/[(s_r - f_1)\pi - f_2]^2 < 0 \quad [8.9b]$$

To avoid terminological confusion, we shall refer to the negative effect of π on u in [8.8] as 'stagnationism'[17] and the negative effect of π on g in [8.9b] as 'wage-led growth' (recall that the real wage is inversely related to π). We also refer to the negative effect of π on r in [8.9a] as 'cooperative stagnationism', for reasons that will be discussed below (see Table 8.1 for definitions of these concepts). However, all of these results depend critically on the

Table 8.1 Alternative concepts of distributional effects on aggregate demand, the profit rate and the growth rate

Concept	Verbal definition	Mathematical definition
Stagnationism (wage-led aggregate demand)	Capacity utilization inversely related to the profit share	$du/d\pi < 0$
Cooperative	Realized profit rate inversely related to the profit share	$dr/d\pi < 0$
Conflictive	Realized profit rate positively related to the profit share	$dr/d\pi > 0$
Exhilarationism (profit-led aggregate demand)	Capacity utilization positively related to the profit share	$du/d\pi > 0$
Cooperative[a]	Total real labour income positively related to the profit share	$d(WN/P)/d\pi > 0$
Conflictive[a]	Total real labour income inversely related to the profit share	$d(WN/P)/d\pi < 0$
Wage-led growth	Capital accumulation rate inversely related to the profit share	$dg/d\pi < 0$
Profit-led growth	Capital accumulation rate positively related to the profit share	$dg/d\pi > 0$

Notes: a. See note 23 on the cooperative and conflictive cases of exhilarationism.

assumption of a positive utilization effect ($f_2 > 0$) in the investment function [8.5], as well as the assumptions of no saving out of wages, no taxes and no foreign trade.

This model thus has very definite and strong political-economy implications. If capital owners want a higher realized profit rate and higher growth rate, they must allow workers to have a higher real wage and a higher share of national income. If the profit recipients instead try to raise their own income share, they will depress aggregate demand by so much that the fall in u ends up more than offsetting the rise in π and hence $r = \pi u$ decreases. This then lays the basis for a policy of 'class compromise', that is, a cooperative solution in which workers get higher real wages and more jobs while capitalists get higher realized profits and faster capital accumulation, as long as the latter are willing to accept a smaller relative share of national income. But, as the rest of this chapter shows, these strong results do *not* necessarily hold in more general neo-Kaleckian models once the simplifying assumptions made here are dropped.

THE INVESTMENT FUNCTION

Marglin and Bhaduri (1990; hereafter 'MB') argue that the assumption that $f_2 > 0$ in the investment function [8.5] amounts to the imposition of a 'strong accelerator condition', that is, the depressing effects of reduced utilization u necessarily dominate the stimulating effects of a rise in the profit share π when income is redistributed to profits. MB observe that, since $f_2 = \partial g^i/\partial u$ is a partial derivative that holds r constant, in order to hold r constant when u increases (given that $r = \pi u$) π must fall equi-proportionately (that is, $dr = 0$ if and only if $d\pi/\pi = -du/u$). Therefore, the assumption that $f_2 > 0$ implies that, if u rises and π falls by the same percentage at the same time, firms *necessarily* desire to invest more.[18] But MB argue that this is not sensible. Whether firms would want to invest more or less in this situation depends on whether they are more concerned with demand and utilization (in which case they would want to invest more) or with profitability (in which case they would want to invest less). The sign of f_2 should therefore be ambiguous, *a priori*.[19]

MB then posit what they consider to be a more general investment function (which we will *not* linearize for reasons that will become clear later):[20]

$$g^i = h(\pi, u) \qquad [8.10]$$

with partial derivatives $h_\pi > 0$ and $h_u > 0$. According to MB, the assumption that $h_u > 0$ is based on the weaker but more plausible presumption that, if u

rises while π stays constant – that is, if there is more demand with the *same* profit share – then firms necessarily desire to invest more.

Using [8.10] in place of [8.5] along with the saving function [8.4] in the equilibrium condition $g^s = g^i$, we get the IS curve

$$s_r \pi u = h(\pi, u) \qquad [8.11]$$

and by total differentiation of [8.11] we obtain:

$$du/d\pi = -(s_r u - h_\pi)/(s_r \pi - h_u) \qquad [8.12]$$

The denominator of [8.12] must be positive for goods market stability, but the numerator can be either positive or negative. Thus, the economy is stagnationist ($du/d\pi < 0$) when $s_r u > h_\pi$ and exhilarationist ($du/d\pi > 0$) when $s_r u < h_\pi$. The key to obtaining the exhilarationist result, then, is a relatively large effect of the profit share on desired accumulation (h_π).[21]

Exhilarationism, as defined here, is a very strong result: it requires that a redistribution of income towards profits stimulates *overall* aggregate demand, not just investment demand. In order to obtain the exhilarationist result in this model, the investment stimulus from a higher profit share must be so large as to more than offset the reduction in consumption spending. Under somewhat weaker conditions, a higher profit share could increase investment and growth, but still depress overall aggregate demand and reduce capacity utilization. MB recognize this possibility with their analysis of 'conflictive' as opposed to 'cooperative' stagnationism. (See Table 8.1 for definitions of all these concepts.)

To see this distinction, consider the effects of a rise in π on r and g. Since $r = \pi u$, $g = s_r \pi u$, and s_r is a constant, the relevant derivatives can be expressed in logarithmic (elasticity) form as follows:

$$\frac{d \ln r}{d \ln \pi} = \frac{d \ln g}{d \ln \pi} = 1 + \frac{d \ln u}{d \ln \pi}. \qquad [8.13]$$

In the stagnationist case, in which $(d \ln u/d \ln \pi) < 0$, [8.13] will be positive (that is, a rise in π will increase r and g even though it reduces u) if and only if (in absolute value terms) $|d \ln u/d \ln \pi| < 1$, that is, if utilization is relatively inelastic with respect to the profit share. This is the case that MB call 'conflictive stagnationism', in the sense that capitalists do not have an incentive to cooperate with workers because they can increase their profit rate and accumulation rate by raising their mark-ups and profit share (and thus cutting the real wage), even though they depress aggregate demand and capacity utilization (and employment) in the process. The opposite case, where

$|d \ln u/d \ln \pi| > 1$, that is, utilization is profit-share elastic, is what MB call 'cooperative stagnationism', which corresponds to the simple stagnationist model presented earlier. Using [8.12] for $du/d\pi$, the condition for cooperative versus conflictive stagnationism can be expressed as whether $h_u(u/g) > h_\pi(\pi/g)$ or $h_\pi(\pi/g) > h_u(u/g)$, that is, whether investment demand is more elastic with respect to the utilization rate or the profit share.[22]

However, the 'conflictive-stagnationist' case allows for a class compromise in another sense. Since $dg/d\pi > 0$ in this case, if workers accept a lower wage share of income (and a lower real wage), they will nevertheless benefit from faster growth that will eventually increase employment opportunities. In this situation, *growth* is profit-led even though *aggregate demand* is wage-led. This situation is possible because growth in the sense of capital accumulation depends on only one element of aggregate demand (investment) and not on the total level. In contrast, in the more extreme exhilarationist case, not only is growth profit-led, but aggregate demand and employment are also stimulated by a redistribution of income towards profits.[23]

Indeed, the MB model requires the assumption of an investment function with what might be called a 'strong profit-share effect' in order to generate exhilarationist results.[24] By using some common explicit functional forms for MB's implicit investment function [8.10], we can show that the possibility of such a strong profit-share effect is more dubious than MB's presentation (using the implicit function [8.10]) makes it appear. For example, using the linear function:

$$g^i = h_0 + h_1\pi + h_2u \qquad [8.10']$$

with $h_j > 0$ ($j = 0, 1, 2$), the equilibrium utilization rate is

$$u = (h_0 + h_1\pi)/(s_r\pi - h_2) \qquad [8.14]$$

with $s_r\pi - h_2 > 0$ for stability, and

$$du/d\pi = (-h_1h_2 - s_rh_0)/(s_r\pi - h_2)^2 < 0. \qquad [8.15]$$

Thus, the profit share effect can never be strong enough in [8.10′] to lead to exhilarationism in this model, no matter how high is the coefficient h_1.[25]

As another example, consider the 'Cobb–Douglas' functional form

$$g^i = A\pi^\alpha u^\beta \qquad [8.10'']$$

with $\alpha > 0$, $\beta > 0$. Setting [8.10″] equal to [8.4] and differentiating logarithmically:

$$\frac{d\ln u}{d\ln \pi} = -\frac{1-\alpha}{1-\beta}. \qquad [8.16]$$

Assuming $\beta < 1$ for goods-market stability, exhilarationism is possible only in the extreme case where $\alpha > 1$, that is, the elasticity of the desired accumulation rate with respect to the profit share exceeds unity. Under less extreme conditions, both conflictive and cooperative stagnationism can result, with the former obtaining when $\beta < \alpha < 1$ and the latter when $\alpha < \beta < 1$.

Thus, the use of two common explicit functional forms for the MB investment function implies that exhilarationism is either impossible or results only under extreme elasticity assumptions, in a model that assumes no workers' saving, no government, and no foreign trade.[26] This suggests that separating the utilization rate and profit share terms in the investment function by itself is unlikely to produce an exhilarationist outcome, although separating these terms easily allows for the 'conflictive' rather than the 'cooperative' variety of stagnationism to occur.

POSITIVE SAVING OUT OF WAGES

This section shows that positive saving out of wages creates possibilities for exhilarationism and increases the likelihood of profit-led growth, even using an investment function that would otherwise imply stagnationism. Suppose that wage-earners save at a rate which is less than the saving rate out of profits ($s_w < s_r$) as a result of the retention of a significant portion of profits by corporations. In this case, the saving function can be written as

$$g^s = [s_r\pi + s_w(1 - \pi)]u \qquad [8.17]$$

in which the functional saving rates are weighted by the income shares of profits and wages, respectively, and multiplied by u for proportionality to the capital stock.

For an investment function, we must choose between the various alternatives discussed above. An intuitively appealing specification that respects MB's critique (and which is similar to one of the investment functions considered by Lavoie, 1996) is the following:

$$g^i = g_0 + g_1\pi v + g_2 u, \qquad [8.18]$$

where v is the 'full-capacity' output-capital ratio (measured at a 'normal' rate of capacity utilization), and thus πv is the full-capacity profit rate ($r = \pi v$ when $u = v$), with $g_j > 0$ ($j = 0, 1, 2$). There is no 'strong accelerator condition' here, since $g_2 > 0$ is assumed holding π (not r) constant. Yet if [8.18] were used in a closed economy model with no saving out of wages, it would only permit a stagnationist outcome since it is just a variant on the linear form [8.10′].[27]

Using [8.17] and [8.18] in the equilibrium condition $g^s = g^i$ yields the IS curve:

$$[(s_r - s_w)\pi + s_w]u = g_0 + g_1\pi v + g_2 u \quad [8.19]$$

which has the explicit solution:

$$u = (g_0 + g_1\pi v)/S(\pi) \quad [8.20]$$

with the denominator $S(\pi) = (s_r - s_w)\pi + s_w - g_2 > 0$ for stability. Differentiating [8.20] with respect to π yields (after some rearranging):

$$du/d\pi = [(s_w - g_2)g_1 v - (s_r - s_w)g_0)]/[S(\pi)]^2 \quad [8.21]$$

which is ambiguous in sign. If s_w is relatively large compared with s_r and g_2, then exhilarationism ($du/d\pi > 0$) may result. Intuitively, if workers are relatively big savers, then there is a relatively small loss in consumption demand from redistributing income to profits, and the positive effects of increased profitability on investment demand dominate.

Even if this model is stagnationist ($du/d\pi < 0$), it can be either cooperative- or conflictive-stagnationist and may exhibit either wage- or profit-led growth because the signs of $dr/d\pi$ and $dg/d\pi$ are ambiguous.[28] The signs of these two derivatives no longer depend on the same parameter conditions, since g is not directly proportional to r when $s_w > 0$. The economy is conflictive-stagnationist ($dr/d\pi > 0$) if $s_w + g_1\pi v > g_2$ (that is, the saving rate out of wages and the profitability effect on investment are relatively large compared with the utilization effect on investment), and is cooperative-stagnationist if $s_w + g_1\pi v < g_2$. Growth is profit-led ($dg/d\pi > 0$) even though the economy is stagnationist if the following condition holds (in absolute value):

$$\left|\frac{du}{d\pi}\cdot\frac{\pi}{u}\right| < \frac{g_1\pi v}{g_2 u}$$

that is, if utilization is relatively profit share-inelastic, and this condition is more likely to hold if investment is relatively responsive to profitability (g_1 is large) and relatively unresponsive to utilization (g_2 is small). Growth is wage-led ($dg/d\pi < 0$) in the opposite case.

FISCAL POLICY AND THE PROGRESSIVITY OF INCOME TAXATION

The results of the previous section may appear to be relevant only to countries with high workers' saving rates, such as the East Asian economies. But the same principles apply to the effects of income taxation, when effective tax rates differ between labour and capital income. Income taxes also constitute 'leakages' from income-expenditure flows, and personal income tax rates can be much larger than household savings rates.[29] Thus, even where savings out of wages are relatively small, the progressivity or regressivity of the tax system can affect whether an economy is stagnationist or exhilarationist and whether growth is wage-led or profit-led.

Suppose the government levies income taxes at the rates t_r on profits and t_w on wages. We define the progressivity of the tax system by the extent to which t_r exceeds t_w. The income shares π and $(1 - \pi)$ are now interpreted as pre-tax shares and we continue to take π as exogenously given for simplicity.[30] Tax revenue, in proportion to the capital stock, is equal to:

$$T/K = [t_r\pi + t_w(1 - \pi)]u \qquad [8.22]$$

Government spending is assumed to be a constant proportion of the capital stock for simplicity:

$$G/K = c_g. \qquad [8.23]$$

Assuming that personal and corporate savings come out of after-tax income, total private saving (in proportion to the capital stock) can be expressed as:

$$g^s = [s_r(1 - t_r)\pi + s_w(1 - t_w)(1 - \pi)]u \qquad [8.17']$$

Assuming that business firms consider after-tax profits in making investment decisions, the investment function [8.18] becomes:

$$g^i = g_0 + g_1(1 - t_r)\pi v + g_2 u \qquad [8.18']$$

With a government sector but no foreign trade, the goods market equilibrium condition can be written as:

$$g^s + (T - G)/K = g^i \qquad [8.24]$$

Substituting [8.22], [8.23], [8.17′] and [8.18′] into [8.24] and rearranging, we get the IS curve:

$$[(\sigma_r - \sigma_w)\pi + \sigma_w - g_2]u = c_g + g_0 + g_1(1 - t_r)\pi v \qquad [8.25]$$

where σ_r and σ_w are 'saving-*cum*-tax rates' for each type of income $[\sigma_j = s_j(1 - t_j) + t_j, j = r, w]$. This yields the solution:

$$u = [c_g + g_0 + g_1(1 - t_r)\pi v]/\sigma(\pi) \qquad [8.26]$$

where $\sigma(\pi) = (\sigma_r - \sigma_w)\pi + \sigma_w - g_2 > 0$ for stability, with slope:

$$du/d\pi = [(\sigma_w - g_2)g_1(1 - t_r)v - (\sigma_r - \sigma_w)(c_g + g_0)]/[\sigma(\pi)]^2 \qquad [8.27]$$

This slope is ambiguous in sign, creating the possibility of either stagnationist or exhilarationist regimes. The bigger is the saving-*cum*-tax rate out of wages σ_w relative to the corresponding rate out of profits σ_r, the higher (that is, more positive or less negative) is the slope $du/d\pi$, and the more likely is an exhilarationist outcome. Thus, a more regressive tax system (in the sense that wage and profit income are taxed at relatively similar rates) makes the economy more likely to be exhilarationist, while a more progressive tax system makes the economy more likely to be stagnationist, holding other factors equal. If the economy is stagnationist, it can be either cooperative or conflictive and it can have either wage-led or profit-led growth. Generally, higher taxation of wages relative to profits makes a stagnationist economy more likely to be conflictive and to have profit-led growth, *ceteris paribus*.

INTERNATIONAL COMPETITION AND CAPITAL MOBILITY

In an open economy, both international competition and capital mobility[31] potentially make it more difficult for either demand or growth to be wage-led, depending on the forms that openness takes. Generally speaking, the more a country's products are exposed to price-based competition with similar types of foreign products in both home and foreign markets (that is, domestic and foreign goods are close substitutes and markets are relatively open), and the more a country's investment is sensitive to relative profitability *vis-à-vis* other countries (for example, because countries are competing for multinational investment based on low unit labour costs), the more likely it is that the country's economy will behave in an exhilarationist (or conflictive-stagnationist) fashion.

For example, if increased nominal wages are passed through (to any extent) into higher goods prices, domestic products become less competitive compared with foreign products and the trade balance is likely to worsen, with a negative impact on aggregate demand. At the same time, international competitive pressures are likely to prevent firms from fully passing through wage increases into higher prices, and thus profit margins are squeezed.[32] As a result, a redistribution of income towards wages puts downward pressure on aggregate demand via the trade channel. Also, if increased wages lead to a reduction in the rate of profit, investment in the home country will become less attractive compared with investment in foreign countries, thus leading to lower domestic investment (by both domestic and foreign capital). If these types of effects are strong enough to outweigh other effects of higher wages (especially the boost to consumption), they can possibly tilt the scales towards an exhilarationist regime, or at least towards conflictive stagnationism and profit-led growth.

There are several qualifications to this analysis. First, these considerations apply only to individual countries that are open to trade and investment flows; the world economy as a whole remains a closed system and hence is not subject to these types of competitive effects. Second, country size matters: the smaller a country, and the greater are its shares of trade and foreign investment in GDP, the more these kinds of competitive effects are likely to impact on the domestic economy. Third, policy regimes also matter: protectionist trade policies and controls on direct investment can make a country's trade and investment relatively insensitive to changes in relative prices or profitability, even if the country is small and the shares of foreign trade and investment are relatively large. Finally, the kinds of price-competitive effects emphasized here may be less significant over longer time horizons than they are in the short run.[33]

Extending the neo-Kaleckian model to incorporate these aspects of international trade and investment requires three modifications. First, the price-cost margin φ in equation [8.1] needs to be made flexible in order to capture firms' reactions to international competitive pressures. For mathematical convenience, the profit margin is determined by the following constant-elasticity function:[34]

$$\varphi = \Phi q^{\theta} \qquad [8.28]$$

where $q = eP^*/P$ is the real exchange rate, e is the nominal exchange rate (home currency price of foreign exchange), P^* is the foreign currency price of competing products from other countries, $\Phi > 1$ is the domestic firms' 'target' profit margin (an exogenously given parameter, reflecting Kalecki's 'degree of monopoly') and $\theta > 0$ is the elasticity of the price-cost margin with respect to the real exchange rate. Foreign prices P^* are taken as exogenously given on the small country assumption, while the nominal exchange rate e is assumed to be either fixed by government policy or else determined by financial factors outside this model.[35] The domestic price P is determined by [8.1], assuming for simplicity that there are no imported intermediate goods and labour is the only variable input. Substituting [8.28] into [8.1], using the definition of q, and solving for φ yields:

$$\varphi = \Phi^{1/(1+\theta)} z^{\theta/(1+\theta)} \qquad [8.29]$$

where $z = eP^*/aW = q\varphi$ is the ratio of the price of foreign goods to domestic unit labour costs.[36] Substituting [8.29] into [8.2], the profit share becomes a positive function of two underlying factors: the target profit margin Φ and the cost-competitiveness ratio z:

$$\pi = [\Phi^{1/(1+\theta)} z^{\theta/(1+\theta)} - 1]/\Phi^{1/(1+\theta)} z^{\theta/(1+\theta)} = \pi(\Phi, z) \qquad [8.30]$$

with $\pi_{\Phi} > 0$ and $\pi_z > 0$.[37]

Second, in the presence of capital mobility, domestic investment may be sensitive to the difference between the domestic and foreign rates of return, that is, profit rates. This suggests modifying the investment function [8.18] as follows:

$$g^i = g_0 + g_1(\pi v - r^*) + g_2 u \qquad [8.18'']$$

where r^* is the foreign rate of profit (taken as exogenously given on the small country assumption).[38] In addition, as suggested by You (1991), capital mobility may imply a relatively high g_1 coefficient (profitability effect on investment), at least in situations where 'footloose' capital chooses production locations based on relative profitability considerations.

Third, the saving-investment equilibrium condition needs to be modified to include the trade balance. We allow for saving out of both wages and profits here, but assume no government spending or taxation for simplicity. This implies the equilibrium condition:

$$g^s = g^i + b \qquad [8.31]$$

where g^s is given by equation [8.17] above, g^i is determined by [8.18″], b is the trade balance (measured as a ratio to the capital stock)[39] and the rest of the current account (net factor income inflows plus net unilateral transfers) is assumed to be zero for simplicity. The trade balance is determined by the following reduced-form specification:

$$b = b(q, u) \qquad [8.32]$$

Assuming the Marshall–Lerner conditions holds,[40] a real depreciation (increase in q) improves the trade balance ($b_q > 0$). Higher capacity utilization increases import demand and thus worsens the trade balance ($b_u < 0$).

Substituting [8.17], [8.18″] and [8.32] into [8.31], and using [8.29] and [8.30], we obtain the IS curve (goods market equilibrium condition):

$$[(s_r - s_w)\pi(\Phi, z) + s_w]u = g_0 + g_1[\pi(\Phi, z)v - r^*] + g_2 u + b[\Phi^{-1/(1+\theta)}z^{1/(1+\theta)}, u] \qquad [8.33]$$

where we have substituted $q = z/\varphi = \Phi^{-1/(1+\theta)}z^{1/(1+\theta)}$. In this model, we cannot consider exogenous variations in π and must instead analyse the effects of changes in its underlying determinants, the target profit margin Φ and the cost-competitiveness ratio z. Although Φ and z have symmetrical, positive effects on π, they have opposite effects (negative and positive, respectively) on the real exchange rate q and therefore on the trade balance b. Thus, whether the economy exhibits stagnationist or exhilarationist behaviour in this open economy model depends on the source of a distributional shift.

Consider first an increase in cost competitiveness z, which could result from a currency depreciation (risen in e), foreign inflation (rise in P^*), productivity improvement (decrease in a) or wage cut (fall in W). Totally differentiating [8.33] with respect to u and z yields:

$$du/dz = \{[-(s_r - s_w)u + g_1 v]\pi_z + [q/z(1 + \theta)]b_q\}/S_o(\pi) \qquad [8.34]$$

where $S_o(\pi) = (s_r - s_w)\pi + s_w - g_2 - b_u > 0$ for goods-market stability (the subscript 'o' stands for 'open economy').[41] The numerator of [8.34] is ambiguous in sign, thus allowing for either stagnationist or exhilarationist outcomes, but the open economy effects tend to push the system more in the latter direction. The sign of the first term in the numerator, $[\cdot]\pi_z$, determines whether the economy would be stagnationist (if negative) or exhilarationist (if positive) if it were closed to foreign trade.[42] This term can also be thought of as the effect of the rise in the profit share on domestic absorption (that is, consumption plus investment).

In addition, the positive term $[q/z(1 + \theta)]b_q$, which reflects the gains in net exports from improved cost competitiveness, makes du/dz more likely to be positive, assuming that the Marshall–Lerner condition is satisfied. Even if the economy would be stagnationist in the absence of trade effects, international competition can make it exhilarationist if the increase in net exports caused by a rise in z (which also increases π) is large enough to outweigh the decrease in domestic absorption.[43] Whether this occurs depends on the magnitude of the Marshall–Lerner elasticities and the ratio of the trade balance to the capital stock, both of which are reflected in b_q. In addition, the profitability effect on investment demand $g_1 v$ is likely to be greater in the presence of capital mobility, which also makes du/dz more likely to be positive and the economy more likely to be exhilarationist.[44]

Second, consider the effect of a higher target profit margin Φ, which is given by:

$$du/d\Phi = \{[-(s_r - s_w)u + g_1 v]\pi_\Phi - [q/\Phi(1 + \theta)]b_q\}/S_o(\pi) \qquad [8.35]$$

Although this derivative is also ambiguous in general, it is much more likely to be negative than [8.34] because in this case the international competitive effect ($-[q/\Phi(1 + \theta)]b_q$) is negative (again assuming Marshall–Lerner). When domestic firms increase their target profit margins, they have to raise their prices and thus their goods become less competitive internationally, causing net exports to fall. Only a strong profitability effect on investment demand ($g_1 v$) combined with a relatively large saving rate out of wages (s_w) could make [8.35] positive. Thus, an open economy is more likely to behave in a stagnationist fashion in response to changes in firms' target profit margins than in response to changes in cost competitiveness. As a result, competition policies that reduce firms' monopoly power and lower their target profit margins are still likely to be expansionary in an open economy, while raising real wages and redistributing income to labour.[45]

Finally, this model can be used to analyse how the impact of a currency devaluation is affected by its distributional impact. Since a devaluation increases z, the effect on utilization (output) is determined by [8.34]: a devaluation is contractionary if the economy is stagnationist ($du/dz < 0$),[46] and expansionary if the economy is exhilarationist ($du/dz > 0$). The effect on the trade balance is given by:

$$db/dz = [q/z(1 + \theta)]b_q + (du/dz)b_u \qquad [8.36]$$

The first term in [8.36] is the the relative price effect, which is positive under the standard Marshall–Lerner condition. The second term is the income effect, which depends on whether the economy's response to the devaluation is stagnationist or exhilarationist. If the economy is stagnationist and the devaluation is contractionary, the fall in utilization reduces the demand for imports and therefore further improves the trade balance (recall that $b_u < 0$). If the economy is exhilarationist and the devaluation is expansionary, however, the rise in utilization increases the demand for imports and thereby reduces the improvement in the trade balance.[47]

CONCLUSIONS

Most early neo-Kaleckian models of demand-constrained growth tended to assume conditions that implied what has become known as 'cooperative stagnationism': a situation in which a rise in the profit mark-up rate (or profit share) depresses aggregate demand, capacity utilization, realized profits and economic growth. Under these conditions, redistributive policies favouring labour are mutually beneficial to all classes in society. However, later models revealed that this optimistic policy implication was implicitly based on a number of highly restrictive assumptions. These assumptions included weak profitability effects and strong accelerator effects on investment demand, negligible workers' saving, progressive tax systems, high trade barriers (or low price elasticities of export and import demand) and immobile capital (or, at least, foreign investment motivated by factors other than profit rate differentials).

If these assumptions are relaxed, the door is opened to other possible outcomes. With relatively strong profitability effects and weak accelerator effects on investment, relatively high workers' saving, regressive tax systems, liberalized trade flows, high price elasticities and high capital mobility, an economy can become 'exhilarationist' in the sense that redistributing income towards profits stimulates aggregate demand and raises capacity utilization. Indeed, an economy need only have some of these conditions, not all, in order to become exhilarationist. In addition, there are a variety of intermediate regimes that are weakly stagnationist (in the sense that a higher profit share only moderately depresses aggregate demand and capacity utilization and raises the realized rate of profit) and in which growth can be profit-led (in the sense that a higher profit share increases desired investment and the capital accumulation rate).

These intermediate regimes have been referred to as 'conflictive-stagnationist', because there is an incentive for capitalists to seek increases in profit margins in order to raise their realized profit rates and increase the growth of their capital, in spite of the negative effects on output and employment. Yet what these intermediate regimes really do is to shift the onus of 'cooperation' from capitalists onto workers: instead of capitalists being forced to accept a lower profit share in order to realize higher profit and growth rates, workers are forced to accept a lower wage share (and lower real wages[48] and employment) in order to obtain faster growth that eventually increases employment in the future.

These theoretical distinctions have important practical implications in light of recent structural changes and policy shifts in the global economy. As a result of both technological advances and liberalization policies, 'globalization' has made most countries more open to international trade and foreign investment than they were in previous decades (Baldwin and Martin, 1999). Many governments have made their tax systems less progressive through fiscal 'reforms' that have effectively shifted the burden of taxation from capital to labour. A number of major countries, especially in East Asia, have very high workers' saving rates. All of these factors suggest that many countries today are at least conflictive-stagnationist if not exhilarationist, and that growth is often profit-led even where aggregate demand constraints on growth are binding.[49] Nevertheless, since the world as a whole remains a closed economy, the entire global economy can still be depressed by policies that repress average wages in most countries, even if some individual countries can gain short-run competitive advantages in the process.

NOTES

1. The author wishes to acknowledge helpful comments and suggestions from Marc Lavoie, Tracy Mott and Lance Taylor, as well as feedback from his graduate students at American University, on earlier versions of this chapter. The usual caveats apply.
2. Kalecki's work on such models, from the earliest versions in the 1930s through the most definitive treatments in the 1950s, is collected in Kalecki (1990, 1991).
3. Steindl also hypothesized that established oligopolistic firms would tend to capture the benefits of cost-reducing technological progress through rising profit margins, rather than pass the cost savings on to consumers through lower prices. Thus, the tendency towards rising profit margins would continue during the stage of mature or oligopolistic capitalism, a view later expanded upon by Baran and Sweezy (1966).
4. I am indebted to Marc Lavoie for pointing out Del Monte's priority in this area. Del Monte's work, which was published in Italian, is little known among Anglo-American economists, and did not influence the later literature developed mostly in the USA and UK. Yet Del Monte obtained the same core results later obtained by Rowthorn, Dutt and Taylor regarding the negative effects of an increased degree of monopoly (profit mark-up) on steady-state capacity utilization and economic growth. Lavoie (1992, p. 297) reports that Rowthorn and Dutt each independently arrived at the same results, and Taylor (1983, p. 210, note 7) acknowledges that Dutt's (1982) doctoral dissertation was the basis for his own work on stagnationism.
5. Taylor (1985) used a slightly different investment function, in which investment depends positively on the net profit rate (after interest costs) and negatively on the profit mark-up (as a 'reduced form' representing the presumptive negative effect of the mark-up on utilization). Amadeo (1986) assumed that investment was a function of the utilization rate only, based on a rather peculiar reading of Steindl. Amadeo also considered positive saving out of wages in an appendix (see note 28 below).
6. Some economists (for example, Skott, 1989; Duménil and Lévy, 1995) object to any model in which capacity utilization is an endogenous variable in the long run. However, Lavoie (1996) shows that utilization can be a variable even in a fully adjusted long-run equilibrium provided that there are hysteresis effects, that is, firms adapt their expectations of normal utilization to actual, past utilization rates. In this chapter, we sidestep this issue by considering only short-run comparative statics.
7. Rowthorn contrasted the neo-Kaleckian case of excess capacity with the neo-Keynesian case of full capacity, arguing that the traditional inverse relationships between the real wage and the profit rate and between the real wage and the growth rate would only hold in the latter case. Rowthorn included overhead labour in his models. Dutt emphasized development issues specific to the Indian economy in his 1984 paper, and stressed conflicting claims

inflation in his 1987 paper (a critique of Marglin, 1984). Taylor also analysed conflicting claims inflation and emphasized asset market interactions and long-run dynamics in his 1985 paper. Taylor's 1983 book included imported intermediate goods in variable costs and focused on applications to development issues.

8. Marglin and Bhaduri also make another distinction, between 'cooperative' and 'conflictive' regimes, which is discussed below.
9. This result requires a flexible or endogenous mark-up rate, while most (although not all) of the purely stagnationist models assume an exogenous mark-up. See also Sarantis (1990–1) and Blecker (1999) for other neo-Kaleckian models of open economies, and Bowles and Boyer (1995) and Stanford (1998) for empirical estimates of open economy effects.
10. The most complete synthesis to date is Mott and Slattery (1994b).
11. Chapters in this book that consider some of these dynamic extensions include those by Cassetti and Lavoie. Neo-Kaleckian macro-models are extended to incorporate finance and expectations in Taylor (1991).
12. This model represents the 'core' analysis of aggregate demand in Rowthorn (1982), Dutt (1984, 1987) and Taylor (1983, 1985), although (as discussed in note 7 above) these authors also considered a variety of other issues.
13. Kalecki's 'degree of monopoly' depends positively on the degree of industrial concentration, the level of overhead costs, and the sales effort, and inversely on the power of trade unions. In an open economy context, the degree of monopoly can be influenced by the degree of foreign competition. See Karier (1988) and the discussion of open economies, below.
14. Note that $u = (Y/Y^*)(Y^*/K)$, where Y/Y^* is the ratio of actual to potential output (the true utilization rate) and Y^*/K is the ratio of potential output (capacity) to the capital stock (defined as v, below), which may be assumed to be technologically fixed.
15. Equation (5) is written in linear form for convenience, but none of the results in this section depend on the assumption of linearity. Steindl (1979) proposed a similar investment function, but did not derive the type of analytical results shown here as did the other authors.
16. Del Monte's (1975) investment function included a true accelerator effect, that is, the growth rate of output. Del Monte used the changes in both the profit rate and the growth rate along with level of the output-capital ratio in his function for $g^i = I/K$.
17. Note that a stagnationist economy need not actually be stagnant. Stagnationism is simply the case of wage-led aggregate demand, in which an increased profit share depresses aggregate demand, but an increased wage share boosts it.
18. Mathematically, substituting [8.3] into [8.5] and totally differentiating yields $dg^i = f_1\pi du + f_1 u d\pi + f_2 du$. If $du/u = -d\pi/\pi$, the first two terms cancel and $dg^i = -f_2(u/\pi)d\pi < 0$ (for $d\pi > 0$). Thus, the 'strong accelerator condition' results from the fact that u is essentially double-counted in [8.5]: $f_2 u$ is the direct effect of u on g^i, but the $f_1 r = f_1 \pi u$ term contains a second, indirect effect of u on g^i as well.
19. Mott and Slattery (1994b) dispute this argument. They respond that investment depends on the level of realized profits because realized profits are the source of the 'cash flow' that relieves financial constraints on investment. Normalizing investment and profits by the capital stock yields an investment function more like [8.5], rather than [8.10]. Mott and Slattery dismiss MB's concerns over the double-counting of utilization effects in [8.5] because there is both theoretical and empirical support for retain profits (cash flow) and utilization rates (or accelerator effects) having independent, positive effects on investment. In contrast, they argue that there is neither theoretical nor empirical support for investment depending on the profit share.
20. MB rationalize this function by asserting, following Robinson (1962), that desired accumulation depends on the *expected* profit rate r^e. They then argue that profit expectations are based on the two variables, u and π, which determine r. Thus, $g^i = h(r^e)$, with $r^e = r^e(\pi, u)$, implies $g^i = h(r^e(\pi, u))$, which is equivalent to [8.10].
21. Just as a stagnationist economy is not necessarily stagnant, an exhilarationist economy is not necessarily booming since it can be subject to a 'profit-squeeze' crisis. Although the terminology can be confusing, a low profit share causes stagnation in an exhilarationist economy.
22. See Marglin and Bhaduri (1990) for a graphical representation of this elasticity condition. However, they write their derivatives and elasticities upside-down as (in our notation) $d\pi/du$

and $(d \ln \pi / d \ln u)$. This is confusing, since π is the independent variable and u is the dependent variable, and it means that all their elasticity conditions are inverses of the ones shown here.

23. The exhilarationist case also allows for cooperative and conflictive sub-cases,, although they have to be defined differently since $dr/d\pi > 0$ and $dg/d\pi > 0$ always hold under exhilarationism. As shown in Table 8.1, the distinction is based on whether a rise in π leads to an increase or decrease in total real labour income, $WN/P = uK/\varphi = (1 - \pi)uK$ (that is, whether the rise in employment is large enough to offset the fall in the real wage or labour share). This condition can also be expressed in terms of the elasticity of the utilization rate with respect to the profit share. Cooperative exhilarationism results when $(d \ln u)/(d \ln \pi) > \pi/(1 - \pi)$ and conflictive exhilarationism results when $(d \ln u)/(d \ln \pi) < \pi/(1 - \pi)$.
24. I am indebted to the editor for suggesting this way of phrasing the point.
25. However, the model with [8.10′] can be either conflictive or cooperative and growth can be either profit- or wage-led, since the signs of $dr/d\pi$ and $dg/d\pi$ are ambiguous.
26. Ironically, one functional form that readily implies the possibility of exhilarationism is [8.5], provided that we allow for $f_2 < 0$ while assuming $f_1\pi + f_2 > 0$ (that is, $\partial g^i/\partial u > 0$, holding π constant).
27. None of the qualitative results in this section depend on using the specific investment function [8.18]. All of these results could be obtained using [8.5] together with [8.17], since with $s_w > 0$ the model need not yield cooperative-stagnationist results in order to satisfy the stability condition. See Taylor (1990) and Mott and Slattery (1994b).
28. The possibility of a conflictive-stagnationist outcome with positive saving out of wages was anticipated (although not recognized) by Amadeo (1986, p. 94). Amadeo shows that (in our notation) $dr/d\pi$ is ambiguous in sign when $s_w > 0$, but $du/d\pi < 0$ and $dg/d\pi < 0$ always hold in his model due to his peculiar investment function (see note 5 above), regardless of whether workers save. The ambiguity in $dr/d\pi$ is buried in a mathematical appendix and not discussed in the text. I am indebted to Marc Lavoie for this reference.
29. For example, wages in the USA today are subject to federal income taxes at either a 15 per cent or 28 per cent marginal rate, a social insurance payroll tax of 15.3 per cent and state and local income taxes of varying rates. In contrast, the US personal saving rate has generally been below 10 per cent in recent decades and fell below 5 per cent in 1996–9, and this is an upper bound on workers' saving since it is an average rate including wealthy households that receive capital income.
30. This assumption avoids the issue of tax incidence, that is, to what degree firms can shift their tax burden onto consumers (most of whom are workers) via higher prices, and to what extent workers can shift their tax burden onto firms via increased wages. This chapter is concerned with the effects of variations in income distribution under a given tax structure rather than the effects of changes in tax rates on different classes of income earners. For a neo-Kaleckian analysis of tax incidence, see Mott and Slattery (1994a).
31. Capital mobility here refers to direct investment by multinational corporations in productive facilities, not to purely financial flows.
32. Profit margins in open economies are sensitive to changes in the real exchange rate (relative price of foreign to domestic goods), as emphasized by Krugman and Taylor (1978). Real appreciation induces firms to 'squeeze' φ in order to preserve market shares (both at home and abroad), while real depreciation allows firms to raise φ without losing market shares. As shown analytically below, a rise in the home country nominal wage is equivalent to a real appreciation.
33. Relative price effects on the trade balance are ruled out by assumption in most models of balance-of-payments-constrained growth, as discussed in the chapters by McCombie and Atesoglu in this volume. In part, this difference can be attributed to the fact that those models take a long-term perspective, and it is more reasonable to assume that relative prices are stable over long periods of time (that is, relative purchasing power parity is more likely to hold in the long run – see Rogoff, 1996). In addition, there are different views about whether price elasticities are large enough to lead to significant competitive effects on the trade balance and economic growth. Finally, the present model does not assume a balance-of-payments constraint; the trade balance is endogenous and any resulting trade imbalance

is assumed to be accommodated by the requisite net capital flows. While these differences cannot be resolved here, the open economy model presented in this chapter is designed to highlight the implications of relative price effects when they are large enough to matter and when trade balances are unconstrained.

34. This approach has been used previously by Blecker (1989) and Blecker and Seguino (2002). For an alternative approach to modelling a flexible mark-up see Blecker (1999).
35. The real exchange rate q is not fixed at unity because domestic and foreign products are assumed to be imperfect substitutes, and hence the 'law of one price' does not apply.
36. The elasticity θ is inversely related to the degree of 'exchange rate pass-through', which is measured by $1 - [\theta/(1 + \theta)] = 1/(1 + \theta)$. Thus, pass-through is full when $\theta = 0$ and $\varphi = \Phi$ is a constant, and approaches zero in the limit as θ approaches infinity and φ becomes more and more sensitive to z.
37. In this specification, the sensitivity of income shares to international competition implies that those shares are sensitive to domestic wage-setting as well. If workers win a higher nominal wage rate W, $z = eP^*/aW$ falls, which lowers the profit share π. This did not occur in the closed economy model, where φ was determined independently of W.
38. A similar specification is used in Blecker (1996) in a two-country setting.
39. Note that b is likely to be inversely related to country size, holding other factors equal, and therefore trade effects will tend to be relatively smaller in larger countries.
40. This requires assuming that the sum of the price elasticities of demand for exports and imports exceeds unity in absolute value. Strictly speaking, this condition requires assuming $b = 0$ initially, but analogous elasticity conditions can be derived with initially imbalanced trade. Of course, if this condition is violated, or if there is a large initial trade imbalance (for example, a large deficit, with the trade balance measured in domestic currency), then $b_q \leq 0$ is possible.
41. Note that since $-b_u > 0$, the stability condition is easier to satisfy in an open economy.
42. It can be shown that $[-(s_r - s_w)u + g_1 v]/S_o(\pi)$ in (34) is equal to $[(s_w - g_2)g_1 v - (s_r - s_w)g_0)]/[S(\pi)]^2$ in [8.21] when trade balance effects are eliminated.
43. Of course, if the domestic absorption effect is positive, then the economy is definitely exhilarationist as long as $b_q > 0$.
44. Although space limitations preclude a full discussion of dr/dz and dg/dz here, it should be noted that even if $du/dz < 0$ (stagnationism), the open economy effects (international competition and capital mobility) tend to make the elasticity $(du/dz)(z/u)$ smaller in absolute value, and hence make the economy more likely to be conflictive-stagnationist ($dr/dz > 0$) and to have profit-led growth ($dg/dz > 0$).
45. A similar result was obtained by Dutt (1984), who assumed a fixed mark-up rate that reflected monopoly power of firms. Thus, Dutt obtained a result similar to [8.35] but could not obtain [8.34].
46. This is the case considered by Krugman and Taylor (1978).
47. See Blecker (1999) for a further analysis of the effects of a devaluation on the trade balance.
48. An exception is the case of an increase in labour productivity (decrease in a) in the open economy model, which can potentially lead to an increase in the real wage even though the wage share falls.
49. As various authors (for example, Rowthorn, 1982; Amadeo, 1986; Taylor, 1991) make clear, once economies reach capacity constraints they are likely to revert to profit-led growth.

REFERENCES

Amadeo, E.J. (1986) 'Notes on capacity utilization, distribution and accumulation,' *Contributions to Political Economy*, 5, 83–94.

Asimakopulos, A. (1975) 'A Kaleckian theory of income distribution.' *Canadian Journal of Economics*, 8, 313–33.

Baldwin, R.E. and P. Martin (1999) 'Two waves of globalization: superficial similarities, fundamental differences,' NBER Working Paper no. 6904, January.

Baran, P.A. and P.M. Sweezy (1966) *Monopoly Capital: An Essay on the American Economic and Social Order*, New York, Monthly Review Press.

Bhaduri, A. and S.A. Marglin (1990) 'Unemployment and the real wage: the economic basis for contesting political ideologies,' *Cambridge Journal of Economics*, 14, 375–93.

Bleaney, M.F. (1976) *Underconsumptionist Theories: A History and Critical Analysis*, New York, International Publishers.

Blecker, R.A. (1989) 'International competition, income distribution and economic growth,' *Cambridge Journal of Economics*, 13, 395–412.

Blecker, R.A. (1996) 'The new economic integration: structuralist models of North–South trade and investment liberalization,' *Structural Change and Economic Dynamics*, 7, 321–45.

Blecker, R.A. (1999) 'Kaleckian macro models for open economies,' in J. Deprez and J.T. Harvey (eds) *Foundations of International Economics: Post Keynesian Perspectives*, London, Routledge, 116–49.

Blecker, R.A. and S. Seguino (2002) 'Macroeconomic effects of reducing gender wage inequality in an export-oriented, semi-industrialized economy,' *Review of Development Economics* 6, forthcoming.

Bowles, S. and R. Boyer (1995) 'Wages, aggregate demand, and employment in an open economy: an empirical investigation,' in G. Epstein and H. Gintis (eds) *Macroeconomic Policy After the Conservative Era*, Cambridge, Cambridge University Press, 143–71.

Chick, V. and M. Caserta (1997) 'Provisional equilibrium and macroeconomic theory,' in P. Arestis, G. Palma and M. Sawyer (eds) *Markets, Unemployment and Economic Policy: Essays in Honour of Geoff Harcourt*, vol. II, London, Routledge, 223–37.

Del Monte, A. (1975) 'Grado di monopolio e sviluppo economico,' *Rivista Internazionale di Scienze Sociale*, 83, 231–63.

Díaz-Alejandro, C.F. (1963) 'A note on the impact of devaluation and the redistributive effect,' *Journal of Political Economy*, 71, 577–80.

Duménil, G. and D. Lévy (1995) 'A Post-Keynesian long-term equilibrium with equalized profit rates?' *Review of Radical Political Economics*, 27, 135–41.

Dutt, A.K. (1982) 'Stagnation, income distribution, and monopoly power,' unpublished Ph.D. dissertation, Massachusetts Institute of Technology.

Dutt, A.K. (1984) 'Stagnation, income distribution, and monopoly power,' *Cambridge Journal of Economics*, 8, 25–40.

Dutt, A.K. (1987) 'Alternative closures again: a comment on "Growth, distribution and inflation",' *Cambridge Journal of Economics*, 11, 75–82.

Harris, D.J. (1974) 'The price policy of firms, the level of employment and distribution of income in the short run,' *Australian Economic Papers*, 13, 144–51.

Kalecki, M. (1937) 'The principle of increasing risk,' *Economica*, 4, 440–47.

Kalecki, M. (1954) *Theory of Economic Dynamics*, London, Unwin. Reprinted New York, Monthly Review Press, 1968.

Kalecki, M. (1990) *Collected Works of Michał Kalecki*, Volume I, *Capitalism: Business Cycles and Full Employment*, ed. J. Osiatyński, trans. C.A. Kisiel, Oxford, Oxford University Press.

Kalecki, M. (1991) *Collected Works of Michał Kalecki*, Volume II, *Capitalism: Economic Dynamics*, ed. J. Osiatyński, trans. C.A. Kisiel, Oxford, Oxford University Press.

Karier, T. (1988) 'New evidence on the effects of unions and imports on monopoly power,' *Journal of Post Keynesian Economics*, 10, 414–27.
Krugman, P.R. and L. Taylor (1978) 'Contractionary effects of devaluation,' *Journal of International Economics*, 8, 445–56.
Lavoie, M. (1992) *Foundations of Post-Keynesian Economic Analysis*, Aldershot, Edward Elgar.
Lavoie, M. (1996) 'Traverse, hysteresis, and normal rates of capacity utilization in Kaleckian models of growth and distribution,' *Review of Radical Political Economics*, 28, 113–47.
Marglin, S.A. (1984) 'Growth, distribution and inflation: a centennial synthesis,' *Cambridge Journal of Economics*, 8, 115–44.
Margin, S.A. and A. Bhaduri (1990) 'Profit squeeze and Keynesian theory,' in S.A. Marglin and J.B. Schor (eds) *The Golden Age of Capitalism*, Oxford, Oxford University Press, 153–86.
Mott, T. and E. Slattery (1994a) 'Tax incidence and macroeconomic effects in a Kaleckian model when profits finance affects investment and prices may respond to taxes,' *Journal of Post Keynesian Economics*, 16, 391–409.
Mott, T. and E. Slattery (1994b) 'The influence of changes in income distribution on aggregate demand in a Kaleckian model: stagnation vs. exhilaration reconsidered,' in P. Davidson and J. Kregel (eds) *Employment, Growth, and Finance*, Cheltenham, Edward Elgar, 69–82.
Robinson, J. (1962) *An Essay on the Theory of Economic Growth*, London, Macmillan.
Rogoff, K. (1996) 'The purchasing power parity puzzle,' *Journal of Economic Literature*, 34, 647–68.
Rowthorn, B. (1982) 'Demand, real wages and economic growth,' *Studi Economici*, 18, 3–53.
Sarantis, N. (1990–1) 'Distribution and terms of trade dynamics, inflation, and growth,' *Journal of Post Keynesian Economics*, 13, 175–98.
Skott, P. (1989) 'Effective demand, class struggle and cyclical growth,' *International Economic Review*, 30, 231–47.
Stanford, J. (1998) 'Openness and equity: regulating labor market outcomes in a globalized economy,' in D. Baker, G. Epstein and R. Pollin (eds) *Globalization and Progressive Economic Policy*, Cambridge, Cambridge University Press, 245–70.
Steindl, J. (1952) *Maturity and Stagnation in American Capitalism*, Oxford, Blackwell. Reprinted New York, Monthly Review Press, 1976.
Steindl, J. (1979) 'Stagnation theory and stagnation policy,' *Cambridge Journal of Economics*, 3, 1–14.
Taylor, L. (1983) *Structuralist Macroeconomics*, New York, Basic Books.
Taylor, L. (1985) 'A stagnationist model of economic growth,' *Cambridge Journal of Economics*, 9, 383–403.
Taylor, L. (1990) 'Real and money wages, output and inflation in the semi-industrialized world,' *Economica*, 57, 329–53.
Taylor, L. (1991) *Income Distribution, Inflation, and Growth*, Cambridge, MA, The MIT Press.
You, J. (1991) 'Capital–labor relations and economic development,' unpublished Ph.D. dissertation, Harvard University.

9. Longer-run aspects of Kaleckian macroeconomics

Tracy Mott[1]

INTRODUCTION

The significance of 'longer-run' factors was soon appealed to as a counter to the conclusions of 'Keynesian' macroeconomics following the publication of J.M. Keynes's *General Theory* in 1936. The first major use of such was by A.C. Pigou (1943). The idea that money wage and price-level changes would eventually occur in response to aggregate demand effects on output and employment was well acknowledged by Keynes. What Keynes denied that Pigou sought to demonstrate was that money wage or price-level movements are capable of restoring the full employment level of output in an economy.

Pigou's argument was never championed as a device that would continuously maintain full employment, and many economists who found the logic of the argument convincing held that its workings would require too long a time for it to have practical significance. Coupled with the notion of the stability of the demand for money, however, 'monetarists', led by Milton Friedman, posited that the return to a level of output consistent with the 'natural rate' of unemployment would occur soon enough as to make the use of activist demand-management policies pointless and perhaps even destabilizing.[2] The occurrence of price inflation at levels of unemployment thought to be significantly above full employment in the industrialized capitalist economies in the 1970s was taken by many as supportive of this view.

Most macroeconomists were willing to agree that in the 'long run', aggregate output and employment are determined by the supplies of labour and capital desiring to be employed at returns equal to their marginal factor productivities. This left plenty of room for argument about how long it would take to reach this 'long run', and so how useful demand-management policies would be in practice. Longer-run factors, in any event, should not be ignored, as these are phenomena that will create change over time, as long as the current state of affairs does not block them. Keynes's (1971 [1923], p. 65) famous remark – '*In the long run* we are all dead' (emphasis in original) – might well still apply to an analysis which ignores everything but the long run, but it need not rule out the notion that there can be longer-run factors at work affecting economic conditions in particular short-run periods.

I would argue that the emphasis on longer-run factors which arose as monetarism was intensified by the theory of 'rational expectations', and as considerations of 'supply-side' matters came more to the fore, has been exaggerated to the point of nonsense. The problem that I wish to focus on here, though, is that the emphasis on long-run factors in macroeconomics has been based *solely on the perspective of neoclassical economic theory.* I want to demonstrate that consideration of longer-run factors in the macroeconomics associated with the work of Michał Kalecki gives us a quite different longer-run analysis of capitalist economies, and one in which aggregate output and employment are *not* determined by the supplies of labour and capital desiring to be employed at return equal to their marginal factor productivities.

THE KALECKIAN SHORT RUN

In Kaleckian analysis, national output at any particular instant is determined by the propensity to spend out of wages (on consumption) and out of profits (on consumption and – mainly – on investment), the distribution of income between wages and profits, and the demand arising from government spending and exports minus imports. Employment is related to output by the labour requirements of producing this output, which reflect labour productivity. Given those requirements, we have a purely demand-side determination of output and employment. Given the spending propensities of workers and capitalists and the level of labour productivity, the level and distribution of national income determine one another recursively. In the simplest case of a fully integrated economy with no government sector in which there is no saving out of wages, spending out of profits determines profits, and the weighted average mark-up of prices above labour costs determines income shares and so, given profit income, total wage income. Labour productivity determines how many person-hours of employment is needed to produce profit plus wage income. Money wages per worker times workers per unit of output determines labour costs per unit. Unit labour costs times the percentage mark-up gives prices.

In a neoclassical macro-model, output and employment are determined ultimately by labour supply and productivity considerations, as the real wage settles at the level where it equals both the marginal disutility and marginal productivity of labour. For Keynes and Kalecki, this is rather an unlikely outcome, because changes in money wages in the short run would largely only change prices. Should falling money wages lead to falling real wages, this would reduce demand as much as costs. Only a Pigou effect, whereby falling money wages leading to falling prices would increase consumption spending out of monetary wealth, or a 'Keynes' effect, whereby falling money wages leading to falling prices would lower interest rates, could automatically eliminate involuntary unemployment.

WHAT LONGER-RUN FACTORS ARE RELEVANT?

If we accept, along with Kalecki and Keynes, the implausibility of these neoclassical mechanisms, we still must examine the impact of whatever longer-run factors can plausibly affect the current short-run situation. Returning to the short-run Kaleckian equilibrium described above, what should we be considering in this regard? I suggest the first set of questions should be these: (1) what determines spending out of profits? (2) what determines the mark-up? (3) what determines labour productivity?

On (1), it may be safe to regard consumption out of profits as a percentage of profits that is not likely to change much over time. Indeed, if the proportion of profits devoted to consumption is small, it may not be worth worrying about anyway. Investment is the most significant type of spending that is related to profits in the Kaleckian framework. Investment spending is either financed from retained profits, borrowing, or new equity issuance, and the availability of the latter two sources of finance are, themselves, strongly affected by the level of profits.[3] For Kalecki, then, investment is largely determined by the level of profits relative to the amount of productive capacity already in place, as an indicator of the additional profitability of investment in more capacity.

It is difficult to answer question (2) precisely, but we start simply with 'the degree of monopoly', to use the term that Kalecki borrowed from Abba Lerner. Perhaps 'the degree of competition' is a better expression, as it captures the idea that economy-wide intensification of competition, other things being equal, should lower the aggregate mark-up, while relaxation of competition should be associated with a rise in the mark-up.[4] Regarding (3), labour productivity is determined by a number of factors, including the amount and type of productive capacity in place, the degree of utilization of this capacity, and decisions about employment practices and methods by firms and workers.

I suggest that the economic variables we should examine in a long-run exploration of the Kaleckian framework are, then, the amount and type of productive capacity, and the degree of competition. Short-run equilibrium, as described above, is determined by spending out of profits and wages and the distribution of national income. Short-run equilibria over time will be different, as amounts and types of capacity and conditions of competition change.

In contrast, the 'supply-side' determinants of economic performance in the neoclassical longer term are labour supply and capital supply, the latter given by the level of saving. Real wage and interest rate adjustments, as described earlier, should automatically correct any short-run deviations from the governance of these variables. Monetary effects (as in monetarist and rational expectations models) or their absence (as in real business cycle and neoclassical growth models) ensure that these adjustments work. Labour and capital supply and technological change determine labour and capital productivity and so the demand for each factor of production.

In the Kaleckian framework, of course, labour and capital supply can only determine the level of output if the aggregate demand for output is greater than what the fully employed labour force can produce with the fully utilized stock of existing productive capacity. The ruling technology and production methods are relevant in both theories, then, though their determinants may be theorized rather differently.

JOSEF STEINDL'S CONTRIBUTION

The most significant work examining long-run conditions in a Kaleckian framework is that of Josef Steindl.[5] Steindl argued that firms tend to build up productive capacity ahead of demand. Firms in any industry that have lower costs than others, or that can have lower costs with higher sales, will want to utilize their extra capacity by lowering their prices or by spending their extra profits on the sales effort, or some combination of the two. This will keep prices close to unit costs. As these lower-cost firms can price below the costs of their rivals, they will grow faster than the industry as a whole. As their scale expands, they likely experience even lower unit costs.

Eventually, the industry reaches a stage at which the only significant competitors left should have sufficiently similar cost structures to make further price competition disadvantageous. Prices cease to respond to cost reductions, so profit margins expand. In this stage of industry – 'maturity' – excess capacity, which is not eliminated by price cuts, emerges, and investment spending on additional capacity slows down.

This depicts a long-run tendency for competition to turn into oligopoly and for excess capacity to emerge. Short-run demand-determined equilibria should thus be affected by long-run tendencies towards a lower average level of investment spending as a percentage of capacity, and towards a rise in the average mark-up and hence the profit share of income.[6] This combination of stagnation in investment spending and the rise in the profit share should retard the growth of short-run aggregate demand and employment.

A reduction in the rate of growth of labour productivity should accompany the stagnation in investment. This will keep labour requirements from falling as much as they might otherwise do. Of course, in times of greater price and cost competition, though productivity should be rising more rapidly, the gains from these productivity increases should be reflected in higher real wages, offsetting the negative effect on the wage share of lower labour requirements.

Steindl (1976 [1952]) attributed the emergence of the Great Depression in the USA to the development of maturity in a majority of its significant industries. He held that the stage had been set by the end of the nineteenth century for the US economy to endure such stagnation,[7] but that its advent had been delayed by the rise in the availability of stock market finance, which kept investment spending high enough to postpone the day of reckoning. Of course, the working-out of theoretical tendencies in actuality must always occur through historical developments that involve offsetting or enhancing tendencies, as other things do not remain equal in history.

HISTORICAL DEVELOPMENTS IN RESPONSE TO STAGNATION

More fundamentally, counter-tendencies may be seen to arise in response to the effects of the original forces at work. In the case of the macroeconomic stagnation, which emerged not only in the USA, but world-wide in the 1930s, World War II was to a great extent a response, but increased governmental responsibility for the macroeconomy (with or without war) was the more general outcome. Along with this came a rise in the power of organized labour, which had the effect of offsetting some of the monopoly power of big business, thus restraining the rise in mark-ups and capturing, in enhanced real wages, some of the gains in labour productivity.

A second result of increased government spending and trade union power was an increased propensity for any threats to the real value of profits or wages to trigger price inflationary responses and more borrowing to finance business and household spending.[8] As noted earlier, conservative economists took these phenomena to conform to a neoclassical view of how the chronic use of fiscal and monetary policy to maintain high employment in an economy tending naturally to stabilize itself in the long run would lead to excessive credit creation and inflation. The rise in international economic interpenetration as Western Europe and Japan recovered from the war also made national price levels and exchange rates greater objects of concern than they had been for some time.

The policy response to the 'stagflation' of the 1970s, supported by conservative neoclassical economists, involved monetary growth restraint, following Friedman's gospel of a money growth rule. As regards fiscal policy, the presumption on the conservative side was that government deficits 'crowd out' an equivalent amount of private spending. As the decade wore on, 'supply-side' economics emerged, which advocated lowering marginal tax rates on labour and capital income on the basis that this would encourage more labour effort and more saving and investment. The neoclassical growth model developed by Solow (1956), who on short-run policy matters eagerly supported 'Keynesian' activist fiscal and monetary measures, countered the demand-determined results of Harrod (1939) and Domar (1946), suggesting that long-run growth is governed by labour force growth and the saving rate.[9] The 'supply-siders' argued that stimulating the supplies of labour and savings was the prescription for non-inflationary growth. In practice, adoption of the versions of monetary restraint and tax rate cutting applied in the USA eventually lowered the inflation rate and allowed an economic recovery weighted towards the wealthy by first squeezing demand and then reviving it through military spending and the luxury consumption of the wealthy. Median real wages were the chief victims of this policy mix.[10]

KALECKIAN SHORT-RUN AND LONG-RUN INTERACTIONS

The Kaleckian perspective would understand the historical developments described above as follows. Stagnation in output and employment growth resulted from demand shortfalls. Inflationary tendencies arose from rising mark-ups pushing up prices, or rigid mark-ups causing increases in money wages exceeding productivity growth to be passed along in the form of higher prices.

This Kaleckian conception is consistent with a version of what has been called 'underconsumption'. The aggregate mark-up largely determines the profit share in national income. The higher it is, the more investment, government spending and net exports are needed to achieve any given level of output and employment. The lower is investment spending, the lower mark-ups will be, so that the consumption spending of wage earners will offset low investment spending.

The following version of a model constructed by Harris (1974) portrays the Kaleckian short run as described above, and helps to show how longer-run factors may affect short-run outcomes over time:[11]

$$pY = W + \Pi \qquad [9.1]$$

$$W = wL \qquad [9.2]$$

$$L = bY \qquad [9.3]$$

$$pI + pA = s_{\Pi}\Pi + pT \qquad [9.4]$$

$$p = \phi wb \qquad [9.5]$$

Equation [9.1] states that the price level, p, multiplied by real national income, Y, equals the wage bill, W, plus money profits, Π. Equation [9.2] describes the wage bill as the money wage, w, multiplied by the level of employment, L. L, in turn, is determined in equation [9.3] by b, the number of workers per unit of output, times Y. Equation [9.4] shows how the Kaleckian macroeconomic equilibrium (injections equal leakages) is related to changes in the level and distribution of national income. The price level multiplied by the level of real investment spending, I, plus p times autonomous spending (net exports plus real government spending), A, equal the propensity to save out of profits, s_{Π}, multiplied by money profits, plus p multiplied by real taxes, T. We are assuming zero saving out of wages, which should not make a difference to the results unless we were to assume that the propensity to save out of wages is implausibly high relative to s_{Π}. Equation [9.5] describes the price level in terms of the index of labour costs, wb, where labour is the only non-produced input, multiplied by the ratio of prices to costs, $\Phi > 1$. This ratio equals one plus the percentage price-cost mark-up. Hereafter, we will call Φ the mark-up.

The endogenous variables are p, Y, W, Π, and L. Some significant equilibrium conditions are:

$$Y^* = \frac{\phi(I + A - T)}{s_{\Pi}(\phi - 1)} \qquad [9.6]$$

$$\left(\frac{\Pi}{p}\right)^* = \frac{I + A - T}{s_{\Pi}} \qquad [9.7]$$

and:

$$\left(\frac{\Pi/p}{Y}\right)^* = \frac{\phi - 1}{\phi} \qquad [9.8]$$

Equation [9.6] describes how national income is determined by autonomous and induced spending. Equation [9.7] shows Kalecki's determination of profits by spending out of profits plus the government deficit and net exports, or Keynes's 'widow's cruise' theory of profits in his *Treatise on Money* (1971 [1930]).[12] Equation [9.8] shows the relation between the profit share and the aggregate mark-up, in which the profit share is wholly determined by the mark-up.

It is straightforward to show that:

$$\frac{\partial Y^*}{\partial(I + A \pm T)} = \frac{\phi}{s_\Pi(\phi - 1)} > 0 \qquad [9.9]$$

and:

$$\frac{\partial Y^*}{\partial \phi} = \frac{-s_\Pi(I + A \pm T)}{[s_\Pi(\phi - 1)]^2} < 0 \qquad [9.10]$$

Equation [9.9] is the Keynesian 'multiplier', which is still the reciprocal of the propensity to save. Since saving only takes place out of profits, the mark-up, which determines the distribution of income and profits, has to be included.

Note that rearranging equation [9.5], we get $w/p = 1/\phi b$. This demonstrates the relationship between the real wage and the mark-up, given labour productivity, and between the real wage and productivity, given the mark-up. Equation [9.10] shows that increasing the aggregate mark-up, other things being equal, decreases national income because part of profit income is saved, while all of wage income is spent.

These relationships show how underconsumption, defined here as the condition that a drop in investment spending is not offset by a rise in consumption spending, is the cause of cyclical and longer-run stagnation. That is, if the aggregate mark-up, Φ, remains rigid, a decrease in investment will decrease aggregate demand. All wages are spent on consumption, while only part of profits is spend on consumption, and sufficient investment plus government spending plus net exports is necessary to ensure that the part of profits saved is either channelled into or offset by such spending.[13] If the aggregate mark-up (and so the profit share) were to change sufficiently with changes in investment spending, aggregate demand would not change, as changes in investment and consumption would offset one another.[14]

Again, none of this would change were we to allow for some saving out of wage income, provided that the propensity to save out of wages were less than the propensity to save out of profits. It is also worth noting here that changes in the mark-up (that is, redistribution of income between wages and profits) as aggregate demand falls below or rises above its full employment level is the method of stabilization used to offset the knife-edge that would otherwise prevail in Kaldor's (1956) 'neo-Keynesian' macroeconomic income distribution model.

Suppose we endogenize investment by making I/Z, where Z is capacity defined in terms of how much output it can produce – that is, full-capacity output – a function of $(\Pi/p)/Z$ and Y/Z,[15] on the grounds presented above that the profitability of investment should largely be a matter of the level of existing capacity utilization (Y/Z), and that profits furnish the preferred source of finance for investment. In the short-run, with rigid mark-ups, we should have cycles due to interactions among I, Π/p, Y, and Z. In this Kalecki–Steindl world, instead of the extremes of the knife-edge, we have short-run cycles in which increases in investment raise profits and output demand, spurring more investment, while increases in investment also increase capacity, which eventually starts to retard the profitability of investment. Decreases in investment then decrease profits and output demand, decreasing the desirability of investment even more, until the wearing-out of existing capacity, or some exogenous spur to aggregate demand or to the profitability of investment, turns investment spending upwards again.

In the long run, in the sense now of long-run average magnitudes, I/Z should be proportional to Y/Z and $(\Pi/p)/Z$, if the long-run sensitivities of I/Z to Y/Z and $(\Pi/p)/Z$ do not change and as Φ is constant, which, as we know, makes $(\Pi/p)/Y$ constant and so Y/Z and $(\Pi/p)/Z$ proportional to one another. Will there be any systematic changes in the long-run average position of these variables over time? This will depend on what is going on in cyclical slumps and recoveries and in the processes of longer-run technical change that would affect I, Y and Z and hence their long-run values, and on what happens to the degree of competition over time. How long slumps persist and what factors are responsible for recoveries will affect the long-run trend, as they foster more or less drastic alterations of the economic environment.

The only ways in which 'supply creates its own demand' are due to forces coming from innovative activity or encouraging policy actions. For example, new products or new processes indicating potential profitability, or high actual or potential unemployment resulting in government action, might be said to describe supply-driven phenomena. Innovative activity or government policy actions of this sort, however, obviously work by creating demand for the supply of new products being created, or for the supply of idle workers seeking employment.

THE LONGER-RUN RESULTS OF ANTI-RECESSIONARY DEMAND MANAGEMENT POLICY

Policy action which limits slumps and hastens recoveries tends to reduce the immediate problem of excess capacity. It may, however, aggravate price-inflationary tendencies over time, and increase the ratio of private debt to income. The reasons for this have to do with the fact that demand-stimulating activity tends to reduce the pressures to lower costs over time and increase competitiveness, or to reduce debt leverage to avoid bankruptcy.

These problems were emphasized by Minsky (1985, 1986), and can be shown using the model presented above. Recall equation [9.5], $p = \phi wb$. Increases in productivity $(1/b)$ with Φ constant allow prices to fall as money wages stay constant, or more likely, money wages to rise as prices stay constant. Following Steindl's argument, when there are strong incentives for price competition due to the emergence of large cost differentials between firms because of technological improvements or scale economies, productivity gains and pressure to keep mark-ups low will be high. When cost differentials are not large, price competition offers little reward, as rivals will normally follow any firm's price-cuts, making no one much better off. Price increases will only be advantageous if all firms in the industry follow suit, but this is much more likely to occur with a rise in costs which is experienced by all the firms in the industry, such as industry-wide trade union wage demands. If the union only asks for gains equal to productivity increases, these can be granted and mark-ups preserved, leaving prices unchanged. If the union asks for wage increases that exceed productivity gains, however, firms are more likely to grant these increases and to preserve mark-ups by raising prices if demand for their products is high. If there is a 'supply shock', like the oil price increases of the 1970s, prices and money wages should chase each other up in attempts to maintain or increase real incomes.[16]

The tendency for the debt-income ratio to rise occurs as follows. Suppose the desired capacity to output ratio (Z/Y) to be unchanging within business cycles. Then the amount of capacity desired will depend upon the expected level of demand. Assuming Φ to be unchanging as well, we know that $(\Pi/p)/Z$ will be constant. If the rate of growth of output, $\dot{Y}/Y$, is greater than the rate of growth capacity, $\dot{Z}/Z$, as it normally is during the first half of a cyclical upswing, the consequent rise in Y/Z will eventually spur an increase in $\dot{Z}/Z = I/Z$. For a time, then, firms will want $\dot{Z}/Z$ to be greater than $\dot{Y}/Y$. This means they must order an increased ratio of investment goods to the level of national income. In other words, desired I/Y will increase in an attempt to maintain the desired capacity output ratio. Since $(\Pi/p)/Y$ will remain the same, the need for investment finance will grow faster than the availability of profits to provide such finance is growing. Thus recourse must be made to borrowing.[17]

To be sure, in the first half of the cyclical upswing and the last half of the downswing, $\dot{Z}/Z$ will be less than $\dot{Y}/Y$, so investment financing needs will tend to fall in relation to the flow of profits, and debt can be retired. From equation [9.7], we know that in equilibrium profits will equal $I + A - T/s_\Pi$.[18] If roughly half of profits are distributed as dividends to shareholders, the government budget and foreign trade are in balance, and s_Π is greater than 0.5, investment spending will exceed the retained profits available for finance in equilibrium. So, if all external finance takes the form of debt, the long-run debt to income ratio will be $(s_\Pi - r)(\Pi/p)/Y$, where r is the rate of retention of profits.[19]

If, however, cyclical downswings are kept shorter than upswings by means of counter-cyclical policy actions, the debt-income ratio should be higher than this, and rising over time. The increase in debt in cyclical upswings comes from the fact that *desired* investment rises. Higher *actual* investment will only be undertaken as finance can be obtained beforehand, but higher profits will only be received as the actual investment spending occurs. As counter-cyclical policies involve government deficits, profits will be greater than otherwise, except as government deficits contribute to increases in trade deficits, which will decrease profits. Minsky's proposition that the use of counter-cyclical policy to shorten slumps will raise the debt-income ratio over time is thus quite plausible.[20]

As the increased use of counter-cyclical policy leads to an upward drift in costs and prices in any one country, it will face a loss in competitiveness relative to foreign producers with lower costs and prices due to newer technology or lower wages. Along with this, the price inflation and currency depreciation, which can aggravate each other without helping to cure the problem of uncompetitiveness, give rise to support for austerity measures in policy. In this way, we see political forces at work, as predicted by Kalecki (1990 [1943]), both within cycles and over longer periods of time. The 'monetarist' and 'supply-side' policies discussed above can thus be understood as having been designed to produce cost restraint by means of wage restraint.

The problem is that wage restraint can only be beneficial to the extent that it reduces wages relative to those paid elsewhere. Moreover, pressure on wages can only be accomplished by a period of high unemployment and lower profits. These are both inimical to productivity, the other major element determining costs and hence prices.[21]

As the debt-income ratio rises over time with policy limiting the duration of slumps, attempts to use policy to limit inflation run the danger of instigating more serious slumps. Anything which impairs the ability of debtors to meet their obligations will amplify decreases in effective demand. Concerns over the impairment of capital, of course, mean that higher debt ratios limit investment spending,[22] putting a heavier burden on policy in the first place. A 'Minsky knife-edge' situation may come into being.[23]

THE ROLE OF INNOVATIONS

Steindl (1990[1979] and 1990 [1981]) acknowledges that one of the assumptions in Steindl (1976 [1952]) – that firms invest only in their own industries – is unnecessarily restrictive, and that new product development is a possible antidote to the stagnation brought about by the emergence of maturity in an economy's major industries.[24] This does not overcome the tendencies towards increases in the mark-up and stagnation, but rather allows for periods of more vigorous competition to interrupt these trends from time to time. Desirable 'supply-side' policies would perhaps be those which stimulate new product development or other innovative research.

We also need to remember that changes in labour required per unit of output are a matter of production technique as well as of economies of scale. Changes in the methods of production as they raise output per worker are capable of affecting economic performance by raising the standard of living for those receiving income, but as income is tied to employment, they can lower incomes by decreasing employment. Minsky though this last consideration could make it desirable to decrease the 'capital intensity' of production. Thinking about this should remind us to note again how matters such as employment, prices, incomes and productivity are interrelated in this framework.

CONCLUSION

The Kaleckian long run would like to be the Kaldorian long run, which avoids the Harrod–Domar knife-edge through mark-up variation. Kalecki thought this would only be possible in a socialist economy.[25] The capitalist economy is doomed to cyclical movements around a level of activity below full employment if counter-cyclical policy is not used, and to cyclical movements *due* to policy actions if it is used, approaching full employment only during wartime. Steindl's analysis depicts the long run as being characterized by a tendency for competition to pass into oligopoly, bringing the stagnation with cycles that Kalecki had proposed. Two key longer-run factors – the aggregate mark-up (or 'degree of monopoly') and the amount and type of productive capacity – affect short-run conditions over time by affecting the distribution of income between wages and profits, the amount of spending out of profits, the level of output per worker, and the desirability and efficacy of policy actions, and thus the levels of national income, employment, prices and the standard of living, both overall and for particular social classes.

NOTES

1. I would like to acknowledge Robert Blecker for helpful comments on an earlier draft, while absolving him of responsibility for any remaining mistakes.
2. Friedman (1968) offers a lucid statement of this view.
3. This follows from Kalecki's 'principle of increasing risk'. See Kalecki (1990 [1937], and 1991 [1954c]).

4. Kalecki (1991 [1954a], pp. 215–6) specified the major influences on the degree of monopoly to be: (1) the degree of industry concentration, which enhances pricing power and allows implicit collusion among firms; (2) the level of sales promotion, which creates product differentiation; (3) the level of overheads, which must be covered over time, relative to prime costs; and (4) the strength of trade unions, which can perhaps push up money wages higher than firms are willing to raise prices. Josef Steindl's (1976 [1952]) formulation of the development of industry competition over time, as we shall see below, provides a dynamic account of the development of such oligopolistic competition.
5. His major work on this is Steindl (1976 [1952]). Kalecki's own work on questions of long-run growth in a capitalist economy, the chief examples of which are Kalecki (1991 [1954d], 1991 [1962], and 1991 [1968]), arrives at conclusions that are similar to much of what is argued in this study. I have chosen also to examine some issues that are not discussed as fully by Kalecki as they are here.
6. Steindl's (1976 [1952], pp. 69–106) study of profit margins in US manufacturing industries from 1899 to 1939 found no tendency for the share of wages in value added to change in the industries he identified as competitive, but in those that were highly concentrated, he found a persistent tendency for the share of wages in value added to decline over the length of this period.
7. Kalecki (1991 [1954a], p. 219) demonstrated a rise in the ratio of proceeds to prime costs (the aggregate mark-up) in US manufacturing between 1879 and 1889.
8. See the data for the US consumer price index in Table 9.A1 in Appendix 9.A.
9. In Solow's model, of course, the rate of growth converges to the rate of labour force growth, no matter what the propensity to save. Changes in the desire to save will only change the equilibrium capital–labour ratio. Only in the recent neoclassical endogenous growth literature do changes in saving actually affect the rate of growth. See, for example, Romer (1986) or Mankiw et al. (1992).
10. See the data on US interest rates and real wages in Table 9.A1 in Appendix 9.A.
11. See also Asimakopulos (1975) and Harcourt (1972, pp. 210–14) for similar models.
12. See also Levy (1943) and Boulding (1950).
13. Ensuring that the 'surplus' is 'absorbed' is the way that Baran and Sweezy (1966) put it.
14. Letting $\Lambda = I + A - T$ in [9.6] and totally differentiating, we see that $dY = s_\Pi[\phi(\phi - 1)d\Lambda - \Lambda d\phi]/[s_\Pi(\phi - 1)]^2$. Thus $dY = 0$ if $\phi(\phi - 1)d\Lambda = \Lambda d\phi$.
15. Note that $\dot{Z} = I$, since investment is defined to be a quantity of the same commodity as output.
16. See the data on mark-ups, money wages, productivity and real wages in the USA in Table 9.A1 at the end of this chapter.
17. This is a modification of an argument presented by Duesenberry (1958, pp. 111–2). See also Mott (1985–6).
18. With overhead labour, of course, the ratio of actual investment to income and the profit share can vary both absolutely and relatively to each other, and indeed both will be pro-cyclical. The argument that investment finance needed will rise relative to profits will still hold, however. See Mott (1985–6).
19. If we modify our model to take into account the influence of profits and output relative to capacity on investment, the long-run debt to income ratio should be something like $(((\alpha(\phi - 1) + \beta\phi)/(\phi - 1)) - r)\,((\Pi/p)/Y)$, where α and β are the sensitivity of investment to profits and output, respectively. See Mott et al. (1997).
20. See the data on corporate and household debt-income ratios in the USA in Table 9.A1 at the end of this chapter.
21. See the data on wages, profits, productivity and unemployment in the USA in Table 9.A1 at the end of this chapter.
22. This follows again from the principle of increasing risk.
23. See the data on US investment spending in Table 9.A1 at the end of this chapter.
24. See also Shapiro (1988). Kalecki (1991 [1954d], pp. 334–5; 1991 [1962]) held that a capitalist economy would lapse into zero growth in the absence of innovations.
25. See Kalecki (1991 [1954b], pp. 254–5).

APPENDIX 9.A

Table 9.A1 Selected US macroeconomic data, 1948–99

Year	Money wages	Productivity	Prices	Real wages	Mark-up	Unemployment rate
1948	1.23	2.7	24.1	5.10	1.58	4.0
1949	1.28	3.4	23.8	5.38	1.59	6.6
1950	1.34	6.9	24.1	5.56	1.63	4.3
1951	1.45	2.5	26.0	5.58	1.60	3.1
1952	1.52	2.1	26.5	5.74	1.56	2.7
1953	1.61	2.3	26.7	6.03	1.53	4.5
1954	1.65	2.0	26.9	6.13	1.54	5.0
1955	1.71	4.2	26.8	6.38	1.58	4.2
1956	1.80	–0.8	27.2	6.62	1.55	4.2
1957	1.89	2.5	28.1	6.73	1.54	5.2
1958	1.95	2.3	28.9	6.75	1.53	6.2
1959	2.02	4.0	29.1	6.94	1.56	5.3
1960	2.09	1.3	29.6	7.06	1.53	6.6
1961	2.14	3.4	29.9	7.16	1.54	6.0
1962	2.22	4.5	30.2	7.35	1.56	5.5
1963	2.28	3.5	30.6	7.45	1.57	5.5
1964	2.36	4.2	31.0	7.61	1.58	5.0
1965	2.46	3.1	31.5	7.81	1.60	4.0
1966	2.56	3.5	32.4	7.90	1.57	3.8
1967	2.68	1.7	33.4	8.02	1.56	3.8
1968	2.85	3.1	34.8	8.19	1.55	3.4
1969	3.04	0.1	36.7	8.28	1.52	3.5
1970	3.23	1.5	38.8	8.32	1.49	6.1
1971	3.45	4.2	40.5	8.52	1.51	6.0
1972	3.70	3.4	41.8	8.85	1.51	5.2
1973	3.94	3.1	44.4	8.87	1.50	4.9
1974	4.24	–1.6	49.3	8.60	1.47	7.2
1975	4.53	2.7	53.8	8.42	1.52	8.2
1976	4.86	3.7	56.9	8.54	1.52	7.8
1977	5.25	1.5	60.6	8.66	1.53	6.4
1978	5.69	1.3	65.2	8.73	1.51	6.0
1979	6.16	–0.4	72.6	8.48	1.48	6.0
1980	6.66	–0.3	82.4	8.08	1.47	7.2
1981	7.25	1.2	90.9	7.98	1.51	8.5
1982	7.68	–0.6	96.5	7.96	1.51	10.8

Year	Money wages	Productivity	Prices	Real wages	Mark-up	Unemployment rate
1983	8.02	4.5	99.6	8.05	1.53	8.3
1984	8.32	2.2	103.9	8.01	1.54	7.3
1985	8.57	1.3	107.6	7.96	1.53	7.0
1986	8.76	3.0	109.6	7.99	1.51	6.6
1987	8.98	0.4	113.6	7.90	1.51	5.7
1988	9.28	1.3	118.3	7.84	1.53	5.3
1989	9.66	0.8	124.0	7.79	1.52	5.4
1990	10.01	1.1	130.7	7.66	1.51	6.3
1991	10.32	1.2	136.2	7.58	1.51	7.3
1992	10.57	3.7	140.3	7.53	1.50	7.4
1993	10.83	0.5	144.5	7.49	1.51	6.5
1994	11.12	1.3	148.2	7.50	1.54	5.5
1995	11.43	0.9	152.4	7.50	1.54	5.6
1996	11.82	2.5	156.9	7.53	1.56	5.4
1997	12.28	1.8	160.5	7.65	1.56	4.7
1998	12.78	2.6	163.0	7.84	1.55	4.4
1999	13.24	2.9	166.6	7.95	1.55	4.1

Table 9.A1 Selected US macroeconomic data, 1948–99 (continued)

Year	Profits	Real Profits	Investment	Real Investment
1948	30.8	127.8	26.8	111.2
1949	28.6	120.2	24.9	104.6
1950	35.4	146.9	27.8	115.4
1951	40.4	155.4	31.8	122.3
1952	38.4	144.9	31.9	120.4
1953	38.7	144.9	35.1	131.5
1954	37.9	140.9	34.7	129.0
1955	48.5	181.0	39.0	145.5
1956	47.4	174.3	44.5	163.6
1957	47.0	167.3	47.5	169.0
1958	42.4	146.7	42.5	147.1
1959	53.7	184.5	46.5	159.8
1960	52.3	176.7	49.4	166.9
1961	53.4	178.6	48.8	163.2
1962	61.6	204.0	53.1	175.8
1963	67.7	221.2	56.0	183.0
1964	74.9	241.6	63.0	203.2
1965	86.0	273.0	74.8	237.5
1966	92.0	284.0	85.4	263.6
1967	89.7	268.6	86.4	258.7
1968	96.6	277.6	93.4	268.4
1969	93.7	255.3	104.7	285.3
1970	81.6	210.3	109.0	280.9
1971	95.2	235.1	114.1	281.7
1972	109.8	262.7	128.8	308.1
1973	123.9	279.1	153.3	345.3
1974	114.5	232.3	169.5	343.8
1975	133.0	247.2	173.7	322.9
1976	160.6	282.2	192.4	338.1
1977	190.9	315.0	228.7	377.4
1978	217.3	333.3	278.6	427.3
1979	222.5	306.5	331.6	456.7
1980	198.5	240.9	360.9	438.0
1981	219.0	240.9	418.4	460.3
1982	201.3	208.6	425.3	440.7
1983	254.1	255.1	417.4	419.1
1984	309.8	298.2	490.3	471.9
1985	322.5	299.7	527.6	490.3
1986	300.7	274.4	522.5	476.7
1987	346.6	305.1	526.7	463.6
1988	405.0	342.3	568.4	480.5
1989	395.7	319.1	613.4	494.7
1990	408.6	312.6	630.3	482.2
1991	431.2	316.6	608.9	447.1
1992	453.0	322.9	626.1	446.3
1993	510.5	353.3	682.2	472.1
1994	573.1	386.7	748.6	505.1
1995	668.8	438.8	825.1	541.4
1996	754.0	480.6	899.4	573.2
1997	833.8	519.5	999.4	622.7
1998	815.1	500.1	1107.5	679.4
1999	856.0	513.8	1203.1	722.1

Aaa Bond Rate	Baa Bond Rate	Corporate Debt/Income	Household Debt/Income
2.8	3.5	0.458	0.285
2.6	3.3	0.467	0.329
2.7	3.2	0.513	0.362
3.0	3.6	0.490	0.367
3.0	3.5	0.481	0.399
3.1	3.8	0.474	0.425
2.9	3.5	0.484	0.463
3.1	3.6	0.506	0.506
3.7	4.3	0.512	0.524
4.0	5.0	0.514	0.536
4.1	4.9	0.536	0.554
4.6	5.3	0.533	0.586
4.3	5.1	0.537	0.610
4.4	5.1	0.547	0.631
4.3	5.0	0.540	0.649
4.3	4.8	0.551	0.686
4.4	4.8	0.553	0.694
4.6	5.0	0.569	0.703
5.4	6.1	0.571	0.693
6.1	6.8	0.582	0.691
6.2	7.0	0.600	0.692
7.4	8.4	0.623	0.686
7.9	9.3	0.644	0.650
7.3	8.4	0.648	0.655
7.1	8.0	0.649	0.676
7.7	8.4	0.675	0.669
9.0	10.5	0.631	0.663
8.8	10.4	0.835	0.649
8.4	9.8	0.817	0.660
8.0	9.0	0.816	0.689
8.7	9.5	0.824	0.714
9.6	10.7	0.862	0.732
11.9	13.7	0.897	0.721
14.1	16.0	0.919	0.698
13.8	16.1	0.943	0.683
12.0	13.6	0.933	0.701
12.7	14.2	0.926	0.701
11.4	12.7	0.979	0.770
9.0	10.4	0.992	0.811
9.4	10.6	0.992	0.836
9.7	10.8	1.010	0.845
9.3	10.2	1.032	0.863
9.3	10.4	1.019	0.873
8.8	9.8	1.015	0.885
8.1	9.0	1.023	0.872
7.2	7.9	1.026	0.891
8.0	8.6	1.013	0.914
7.6	8.2	1.023	0.940
7.4	8.1	1.027	0.959
7.3	7.9	1.002	0.978
6.5	7.2	1.006	1.005
7.1	7.9	1.053	1.052

APPENDIX 9.B

Data Definitions and Sources

Money wages average hourly earnings of production works, US Bureau of Labour Statistics.
Productivity annual percentage change in output per hour, US Bureau of Labour Statistics.
Prices Consumer price index, all urban consumers, US Bureau of Labour Statistics.
Real wages computed by dividing the money wages series by the price series.
Mark-up price per unit labour cost, Bureau of Economic Analysis, US Commerce Department.
Unemployment rate unemployment rate for civilian labour force in December of each year, US Bureau of Labour Statistics.
Profits corporate profits with inventory valuation and capital consumption adjustments, Board of Governors of the Federal Reserve System.
Real profits computed by dividing the profits series by the price series.
Investment private non-residential fixed investment, Bureau of Economic Analysis, US Commerce Department.
Real investment computed by dividing the investment series by the price series.
Aaa bond rate Average yield to maturity on selected long-term bonds rated Aaa by Moody's Investor Service, Board of Governors of the Federal Reserve System.
Baa bond rate average yield to maturity on selected long-term bonds rated Baa by Moody's Investor Service, Board of Governors of the Federal Reserve System.
Corporate debt/income computed by dividing total liabilities of non-farm non-financial corporate business by national bond, Board of Governors of the Federal Reserve System.
Household debt/income computed by dividing liabilities of household and non-profit organizations by disposable personal income, Board of Governors of the Federal Reserve System.

REFERENCES

Asimakopulos, A. (1975) 'A Kaleckian theory of income distribution,' *Canadian Journal of Economics*, 8, 313–33.
Baran, P. and P. Sweezy (1966) *Monopoly Capital*, New York, Monthly Review Press.
Boulding, K. (1950) *A Reconstruction of Economics*, New York, John Wiley & Sons.
Domar, E. (1946) 'Capital expansion, rate of growth, and employment,' *Econometrica*, 14, 137–47.
Duesenberry, J. (1958) *Business Cycles and Economic Growth*, New York, McGraw-Hill.
Friedman, M. (1968) 'The role of monetary policy,' *American Economic Review*, 58, 1–17.
Harcourt, G.C. (1972) *Some Cambridge Controversies in the Theory of Capital*, Cambridge, Cambridge University Press.
Harris, D. (1974) 'The price policy of firms, the level of employment, and the distribution of income in the short run,' *Australian Economic Papers*, 13, 144–51.
Harrod, R.F. (1939) 'An essay in dynamic theory,' *Economic Journal*, 49, 14–33.

Kaldor, N. (1956) 'Alternative theories of distribution,' *Review of Economic Studies*, 23, 83–100.
Kalecki, M. (1990 [1937]) 'The principle of increasing risk,' in J. Osiatyński (ed.) *Collected Works of Michał Kalecki*, vol. I, Oxford, Clarendon Press, 285–93.
Kalecki, M. (1990 [1943]) 'Political aspects of full employment,' in J. Osiatyński (ed.) *Collected Works of Michał Kalecki*, vol. I, Oxford, Clarendon Press, 347–56.
Kalecki, M. (1991 [9154a]) 'Costs and prices,' in J. Osiatyński (ed.) *Collected Works of Michał Kalecki*, vol. II, Oxford, Clarendon Press, 209–25.
Kalecki, M. (1991 [1954b]) 'Determination of national income and consumption,' in J. Osiatyński (ed.) *Collected Works of Michał Kalecki,* vol. II, Oxford, Clarendon Press, 251–61.
Kalecki, M. (1991 [1954c]) 'Entrepreneurial capital and investment,' in J. Osiatyński (ed.) *Collected Works of Michał Kalecki*, vol. II, Oxford, Clarendon Press, 277–81.
Kalecki, M. (1991 [1954d]) 'Long-run economic development,' in J. Osiatyński (ed.) *Collected Works of Michał Kalecki*, vol. II, Oxford, Clarendon Press, 322–37.
Kalecki, M. (1991 [1962]) 'Observations on the theory of growth,' in J. Osiatyński (ed.) *Collected Works of Michał Kalecki*, vol. II, Oxford, Clarendon Press, 411–34.
Kalecki, M. (1991 [1968]) 'Trend and the business cycle,' in J. Osiatyński (ed.) *Collected Works of Michał Kalecki*, vol. II, Oxford, Clarendon Press, 435–50.
Keynes, J.M. (1971 [1923]) *A Tract on Monetary Reform*, London, Macmillan.
Keynes, J.M. (1971 [1930]) *A Treatise on Money*, London, Macmillan.
Keynes, J.M. (1964 [1936]) *The General Theory of Employment, Interest and Money*, New York, Harcourt Brace.
Levy, J. (1943) *Economics Is an Exact Science*, New York, New Economic Library.
Mankiw, G., D. Romer and D. Weil (1992) 'A contribution to the empirics of economic growth,' *Quarterly Journal of Economics*, 107, 407–37.
Minsky, H. (1985) 'The financial instability hypothesis: a restatement,' in P. Arestis and T. Skouras (eds) *Post Keynesian Economic Theory*, Brighton, Wheatsheaf Books, 24–55.
Minsky, Hyman (1986) *Stabilizing an Unstable Economy*, New Haven, Yale University Press.
Mott, T. (1985–6) 'Kalecki's principle of increasing risk and the relation among mark-up pricing, investment fluctuations, and liquidity preference,' *Economic Forum*, 15, 65–76.
Mott, T., E. Slattery and G. Caudle (1997) 'The cycle, growth, and distributional dynamics of a Kalecki–Minsky macroeconomic model,' mimeo, University of Denver.
Pigou, A.C. (1943) 'The Classical stationary state,' *Economic Journal*, 53, 343–51.
Romer, P. (1986) 'Increasing returns and long run growth,' *Journal of Political Economy*, 94, 1002–37.
Shapiro, N. (1988) 'Market structure and economic growth: Steindl's contribution,' in *Social Concept*, 4, 72–83.
Solow, R. (1956) 'A contribution to the theory of economic growth,' *Quarterly Journal of Economics*, 70, 65–94.
Steindl, J. (1976 [1952]) *Maturity and Stagnation in American Capitalism*, New York, Monthly Review Press.
Steindl, J. (1990 [1979]) 'Stagnation theory and stagnation policy,' in *Economic Papers 1914–88*, New York, St. Martin's Press, 107–26.
Steindl, J. (1990 [1981]) 'Ideas and concepts of long run growth,' in *Economic Papers 1941–88*, New York, St. Martin's Press, 127–38.

10. The Kaleckian growth model with target return pricing and conflict inflation

Marc Lavoie[1]

INTRODUCTION

The Kaleckian model of growth is a demand-led model of growth. The rates of accumulation and the rates of profit and capacity utilization are determined by effective demand. In all variants, as in the old post-Keynesian models of growth *à la* Robinson and Kaldor, an increase in the propensity to save leads to a reduction in all of the above mentioned variables – the so-called paradox of thrift. Also, as first argued by Rowthorn (1981), increases in real wages may lead to accelerating accumulation. These features have been obtained at some cost, however: in these models, in contrast to what most economists would expect, neither the equilibrium rate of capacity utilization nor the equilibrium rate of profit are equal to their normal values.

Several authors, be they Sraffians or Marxists, have claimed that long-run models in which the rate of utilization is not equal to its normal value lack logical consistency. For these authors, only fully adjusted positions are logically consistent in a long-run analysis. In other words, in one-sector models, only equilibria where the realized and normal rates of profit are equal, and where the realized and normal rates of capacity utilization are equal, are admissible. Only these equilibria are *final*, because otherwise there would exist economic forces that would change the long-run equilibrium configuration. One response to this critique has been to redefine the long run. Hence Chick and Caserta (1997) label as *medium-run models* or *provisional equilibria* those models that achieve an equilibrium rate of growth without the actual and the normal utilization rates being equal. The other response has been to study the mechanisms that could lead these utilization rates to become equal, and to analyse the consequences of these mechanisms for the theory of effective demand. This is the approach taken here, where a specific mechanism, based on a conflict theory of inflation, will be shown to yield a determinate solution to our problem.

The chapter proceeds as follows. In the next section we present the essentials of a Kaleckian model of growth with target return pricing. In the third section, a simple mechanism is proposed to bring the economy back to a fully adjusted position. In the fourth section, we introduce a conflict-based theory of inflation. In the fifth section, it is shown that an adjustment process that takes into account the bargaining power of workers does not bring back the economy to a fully adjusted position. Although target rates of return and realized rates of return are equated, actual rates of capacity utilization do not converge towards normal rates. The final section offers some conclusions.

THE BASIC MODEL

The Profits Cost Equation

There are two crucial equations in the Kaleckian model of growth and distribution: one identifies the rate of profit from the supply side, the other from the demand side. We start with the supply side. From the national accounts, it follows that the value of net aggregate output is equal to the sum of wage costs and the profits on capital:

$$pq = wL + rpK$$

where p is the price level, q is the level of real output, w is the nominal wage rate, L is the level of labour employment, r is the rate of profit and K is the stock of capital in real terms. Thus,

$$p = w(L/q) + rpK/q \qquad [10.1]$$

We then make the following definitions:

$$l = L/q$$

$$u = q/q_{fc}$$

$$v = K/q_{fc}$$

The first equation defines labour per unit of output, assuming away (as is conventional) overhead labour. The second equation defines the rate of capacity utilization, with q_{fc} representing full capacity output. The third equation defines the capital to capacity ratio, which is assumed to depend on technology. Using these definitions, equation [10.1] can be rewritten as:

$$p = wl + rpv/u \qquad [10.2]$$

Equation [10.2] gives the price of a unit of output in terms of the labour costs per unit of output and the profits per unit of output. From this equation, we obtain the rate of profit in terms of the real wage rate:

$$r = (u/v)[1 - (w/p)l] \qquad [10.3]$$

The *realized* rate of profit thus depends on the exogenous real wage rate and the degree of capacity utilization.

At this stage, we need to introduce a pricing equation. Kaleckians have traditionally favoured mark-up pricing, such that:

$$p = (1 + \theta)wl$$

where θ is the size of the mark-up. It is not necessary to accept this cost-plus pricing procedure, however. Indeed, it has been argued by Lee (1994) that pricing procedures are to a large extent dependent on accounting practices, and that the latter have long been sophisticated enough to support normal cost pricing procedures, sometimes called full-cost pricing. Such pricing is based on unit costs, or more specifically standard unit costs, rather than unit direct costs only. A particular specification of normal cost pricing is target return pricing, a practice that seems to have been prevalent for some time, both among large and smaller firms (Lanzillotti, 1958; Shipley, 1981). Prices are set according to the normal unit costs of the price leader, assessed at some *standard* volume of production, on the basis of a *target rate of return*. There is no presumption that this target rate of return will be the realized rate of profit: the former will be achieved only if actual sales are equivalent to the standard volume of output.

There exists an explicit pricing formula for target return procedures that is almost as simple as the mark-up equation. What, then, would the mark-up proxy θ be equal to? Suppose that the replacement value of the stock of capital is pK, while the target rate of return, which we might want to call the *normal* or the *standard* rate of profit, is r_s. Required profits for the period are then $r_s pK$. With a normal (or standard) rate of capacity utilization, u_s, corresponding within the period to the level of output of q_s, the required profits for the period must be equal to $r_s vpq_s/u_s$. This must be equated to the total profits that are to be obtained by marking up unit costs at the standard rate of utilization of capacity: θwl. After some manipulation, a simple pricing formula for target pricing procedures can be found:[2]

$$p = \left(\frac{u_s}{u_s - r_s v}\right) wl \qquad [10.4]$$

Of course, the equation makes sense only if the denominator is positive, that is if $u_s > r_s v$. This inequality must be fulfilled since it implies that wages are positive (that is, profit income is smaller than total income). When this target return pricing formula is combined with equation [10.3], we obtain the rate of profit seen from the cost side, i.e., the profits cost function:

$$r^{PC} = r_s(u/u_s) \qquad [10.5]$$

One should note that if the actual rate of capacity utilization u turns out to be equal to the standard rate of utilization of capacity u_s, the actual rate of profit r is then equal to the target rate of return r_s embodied in the costing margin of the pricing procedure. Since equation [10.5] is linear in u, it clearly shows that the standard and the actual rates of profit cannot be equal unless the standard and the actual rates of capacity utilization are equal. This result will be useful when the target rate of return is endogenized later on.

The Effective Demand Side

The previous equations define a rate of profit seen from the cost accounting side. The rate of profit that will be realized depends on the actual rate of capacity utilization. Effective demand, which has not yet been taken into account, helps determine the rate of capacity utilization. In the old post-Keynesian models, the rate of accumulation is taken to be exogenous. The impact of effective demand in the Cambridge equation is felt on the realized rate of profit, which is the endogenous variable. A crucial feature of the Kaleckian model is its investment function. The Cambridge equation must thus be reinterpreted as a savings function. Using the standard assumption that there are no savings out of wages, the savings function in growth terms becomes:

$$g^s = rs_p$$

with s_p the overall propensity to save out of profits.

We now come to the investment function, which has been an important subject of contention.[3] Let us present a version of it which has often been used by Kaleckian authors. The rate of accumulation set by firms depends on the rate of capacity utilization and on the realized rate of profit:

$$g^i = \gamma + \gamma_u u + \gamma_r r$$

where γ is some parameter, which must be positive in models without overhead labour (Dutt 1990, p. 25), while γ_u and γ_r are positive reaction parameters.

Putting together the previous two equations, one obtains what Rowthorn (1981, p. 12) calls the realization curve. To avoid confusion, and to emphasize the role of effective demand, we shall call it the effective demand equation:

$$r^{ED} = (\gamma_u u + \gamma)/(s_p - \gamma_r) \quad [10.6]$$

The steady-state solution to this Kaleckian model of growth and distribution can be obtained by combining the profits cost equation [10.5] and the effective demand equation [10.6]. Doing so yields:

$$u^* = \gamma u_s/[r_s(s_p - \gamma_r) - \gamma_u u_s]$$

$$r^* = \gamma r_s/[r_s(s_p - \gamma_r) - \gamma_u u_s] \quad [10.7]$$

As is standard with this kind of model, the solutions are positive and the model is stable provided:

$$s_p > \gamma_r + \gamma_u u_s/r_s$$

A FULLY ADJUSTED POSITION WITH AN ENDOGENOUS NORMAL RATE OF PROFIT

As is well known, the basic Kaleckian growth model exhibits two features. First, Keynes's paradox of thrift holds, even in the long run (an increase in the propensity to save decreases u^* and r^*, and hence the rate of accumulation). Second, there is the paradox of cost: any increase in costs raises the realized rate of profit (Rowthorn, 1981, p. 18). A higher target rate of return (that is, a lower real wage) is associated with a lower rate of utilization, a lower realized rate of profit and hence a lower rate of accumulation. Not all Kaleckians endorse the sort of investment function that gives rise to the paradox of costs, but there is agreement, nonetheless, that the paradox of costs may occur under some circumstances.[4]

Another controversy – central to the focus of this chapter – is the discrepancy between the target rate of return and the realized rate of profit. While there is no objection to these two rates being different in the short run, several authors believe that any discrepancy between the two rates contradicts the notion of a long-run equilibrium – a final equilibrium where there should exist no inducement to modify the values taken by the main variables. Sraffian authors, such as Vianello (1985), Committeri (1986) or Park (1997a), and Marxist authors, such as Duménil and Lévy (1995, 1999) or Auerbach and Skott (1988), insist that, in the long run, targets should be achieved. The steady-state solutions of the Kaleckian growth model in equation [10.7] may thus be interpreted as a provisional equilibrium. How, then, can we arrive at a final equilibrium? And would this final equilibrium be a fully adjusted position?

One mechanism capable of generating a final, long-run position involves the normal rate of profit (or, more precisely, the target rate of return) being influenced by the actual rate of profit. Whenever the rate of profit exceeds the target rate of return, firms react by (slowly) increasing the target rate of return and the costing margin. A straightforward representation of this intuition yields the following difference equation:

$$\dot{r}_s = \varphi(r^* - r_s) \qquad [10.8]$$

Will the operation of equation [10.8] assure convergence between the actual rate of profit and the target rate of return? When the actual rate of profit is higher than the target rate of return, the latter is set at a higher value. The profit margin is thus increased. The higher profit margin (the lower real wage) slows down effective demand growth, thus reducing the rate of utilization and the realized rate of profit, despite the higher target rate of return. This process will go on until the target rate of return is such that it generates an equivalent actual rate of profit. More formally, this can be seen by taking the derivative of the equilibrium rate of profit in equation [110.7] with respect to the target rate of return:

$$dr^*/dr_s = -\gamma\gamma_u u_s/D^2 < 0$$

where D is the denominator of [10.7].

This process, however, will also bring together the realized rate of capacity utilization and the standard rate of utilization. The actual rate of utilization in the fully adjusted position thus becomes a predetermined variable, equal to the given conventional standard rate u_s. As a result, the paradox of costs disappears. An increase in the rate of growth is associated with a decrease in the real wage rate (and an increase in the target rate of return).

On the other hand, the paradox of thrift is sustained even in this fully adjusted position. An increase in the propensity to save has a negative impact, from one fully adjusted position to the next, on the rate of accumulation. This can be seen by putting together equations [10.5] and [10.6], defining the profits cost function and the effective demand function. In a fully adjusted position, the realized rate of capacity utilization is always equal to its standard level, so that $u^* = u_s$. When solving for the long-run, when all adjustments corresponding to equation [10.8] have been exhausted, it is the target rate of return r_s which becomes the endogenous variable. Solving for this variable, and making use of the Cambridge equation, we obtain:

$$r_s^{**} = (\gamma_u u_s + \gamma)/(s_p - \gamma_r)$$

$$g^{**} = (\gamma_u u_s + \gamma)/[1 - (\gamma_r/s_p)]$$

An increase in the propensity to save s_p yields a fully adjusted position with a lower rate of accumulation. The paradox of thrift thus appears to be quite resilient. Indeed, the results that are achieved with the addition of the adjustment process described by equation [10.8] are akin to those that were defended by post-Keynesians such as Joan Robinson with the help of the old Cambridge model (Lavoie 1992, p. 357).

Are there other means to recover the paradox of thrift or the paradox of costs? It is possible to argue that the standard rate of utilization depends on actual utilization rates (Lavoie, 1996; Dutt, 1996; Park, 1997b). This line of research, which generates a multiplicity of solutions, many of which retain their Kaleckian properties, will not be pursued here. We shall, instead, follow a new avenue, based on the addition of a conflict-based model of inflation. This will allow us, within a fully determined model, to retain the flexibility of the rate of capacity utilization and the positive relation between the real wage rate and the rate of accumulation, while assuming equalization of the realized and normal rates of profit.

A MODEL OF CONFLICT INFLATION

We now present a model of inflation which does not rely on excess demand. The model is based on the inconsistent income claims of firms and workers, that is, on what has variously been described as *real wage resistance* or the *aspiration gap*. In standard terminology, the focus of the analysis is on the wage-price spiral. As a first approximation, wage–wage inflation and other income conflicts will be omitted, as will be feedback effects from the real economy. This will allows us to understand the essentials of the model and to integrate it with target return pricing.

The conflict inflation model is Kaleckian because it has some affinity with Kalecki's last article (Kalecki, 1971, chapter 14). Whereas previously Kalecki took the degree of monopoly to be an exogenous variable, he argues in this article that trade unions have the power to achieve reductions in the mark-up, by demanding and achieving large increases in money wage rates.

Several post-Keynesian, neo-Marxian and even mainstream authors have constructed models of conflict inflation, as first presented by Rowthorn (1977). In these models, the rate of inflation is a function of the degree of inconsistency between the mark-up that firms wish to target and the real wage rate that the leading labour bargaining units consider to be fair. As is clear from the mark-up pricing equation, $p = (1 + \theta)wl$, a target set in terms of real wages can always be made equivalent to a target set in terms of a mark-up. With target return pricing procedures, this target corresponds precisely to a target rate of return. Provided there is no change in productivity, it is thus unimportant whether we assume that firms and workers set real wage targets or mark-up targets. Here, we shall formulate the model in terms of target rates of return.

The basic model of conflict inflation is based on two equations (see for example Dutt, 1990, p. 83). It is assumed first that the rate of growth of money wages, which labour unions manage to negotiate, is a function of the discrepancy between their real wage target and the actual real wage rate. In terms of target rates of return, this means that the target real wage rate of workers is equivalent to a target rate of return r_{sw}. It is the discrepancy between a high actual target rate of return and a low desired target rate of return, seen from the workers' point of view, which drives up wage demands. It is also assumed that the rate of growth of money wages depends on the expected rate of price inflation, $\hat{p}^e$. In its simplest form, these ideas can be expressed as:

$$\hat{w} = \Omega_1(r_s - r_{sw}) + \Omega_2\hat{p}^e$$

Similarly, it may be assumed that firms increase prices when the actual mark-up is below the mark-up that they desire, and that the larger the differential between these mark-ups, the higher the rate of price inflation will be. This may be formalized in terms of a target rate of return, which for the firm we may denote as r_{sf}. The target rate of return as *assessed* by firms may be different from the actual target rate of return *incorporated into prices*. When firms aim for higher mark-ups, given the current actual mark-up, they will speed up the rate of price inflation, subject to the constraint of their bargaining power *vis à vis* labour and in product markets. Assuming that firms may have to list prices before wage increases have been settled, and taking into account expected wage inflation, we have:

$$\hat{p} = \Psi_1(r_{sf} - r_s) + \Psi_2\hat{w}^e$$

We are now able to give an explanation of why the target rate of return may fully adjust to the actual rate of profit, without the rate of capacity utilization becoming exogenous. To do so, it has to be recognized that firms are not in a position to set the exact mark-up of their choice. One must thus distinguish between two sorts of gross costing margins: the actual costing margin, which arises from the bargaining process; and the desired costing margin, which corresponds to the target rate of return and the standard rate of capacity utilization that firms would like to incorporate into their pricing strategy. In terms of wage rates, one would have to distinguish between two wage rates: the actual real wage rate arising from bargaining; and the real wage rate targeted by firms, corresponding to the standard rate of profit r_{sf} *assessed* by firms.

A steady state in a model without technical progress occurs when the actual real wage rate is constant, that is, when the actual and the expected rates of wage inflation are equal to the actual and expected rates of price inflation. In such an equilibrium, the profit margin is constant, and equating the two equations describing wage and price inflation, we get:

$$\hat{p} = \frac{\Omega_1(r_s - r_{sw})}{1-\Omega_2} = \frac{\Psi_1(r_{sf} - r_s)}{1-\Psi_2}$$

By solving the above equation for the target rate of return actually incorporated into prices, r_s, the distinction between this concept and the target rate of return r_{sf} assessed by firms becomes clearer. There is a simple relationship between the two concepts: the actual target rate of return r_s is a weighted average of both the target rate of return assessed by firms and the target rate of return assessed by workers, where the sum of the weights (Ω and Ψ) is equal to one, such that:

$$r_s = \Psi r_{sf} + \Omega r_{sw} \qquad [10.9]$$

where:

$$\Omega = \frac{\Omega_1(1-\Psi_2)}{\Omega_1(1-\Psi_2)+\Psi_1(1-\Omega_2)}$$

$$\Psi = \frac{\Psi_1(1-\Omega_2)}{\Omega_1(1-\Psi_2)+\Psi_1(1-\Omega_2)}$$

The resulting model of accumulation is exactly like the model first presented in the second section, which involved no complications related to inflation. In equations [10.4] and [10.5], we may now introduce the value of the actual target rate of return as given by the weighted average in equation [10.9]. Combining equations [10.7] and [10.9], one obtains:

$$r^* = \frac{\gamma(\Psi r_{sf} + \Omega r_{sw})}{(s_p - \gamma_r)(\Psi r_{sf} + \Omega r_{sw}) - \gamma_u u_s} \qquad [10.10]$$

An increase in the target rate of return as assessed by firms, r_{sf}, will lead to an increase in the target rate of return incorporated into prices, r_s, and hence, as shown in the third section, to a fall in the realized rate of profit r^*, that is:

$$dr^*/dr_{sf} < 0 \qquad [10.11]$$

CONFLICT INFLATION WITH AN ENDOGENOUS TARGET RATE OF RETURN

Let us now endogenize the target rate of return as assessed by firms. This means that higher realized rates of profit will modify what firms consider to be the normal rate of profit. Let us assume, then, that firms slowly adjust their assessed target rate of return (r_{sf}) according to the actual rate of profit (r), in the manner of equation [10.8] above. More precisely, as suggested in Lavoie (1992, p. 418), equation [10.8] must now be written as:

$$\dot{r}_{sf} = \varphi(r^* - r_{sf}) \qquad [10.12]$$

In the third section, it was argued that a long-run equilibrium is reached when the target rate of return, r_s, is the same in two successive periods – that is, when the target rate of return and the actual rate of profit are equal, due to the process in equation [10.8]. Here, in a world where trade unions have some bargaining power, the process of adjustment instead involves the target rate of return r_{sf} assessed by firms and equation [10.12]. In general, the process described by equation [10.12] will thus come to an end without the fully adjusted rate of return being actually incorporated in prices. This means that the rate of capacity utilization emerging from the adjustment process is not necessarily the standard rate of utilization, and that as a consequence the rate of capacity utilization is endogenous despite the existence of this adjustment process. *The long-run equilibrium is not, in general, a fully-adjusted position.*

The final equilibrium of such an economy with evolving bargaining power thus requires the additional equation, $r^* = r_{sf}$. Unfortunately, adding this condition in equations [10.7] and [10.10] yields a quadratic equation. It is thus easier to assess the adjustment process from a graphical point of view. We can first look at this adjustment process by considering the rate of profit only. This is done in Figure 10.1. The r^* curve represents the negative link between the target rate of return assessed by firms, r_{sf}, and the actual rate of profit that arises from effective demand considerations. For instance, when the actual rate of profit is above the target rate of return as assessed by firms, firms react by raising what they perceive to be the normal target rate of return. This, as shown by equation [10.11], leads to a decrease in the realized rate of profit.

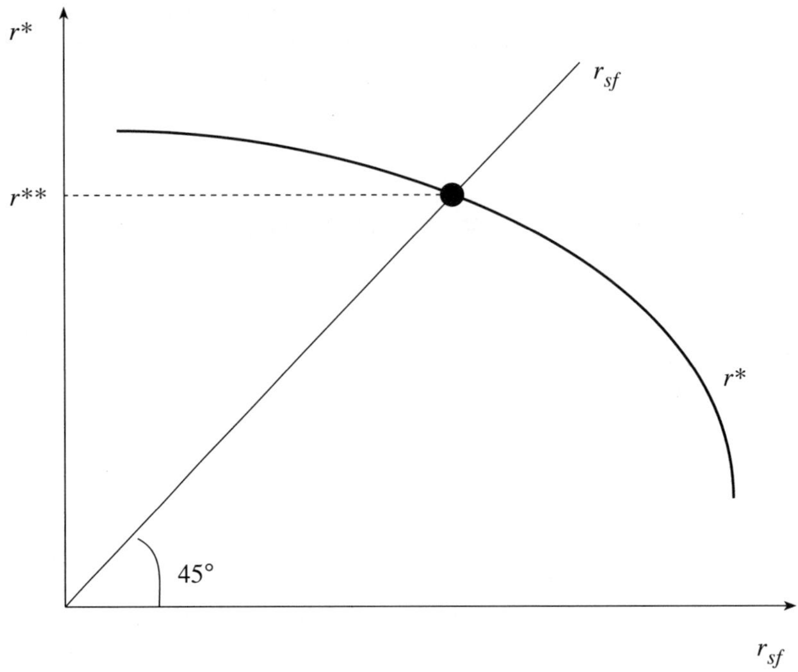

Figure 10.1 Reconciliation of the target rate of return assessed by firms and the actual rate of profit

There is thus a convergence process between the two rates, achieved at r^{**}. This is the long-run rate of profit.[5]

The adjustment process is more completely represented in Figure 10.2. Let us start from a situation in which the real wage rates desired by firms and by workers coincide, as shown on the left-hand side of the figure, where the $\hat{w}$ and $\hat{p}$ curves intersect on the vertical axis (so that $\hat{p} = 0$). This implies that the target rate of return initially assessed by firms, called r_{sf1}, and the target rate of return embodied in the pricing formula, called r_{s1}, are equal. We have the triple equality: $r_{sw} = r_{sf1} = r_{s1}$. We can draw the profits cost curve corresponding to this situation, shown on the right-hand side of the figure as PC(r_{s1}). Suppose that the initial conditions, from the effective demand point of view, were such that the target rate of return incorporated into prices was being realized at the standard rate of capacity utilization u_s, that is, $r_{s1} = r_1^{**}$ (as shown by the curve ED$_1$). Suppose now that there is a sudden increase in demand, as shown by the shift of the ED curve from ED$_1$ to ED$_2$. Under the new demand conditions, the actual rate of capacity utilization is u_2, and the actual rate of profit is r_2. The actual rate of profit r_2 is thus much higher than the target rate of return $r_{sf1} = r_1^{**}$. As a result, firms will slowly revise upwards their assessed target rate of return r_{sf}, along the lines of equation [10.12], as is illustrated in Figure 10.1.

Three phenomena will now arise. First, as firms revise their estimate of what the target rate of return is, a discrepancy arises between the real wage rate targeted by firms and the real wage rate targeted by workers. This will induce wage and price inflation, along the lines of our conflict inflation model, while the actual real wage rate becomes different from the real wage targeted by firms. Second, a similar wedge arises between the target rate of return *assessed by firms* and the target rate of return *incorporated into prices*. Third, as real wages diminish, the actual rate of profit falls. There is thus a convergence between the realized rate of profit, which falls, and the target rate of return assessed by firms, which rises.

The end result of this convergence process is shown in Figure 10.2. Firms are assessing a target rate of return of r_{sf2}. Because of the bargaining power of labour, inflation occurs at a rate of $\hat{p}_2^*$.[6] The new profits cost curve PC(r_{s2}) is

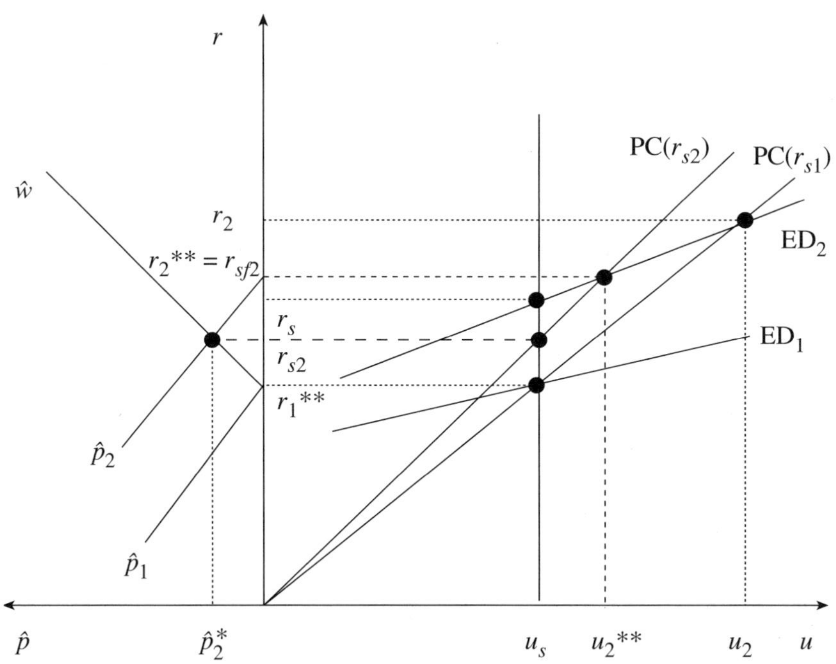

Figure 10.2 Adjustment to long-run equilibrium following a change in demand conditions

such that the actual rate of profit, r_2^{**}, and the target rate of return *assessed by firms*, r_{sf2}, are equated. The adjustment process of the target rate of return has led to a new rate of capacity utilization u_2^{**}, which is different from the standard rate of utilization, u_s. The rate of capacity utilization in the long-run position is thus still endogenous, despite the presence of an adjustment mechanism.

The introduction of real wage resistance by workers thus yields a model where the equilibrium rate of capacity utilization remains endogenous (that is, does not have to equal its exogenously given standard rate), despite the adoption of a mechanism that brings the target rate of return and the actual rate of profit into equality. The realized rate of profit is equalized to the target rate of return assessed by entrepreneurs, although this assessed normal rate of profit is not exactly incorporated into prices because of real wage resistance. The key characteristic of the Kaleckian model, that is the endogeneity of the rate of capacity utilization, even in the long run, is thus preserved within a model with definite solutions.

One last issue must be dealt with: does the paradox of costs still hold in the new model? From the analysis portrayed in Figure 10.2, it is clear that the higher fully adjusted rate of accumulation (induced by higher animal spirits or a lower propensity to save) has led to an increase in the profit margin and hence to a fall in the real wage rate. Thus, while the paradox of thrift has been recovered once again, one may wonder whether the attempt to extend the Kaleckian model has resulted in the abandonment of key features of Kaleckian analysis? This is not the case however. Even with adjustment mechanisms of the type entertained in equation [10.12], a rise in the rate of accumulation may be accompanied by increases in the real wage rate.

This possibility is illustrated in Figure 10.3. Suppose again that we start from a fully adjusted position, where conditions are such that the actual rate of capacity utilization is equal to the standard rate of utilization, and where the targets of workers and firms coincide. The rates of profit are then $r_1^{**} = r_{s1} = r_{sf1} = r_{sw1}$. The economy is at the intersection of the ED and PC(r_{s1}) curves, while on the left-hand side of the figure, the $\hat{w}_1$ and $\hat{p}_1$ curves intersect on the vertical axis. Now consider the case where workers are more militant and request a higher real wage rate, equivalent to a lower target rate of return, say r_{sw2}. Given this new target real wage, the wage inflation curve in the left-hand quadrant will shift from $\hat{w}_1$ and $\hat{w}_2$. Assume, for didactic purposes, that the actual real wage quickly settles to its stationary level, where wage inflation and price inflation are equated. This implies that the rate of profit incorporated into prices will be r_{sp}, given by the intersection of the $\hat{w}_2$ and $\hat{p}_1$ curves. The profits cost curve will thus rotate down from PC(r_{s1}) to PC(r_{sp}). The higher real wages will induce a higher rate of capacity utilization (u_2), a higher rate of accumulation and higher realized rates of profit (r_2). This is the

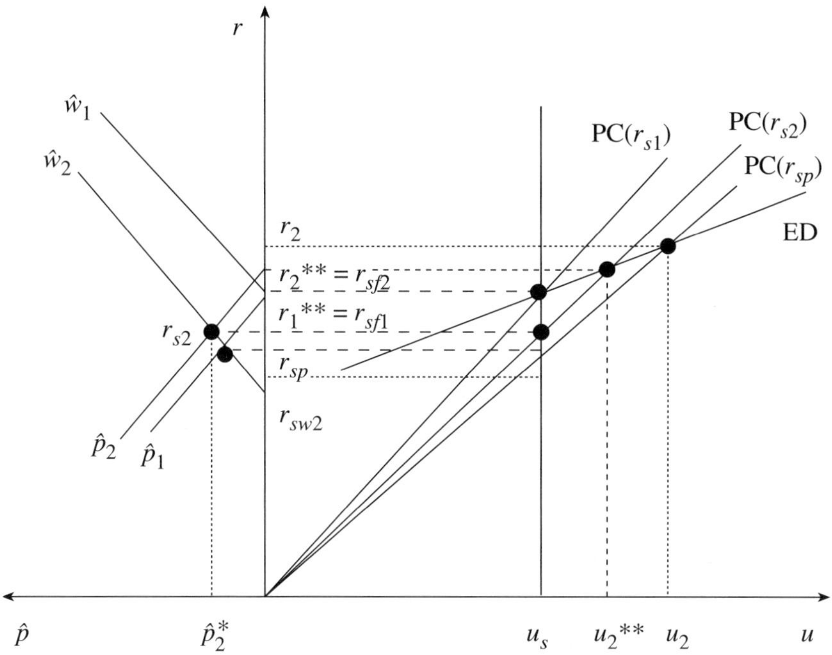

Figure 10.3 Adjustment to long-run equilibrium following a change in cost conditions

usual Kaleckian result, but it is a provisional one. In the long run, the high realized rate of profit will induce entrepreneurs to increase what they consider to be the assessed target rate of return. In Figure 10.3, this is represented both by a displacement of the $\hat{p}$ price inflation curve, from $\hat{p}_1$ to $\hat{p}_2$, and by an upward rotation of the PC curve, from PC(r_{sp}) to PC(r_{s2}), until finally, the falling realized rate of profit equates the increasing assessed target rate of return, such that in the end $r_{sf2} = r_2^{**}$. At this point, the new long-run rate of return incorporated into prices is given by r_{s2}, with $r_{s2} < r_{s1}$. The new $\hat{w}_2$ and $\hat{p}_2$ curves intersect at this rate of profit. The new long-run rate of utilization, u_2^{**}, is necessarily on the given ED curve, between the initial rate u_s and the provisional rate u_2. Thus comparing long-run positions, where the assessed target rates of return and the realized rate of profit are equated, it follows that, in this case, a higher rate of capital accumulation is associated with a lower incorporated target rate of return, and hence with a higher real wage.[7] The key Sraffian and Kaleckian belief, that higher rates of accumulation need not be associated with lower real wages, is thus confirmed, even across long-run positions.

CONCLUSION

In contrast to what was initially assumed both by Marxists and neo-Keynesians *à la* Joan Robinson and Nicholas Kaldor, Kaleckians (and some Sraffians) contend that higher rates of accumulation need not be associated with lower real wages, even without technical progress. This result is linked to the endogeneity of the rate of capacity utilization. However valid within the short-run context, the result has been questioned on the basis that it relies on discrepancies between the standard and realized rates of capacity utilization, or between normal and realized rates of profit, discrepancies that are judged to be unwarranted in long-run analysis. Other solutions have been offered in the past to avoid this logical problem, such as the distinction between normal and average values (Park, 1997a; 1997b), as well as the possibility of endogenous normal rates of capacity utilization, which generates models of hysteresis (Dutt, 1997; Lavoie, 1996). There is also the solution offered by Duménil and Lévy (1999), where a short-run Kaleckian growth model, with demand-led features, is transformed into a long-run supply-led classical model of accumulation. In this model, faster growth in fully adjusted positions requires higher savings rates and higher normal profit rates.

Two other solutions, that do not forsake the long-run, demand-led approach to growth, were considered here. The first solution, where the normal profit rate is endogenous, responding to the values taken by the realized profit rate, transforms the Kaleckian model into the old Cambridge growth model *à la* Joan Robinson. When the adjustment process has been completed, the long-run equilibria are fully adjusted positions running at their normal rates of capacity utilization, where higher rates of accumulation require lower real wages and higher normal profit rates. Still, these fully adjusted positions exhibit some demand-led features, namely the paradox of thrift.

The solution examined in greatest detail is also based on the endogeneity of the value taken by the normal rate of profit. But, in addition, we considered the possibility of a divergence between the rates of return assessed and targeted by firms on the one hand, and the rate of return which is actually incorporated into prices on the other. This divergence arises because of the bargaining power of workers and their real wage resistance. There is convergence, however, between the realized rate of profit and the rate of profit targeted by firms. Under this conditions, the demand-led characteristics of the Kaleckian model are sustained, even in long-run equilibrium. Such long-run equilibria are not fully adjusted positions, where the equilibrium rate of capacity utilization equals its normal value. The utilization rate remains an endogenous variable, even in long-run equilibrium. The paradox of thrift remains true in all cases, while the paradox of costs remains valid, in some cases, that is, higher rates of accumulation need not be associated with lower real wages, even across long-run positions.

The model is a highly simplified one. For instance, technical progress has been set aside; it has also been implicitly assumed that there is a reserve army of workers and that fluctuations in employment do not have feedback effects on the real wage targeted by workers. However, realistic complications that go beyond the above-mentioned heuristic simplifications can be added to the model, without affecting the main results (Cassetti 2000).

NOTES

1. This chapter was presented at the annual meeting of the Eastern Economic Association, in Boston, in March 1999, and also at a seminar organized by Ramon Tortajada at the University Pierre Mendès-France, Grenoble, in March 2000. I wish to thank participants in both events for their comments.
2. A similar but more complicated formula could be derived in a two-sector case, as is done in Lavoie and Ramirez-Gaston (1997).
3. See the chapter by Blecker in this volume for a review of this debate.
4. Sraffian and Marxist authors, as is explicit in Kurz (1991, 1994) and Bhaduri and Marglin (1990), generally endorse an investment function of the type: $g^i = \gamma + \gamma_u u + \gamma_r r_s$. The paradox of costs will only arise under some parameter constellations. This sort of investment function, however, creates some additional stability problems, as can be deduced from the work of Bruno (1999).
5. As can be seen, given the necessary negative relationship between the target rate of return and the actual rate of profit, there can only be one economically relevant long-run equilibrium; the other solution would yield a negative rate of profit.
6. This rate of inflation is a steady-state rate of inflation, and not just a transitory phenomenon.
7. We would still get this result if we had started from a situation where the steady-state rate of inflation were greater than zero.

REFERENCES

Auerbach, P. and P. Skott (1988) 'Concentration, competition and distribution,' *International Review of Applied Economics*, 2, 42–61.

Bhaduri, A. and S. Marglin (1990) 'Unemployment and the real wage: the economic basis for contesting political ideologies,' *Cambridge Journal of Economics*, 14, 375–93.

Bruno, O. (1999) 'Long-run positions and short-run dynamics in a classical growth model,' *Metroeconomica*, 50, 119–37.

Cassetti, M. (2000) 'Conflict, inflation, distribution and terms of trade in the Kaleckian model,' this volume.

Chick, V. and M. Caserta (1997) 'Provisional equilibrium and macroeconomic theory,' in P. Arestis, G. Palma and M. Sawyer (eds) *Markets, Unemployment and Economic Policy: Essays in Honour of Geoff Harcourt*, vol. II, London, Routledge, 223–37.

Committeri, M. (1986) 'Some comments on recent contributions on capital accumulation, income distribution and capacity utilization,' *Surplus Studies in Political Economy*, 2, 161–86.

Duménil, G. and D. Lévy (1995) 'A post-Keynesian long-term equilibrium with equalized profit rates? A rejoinder to Amitava Dutt's synthesis,' *Review of Radical Political Economics*, 27, 135–41.
Duménil, G. and D. Lévy (1999) 'Being Keynesian in the short term and classical in the long term: the traverse to classical long term equilibrium,' *Manchester School of Economics and Social Studies*, 67, 684–716.
Dutt, A.K. (1990) *Growth, Distribution and Uneven Development*, Cambridge, Cambridge University Press.
Dutt, A.K. (1997) 'Equilibrium, path dependence and hysteresis in post-Keynesian models,' in P. Arestis, G. Palma and M. Sawyer (eds) *Markets, Unemployment and Economic Policy: Essays in Honour of Geoff Harcourt*, vol. II, London, Routledge, 238–53.
Kalecki, M. (1971) *Selected Essays in the Dynamics of the Capitalist Economy*, Cambridge, Cambridge University Press.
Kurz, H.D. (1991) 'Technical change, growth and distribution: a steady state approach to unsteady growth on Kaldorian lines,' in E.J. Nell and W. Semmler (eds) *Nicholas Kaldor and Mainstream Economics*, London, Macmillan, 421–48.
Kurz, H.D. (1994) 'Growth and distribution,' *Review of Political Economy*, 6, 393–420.
Lanzillotti, R.F. (1958) 'Pricing objectives in large companies,' *American Economic Review*, 48, 921–40.
Lavoie, M. (1992) *Foundations of Post-Keynesian Economic Analysis*, Aldershot, Edward Elgar .
Lavoie, M. (1996) 'Traverse, hysteresis and normal rates of capacity utilization in Kaleckian models of growth and distribution,' *Review of Radical Political Economics*, 28, 113–47.
Lavoie, M. and P. Ramirez-Gaston (1997) 'Traverse in a two-sector Kaleckian model of growth with target-return pricing,' *Manchester School of Economic and Social Studies*, 65, 45–69.
Lee, F.S. (1994) 'From post-Keynesian to historical price theory, part 1: facts, theory and empirically grounded pricing model,' *Review of Political Economy*, 6, 303–36.
Park, M.S. (1997a) 'Normal values and average values,' *Metroeconomica*, 48, 188–99.
Park, M.S. (1997b) 'Accumulation, capacity utilization and distribution,' *Contributions to Political Economy*, 16, 87–101.
Rowthorn, R.E. (1977) 'Conflict, inflation and money,' *Cambridge Journal of Economics*, 1, 215–39.
Rowthorn, B. (1981) 'Demand, real wages and economic growth,' *Thames Papers in Political Economy*, London, Thames Polytechnic.
Shipley, D.D. (1981) 'Pricing objectives in British manufacturing industry,' *Journal of Industrial Economics*, 29, 429–43.
Vianello, F. (1985) 'The pace of accumulation,' *Political Economy: Studies in the Surplus Approach*, 1, 69–87.

11. Conflict, inflation, distribution and terms of trade in the Kaleckian model

Mario Cassetti

INTRODUCTION

Recently, a new generation of models of growth and distribution, inspired by the Kaleckian tradition, has emerged.[1] As noted by Lavoie (1992, 1995), these models differ from the standard Cambridgian growth models in two respects. First, they assume an oligopolistic environment, that is, firms have discretionary power and set their margins above production costs in order to generate funds for investment. Also, unions negotiate money wages with a view to achieving a 'fair' or historic share of total real income. Second, the new models treat capacity utilization as endogenous, even in the long period. As a result, the real wage rate and the rates of capacity utilization, accumulation and profit are correlated both in the short and in the long period.

There is also a substantial difference between the standard Cambridgian and later Kaleckian models as regards the role of changes in income distribution. Such changes are confined to full employment (Kaldor, 1961) or full capacity situations (Robinson, 1962) in the earlier post-Keynesian models, where Keynes's multiplier theory has two different uses. In the short period, the principle of effective demand is put to work to determine real income and employment, *given the distribution of income*. In the long period, it is applied to the determination of prices relative to wages, that is, to changes in the distribution of income, *given the level of capacity or of employment*. In this situation, an increase in investment results in an increase in the profit share and in savings. This is the long-period mechanism by which savings are adjusted to investment. In the new Kaleckian models, in the long run, the capacity utilization rate (which may diverge from full capacity), the rate of growth and income distribution are all jointly determined.

This chapter shows how to combine, in a Kaleckian framework, the theory of effective demand and the conflict theory of inflation. In particular, it is assumed that the relative bargaining power of capitalists and workers affects the dynamics of prices and wages, and therefore modifies their income shares. The subsequent changes in investment and saving decisions influence growth, capacity utilization and employment levels. These, in turn, feed back to affect workers' and capitalists' bargaining strength.

Before summarizing this chapter, we first briefly discuss the existing literature. Basic insights into the problem studied here can be found in Rowthorn (1977, 1981), Del Monte (1975), Marglin (1984, especially chapter 20), Taylor (1985), Skott (1989, especially chapter 8), Dutt (1984, 1990, 1992) and Lavoie (1992, 1995). None of these works, except for Dutt (1992), treats the distribution of income as endogenous.

Rowthorn's fundamental papers deal with both growth and distribution, but separately. Taylor combines aspects of Kaleckian growth with the conflict theory of inflation. Unfortunately, he linearizes all functions, thus eliminating the possibility of multiple equilibria. Del Monte (1975) and Dutt (1984) explicitly consider the relationship between growth and distribution, but analyse only the effects of exogenous changes in the mark-up.

The aim of Dutt's (1992) model is essentially the same as ours, but its dynamics are different.[2] A long and comprehensive discussion of the Kaleckian model and its extensions can be found in Lavoie (1992): this chapter explicitly models chapter 7 of Lavoie's book.

The rest of the chapter is organized as follows. The second section describes a closed economy model that displays effective demand and conflicting claims features. Its dynamic and static implications are then discussed in the third and fourth sections. The model is extended in the fifth section to include foreign trade, by bringing the terms of trade and the trade balance into play. A final section considers instability in the long run.

THE CLOSED ECONOMY MODEL[3]

In this section, we describe the basic Kaleckian model of a closed economy. We begin with a list of assumptions sufficient to specify effective demand, and then deduce their implications. Income distribution and inflation are introduced afterwards.

There are two social classes: workers, and capitalist who own firms. Firms produce outputs that are used both for consumption and investment.

The money supply is passive, that is, either monetary policy accommodates fully all wage claims and pricing decisions, or the velocity of money adjusts instantly to reestablish equilibrium.

At any time t, workers consume all their income, while capitalists save a constant fraction, s_p, of profits, Π_t.[4] The ratio of the capital stock, K_t, to real, full capacity output, Y_t^*, denoted by k, is constant. Capital does not depreciate.

We also assume that the ratio of government expenditure to the stock of capital is constant, say b.

Since investment and savings are always equal, the well-known Cambridge equation holds:

$$g_t = s_p r_t - b \qquad [11.1]$$

where g_t is the 'effective' rate of growth and r_t is the rate of profit.

As is usually the case in Keynesian models, below full capacity, the short-run supply of output adjusts immediately to demand. This means that equation [11.1] is always satisfied, and that g_t is the 'effective' rate of growth.

The desired rate of accumulation, g_t^d, is a linear function of the expected rate of profit, r_t^e, and of the expected rate of capacity utilization, u^e:

$$g_t^d = \gamma + \delta r_t^e + \varepsilon u_t^e \qquad \gamma \gtrless 0; \quad \delta, \varepsilon > 0 \qquad [11.2]$$

where γ is the autonomous rate of growth of capital, and δ and ε reflect the sensitivity of investors to the rates of profit and capacity utilization, respectively. The actual utilization rate is $u_t = Y_t / Y_t^*$, where Y_t stands for real output. Equation [11.2] is the standard Kalecki–Steindl–Kaldor investment function.[5]

The assumptions given are sufficient to describe the effective demand side of the model, which will be in equilibrium if $g_t = g_t^d$. We turn now to the conflicting claims side of the model.

In all post-Keynesian literature, the basic idea is that the wage rate is not an ordinary price. Money wages depend largely on the balance of power between workers and capitalists. Commodity prices, meanwhile, depend on the market power of firms and on their needs for internal funds. Real wages and income distribution, therefore, result from changes in money wages and prices.

Firms set the price as a mark-up, μ_t, on prime costs (which here consist only of labour costs), that is:

$$p_t = \frac{w_t}{a}(1 + \mu_t) \qquad [11.3]$$

where p_t is the price level, w_t the money wage rate, and a the average productivity of labour, which we assume constant. From [11.3] we can now derive an expression for the rate of growth of prices.

Let E_t denote the level of employment. Then total profits are:

$$\Pi_t = p_t Y_t - w_t E_t \qquad [11.4]$$

Combining [11.3] and [11.4], the share of profits, m_t can be written as:

$$m_t = \frac{\Pi_t}{p_t Y_t} = \frac{\mu_t}{1+\mu_t} \qquad [11.5]$$

and the price equation [11.3] may be rewritten as:

$$p_t = \frac{w_t}{a}\left(\frac{1}{1-m_t}\right) \qquad [11.6]$$

Finally, diffentiating [11.6] with respect to time, we obtain:

$$\frac{\dot{p}_t}{p_t} = \frac{\dot{w}_t}{w_t} + \frac{\dot{m}_t}{1-m_t} \qquad [11.7]$$

Now assume that workers set the nominal wage in order to achieve the real wage target v_w. In terms of the share of profits, this means that workers try to fix the profit share at the target value $m_w = 1 - v_w/a$. Similarly, firms set prices so as to achieve their target mark-up, which, in view of [11.5], corresponds to a target income share m_f.

Expectations are adaptive. If the wage share is low, workers will press for higher money wages until the wage share reaches the desired level. The equation determining the rate of wage inflation is:

$$\frac{\dot{w}_t}{w_t} = \theta_w(m_t - m_w) \qquad \theta_w > 0 \qquad [11.8]$$

where θ_w measures the reaction speed of labour unions to a discrepancy between the actual and workers' desired profit share of income.

Symmetrically, firms try to close the gap between the actual and their target profit share by increasing prices. The price change equation is given by:

$$\frac{\dot{p}_t}{p_t} = \theta_f(m_f - m_t) \qquad \theta_f > 0 \qquad [11.9]$$

where θ_f is the speed of adjustment of firms.

Both θ_w and θ_f depend on the bargaining power of workers and capitalists, respectively. Since both are positive and finite, the actual distribution of income will lie somewhere between the targets of the two groups.

The share targeted by firms is directly related to the ratio of demand to total productive capacity. The target set by labour unions, meanwhile, is positively influenced by the rate of employment e_t. Thus, the target share of firms is:

$$m_f = m_0 + m_1 u_t \qquad m_0, m_1 > 0 \qquad [11.10]$$

while workers' desired profit share is given by:

$$m_w = v_0 - v'_1 e_t \qquad v_0, v'_1 > 0 \qquad [11.11]$$

where $e_t = E_t/L_t$ is the employment rate, L_t being the total workforce, that is, the profit share that workers are willing to leave to firms is inversely related to the rate of employment, and directly related to the rate of unemployment. The rationale behind these relations is that when demand is high with respect to capacity, entrepreneurs try to take advantage of reduced competition in the product market by increasing their mark-ups and profits. The bargaining power of workers increases with tightening of the labour market. This is the Marxian connection between the reserve army of the unemployed and the strength of the working class.[6]

Notice that, given the stock of capital, K_t, and the size of the total work force, L_t, there is a link between the employment and the utilization rate:

$$e_t = \frac{E_t}{Y_t}\frac{Y_t}{Y_t^*}\frac{Y_t^*}{K_t}\frac{K_t}{L_t} = \frac{1}{ka}\frac{K_t}{L_t}u_t \qquad [11.12]$$

Equation [11.12] enables us to introduce another assumption of the neo-Marxian approach. The labour force is endogenous, and grows at the same rate as capital since the capitalistic sector of the economy can draw on labour from the other sectors (see Marglin, 1984, where this assumption is justified at length).[7] Thus, in steady-state equilibrium, the ratio K/L is fixed, and the target share of workers may be written as a function of the utilization rate:

$$m_w = v_0 - v_1 u_t \qquad \text{where} \qquad v_1 = v'_1(1/ka)\,(K/L) > 0 \qquad [11.13]$$

Here, v_1 reflects the rate at which workers' target profit share is revised in response to changes in the capacity utilization rate.

Notice now that, from [11.7], it follows that $\dot{m}_t/(1 - m_t) = 0$ whenever $\dot{p}_t/p_t = \dot{w}_t/w_t$. that is, given [11.8] and [11.9], the inflation rate, the profits share and the real wage bill will be constant.

We next derive a curve representing all the pairings of m_t and u_t for which the inflation rate is constant. Let us define $\hat{p}_t$ as a constant inflation rate, and $\bar{m}_t$ the non-accelerating inflation profit share. Equating [11.8] and [11.9], substituting from [11.10] and [11.13], and rearranging, we have:

$$\bar{m}_t = z_1 + z_2 u_t \qquad [11.14]$$

where:

$$z_1 = \frac{\theta_f m_0 + \theta_w v_0}{\theta_f + \theta_w} > 0 \quad \text{and} \quad z_2 = \frac{\theta_f m_1 - \theta_w v_1}{\theta_f + \theta_w} \gtrless 0 \qquad [11.15]$$

If $\theta_f m_1 > \theta_w v_1$, then $z_2 > 0$, which implies that the firms' bargaining power is stronger than that of workers'. This means that, as capacity utilization increases, the non-accelerating inflation profit share, $\bar{m}$, also increases. We will refer to this case (that is, $z_2 > 0$) as the firms' strength case (FS). If, instead, $\theta_f m_1 < \theta_w v_1$ and $z_2 < 0$, we will have the workers' strength case (WS). For completeness, notice that the same two cases can be renamed as the 'great firms' strength' case (GFS) and the 'great workers' strength' case (GWS) when the absolute value of z_2 exceeds a properly defined numerical value.

In a constant inflation equilibrium, the equilibrium profit share depends on the relative bargaining position of the two groups. The constant inflation equilibrium profit share changes along with the equilibrium utilization rate. Figures 11.1(a) and (b), where the m_f, m_w and $\bar{m}_t$ curves are plotted against the utilization rate, illustrate all this.

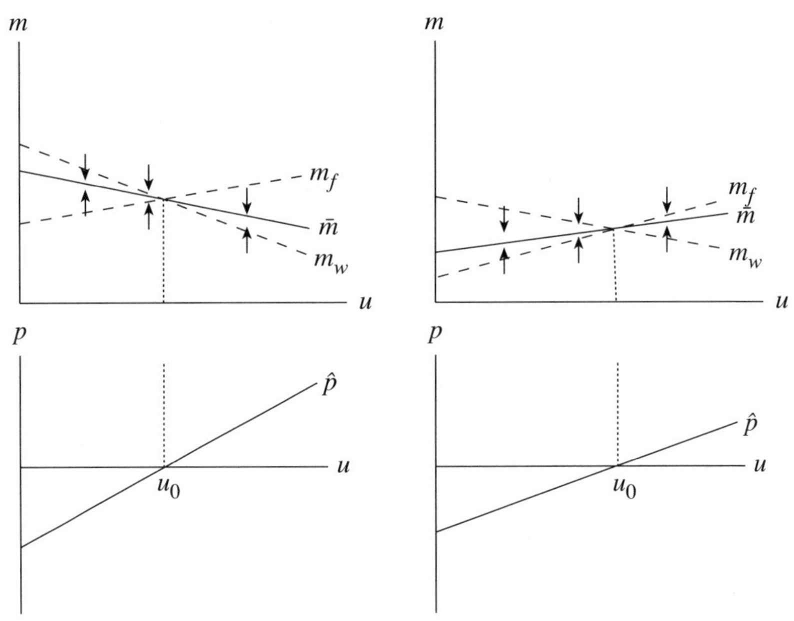

(a) Workers' strength (b) Firms' strength

Figure 11.1 Conflicting-claims profit shares and inflation

The $\bar{m}_t$ curve is decreasing in the utilization rate when $z_2 < 0$ (Figure 11.1(a)), and is increasing when $z_2 > 0$ (Figure 11.1(b)). The arrows indicate the direction of the movement that, at any given u, brings m to the $\bar{m}$ line. All points that lie off the $\bar{m}$ curve imply a rate of wage inflation that differs from the rate of price inflation, and therefore a profit share that is subject to change. The convergence to a constant m is implied by the proportionality hypothesis of equations [11.8] and [11.9]. If firms get near m_f, and thus workers depart from m_w, the increasing push for wages must eventually offset exactly the decreasing pressure on prices.

The relation between the constant price inflation rate $\hat{p}$ and u can be obtained from:

$$\hat{p} = \hat{w} = \theta_w(\bar{m} - v_0 + v_1 u_t) \qquad [11.16]$$

Substituting [11.14] into [11.16] we obtain:

$$\hat{p} = h_1 + h_2 u_t \qquad [11.17]$$

where:

$$h_1 = \frac{\theta_f \theta_w (m_0 - v_0)}{\theta_f + \theta_w} < 0 \quad \text{and} \quad h_2 = \frac{\theta_f \theta_w (m_1 + v_1)}{\theta_f + \theta_w} > 0 \qquad [11.18]$$

The slope of equation [11.17] depends on the adjustment coefficients θ_f and θ_w, and on the parameters m_1 and v_1. Notice that at the utilization rate $u_0 = (v_0 - m_0)/(m_1 + v_1)$, $m_f = m_w$ and $\hat{p} = 0$. Below u_0, $\hat{p}$ is negative, and above it is positive (see the bottom panels of Figure 11.1(a) and (b)). To understand better the determinants of inflation, we rearrange [11.17] to give:

$$\hat{p} = \frac{\theta_f \theta_w}{\theta_f + \theta_w}(m_f - m_w) \qquad [11.19]$$

Inflation (or deflation) is generated by the aspiration gap $(m_f - m_w)$, and is exacerbated by indexation mechanisms, represented by the term $\theta_f \theta_w/(\theta_f + \theta_w)$. An increase in the utilization rate always leads to greater inflation.

It should be noted that conflict arises only when $u > u_0$. It is only then that workers try to obtain higher real wages than firms are willing to allow. Instead, when capacity is below u_0, targets may be reconciled, making it possible for the equilibrium inflation rate to become negative.

DYNAMICS AND STABILITY

We now examine the dynamics of the model and in particular its stability. Distributional changes and investment savings decisions combine to determine the long-run rate of growth. Write the profit rate, r_t, as:

$$r_t = \frac{\Pi_t}{K_t} = \frac{m_t Y_t}{K_t} = \frac{m_t Y_t}{K_t}\frac{Y_t^*}{Y_t^*} = \frac{1}{k} m_t u_t \qquad [11.20]$$

From equation [11.1] and [11.20] the equilibrium rate of capacity utilization can be written as:

$$u_t = \frac{k}{s_p m_t}(g_t + b) \qquad [11.21]$$

Suppose that firms adjust the rate of growth of capital to maintain the desired rate of growth. If entrepreneurial expectations are adaptive, we can write:

$$\dot{g}_t = \alpha(g_t^d - g_t) \qquad \alpha > 0 \qquad [11.22]$$

Equation [11.22] is the first dynamic equation of our model.

A second dynamic equation follows from [11.17], after substitution from [11.8] and [11.9]:

$$\frac{\dot{m}_t}{1 - m_t} = \frac{\dot{p}_t}{p_t} - \frac{\dot{w}_t}{w_t} = \theta_f(m_f - m_t) - \theta_w(m_t - m_w) \qquad [11.23]$$

Solving [11.21] for g_t, substituting the resulting expression into [11.22], and then inserting [11.10], [11.13] and [11.21] into [11.23], we get the system of nonlinear equations:

$$\dot{g}_t = \alpha\left[\gamma + \frac{\delta m_t + ek}{s_p m_t} b - \left(1 - \frac{\delta m_t + ek}{s_p m_t}\right) g_t\right] \qquad [11.24]$$

$$\dot{m}_t = (\theta_f + \theta_w)\left[z_1 - m_t + \frac{z_2 k}{s_p m_t}(g_t + b)\right](1 - m_t) \qquad [11.25]$$

Notice that equation [11.24] holds only when there is excess capacity, so that when $g^d > g$ investment can increase along with consumption. Instead, when capacity is fully utilized, $u_t = 1$ and investment can grow only by increasing savings to the detriment of consumption. In this case, substituting [11.20] into [11.1] and differentiating, we obtain:

$$\dot{g}_t = \frac{s_p}{k}\dot{m}_t \qquad [11.26]$$

This equation replaces [11.24] when capacity is fully utilized.

We next analyse the existence and stability of all possible equilibria, starting with those involving excess capacity.

Equations [11.22] and [11.23] imply that, for an equilibrium to exist, it must be true that $g_t = g_t^d$ and that $m_t = \bar{m}_t$. Taking into account that, in equilibrium, the expected values r^e and u^e equal the corresponding actual values, we get from equations [11.1], [11.2], [11.14] and [11.20], the non-linear equilibrium equations:

$$\frac{s_p}{k}\bar{m}_t u_t - b = \gamma + \left(\frac{\delta}{k}\bar{m}_t + \varepsilon\right) u_t \qquad [11.27]$$

$$\bar{m}_t = z_1 + z_2 u_t$$

Solutions for u are given here by:

$$u_1^*, u_2^* = \frac{-(s_p - \delta)z_1 + k\varepsilon \pm \sqrt{\Delta}}{2z_2(s_p - \delta)} \qquad [11.28]$$

where the '+' part of the '±' sign yields u_1^*, and the '–' part yields u_2^*, while $\Delta = 4kz_2(b + \gamma)(s_p - \delta) + [-(s_p - \delta)z_1 + k\varepsilon]^2$.[8]

Now an excess capacity equilibrium u^* is locally stable if

$$\left.\frac{dg_t}{du_t}\right|_{u=u^*} > \left.\frac{dg_t^d}{du_t}\right|_{u=u^*}$$

or:

$$(s_p - \delta)(z_1 + 2z_2 u^*_{1,2}) > k\varepsilon \qquad [11.29]$$

Only one of the solutions in [11.28] can be stable. In fact, expression [11.29] holds true, after substituting from [11.28], only for u_1^*.[9]

A number of different equilibria are possible, depending on the signs of $(s_p - \delta)$, z_2 and $(b + \gamma)$, and on the magnitude $|z_2|$. These equilibria are shown in Table 11.1.

Table 11.1 Types of excess capacity equilibria

	Stagnationist regime ($s_p > \delta$)				Exhilarationist regime ($s_p < \delta$)			
□	FS	GFS	WS	GWS	FS	GFS	WS	GWS
$b + \gamma > 0$	1 stable	1 stable	1 stable	1 stable 1 unstable	–	–	–	–
$b + \gamma < 0$	1 unstable	1 unstable 1 stable	1 unstable	1 unstable	1 unstable	1 unstable	1 unstable	1 stable 1 unstable

Table 11.2 Types of full capacity equilibria

	Stagnationist regime ($s_p > \delta$)				Exhilarationist regime ($s_p < \delta$)			
	FS	GFS	WS	GWS	FS	GFS	WS	GWS
$b + \gamma > 0$	unstable	unstable	unstable	stable	stable	stable	–	–
$b + \gamma < 0$	stable	unstable	stable	stable	–	–	stable	unstable

Let us now consider the fully capacity equilibrium. This is necessarily unique, and implies an equilibrium profit share fixed at $\bar{m} = z_1 + z_2$. This kind of equilibrium can be maintained as long as firms do not reduce investment, that is, as long as $g_t^d \geq g_t$. The level of investment, however, is bounded from above by savings generated by the constant inflation share of profits. Therefore, firms are rationed and accumulation is determined by the condition:

$$g_t = \frac{s_p}{k}(z_1 + z_2) - b \qquad [11.30]$$

All of the possible full capacity equilibria and corresponding parameter combinations are given in Table 11.2.

Numerous post-Keynesian authors assume that $s_p > \delta$, a stability requirement which turns the model into an unmistakable stagnationist or underconsumptionist version of the Kaleckian model. In an excess capacity equilibrium, any increase in real wages will stimulate the economy and lead to greater output and growth. From Table 11.1 it is clear that for the model developed above to be stable, the same hypothesis is necessary, together with the condition $b + \gamma > 0$. The antithetical assumption, $s_p < \delta$, which gives rise to the *exhilarationist regime* of the model,[10] leads to an unstable excess capacity equilibrium both in the FS case and in the WS case. It is only with the GWS case, coupled with $b + \gamma < 0$, that the *exhilarationist* version yields a stable excess capacity equilibrium. The dynamics of the stagnationist case are illustrated in Appendix 11.A.

Full capacity stable equilibria exist in both regimes (as illustrated in Table 11.2) as a result of a permanent pressure to accumulate. But note, again, that in the exhilarationist regime, an equilibrium does not exist for half of the possible parameter combinations.

Following the Kaleckian tradition, we next examine the main implications of the stagnationist model, in the case where both $s_p > \delta$ and $b + \gamma > 0$.

THE COMPARATIVE DYNAMICS OF THE MODEL

We now turn to the effects on equilibrium of changes in the various parameters of our model. In Figure 11.2 panels (a) and (b) depict the relationships between g^d, g and r (the realized rate of profit), and the rate of capacity utilization. Panels (c) and (d), meanwhile, plot m_f, m_w, $\bar{m}$ and $\hat{p}$ against u. In panel (a), we find the FS and GFS case, which are similar when $b + \gamma > 0$. In panel (b), the GWS case is depicted. The WS case is similar to the GWS case illustrated in panel (b), but with the full capacity vertical line lying between points A and B.

Note that, in the FS/GFS case, as u increases, the strength of firms also

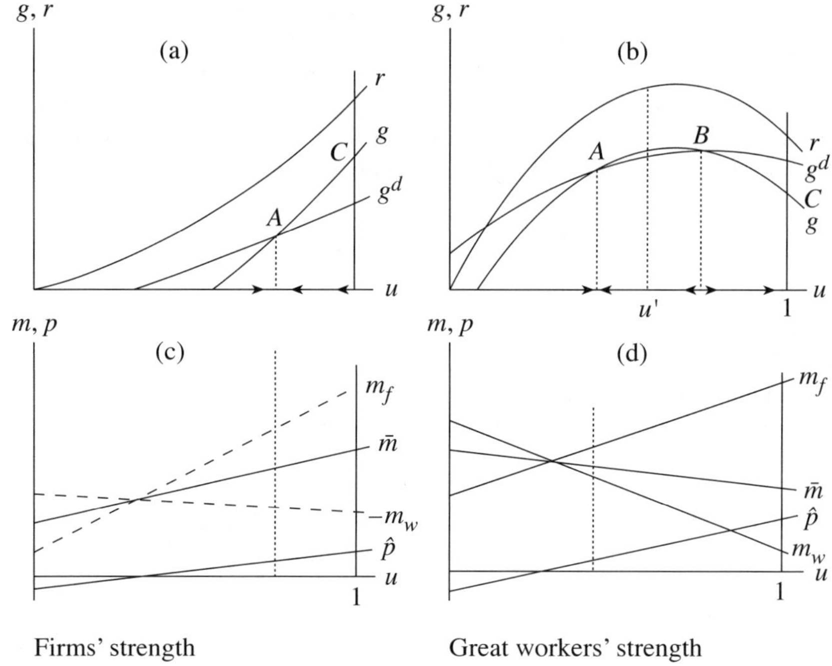

Figure 11.2 Equilibrium positions in the FS/GFS and GWS cases

increases, making the share of profits (see panel (c)), and thus savings, grow. This explains why the 'effective' as well as the desired rate of growth curves are upward-sloping. In view of [11.20], the same is true for the realized rate of profit curve. In the other case (see panel (b)), where the bargaining power of the workers is strong, all of the schedules slope upward as long as the positive effect of an increase in the capacity utilization rate prevails over the negative effect of the fall in the profit share. After a maximum is reached, the curves start sloping downwards, as the capacity effect is insufficient to compensate for the decline in the profit share (see panel (d)).

At point A in panel (a) and (b), the economy is in a stable equilibrium. Points C are full capacity equilibria. C is an unstable point in the FS/GFS/WS case, and stable in the GWS case. Point B in panel (b) is an unstable equilibrium position. Here, $u' = z_1/(2\,|z_2|) - \varepsilon k/(2\,|z_2|(s_p - \delta))$ is the maximum possible excess capacity equilibrium rate of capacity utilization. Any change that pushes the utilization rate beyond u' leads to a full capacity, stable equilibrium, and to a decline in the rates of growth and profit.

Let us now consider how changes in the various parameters affect the equilibrium position of the economy. We shall consider only stable equilibria.

In our model, two crucial features of the Kaleckian model, the paradox of thrift and the paradox of costs (emphasized by Rowthorn (1981) and Lavoie (1992, chapter 6)) are confirmed, provided the rate of capacity utilization stays below unity. The paradox of thrift can be shown by considering the impact of a change in s_p on the utilization rate:

$$\frac{\partial u}{\partial s_p} = -\frac{k[(\gamma + b) + \varepsilon u^*]}{(s_p - \delta)\sqrt{\Delta}} < 0 \qquad [11.31]$$

That is, an increase in the propensity to save out of profits leads to a lower rate of utilization of capacity. Since, in the case of stable excess capacity equilibria, there exist linear and positive relationships between the equilibrium profit and utilization rates, and between the equilibrium growth and utilization rates, an increase in s_p also leads to a lower rate of profit and a lower rate of growth.

As an illustration of the paradox of costs, consider an increase in costs, that is, in the parameter k. Its impact on the rate of utilization is given by:

$$\frac{\partial u}{\partial k} = \frac{\gamma + b + \varepsilon u^*}{\sqrt{\Delta}} > 0$$

In other words, a rise in costs initially reduces profits, and hence savings, and creates an excess demand. As firms respond by increasing utilization and output, investment will also rise because of the accelerator effect (as $\varepsilon > 0$), so that, finally, profits, the rate of profit, and the rate of growth, will recover and exceed their previous levels. This is the 'effective demand' mechanism of the model: whatever increases (reduces) the amount of savings, for a given income, creates an excess supply (demand) which induces less (more) output and income.[11]

As for the inflation rate, except for changes in the bargaining position parameters, any change that increases the utilization rate also increases the inflation rate. Inflation is fuelled by any expansionary pressure because of the positive incentive that an increase in u transmits to both wage and profit aspirations.

Consider now changes in the parameters θ_w, θ_f, and in the target shares m_w and m_f. Let us first examine the impact of changes in workers' bargaining position in terms of the parameters v_0 and v_1 of the function m_w. Here, a decrease in v_0 or an increase in v_1 imply a decrease in the share of profits that workers are willing to leave to firms. The resulting decrease in the actual profit share raises consumption spending, the degree of capacity utilization, and the rates of profit and accumulation. An increase in the inflation rate will follow.

By contrast, an increase in m_0 or m_1 depresses the rates of growth and utilization, as it tends to push upwards the equilibrium profit share through a change in the $\bar{m}$ curve. The impact on the inflation rate of an increase in firms' profit share target is, however, ambiguous. This can be seen by considering, for example, the impact on $\hat{p}$ of an increase in m_0. We see that:

$$\frac{\partial \hat{p}}{\partial m_0} \gtrless 0 \quad \text{if} \quad \frac{\theta_f}{\theta_f + \theta_w}(v_1 + m_1) \lessgtr \frac{\sqrt{\Delta}}{(s_p - \delta)u^*} \qquad [11.32]$$

It is possible that a high θ_w combined with a low v_1 and low m_1 may maintain the inflationary process even if the economy falls into a recession. Under these conditions, therefore, an upward revision of firms' profit targets may give rise to stagflation, whereas a downward revision may stimulate both an expansion and a decrease in the inflation rate. In this particular case, a decrease in the target profit share is the only change that has an expansionary effect while reducing inflation.

Finally, consider the effects of changes in the bargaining strength parameters θ_w and θ_f. Remember that $u_0 = (v_0 - m_0)/(m_1 + v_1)$ is the value of the capacity utilization rate when $m_f = m_w$, and $\hat{p} = 0$. It is useful to distinguish between a change in θ_w or θ_f when $u^* > u_0$, and a change in θ_w or θ_f when $u^* < u_0$. We confine our attention to the first case. Not surprisingly, an increase in workers' bargaining power increases the inflation rate. Since the wage share increases, the utilization rate will also go up. However, an increase in θ_f has a negative impact on the capacity utilization rate, due to an increase in the profit share, but an uncertain effect on the inflation rate. The positive impulse on the inflation rate resulting directly from the rise in θ_f may be offset by the negative effect of the decreasing utilization rate.

To conclude this section, we can show that the multipliers differ under the two bargaining regimes. Consider for example:

$$\frac{\partial u}{\partial b} = \frac{k}{(s_p - \delta)(m^* + 2z_2 u^*) - \varepsilon k} \qquad [11.33]$$

The multiplier is higher when $z_2 < 0$, that is, when workers are stronger. In this case, the resulting reduction in the share of profits, $-2|z_2|u^*$, implies larger increases in the capacity utilization rate in any round of the multiplier process. The multiplier will be lower when the bargaining position of firms is stronger.

CONFLICTING-CLAIMS, INFLATION AND INTERNATIONAL COMPETITIVENESS

The aim of this section is to extend the model to an open economy with flexible exchange rates and competitive imports and exports. We will show that the previous results hold only if the nominal exchange rate is allowed to depreciate or appreciate. Otherwise, some adjustments are required in policy or in bargaining parameters.

Assume that, for analytical simplicity, only consumption goods are traded. Thus, consumption demand is divided into:

$$C_t^D = [W_t + (1 - s_p)\Pi_t]\lambda(\rho_t) \qquad [11.34]$$

and:

$$C_t^M = \frac{[W_t + (1 - s_p)\Pi_t][1 - \lambda(\rho_t)]}{\rho_t} \qquad [11.35]$$

where $W_t = w_t E_t$ is the wage bill,, and C^D and C^M are the demand for domestic and foreign consumption goods, respectively. The function $\lambda(\rho_t)$ is increasing in the real exchange rate, ρ_t. Moreover, $\lambda \rightarrow 1$ when $\rho \rightarrow \infty$ and $0 < \lambda(0) < 1$. As usual, $\rho_t = (d_t p_t^w)/p_t$ is the real exchange rate, where d_t stands for the nominal exchange rate, p_t^w is the price of foreign goods, and p_t is, as before, the price of domestic goods. All this means that a depreciation (appreciation) of the real exchange rate makes domestic goods more (less) attractive to foreign as well as to domestic buyers. Exports and the domestic demand for consumption goods will therefore increase (decrease) and imports will decrease (increase).

We also assume that the demand for real exports per unit of capital is:

$$x = x_0 \rho_t \qquad [11.36]$$

Equation [11.36] implies a unitary elasticity of exports, so that the Marshall–Lerner condition is always satisfied.[12]

The equilibrium balance of trade per unit of capital (bt) is:

$$bt = x_0 \rho_t - \rho_t c_t^M = 0 \qquad [11.37]$$

where c_t^M is the demand for foreign consumption goods per unit of capital. Since $W_t = (1 - m_t)Y_t$ and $\Pi_t = m_t Y_t$, and recalling that $Y_t/K_t = u_t/k$, after substitution and rearrangement, equation [11.37] may be rewritten as:

$$bt = x_0 \rho_t - [1 - \lambda(\rho_t)]\,(1 - s_p m_t)\frac{u_t}{k} = 0 \qquad [11.38]$$

The 'effective' rate of growth now becomes:

$$g_t = -\,b - x_0 \rho_t + [1 - \lambda(\rho_t)]\,\frac{u_t}{k} + \lambda(\rho_t) s_p r_t \qquad [11.39]$$

By substitution from [11.38], equation [11.39] reduces to equation [11.1] for the closed economy, whereas the function g_t^d remains unchanged. Thus when $bt = 0$, we have the same solutions for u, g, m and r as in the closed model. Given these solutions, equation [11.38] determines ρ.

The dynamics of the model, after eliminating r_t, are now represented by the following three-equation system:

$$\begin{aligned} \dot{g}_t &= \alpha\{g^d[u(g_t, \rho_t, m_t), \rho_t] - g[u(g_t, \rho_t, m_t), \rho_t]\} \\ &= F_1(g_t, \rho_t, m_t) \qquad \alpha > 0 \\ \dot{m} &= (\theta_w + \theta_f)[z_1 - m_t + z_2 u_t(g_t, \rho_t, m_t)](1 - m_t) \\ &= F_2(g_t, \rho_t, m_t) \\ \dot{\rho}_t &= \beta\{c^M[u(g_t, \rho_t, m_t), \rho_t] - x(\rho_t)\} \\ &= F_3(g_t, \rho_t, m_t) \qquad \beta > 0 \end{aligned} \qquad [11.40]$$

In order to analyse local stability, consider the Jacobian matrix, J, of the functions F_i of the system [11.40], linearized in the neighbourhood of the equilibrium solution. A necessary stability condition is that the trace of J is negative. It can be shown that the following condition:

$$[\lambda(\rho_t)s_p - \delta](z_1 + 2z_2u^*) > k\varepsilon - [1 - \lambda(\rho_t)] \qquad [11.41]$$

implies that both J_{11} and J_{22} are negative. This condition is more stringent than that in the closed economy model (see [11.29]), but coincides with this earlier condition when $\lambda(\rho_t) \to 1$.

Finally, J_{33} is also negative because:

$$x_0 + (1 - s_p m^*)\frac{u^*}{k}\frac{\partial\lambda}{\partial\rho} > 0 \qquad [11.42]$$

a condition which is always true. Thus, if [11.41] and [11.42] hold true, $J_{11} + J_{22} + J_{33} < 0$.

The central problem of the open Kaleckian model is that the equilibrium inflation rate, $\hat{p}$, that originates from the conflicting claims of workers and firms, may differ from that prevailing in the rest of the world, $\hat{p}_w$. Since, in equilibrium:

$$\frac{\dot{\rho}}{\rho} = \hat{p}_w - \hat{p} + \hat{d} = 0 \qquad [11.43]$$

the equilibrium inflation rate is compatible with foreign inflation only if the nominal exchange rate matches the gap between $\hat{p}$ and $\hat{p}_w$ through steady depreciation or appreciation. If this adjustment of the exchange rate is not possible, it must be true that $\hat{p} = \hat{p}_w$ and $\hat{d} = 0$. But then, from equation [11.17], it follows that:

$$u_F^* = \frac{\hat{p}_w - h_1}{h_2} \qquad [11.44]$$

where u_F^* is the capacity utilization rate imposed by foreign price competition.

Thus, there exists a tension between u_F^* and the equilibrium rate of capacity utilization in the domestic market, u_D^*. When $u_F^* < u_D^*$, an adjustment must take place, through a decrease in the budget deficit or through an attenuation of social groups' income claims. This can be seen by recalling, from equation [11.19], that $u_F^* < u_D^*$ implies:

$$\hat{p} = \frac{\theta_f \theta_w}{\theta_f + \theta_w}(m_f - m_w) > \hat{p}_w$$

At this point, one choice is to depress aggregate demand to reduce m_f and increase m_w through a contraction in economic activity. This option recalls the anti-inflationary policies of the 1980s, often interpreted as an attempt to weaken labour power.[13] The other, less costly, way to reduce inflationary pressure involves a voluntary incomes policy that reduces the income targets of both firms and workers, and mitigates the indexation parameters θ_f and θ_w.

INSTABILITY PROBLEMS IN THE VERY LONG RUN

There are two problems, in the long run, with the model presented in this chapter. The first arises when the labour force grows at an exogenous rate, the second when the equilibrium capacity utilization rate differs from that desired by entrepreneurs. Both problems can lead to instability.

We assumed earlier that labour in the capitalistic sector expands (or contracts) according to this sector's rate of expansion. Workers are recruited from elsewhere to fill the gap between labour required and labour already engaged in production. In the event that the growth of capitalistic production is slow, employment outside the capitalistic sector prevents long-run overt unemployment. For this reason we consider v_1 to be constant, subject only to exogenous changes. If, however, in the very long run, the labour force grows at a different rate than the capital stock, the equilibrium rate of growth g^* is no longer a steady rate since it changes with the K/L ratio. To see this, differentiate v_1 with respect to a, K and L. Recalling that $v_1 = v'_1\,(K/kaL)$, and writing $\dot{a}/a = \lambda$, we obtain:

$$\frac{\dot{v}_1}{v_1} = g - n - \lambda$$

In the very long period, the steady-state condition is $g^* = n + \lambda$, where $n + \lambda$ is Harrod's natural rate of growth. If $g^* > n + \lambda$, v_1 increases causing an increase in g^*. If $g^* < n + \lambda$, v_1 decreases and g^* will fall further.

As regards the second problem mentioned above, the equilibrium capital-capacity ratio may not be judged satisfactory by entrepreneurs. They can try to adjust it by changing the term γ in their investment function. Thus, the economy will slip off the Harrodian knife-edge. Obviously, a symmetric unstable upward movement will take place when producers find themselves short of capital. Only when actual and normal rates of capacity utilization are equal will firms be in a final steady-state equilibrium. This latter argument is based on the notion of a unique desired (or normal) utilization rate which is independent, in the long period, from the process that generates u^*, and g^*.

The meaning of a *normal* rate of capacity utilization, as well as that of a *normal* rate of profit, is the subject of a debate between neo-Ricardians and neo-Marxian authors, on one side, and Kaleckian authors, on the other. As a discussion on these methodological issues is beyond the purpose of the present exposition, we refer the reader to Lavoie (1995) for an account of this debate, and especially to Lavoie (1996, 2002) where a solution to this problem, based on hysteresis effects, is advanced.

CONCLUSION

The Kaleckian growth model developed in this chapter endogenizes the distribution of income. This combination of effective demand and conflict inflation theories seems to be a natural completion of the post-Keynesian view of the dynamics of capitalism, that is, the simultaneous achievement of full employment and low rates of inflation is not automatic.

All of the typical results of the standard Kaleckian model (the paradox of thrift, the paradox of costs and the direct relationship between wages and accumulation) are confirmed, at least for the closed economy. However, economic growth may suffer from an inflationary bias. The larger is the aspiration gap between workers and firms, the greater this bias will be.

It has also been shown that, when international competition is introduced, countries which experience inflation rates higher than that of competitors are forced to adopt adjustment policies. Three alternative policies become relevant at this point. The first and the most painful is the implementation of contractionary measures, since these create higher unemployment. The second is to allow continuous depreciation in order to maintain the competitiveness of domestic industries. The third policy, traditionally recommended by post-Keynesians, is to reform the institutions that give rise to the inflationary bias. This involves introducing a higher degree of cooperation into the system of industrial relations through voluntary income policies. According to well-established literature on the subject, the countries best equipped for this task are those with highly centralized collective bargaining systems.

The distribution of income also depends on a number of non-economic factors, such as demographic, institutional and historical factors. Taking these into account is a challenging task. The classical and post-Keynesian schemes of analysis, which do not reduce distribution to a mere technological issue, would seem to offer the most promising starting point for future research in this direction.

ACKNOWLEDGEMENT

I would like to thank Marc Lavoie for his helpful comments. Errors and omissions are, of course, solely my responsibility.

NOTES

1. The Kaleckian model has been discussed at length by Lavoie (see, for instance, Lavoie, 1992, 1995, 2002). Previous insights into the Kaleckian model are found in Rowthorn (1977, 1981).
2. In Dutt's model, the long-run dynamics of capital accumulation are determined by the savings function only, while in the present model, the equilibrium rates of growth and capacity utilization are determined simultaneously both by saving and investment decisions, on the one hand, and by the conflicting claims of workers and firms on the other. In Dutt's article, the two processes are separated: the former is modelled in the short run, and the latter in the long run. Moreover, Dutt assumes that the labour force grows through time at a constant rate.
3. A version of this model that includes the effects of technical progress can be found in Cassetti (2000).
4. This is the classical savings hypothesis. It is well known that workers savings do not alter the conclusions of the model, as demonstrated in Cassetti (2000).
5. See Steindl (1952) and Kaldor (1957). This investment function has been fully discussed by, among others, Lavoie (1992, 1995). In equation [11.2], γ assumes the meaning of a rate of growth independent from profitability and capacity conditions. A discussion over possible interpretations of γ, for instance as the expected trend of future sales, can be found in Lavoie (1995). For our purposes, γ can assume positive or negative values, or even a value of zero, without compromising our results.
6. See Rowthorn (1977), Skott (1989, chapter 8), Dutt (1992) and Lavoie (1992, chapter 7).
7. See Marglin (1984, pp. 349–50).
8. Δ is the discriminant of the solutions for g^*, m^* and u^*. In order to have real roots, Δ must be non-negative.

9. The system represented by the equations [11.24] and [11.25] can be written as follows:

$$\dot{g}_t = F_1(g_t, m_t)$$

$$\dot{m}_t = F_2(g_t, m_t)$$

Let J be the Jacobian matrix of the functions obtained through expansion of the right-hand side of this system in Taylor's series about the equilibrium solution. A necessary condition for local stability is that the trace of J must be negative. It can be demonstrated that condition [11.29] implies that both J_{11} and J_{22} are negative, so that $J_{11} + J_{22} < 0$.

10. Along with all of the authors cited above, we use the terms '*stagnationist*' (or '*underconsumptionist*') to characterize an economy in which the response of savings to income (here, total profits) is stronger than the response of investment to profitability (that is, $s_p > \delta$). In this case, consumption necessarily dominates effective demand and a higher real wage leads to higher aggregate demand as well as capacity utilization. In our model, as far as excess capacity equilibria are concerned, it leads also to a higher rate of growth. In the opposite situation, when $s_p > \delta$, an *exhilarationist regime* obtains, where investment plays the dominant role in expanding aggregate demand. That is, a reduction in consumption due to a lower real wage is more than offset by the increase in investment. On this point, see Bhaduri and Marglin (1990).
11. Expressions for the effects of all possible shifts in the parameters of the model can be found in Cassetti (2000, Appendices A and B).
12. As also noted by Blecker (2000, this volume), the assumption that changes in relative prices have an important effect on international trade flows in Kaleckian open-economy models contrasts with the assumption made about their unimportance in balance-of-payments-constrained growth models of demand-led growth. See, for example, the papers by Atesoglu and McCombie and Roberts in this volume.
13. See, for instance, Cornwall (1989).

APPENDIX 11.A

The dynamic behaviour of the stagnationist model is shown in the (g, m) plane in Figures A.11.3 and A.11.4. Figure A.11.3(a) shows the FS case, with $s_p > \delta$ and $b + \gamma > 0$. Point A is a locally stable equilibrium. Point C is an unstable, full capacity

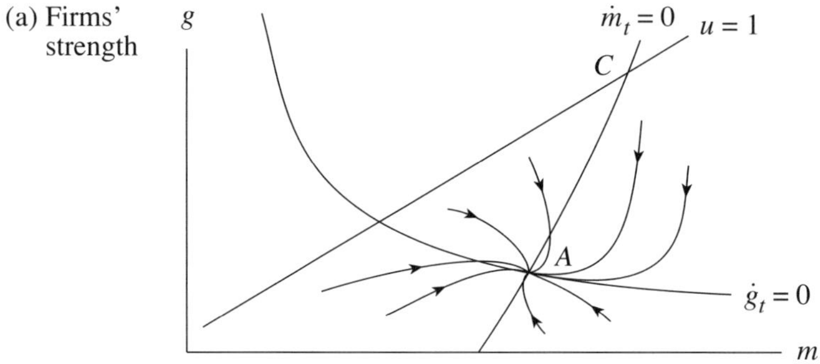

Figure A.11.3 The stagnationist case: one stable excess capacity equilibrium

(b) Workers' strength

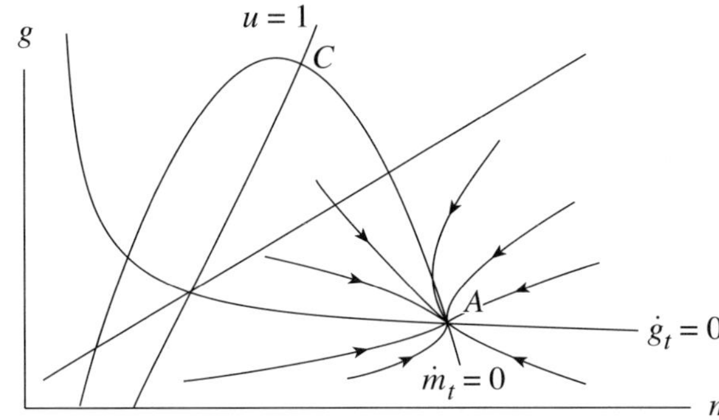

Figure A.11.3 (continued)

equilibrium. In Figure A.11.3(b) we have the WS case with $s_p > \delta$, and $b + \gamma > 0$. Again, we have a stable equilibrium point at A and an unstable, full capacity equilibrium C.

In Figure A.11.4(a) we illustrate the GFS case with $s_p > \delta$ and $b + \gamma < 0$. Here, points A and B are excess capacity equilibria: A is locally stable, B is unstable. C is a locally stable full capacity equilibrium. Figure A.11.4(b) shows the GWS case with $s_p > \delta$ and

(a) Great firms' strength

(b) Great workers' strength

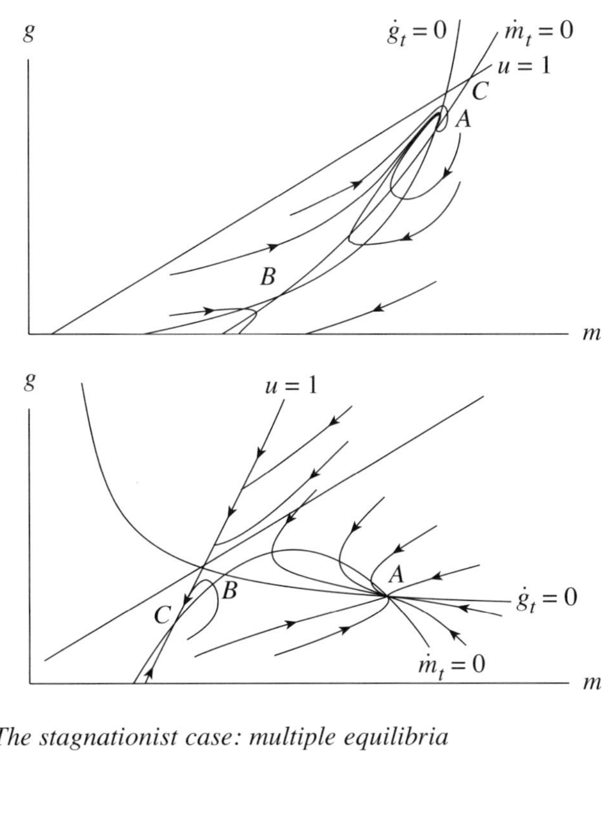

Figure A.11.4 The stagnationist case: multiple equilibria

$b + \gamma > 0$. Again, there are three equilibrium points. A (which is locally stable) and B (which is unstable) are excess capacity equilibria. Finally, C is a stable, full capacity equilibrium.

REFERENCES

Bhaduri A. and S. Marglin (1990) 'Unemployment and the real wage: the economic basis for contesting political ideologies,' *Cambridge Journal of Economics*, 14, 375–93.

Cassetti, M. (2000) 'Endogenizing the conflict over income distribution in the Kaleckian model,' Dipartimento di Scienze Economiche, Università di Brescia, Discussion Paper no. 0002.

Cornwall, J. (1989) 'Inflation as a cause of economic stagnation: a dual model,' in J.A. Kregel (ed.) *Inflation and Income Distribution in Capitalist Crisis: Essays in Memory of Sidney Weintraub*, New York, New York University Press, 99–122.

Del Monte, A. (1975) 'Grado di monopolio e sviluppo economico,' *Rivista Internazionale di Scienze Sociali*, 83, 231–63.

Dutt, A.K. (1984) 'Stagnation, income distribution and monopoly power,' *Cambridge Journal of Economics*, 8, 25–40.

Dutt, A.K. (1990) *Growth, Distribution, and Uneven Development*, Cambridge, Cambridge University Press.

Dutt, A.K. (1992) 'Conflict inflation, distribution, cyclical accumulation and crises,' *European Journal of Political Economy*, 8, 579–97.

Kaldor, N. (1957) 'A model of economic growth,' *Economic Journal*, 67, 591–624.

Kaldor, N. (1961) 'Capital accumulation and economic growth,' in F.A. Lutz and D.C. Hague (eds) *The Theory of Capital*, New York, St. Martin's Press, 177–228.

Kalecki, M. (1943) 'Political aspects of full employment,' *Political Quarterly*, 4, 322–31.

Kalecki, M. (1971) *Selected Essays in the Dynamics of the Capitalist Economy*, Cambridge, Cambridge University Press.

Lavoie, M. (1992) *Foundations of Post-Keynesian Economic Analysis*, Aldershot, Edward Elgar.

Lavoie, M. (1995) 'The Kaleckian model of growth and distribution and its neo-Ricardian and neo-Marxian critiques,' *Cambridge Journal of Economics*, 19, 789–818.

Lavoie, M. (1996) 'Traverse, hysteresis, and normal rates of capacity utilization in Kaleckian models of growth and distribution,' *Review of Radical Political Economics*, 28, 113–47.

Lavoie, M. (2002) 'The Kaleckian growth model with target return pricing and conflict inflation,' this volume.

Marglin, S. (1984) *Growth, Distribution and Prices*, Cambridge, MA, Harvard University Press.

Robinson, J. (1962) *Essays in the Theory of Economic Growth*, London, Macmillan

Rowthorn, R.E. (1977) 'Conflict, inflation and money,' *Cambridge Journal of Economics*, 1, 215–39.

Rowthorn, R.E. (1981) 'Demand, real wages and economic growth,' *Thames Papers in Political Economy*, Autumn, 1–39.

Sarantis, N. (1990–1) 'Distribution and terms of trade dynamics, inflation and growth,' *Journal of Post-Keynesian Economics*, 13, 175–98.

Skott, P. (1989) *Conflict and Effective Demand in Economic Growth*, Cambridge, Cambridge University Press.

Steindl, J. (1952) *Maturity and Stagnation in American Capitalism*, Oxford, Basil Blackwell.

Taylor, L. (1985) 'A stagnationist model of economic growth,' *Cambridge Journal of Economics*, 9, 383–403.

PART FOUR

Traverse Analysis and Demand-led Growth

12. A model of Kaldorian traverse: cumulative causation, structural change and evolutionary hysteresis

Mark Setterfield

INTRODUCTION

In his celebrated critique of equilibrium economics,[1] Nicholas Kaldor argued that history rather than equilibrium should be the central organizing concept on which economic analysis is based. This methodological contribution emerged in the context of Kaldor's rethinking of the economics of long-run growth. Kaldor favoured the Veblen–Myrdal notion of cumulative causation as a vehicle for analysing growth, not least because it eschewed the conventional notion of equilibrium as a strong attractor defined and reached independently of the path taken towards it. Instead, models of cumulative causation provide a recursive analysis of growth as a self-reinforcing process, indelibly influenced by its own past history.

However, not all commentators have shared Kaldor's enthusiasm for analysing growth in terms of cumulative causation. If growth is inherently self-reinforcing, then this suggests that once 'initial conditions' are specified, and in the absence of unexplained shocks, so is the subsequent growth trajectory of the economy.[2] As Hargreaves Heap (1989, p. 142) argues, cumulative causation is, at its core, a model of historical continuity, not one of historical change. On this basis, Gordon (1991) has argued that models of cumulative causation display 'too much cumulation' in order for them to successfully explain the comparative historical growth record of capitalist economies – despite the conclusion of authors such as Amable (1993) that cumulative and divergent forces are of the greatest general relevance for the description of realized growth outcomes over the post-war period.

Building on Setterfield (1997a, 1997b), the purpose of this chapter is to carry forward the spirit of Kaldor's growth analysis and attendant methodological emphasis on history. Importance is attached to the presence of self-reinforcing, cumulative processes in macrodynamics, but the problem, inherent in models of cumulative causation, of there being 'too much cumulation', is avoided. This is achieved by *retaining* rather than dispensing with the notion of equilibrium, and therefore allowing for the existence of point attractors or 'centres of gravity' in the economy.[3] Furthermore, Kaldor's cumulative growth schema, central to which is a positive feedback from output growth to productivity growth, is treated as only one source of path dependency in the growth process; others, including sources of *negative* feedback from output growth to productivity growth, are also postulated.[4] What emerges from all this is ultimately an exercise in traverse analysis: specifically, a model of Kaldorian traverse. The spirit (if not the letter) of Kaldor's cumulative growth schema emerges as the predominant influence on growth in the medium run, but this cumulative causation is couched in the context of growth 'regimes' which may, themselves, be influenced by an economy's past growth trajectory. This results in a model in which medium-term growth – itself described as 'weakly' path dependent – affects the centre of gravity towards which the economy is tending, thus redefining the conditions and position of this centre of gravity and hence the economy's subsequent medium-term growth trajectory, and so on. Growth is thus characterized as a process of traverse towards path dependent, provisional equilibria in what is ultimately described as a model of *evolutionary hysteresis*.[5] It is argued that evolutionary hysteresis provides a better approximation of historical process than either equilibrium or cumulative causation, and thus provides a more satisfactory basis for modelling Kaldorian dynamics.

The remainder of the chapter is organized as follows. The next section discusses the potential of traverse analysis as a general method for all macrodynamic analysis. In the third section, a model of Kaldorian traverse is constructed, in which cumulative causation is 'nested' within an encompassing, evolutionary hysteretic vision of growth. The methodological significance of this analysis for Kaldorian macrodynamics is next discussed, while the final section offers some conclusions.

THE TRAVERSE AND MACRODYNAMIC ANALYSIS

As originally conceived by Hicks (1965), the traverse describes the passage of an economy between two steady states. More generally, following Henry and Lavoie (1997, p. 158) and Kriesler (1999, pp. 401–2), the traverse can be defined as the transition of an economic system between any two states, regardless of whether or not either of these states are equilibria. Traverse analyses usually take initial conditions as given, conjecture the end state of the traverse and are then concerned with the question as to how (if at all) it is possible to get 'there' from 'here' – that is, whether or not it is possible for the economy to effect the conjectured transition between beginning and end states, and if so, how. It is important to realize that this transition may not be possible at all – much depends on the precise sequence of adjustments that the economy must undertake over time in order to complete the conjectured transformation between states. What this means, of course, is that the economy's *realized* traverse path may lead it elsewhere, towards an 'end' or 'final' state (to the extent that such end or final states exist in any but the arbitrary sense of their being attained by some specific date in calendar time) that differs from the end state originally conjectured. In this sense, there is a distinct affinity between traverse analysis and the Robinsonian notion of historical time, in which events take place in a unidirectional sequence such that activities in the present are shaped and constrained by those undertaken in a given and immutable past, and will in turn shape and constrain behaviour in the future (Halevi and Kriesler, 1992, p. 225; Henry and Lavoie, 1997, p. 157; Kriesler, 1999, p. 402).[6]

According to Kriesler (1999, p. 401), 'the traverse is at the same time one of the most important concepts in economic theory, and also one of the most neglected'. It has failed to find its way into economics textbooks that are otherwise laden with Hicksian concepts and contributions (Henry and Lavoie, 1995, p. 157). Meanwhile, Bliss's (1987, p. 645) biography of Hicks dismisses *Capital and Growth*, in which Hicks first introduced the concept of the traverse, as being uninfluential because '. . . equilibrium theory and its sister economic dynamics had moved on a great deal since *Value and Capital* [and] Hicks . . . was no longer talking a language that most economic theorists found congenial'. And yet, any idiosyncracies of Hicks's original traverse analysis aside, no amount of 'moving on' can be allowed to obscure the central importance of the principle of the traverse for economic analysis – no matter how 'uncongenial' economic theorists might find the issues that it raises. As Setterfield (1997a, chapter 2) argues, no economic analysis can completely escape the need to consider the sequential adjustment processes that are the essence of traverse analysis. First, even if equilibria defined independently of the adjustment path taken towards them exist, it is necessary to account for how the economy might 'get into' these equilibria – if, indeed, it can – if they are to serve as useful descriptions of the realized configurations of the economy.[7] Second, consideration of adjustment processes raises the spectre of path dependence. Even equilibria that act as 'attractors' or 'centres of gravity' may be such that their conditions and hence positions are prone to revision in response to the sequential adjustments taken towards them. As such, rather than being an anachronism, the general notion of the traverse is (or should be) central to economic analysis, the subject matter of which is always ultimately concerned with adjustments through time. A central feature of this chapter, then, is that it takes the traverse seriously, positing the relevance of traverse analysis as a general methodology for all dynamic economic analysis.

A MODEL OF KALDORIAN TRAVERSE

A Stylized Model of Cumulative Causation

Following the work of Dixon and Thirlwall (1975) and McCombie and Thirlwall (1994), we begin by characterizing Kaldor's cumulative growth schema in terms of the following structural equations:

$$q_{jt} = r + \alpha_{jt} y_{jt-1}, \qquad \alpha_{jt} > 0 \tag{12.1}$$

$$p_{jt} = w_{jt} - q_{jt} \tag{12.2}$$

$$x_{jt} = \beta(p_{wt} - p_{jt}) + \gamma y_{wt}, \qquad \beta, \gamma > 0 \tag{12.3}$$

$$y_{jt} = \lambda x_{jt}, \qquad \lambda > 0 \tag{12.4}$$

where for any region j, q is the rate of productivity growth, r denotes exogenous influences on q, y is the rate of growth of output, p and w are the rates of price and wage inflation, respectively, and x is the rate of growth of exports. The variables p_w and y_w denote, respectively, price inflation and growth in the 'rest of the world', and t-subscripts denote time periods.[8]

Equations [12.1]–[12.4] capture the joint interaction between demand and supply that is typical of Kaldor's growth schema. Beginning with equation [12.1], output growth in the previous period impacts current productivity growth through the realization of dynamic increasing returns (the Verdoorn Law). Productivity growth then affects inflation, thanks to its negative impact on the growth of unit labour costs (equation [12.2]). These supply-side developments then impact the growth of aggregate demand in equation [12.3], in which export growth responds positively to any increase in the difference between foreign and domestic inflation. Finally, the rate of growth of demand is described as the proximate source of output growth in equation [12.4]. Hence the demand side will subsequently feed back to influence the supply side as demand and hence output growth (equation [12.4]) influence future productivity growth via the Verdoorn Law (equation [12.1]). The recursive interaction of these structural equations, in which productivity growth and demand-led output growth are mutually self-reinforcing, is the essence of Kaldor's cumulative growth schema.

In order to emphasize the self-reinforcing nature of growth outcomes in the model described above, we can substitute equations [12.3], [12.2] and then [12.1] into equation [12.4] to arrive at:

$$y_{jt} = \alpha_{jt} \lambda \beta y_{jt-1} + \lambda \beta (p_{wt} - w_{jt} + r) + \lambda \gamma y_{wt} \tag{12.5}$$

Assuming that conditions analogous to those in equations [12.1] and [12.2] are prevalent in the rest of the world, we can write:

$$q_{wt} = r + \alpha_w y_{wt-1} \tag{12.1a}$$

$$p_{wt} = w_{wt} - q_{wt} \tag{12.2a}$$

$$\Rightarrow \quad p_{wt} = w_{wt} - r - \alpha_w y_{wt-1} \tag{12.6}$$

Suppose we now assume that $w_{jt} = w_{wt}$ and $y_{wt} = y_{wt-1} = y_w$.[9] Given these assumptions, substitution of [12.6] into [12.5] yields:

$$y_{jt} = \alpha_{jt}\lambda\beta y_{jt-1} + \lambda(\gamma - \alpha_w\beta)y_w$$

or:

$$y_{jt} = \alpha_{jt}\eta y_{jt-1} + \theta y_w \tag{12.7}$$

where $\eta = \lambda\beta$ and $\theta = \lambda(\gamma - \alpha_w\beta)$. For all values of $t \geq 2$, equation [12.7] can, in turn, be rewritten as:

$$y_{jt} = \eta^t y_0 \cdot \prod_{i=1}^{t} \alpha_{ji} + \theta y_w \left[1 + \sum_{i=1}^{t-1}\left(\eta^i \cdot \prod_{k=0}^{i-1} \alpha_{jt-k}\right)\right] \tag{12.8}$$

where y_{j0} is the rate of growth in region j in some initial period.

Suppose we now assume that $\alpha_{jt} = \alpha_{j1}\ \forall t$, where α_{j1} represents the initial value of α_j. In other words, we assume that the Verdoorn coefficient in equation [12.1], which describes the ability of region j to capture dynamic increasing returns and hence productivity gains on the basis of any given rate of growth, remains constant.[10] Then equation [12.8] reduces to:

$$y_{jt} = (\eta\alpha_{j1})^t y_0 + \theta y_w \cdot \sum_{i=1}^{t} (\eta\alpha_{j1})^{i-1} \tag{12.9}$$

from which, assuming that $0 < \eta\alpha_{j1} < 1$,[11] it follows that:

$$\lim_{t\to\infty} y_{jt} = \frac{\theta y_w}{1 - \eta\alpha_{j1}} = y_j^* \tag{12.10}$$

Under these conditions, the evolution of the growth rate in region j would appear to be determined by a traditional equilibrium, defined and reached without reference to the path taken towards it. In some respects, this is a very un-Kaldorian result. In his descriptions of cumulative causation (see, for example, Kaldor, 1985, pp. 61–3), Kaldor emphasizes the lasting influence of initial growth outcomes on long-run growth rates in a system that does not gravitate towards an equilibrium defined independently of these initial conditions.[12] At this point, however, we can begin to introduce the first vestiges of traverse analysis in order to reconcile the model developed thus far with the principle of cumulative causation as described by Kaldor. According to the basic principles of traverse analysis, unless we begin from an initial position of equilibrium ($y_{j0} = y_j^*$), it is necessary to contemplate whether or not the latter can, in fact, be reached. Note, for example, that even if $0 < \eta\alpha_{j1} < 1$ so that the equilibrium in [12.10] exists and is (in principle) stable, it will not be possible to 'get into' this equilibrium if the speed of adjustment towards it is slow, relative to the speed at which the 'data' defining the equilibrium are, themselves, changing over time (Harcourt, 1981, p. 218; Fisher, 1983, p. 3; Cornwall, 1991, p. 107; Halevi and Kriesler, 1992, p. 229).

What all this means is that in the model developed above, there may exist an equilibrium such as that in [12.10] which influences the dynamics of the model (and hence the evolution of the growth rate) in its capacity as a point attractor. But this equilibrium need never be relevant as a description of the actual growth rate prevailing in the economy at any point in time. Instead, for any era during which the 'data' defining the expression in [12.10] are, indeed, constant, the actual rate of growth in any period t will be described by equation [12.9], in which initial conditions have precisely the self-reinforcing impact on subsequent growth outcomes accorded to them by Kaldor.[13] We thus have a model of 'weak' path-dependent growth, in which initial conditions, but no other feature of the economy's growth trajectory, influence subsequent growth outcomes in a purely self-reinforcing manner.[14] This demonstrates that a disequilibrium or traverse interpretation of the Dixon–Thirlwall model captures the *spirit* of Kaldor's cumulative growth schema – by restoring initial conditions to their role as a self-reinforcing determinant of subsequent growth outcomes – if not the *letter* of this schema (since the model does allow for the existence of a growth equilibrium defined independently of initial conditions, and for this equilibrium to impact on the evolution of realized growth outcomes in its capacity as an attractor).

Technical Progress and Growth: Positive and Negative Feedbacks

In the previous section, in order to justify a disequilibrium or traverse interpretation of the Dixon–Thirlwall model as an approximation of Kaldor's cumulative growth schema, we alluded to the notion that the 'data' defining the position of an equilibrium need not be immutable, and that structural changes in these conditions of equilibrium may accompany disequilibrium growth. We now turn to consider this possibility more explicitly, in an effort to show how and to what effect such structural change may, in fact, be *endemic* to the growth process.

The traverse path described in equation [12.9] may be accompanied by various, qualitatively different, types of structural change. One example is institutional change – that is, changes in conventions, norms, rules, etc., and hence the internal structure of and relationships between the organizations and individuals of which these institutions are constituent parts. Other examples include technological change and changes in the composition of demand and hence output. Of these sources of structural change, one – technological change – is already an important feature of the model developed in the previous section. Equation [12.1], the Verdoorn law, models productivity growth as an increasing function of past output growth, on the basis that the latter induces technological progress. This arises through such channels as learning-by-doing and, given that firms face indivisibilities in the capital stock and assuming that they are demand-constrained and form expectations of future market expansion that are influenced by past realized growth, the adoption of more capital-intensive techniques of production.[15]

However, while the Verdoorn law as described thus far embodies important sources of positive feedback from output growth to technological progress, it may be useful to think of this law itself as being subject to growth-induced structural change. Recall that α_{jt} – the Verdoorn coefficient – measures the ability of an economy to realize productivity gains on the basis of any given rate of growth. It may be the case that α_{jt} itself is the subject of feedback effects in the course of growth. This would cause the Verdoorn law to experience structural change over time, giving rise to a discrete succession of historically contingent 'productivity regimes' which condition and, in turn, are conditioned by, the growth rate.[16] For example, as growth yields an ever-larger surplus over subsistence needs and ever-increasing specialization in the process of production, so processes associated with learning may become more formally organized, thus raising the value of α_{jt}. This would provide another example of positive feedback from output growth to productivity growth, operating this time, however, not through a given productivity regime, but through the transformation of the productivity regime itself.

Such positive feedback would, of course, only serve to enhance the cumulative growth dynamics already inherent in Kaldor's growth schema. However, the productivity regime may also be subject to *negative* feedback: faster growth in the past may ultimately *impair* the ability of a region to realize induced technological progress. One way in which this can occur is if fast growth causes a region to become 'locked-in' to a particular technological base that becomes difficult to transform in the pursuit of subsequent technological progress.

Lock-in occurs when a system gets stuck in a 'rut' or 'groove' from which it is subsequently difficult to deviate, even if change is, in principle, demonstrably desirable (see, for example, Arthur, 1994). This can happen if the extent to which an activity (such as accumulating specific types of fixed capital) has been practised in the past makes it difficult to change behaviour in the present, by virtue of the prohibitive costs associated with change and/or difficulties associated with coordinating change in an environment of decentralized decision making. In the case of embodied technological progress, such dependence of current decisions on those made in the past can arise because of *interrelatedness* – interconnections between components of the production process (including plant, equipment, human capital and organizational structures) that proliferate as the scale of economic activity increases (Frankel, 1955).[17] Interrelatedness demands that capital accumulated in the present conform to technical and social standards inherited from the past, unless more radical (non-marginal) changes in the production process are to be contemplated.[18] Lock-in results if interrelatedness has advanced to such a degree that these non-marginal changes appear infeasible, with the result that technological progress is inhibited.

The problems of interrelatedness and lock-in suggest a potential source of negative feedback from output growth to a region's productivity regime that would effect structural change in the model developed earlier. This, in turn, would alter the conditions and hence position of the region's growth equilibrium (and hence the subsequent evolution of its growth rate) – all as a result of the region's having previously followed a particular traverse path towards its former equilibrium position. To see this, consider the example of a region that has experienced a virtuous circle of self-reinforcing high growth. In equation [12.9], this would be represented by a 'high' initial rate of growth ($y_{j0} > y_j^* = y_w$) fostering 'high' growth rates in all subsequent periods ($y_{jt} > y_j^* = y_w \; \forall t > 0$, *ceteris paribus*).[19] Now it is self-evident that:

$$Y_{jt} = Y(Y_{j0}; y_{j1}, \ldots, y_{jt}), \qquad Y'_Y, Y'_y > 0 \qquad [12.11]$$

where Y denotes the level of output. In view of what has just been said about interrelatedness and lock-in, however, equation [12.11] may be of some significance for a virtuous circle region. This is because it follows from [12.11] that as the result of a virtuous circle, Y_{jn} in any period $t = n$ will be higher than it would otherwise have been in the absence of a virtuous circle (that is, had we observed $y_{j0} \leq y_j^*$). Furthermore, following Frankel (1955), we have:

$$i_{jt} = i(Y_{jt}), \qquad i' > 0 \qquad [12.12]$$

where i denotes the level of interrelatedness. We can also write:

$$\kappa_{jt} = \kappa(i_{jt}), \qquad \kappa' > 0 \qquad [12.13]$$

where κ denotes the costs – including direct costs of scrapping and removal, and indirect costs associated with the writing-down or writing-off of existing assets – associated solely with the act of *changing* components of the production process. Now consider a single regional decision maker contemplating investment in a new component that embodies technological progress when compared to similar components of an earlier vintage. Suppose that:

$$\pi_A = \sum_{i=n}^{n+T} (R_{Ai} - C_{Ai}) \cdot (1+r)^{-i} > \sum_{i=n}^{n+T} (R_{Bi} - C_{Bi}) \cdot (1+r)^{-1} = \pi_B \qquad [12.14]$$

where R represents revenues, C total costs, π denotes profit flows, T is the decision maker's time horizon and r its rate of time preference, and A and B denote, respectively, the new component of the production process and the old component that it is designed to replace. Considered in isolation, then, the new component is unambiguously more profitable.[20] However, the spectre of interrelatedness means that other changes to the production process may be required in order to accommodate the new component, which thus begs the question as to whether:

$$\pi_A - \kappa_{jn} \gtreqless \pi_B \qquad [12.15]$$

Suppose, in fact, that $Y_{jn} \geq Y_{jL}$, so that $i_{nj} \geq i_{jL}$ and hence $\kappa_{jn} \geq \kappa_{jL}$, where κ_{jL} is the minimum value of κ_j necessary to satisfy the inequality:

$$\pi_A - \kappa_{jn} < \pi_B \qquad [12.16]$$

If, by period n, region j's virtuous circle of growth has raised its level of development to the point where $Y_{jn} \geq Y_{jL}$, then the flow of induced technological progress on which this virtuous circle is based will be adversely affected. By virtue of the proliferation of interrelatedness, the inequality in [12.16] suggests that region j will be locked-in to the inferior technology inherent in component B by virtue of it being prohibitively costly to make the variety of changes within an interrelated production process necessary to accommodate component A. This impact of interrelatedness and lock-in on the productivity regime of region j can be captured by the expression:

$$\alpha_{jt} = \alpha(\kappa_{jt}) = \begin{cases} \phi\alpha_{jt-1} & \text{if} \quad \kappa_{jt} \geq \kappa_{jL} > \kappa_{jt-1} \\ \alpha_{jt-1} & \text{otherwise} \end{cases} \qquad [12.17]$$

where $0 < \phi < 1$ is a constant that captures the impairment of region j's ability to realize induced technological progress brought about by lock-in. In the situation that we are contemplating, equation [12.17] implies that:[21]

$$\alpha_{jt} = \alpha_{j1} \quad \forall t = 1, \ldots, n-1$$

$$\alpha_{jt} = \phi\alpha_{j1} \quad \forall t \geq n$$

The discontinuous adjustments in the Verdoorn coefficient, α_j, described here mirror the discontinuous impact of interrelatedness on the productivity regime of region j, which turns on the threshold or boundary condition captured by κ_{jL}.

All that now remains is to spell out the implications of the change in productivity regime modelled above for the evolution of the growth rate in region j. Recall that, in general, the evolution of the growth rate is given by:

$$y_{jt} = \eta^t y_0 \cdot \prod_{i=1}^{t} \alpha_{ji} + \theta y_w \left[1 + \sum_{i=1}^{t-1} \left(\eta^i \cdot \prod_{k=0}^{i-1} \alpha_{jt-k} \right) \right] \qquad [12.8]$$

Given the solution to [12.17] described above, for all $t \geq n$, equation [12.8] can be evaluated as:

$$y_{jt} = \eta^t \alpha_{j1}^{n-1} (\phi\alpha_{j1})^{t-n+1} \cdot y_{j0}$$
$$+ \theta y_w \cdot \left[\sum_{i=n-1}^{t} (\eta\phi\alpha_{j1})^{t-i} + (\eta\phi\alpha_{j1})^{t-n+1} \cdot \sum_{k=1}^{n-1} (\eta\alpha_{j1})^k \right]$$

or:

$$y_{jt} = \phi^{t-n+1} (\eta\alpha_{j1})^t \cdot y_{j0}$$
$$+ \theta y_w \cdot \left[\sum_{i=n-1}^{t} (\eta\phi\alpha_{j1})^{t-i} + \phi^{t-n+1} \cdot \sum_{k=1}^{n-1} (\eta\alpha_{j1})^{k+(t-n+1)} \right] \qquad [12.18]$$

Furthermore, note that it follows from [12.18] that:

$$\lim_{t\to\infty} y_{jt} = \frac{\theta y_w}{1 - \eta\phi\alpha_{j1}} = y_j^{**} \qquad [12.19]$$

Comparison of equations [12.18] and [12.19] with equations [12.9] and [12.10] (which describe the benchmark case where $\alpha_{jt} = \alpha_{j1}\ \forall t$) reveals how the evolution of the growth rate and the position of the equilibrium implicit in the model are affected by the change in region *j*'s productivity regime that is postulated to have arisen as a consequence of its prior virtuous circle. Specifically, since $0 < \phi < 1$ by hypothesis, it is clear on inspection that the lock-in induced decay in region *j*'s productivity regime adversely affects the region's medium-and long-run growth rates. Indeed, region *j*'s declining growth fortunes will also have an important qualitative impact on its relative growth performance. Recall that region *j* was initially identified as experiencing a virtuous circle of growth, because $y_{j0} > y_j^* = y_w$. Other things being equal, this implied $y_{jt} > y_w$ for all finite values of *t*. However, the structural changes in region *j*'s productivity regime described above mean that the limit value of the region's growth rate is now given by $y_j^{**} < y_j^* = y_w$. In its capacity as an attractor, and in the absence of further, growth-enhancing, structural changes induced by the traverse towards this attractor in the intervening period, y_j^{**} will eventually draw the value of y_t below $y_j^* = y_w$ in some period $n + s$.[22] As a result, region *j* will find itself transformed from a growth leader into a growth laggard, its original virtuous circle of relatively high growth now replaced with a vicious circle of self-reinforcing slow growth ($y_{jt} < y_w \ \forall t \geq n + s$). Note, then, that the model developed here solves the 'too much cumulation' problem associated with Kaldor's growth schema, as identified earlier. It retains the essential self-reinforcing components of this schema, but places them in the context of structural 'regimes' that are themselves endogenous to a region's past growth history. This allows for the possibility that a period of self-reinforcing fast or slow growth may induce structural change in the regime within which it is contextualized, thus altering a region's relative growth performance.

METHODOLOGICAL CONSIDERATIONS

As emphasized above, the central result of the model developed in this chapter is that a virtuous circle of self-reinforcing growth need not be indefinitely self-perpetuating. As such, the model avoids the 'too much cumulation' problem associated with Kaldor's original growth schema without eschewing Kaldor's central insights regarding positive feedback and cumulative causation in the growth process. What remains is for us to emphasize the *methodological* aspects of this exercise and their lessons for Kaldorian macrodynamic analysis.

On the Role of the Traverse in Macrodynamic Analysis

Kriesler (1999, pp. 402–4) identifies three approaches to the role of the traverse in economics, two of which suggest that the traverse matters. First, he identifies a 'life is a traverse' approach in the works of Kalecki, Robinson and Lowe. According to this view, the economy is never in equilibrium and does not 'tend towards' equilibrium – so that dynamic analysis without reference to equilibrium is of the 'utmost analytical value' (p. 403). This position is reflected in Kalecki's claim that 'the long-run trend is but a slowly changing component of a chain of short-period situations; it has no independent identity' (Kalecki, 1971, p. 165). The fact that the long-run trend (read 'equilibrium') has no identity independent of the series of short-run outcomes of which it is ultimately just an average means that it (long-run equilibrium) is not something 'out there', acting as a centre of gravity towards which the economy inexorably 'tends'. Nor is it a state that the economy can ever usefully be described as having 'got into'. In this situation, *non*-equilibrium analysis is all that remains.

Kriesler contrasts this 'life is a traverse' approach with an 'equilibrium and traverse' position, in which the concept of equilibrium is retained, but the need to study the path towards equilibrium is taken seriously. This approach includes models of hysteresis in which the path towards equilibrium affects the conditions and hence position of equilibrium, so that the final equilibrium achieved is path dependent. A wide range of models fit into this category, including *non-tâtonnement* general equilibrium models (Fisher, 1983) and models that have a Kalecki–Robinson pedigree (Lavoie, 1996).

At first sight, the model of Kaldorian traverse developed above seems to fit squarely into the second of these approaches. A steady-state growth equilibrium is postulated as existing at any point in time, and is accredited with the role of a weak attractor in the system's dynamics.[23]

Further reflection reveals that this categorization may not be compelling, however. This is because the conditions necessary for the existence and stability of equilibrium in the model developed above are inessential. They can be dispensed with, and the model will continue to behave as described earlier (periods of cumulative causation in the medium term being punctuated by structural changes, themselves induced by past growth outcomes, in the long term), but without equilibrium existing or acting as a centre of gravity.[24] What this draws to attention is that in the model of Kaldorian traverse, equilibrium is being used as a reference point or organizing concept – it is not essential to the vision of macrodynamics that the model expounds. Instead, equilibrium plays a role similar to that of the point of effective demand in Keynes's *General Theory* (Kregel, 1976; Setterfield, 1997c). This, in turn, suggests that the distinction between the 'life is a traverse' and 'equilibrium and traverse' approaches to the role of the traverse, although useful for taxonomic purposes, may not always involve the concrete methodological differences with respect to the role of equilibrium that it appears to.

From Cumulative Causation to Evolutionary Hysteresis

The model developed above suggests that Kaldorian analysis, in its pursuit of a historical theory of growth, need not abandon the notion of equilibrium *per se*. Cumulative causation can be represented as a traverse path within a system that has a 'centre of gravity' acting as a weak attractor, and in which the traverse path itself affects the conditions and hence the position of this attractor.

Note that this latter property imbues the model with the property of strong path dependence (involving structural change within a model in response to its prior trajectory) or *hysteresis*.[25] Furthermore, this hysteresis is ultimately both endogenous and non-deterministic. It is properly conceived as non-deterministic since lock-in is not inevitable. This is not so much because a region may not reach the critical level of development Y_{jL} before being required to effect non-marginal changes in the production process (although this is quite possible), but because Y_{jL} itself is partly a product of factors such as decision makers' time horizons and rates of time preference, and hence ultimately the nature of *entrepreneurship* within a region.[26] If entrepreneurial activity is best conceived as an open rather than a foreclosed and determinate process, then the hysteretic change we are currently contemplating is necessarily non-deterministic. It will arise over time as an *emergent property* of the system – that is, as an outcome that cannot be reduced to foreclosed explanation in terms of the more 'primitive' causes that are purported to have brought it about.[27] This is not a denial of cause and effect relationships in growth analysis. Instead, what it effectively means is that the same regional decision maker confronted with the same non-marginal change in the production process at the same level of development Y_n may not make uniform choices in a hypothetical series of repeated trials. This is ultimately an assertion that growth and development are not closed, mechanical processes but rather open, social processes involving *creative* or *effective choice* – that is, an ability on the part of decision makers to always have acted differently.[28]

That hysteretic change in the model of Kaldorian traverse is also endogenous is obvious from the fact that the regimes within which cumulative causation occurs are prone to either reinforcement or decay in response to positive and/or negative feedbacks arising from the legacy of the growth outcomes associated with the process of cumulative causation itself. In other words, structural change is modelled as an intrinsic feature of the very adjustments of the economic system through time, rather than being the product of extraneous shocks.

A process may be defined as evolutionary if it is characterized by endogenously generated structural change involving novelty.[29] Given this definition, and in view of what has been said above, the model of Kaldorian traverse may be described as displaying *evolutionary hysteresis* – that is, strong path dependence arising from endogenous but non-deterministic structural change.

In sum, the model developed in this chapter reinterprets Kaldor's cumulative growth schema as a traverse path within a system that has a centre of gravity, while simultaneously extending traditional Kaldorian analysis by interpreting this weak attractor (and hence, to an extent, the traverse path itself) as the product of a growth 'regime' which is historically specific and may be affected by the traverse path.[30] Note that this extension resolves the tension identified earlier, between the model of Kaldorian traverse and the *letter* (as opposed to just the spirit) of Kaldor's growth schema. This is because the attractor in the model is now, itself, a historical construct. It is not independent of the path that the economy takes towards it in the manner in which it was first made to appear. What all this suggests is that in Kaldorian growth analysis, importance ultimately attaches not to the non-existence of equilibria, but to the absence of the mechanical stability properties that are conventionally associated with these equilibria. Kaldorians can thus appeal to the traverse method, coupled with the notion of evolutionary hysteresis, in order to strike a middle ground between abandoning the concept of equilibrium (which Kaldor's (1972) claims about the 'irrelevance of equilibrium economics' may appear, upon first sight, to demand) and acceptance of the economy as being essentially ahistorical. Ultimately, it is traditional equilibrium or equilibrist methodology, which conceives economic outcomes as equilibria defined and reached independently of the path taken towards them, rather than the notion of equilibrium *per se* that Kaldorians and other researchers interested in the historical dynamics of capitalism must abandon.[31] A central purpose of the model developed in this chapter has been to suggest how macrodynamic analysis can proceed in such non-equilibrist terms.

CONCLUSIONS

This chapter both reinterprets and extends Kaldorian growth analysis, casting Kaldor's cumulative growth schema as a process of traverse towards a weak point attractor, the conditions and hence position of which can be altered by the traverse path itself. What emerges is a model in which growth is subject to evolutionary hysteresis. Self-reinforcing growth outcomes, the product of cumulative causation, are the norm in the medium term. But this self-reinforcing growth can affect the very 'regime' of which it is, in part, a product, and which also defines the (unrealized) equilibrium of the system. An episode of cumulative, non-equilibrium growth in the medium term can, therefore, affect the conditions and hence the position of the system's equilibrium which, in its capacity as a weak attractor, will then draw the economy onto a new medium-term growth path that may be both quantitatively and qualitatively different from its predecessor. The economy is thus in a state of permanent traverse towards provisional, path-dependent equilibria, its evolution characterized by a series of transitions between different growth regimes, each of which supports a medium-term episode of cumulative causation manifesting itself (in comparative terms) as either a vicious or a virtuous circle.

The importance of this analysis is twofold. First, at a theoretical level, by nesting Kaldor's cumulative growth schema as a subset of the feedbacks that occur in the course of growth, the evolutionary hysteretic growth schema developed above permits an appreciation of the growth process as being generally subject to self-reinforcing tendencies (which, as noted by studies such as Amable (1993), appears to be empirically appropriate), while simultaneously avoiding the 'too much cumulation' problem that authors such as Gordon (1991) identify. Second, at a methodological level, the model developed above reconciles the belief that growth and development are essentially historical processes (and that they should therefore be analysed as such) with the concept of equilibrium. This is done by harnessing the dynamic properties of equilibrium as a point attractor, without conceiving the latter as a determinate outcome that is defined and reached independently of the path taken towards it. A central feature of this framework is its treatment of the traverse as a general property of economic life. This, coupled with the notion of evolutionary hysteresis, is suggestive of a general approach to macrodynamics that is consistent with Kaldor's own desire to use history as the central organizing concept in economic analysis.

NOTES

1. See, for example, Kaldor (1972, 1985).
2. See also the discussion of methodological aspects of Kaldorian growth modelling in McCombie and Robert's chapter in this volume.
3. This may appear to flatly contradict Kaldor's own preferred methodology, as briefly described above. See, however, Thirlwall (1987), Setterfield (1998a) and the discussion below.
4. These negative feedbacks, which are associated with the problem of lock-in along a particular cumulative growth path, are more explicitly modelled than in the earlier papers cited above.
5. See Chick and Caserta (1997) on the notion of provisional equilibrium, and Setterfield (1997c) on the related concept of conditional equilibrium.
6. See, for example, Setterfield (1995) for discussion of Robinson on historical time.
7. This even applies to models based on strong form rational expectations, in which the economy appears to jump instantaneously from one equilibrium state to another. These models need to explain where knowledge of the 'true model' comes from. They usually posit learning in order to do so – something that is, of course, a type of adjustment process.
8. We assume that $y_{it} > 0\ \forall t, i = j, w$, based on the stylized facts of long-run growth in advanced capitalist economies.
9. The relative merits of these assumptions are discussed in greater detail in Setterfield (1997a, p. 369). The first assumption, which essentially claims that wage relativities are constant across regions, is one of Kaldor's stylized facts of growth.

10. The potential importance of treating α_j as non-constant over time will become clear in the following section.
11. According to Dixon and Thirlwall (1978), this assumption is consistent with the stylized facts concerning the size of the coefficients α, λ and β.
12. In fact, it is far from obvious that there is any place at all for equilibrium in Kaldor's growth schema.
13. It is straightforward to verify that $\partial y_{jt}/\partial y_{j0} = (\eta\alpha_{j1})^t > 0\ \forall t$ in [12.9], since $\eta\alpha_{j1} > 0$ by hypothesis.
14. Weak path dependence, in which initial conditions influence subsequent outcomes but without affecting the *structure* (or data) of a system (as, for example, in conventional models of multiple equilibrium), can be contrasted with strong path dependence or hysteresis, in which the adjustment path of a system does affect its structure (and hence its subsequent outcomes). We return to this distinction below – see also Halevi and Kriesler (1992, p. 228).
15. For further discussion of the channels through which these dynamic increasing returns accrue, see Boyer and Petit (1991) and Setterfield (1997a, chapter 3).
16. That this succession is discrete implies that each productivity regime – captured by a specific value of $\alpha_{jt}\ \forall t = 1, \ldots, n$, where the value of n is free to vary between regimes – is relatively enduring and subject only to discontinuous change. While this is, in general, an assumption, it is certainly justified in the formal example of a regime change modelled below. See also the chapter by Setterfield and Cornwall in this volume.
17. These interconnections may proliferate both within and between productive units, including, of course, those under different ownership.
18. That these 'common standards' are both technical *and* social in nature is due to the fact that interrelatedness as described above involves not just physical and human capital (which may be conceived in purely technical terms), but also the organizational structures within which productive activity occurs, and in which the roles of and relationships between a firm's workers, managers and owners are manifest. For example, Fordism is characterized not just by dedicated assembly line capital but also by specific, hierarchical organizational structures that define the location of knowledge about and hence control over the production process within the enterprise (see, for example, Lazonick, 1990).
19. We assume that $y_j^* = y_w$ in order to simplify both the initial identification of region j as a virtuous circle region, and subsequent discussion of the region's relative growth rate (on which, see below). Note, however, that we must have $y_j^* \geq y_w$ in order to avoid difficulties in interpreting the model developed earlier in Kaldorian terms, since otherwise, we will observe $y_{j0} > y_w$ initially but $y_{jt} < y_w$ for sufficiently large *t ceteris paribus*, which would not allows us to unambiguously interpret region j's initial disequilibrium growth path as a virtuous circle of sustained relatively high growth. This restriction points to an obvious limitation of the model developed earlier as an interpretation of Kaldor's cumulative growth schema.
20. Strictly speaking, of course, these are *expected* profitability comparisons. Here and in what follows, we assume a uniform state of long-run expectations in order to abstract from any potential differences in the confidence of the decision maker in its forecasts of the returns to different assets. This allows us to focus solely on the impact of interrelatedness and lock-in on the investment decision.
21. Note that since $y_{jt} > 0$ by hypothesis, Y_{jt} and hence i_{jt} and κ_{jt} are strictly increasing in t. Only in period n, then, will we observe $\kappa_{jt} \geq \kappa_{jL} > \kappa_{jt-1}$. Note that this also implies that once it is locked-in to the technology inherent in component B, region j will *remain* locked-in – even if, as discussed below, its growth performance is adversely affected. If absolute decline were possible, however, even – in a less aggregative setting – in certain key industries affected by lock-in, then the problem posed above need not persist indefinitely. This does not, of course, mean that the region's subsequent growth and development will necessarily benefit from such absolute decline, owing to the many other effects on the region, which lie beyond the scope of this chapter, that the latter may have.

    Note also that changes in the value of α_j other than those resulting from lock-in as described above may, of course, occur after period $t = n$. We abstract from these here, however, in order to focus on the impact on region j of a single episode of lock-in, *ceertis paribus*.

22. The precise value of s will depend on the speed of adjustment towards y_j^{**}, something which will, of course, vary directly with the size of ϕ.
23. The equilibrium in the model developed above is a weak attractor in the sense that it affects the dynamic adjustment path of the system, without the latter ever 'getting into' equilibrium.
    The fact that it never 'gets into' a position of equilibrium may appear to distinguish the model of Kaldorian traverse from 'equilibrium and traverse' models. But in truth, this may be a common property of models of hysteresis, which can require restrictive conditions if they are to eventually converge to a (path dependent) equilibrium (see, for example, Fisher, 1983). Whether or not sufficient attention is generally paid to these problems of convergence in the 'equilibrium and traverse' approach is, however, a different matter.
24. For example, it can be assumed that $\eta\alpha_{jt} > 1$, so that no (positive) equilibrium exists, and the growth rate increases over time in the course of any episode of cumulative causation.
25. On the central role of structural change in the process of hysteresis, see Amable et al. (1995) and Setterfield (1998b).
26. The lock in threshold, Y_{jL}, is also endogenous to the technique of production employed. See Setterfield (2001, p. 110).
27. The term 'emergence' is usually used to denote a situation in which a system possesses properties that cannot be inferred from the properties of its constituent parts at a lower level of aggregation. The term is used here, however, in a dynamic context to denote a situation in which there are properties of a period/event in historical time that cannot be inferred from the properties of earlier periods/events that, in the context of path dependence, are understood to have influenced its constitution. Note also that the term is being used in a manner that connotes an absence of foreclosure in this dynamic process.
28. Note that this does not mean that the model degenerates into nihilism. In practice – that is, in concrete historical circumstances – decision makers can be expected to develop conventions to guide behaviour in the open environment we are not contemplating. These conventions lend *conditional closure* to the macroeconomic system, the conditionality arising from the fact that system closure is historically specific and contingent on the reproduction of conventions which are, themselves, ultimately arbitrary and subject to effective choice. Part of the art of macrodynamic analysis is thus the identification of relatively enduring institutions that define conditionally closed macroeconomic epochs, which in turn permit concrete historical explanation and even (within a particular epoch) conditional prediction. See Setterfield (1997c).
29. This does not mean that change within an evolutionary system cannot arise from without – only that exogenous events are not the source of *all* change.
30. The traverse path is only partly determined by the structure of the growth regime because, of course, it also depends on the rate of growth achieved in the initial period.
31. See also Setterfield (1997c). This view is arguably compatible with Kaldor's own on the subject (see, for example, Thirlwall (1987, p. 316; 1991, p. 41) and Setterfield (1998a)).

REFERENCES

Amable, B. (1993) 'Catch-up and convergence: a model of cumulative growth,' *International Review of Applied Economics*, 7, 1–25.

Amable, B. et al. (1995) 'Hysteresis revisited: a methodological approach,' in R. Cross (ed.) *The Natural Rate of Unemployment: Reflections on 25 Years of the Hypothesis*, Cambridge, Cambridge University Press, 153–80.

Arthur, W.B. (1994) *Increasing Returns and Path Dependence in the Economy*, Ann Arbor, University of Michigan Press.

Bliss, C. (1987) 'Hicks, John Richard (born 1904),' in J. Eatwell, M. Milgate and P. Newman (eds) *The New Palgrave: A Dictionary of Economics*, London, Macmillan, 641–6.

Boyer, R. and P. Petit (1991) 'Kaldor's growth theories: past, present and prospects for the future,' in E.J. Nell and W. Semmler (eds) *op. cit.*, 485–517.
Chick, V. and M. Caserta (1997) 'Provisional equilibrium in macroeconomic theory,' in P. Arestis, G. Palma and M. Sawyer (eds) *Markets, Unemployment and Economic Policy: Essays in Honour of Geoff Harcourt*, vol. II, London, Routledge.
Cornwall, J. (1991) 'Prospects for unemployment in the 1990s with hysteresis,' in J. Cornwall (ed.) *The Capitalist Economies: Prospects for the 1990s*, Aldershot, Edward Elgar, 107–24.
Dixon, R. and A.P. Thirlwall (1975) 'A model of regional growth rate differences along Kaldorian lines,' *Oxford Economic Papers*, 27, 201–14.
Dixon, R. and A.P. Thirlwall (1978) 'Growth rate stability in the Kaldorian regional model,' *Scottish Journal of Political Economy*, 25, 97–9.
Fisher, F.M. (1983) *Disequilibrium Foundations of Equilibrium Economics*, Cambridge, Cambridge University Press.
Frankel, M. (1955) 'Obsolescence and technological change in a maturing economy,' *American Economic Review*, 45, 296–319.
Gordon, D. (1991) 'Kaldor's macro system: too much cumulation, too few contradictions,' in Nell, E.J. and W. Semmler (eds) *op. cit.*, 518–48.
Halevi, J. and P. Kriesler (1992) 'An introduction to the traverse in economic theory,' in J. Halevi, D. Laibman and E.J. Nell (eds) *Beyond the Steady State: A Revival of Growth Theory*, New York, St. Martin's Press, 225–34.
Harcourt, G.C. (1981) 'Marshall, Sraffa and Keynes: incompatible bedfellows?' reprinted in P. Kerr (ed.) (1982) *The Social Science Imperialists: Selected Essays of G.C. Harcourt*, London, Routledge, 205–21.
Hargreaves Heap, S.P. (1989) *Rationality in Economics*, Oxford, Basil Blackwell.
Henry, J. and M. Lavoie (1997) 'The Hicksian traverse as a process of reproportioning: some structural dynamics,' *Structural Change and Economic Dynamics*, 8, 157–75
Hicks, J.R. (1965) *Capital and Growth*, Oxford, Oxford University Press.
Kaldor, N. (1972) 'The irrelevance of equilibrium economics,' *The Economic Journal*, 82, 1237–55.
Kaldor, N. (1985) *Economics Without Equilibrium*, Cardiff, University College of Cardiff Press.
Kalecki, M. (1971) *Selected Essays on the Dynamics of the Capitalist Economy*, Cambridge, Cambridge University Press.
Kregel, J. (1976) 'Economic methodology in the face of uncertainty: The modelling methods of Keynes and the post-Keynesians,' *Economic Journal*, 86, 209-25.
Kriesler, P. (1999) 'Harcourt, Hicks and Lowe: incompatible bedfellows?' in C. Sardoni and P. Kriesler (eds) *Themes in Political Economy: Essays in Honour of Geoff Harcourt*, London, Routledge, 400–17.
Lavoie, M. (1996) 'Traverse, hysteresis and normal rates of capacity utilization in Kaleckian models of growth and distribution,' *Review of Radical Political Economics*, 28, 113–47.
Lazonick, W. (1990) *Competitive Advantage on the Shopfloor*, Cambridge, MA, Harvard University Press.
McCombie, J.S.L. and A.P. Thirlwall (1994) *Economic Growth and the Balance of Payments Constraint*, London, Macmillan.
Nell, E.J. and W. Semmler (eds) (1991) *Nicholas Kaldor and Mainstream Economics: Confrontation or Convergence?* New York, St. Martin's Press.
Setterfield, M.A. (1995) 'Historical time and economic theory,' *Review of Political Economy*, 7, 1–27.

Setterfield, M.A. (1997a) *Rapid Growth and Relative Decline: Modelling Macroeconomic Dynamics with Hysteresis*, London, Macmillan.

Setterfield, M.A. (1997b) 'History versus equilibrium and the theory of economic growth,' *Cambridge Journal of Economics*, 21, 365–78.

Setterfield, M.A. (1997c) 'Should economists dispense with the notion of equilibrium?' *Journal of Post Keynesian Economics*, 20, 47–76.

Setterfield, M.A. (1998a) 'History versus equilibrium: Nicholas Kaldor on historical time and economic theory,' *Cambridge Journal of Economics*, 22, 521–37.

Setterfield, M.A. (1998b) 'Adjustment asymmetries and hysteresis in simple dynamic models,' *The Manchester School*, 66, 283–301.

Setterfield, M.A. (2001) 'Cumulative causation, interrelatedness and the theory of economic growth: a reply to Argyrous and Toner,' *Cambridge Journal of Economics*, 25, 107–12.

Thirlwall, A.P. (1987) *Nicholas Kaldor*, Brighton, Wheatsheaf.

Thirlwall, A.P. (1991) 'Nicholas Kaldor, 1908–86,' in E.J. Nell and W. Semmler (eds) *op. cit.*, 13–47.

PART FIVE

Structural Change and Demand-led Growth

13. Endogenous demand in the theory of transformational growth

George Argyrous

INTRODUCTION

Neoclassical economics takes as given the tastes and preferences of consumers, and seeks to determine the set of relative prices that will reconcile these given tastes and preferences with the limited resources and technological capacity available to satisfy them. At the micro-level, demand is exogenous since the tastes and preferences of consumers are given from the outset. At the macro-level, the sum of these preferences – aggregate consumer demand – adjusts passively to changes in prices at the micro-level, so that aggregate demand equals aggregate supply. The focus is thereby shifted onto aggregate supply and its components, as in both the Solow growth model and the neoclassical endogenous growth theory. Demand is essentially exogenous.

Post-Keynesian theory, on the other hand, treats aggregate effective demand as a variable that determines the growth part of the economy. Yet within the post-Keynesian literature there remains a lacuna in the explanation of effective demand: what determines its evolution? This is particularly worrisome given the often-stated desire to use history rather than equilibrium as the methodological guidepost for analysis. Despite this desire, a historically based theory of the growth of markets has not been fully developed.

The theory of transformational growth (TG), on the other hand, provides such a historically based theory of the growth of demand. Moreover, the forces it identifies to explain the growth of demand are endogenous to the growth process itself. TG identifies feedback loops between the growth of individual markets and aggregate expansion in general, and these feedbacks provide an endogenous theory of qualitative change; hence the adjective in the term 'transformational growth'. The natural tendency of the system is change and development.[1]

The theory of TG juxtaposes two distinct periods of capitalist development. The first period, which characterized the pre-First World War era, is a system in which craft technology was the dominant method of production. The second period, corresponding with the post-Second World War era, features mass production technology, or what has elsewhere been termed a Fordist regime. These are very much idealized types; mass production technology was evident in some industries during the nineteenth century, and similarly craft technology persisted beyond the end of the Second World War. The dominance of one technology over the other in each period is nevertheless clear.

This chapter discusses the way in which the growth of demand is endogenous to the system itself, and that this endogenous process is an essential element in explaining the transition from craft to mass production. Market expansion is inherently endogenous: supply and demand do not seek an equilibrium, but rather induce feedback effects on each other resulting in perpetual change.

THE EMERGENCE OF WAGE LABOUR AND THE ORIGINS OF MASS MARKETS

The theory of TG emphasizes the role of mass production technology in altering the fundamental operations of a capitalist economy (Nell, 1998b). Of equal importance, though, is the rise of mass markets that make such a technology viable. TG therefore also seeks to explain the rise of mass markets and the consumer behaviour that underpins them. In particular, the theory of TG argues that the rise of mass markets is a historical process involving complex changes in the way household production and consumption are related to industrial production.

Three distinct processes are involved in the rise of mass markets; each of varying importance at different stages of development. The first is the formation of an industrial working class that purchases subsistence goods in the market rather than producing them within a largely self-sufficient household. The second process by which mass markets form is through the productivity-enhancing effects of mass production technology on the aggregate incomes of workers, once this technology becomes established as a result of the formation of an industrial working class. The third is changes in the composition of demand resulting from income growth.

The theory of TG draws a distinction between pre-industrial, predominantly agrarian, societies and modern mass production economies. The family unit in traditional society produced for itself the goods its members consumed. Each family had access to the raw materials it needed, such as cotton, wool, and grains, and applied domestic labour to transform these raw inputs into usable goods, often drawing on the extended family when labour was required for major tasks such as homebuilding. 'Our forefathers in colonial America lived on their own farms, built their own houses, raised their own food, and made their own clothes. Each family was a little world in itself, capable of meeting most of the needs of its existence. Today, an individual produces few of the commodities he consumes' (Andrews and Michels, 1937, p. 44). Households within a village community interacted with each other, exchanging goods that each may have produced in surplus, but the pattern of exchanges between households was regulated by custom and tradition (Nell, 1992, pp. 364–6).

Thus, for the bulk of the population, consumption was satisfied through direct production by the consuming household. Alongside this system of household production, there existed commercial producers who sold commodities in a market. But these markets were based largely on the discretionary needs of aristocratic households or the occasional needs of village households for specialized goods they could not make for themselves. Thus, these firms were characterized by craft technology that could be adapted to meet the discretionary needs of such expenditure. The need to literally tailor-make goods to the specific demands of individual consumers restricted production technology to small-scale craft technology using very simple equipment. Producers knew who would consume their product and were geared towards adapting production to the particular needs of these consumers.

The basis of this system was the access of the peasantry to land, from which they could obtain raw material inputs into domestic production, and the availability to the household of the labour time of its members. The breakdown of this system can therefore be found in the alienation of the peasantry from land, or the removal of members of the household so that their labour time was no longer available (as when male members were conscripted into the army). Without access to land and the raw materials it provides, or the domestic labour to produce subsistence goods, previously self-sufficient peasants are forced to purchase the inputs to domestic production on the market. And their only means for doing this is to offer their labour power for sale in return for wages.

Thus the process of alienating the peasantry from the material inputs to domestic production, as in the enclosure movement in the UK, creates markets for goods that were previously produced by the household. As Marx cogently summarized, 'in fact, the events that transformed the small peasants into wage-labourers, and their means of subsistence and of labour into material elements of capital, created, at the same time, a home market for capital' (1886, p. 910).

As workers are created out of this breakdown of the traditional system, they have to spend their wages on the materials or finished goods that they once produced for themselves. With the market for such goods expanding, more labour is drawn away from the countryside and into industrial production. These additional workers, in turn, can no longer devote their time to domestic production, and therefore add to the demand for industrially produced goods. Workers are pulled off the land as new industries spring up and require abundant supplies of cheap labour, and these workers themselves then add to the growth of markets. Thus when a critical mass of wage labourers forms, the process becomes cumulative and draws more of the peasantry into its orbit.

Moreover, this mechanism by which market demand expands through the breakdown of the household system carries forward even into later stages of capitalist development and provides a means by which crises of underconsumption may endogenously create the conditions for future market expansion. In periods of recession, the decline in household wage income upsets the balance between labour supplied to the market and labour devoted to domestic production. With less money income from wage labor, the inputs needed for domestic production will be more difficult to purchase. And without their own land to cultivate, the family will not be able to maintain its standard of living by opting out of industrial production. More members of the family will have to offer their labour power in the market, or existing workers will put in overtime in order to maintain the flow of money income. But this means that there is less labour available for household production. Households will thereby use their income to purchase final commodities, or labour-saving inputs to domestic production, which embody a higher degree of industrial production. These changes imply a rearrangement of the entire lifestyle of the household and its operation.

The impact of all of this on consumer demand is not due to an increase in total household income: in fact, the process has come about precisely because incomes have declined to a level that undermine the normal standard of living. A family's response to this through the reallocation of labour between industry and the household, however, alters the pattern of demand so that the nature of the things purchased changes. Households no longer purchase raw materials to be used as inputs to household production. Instead, they require finished consumer goods and appliances that are complementary to the consumption of these goods, especially consumer durables.

It is important to note that the rise in money income as a means for satisfying demand is not necessarily equated with an improvement in the living standards of the working class. Indeed, it is sometimes the impoverishment of households brought about by their alienation from the means of household production that forces them to seek wage labour, thereby simultaneously creating and expanding consumer markets. Bernstein (1987), for example, has argued that the mass unemployment of the 1930s in the USA lowered the money wage level of many working-classes households. In order to maintain the money income of the family, other members of the household, especially housewives, had to seek employment. With less time available to devote to household production, activities such as the preparation and storage of food could no longer be undertaken domestically. This created a market for consumer durables and for packaged food, which, in turn, fostered expansion of the canning and bottling industries. Bernstein argues that with sufficient time, these processes may have allowed the economy to move out of depression, albeit very slowly.

THE DEMAND EFFECTS OF PRODUCTIVITY GROWTH

With the formation of an industrial working class, the consumption goods market can continue to grow by cheapening the commodities that make up the consumption basket, thereby raising the real incomes of consumers. This has been a focal point of the cumulative causation literature, particularly that of Allyn Young and Nicholas Kaldor. The division of labour raises productivity and allows a cheapening of commodities, which leads to an expansion of the market for that commodity, which then induces further division of labour and the extension of the mass production system. This mutually reinforcing feedback between technology and market demand led Young (1928) to amend Adam Smith's famous dictum such that 'the division of labor is limited by the division of labor'. He could alternatively have stated this apparent tautology by arguing that the extent of the market is limited by the extent of the market. In fact, neither statement is a tautology, since they are backed by a theory that explains the self-reinforcing feedbacks between productivity growth and market demand.

It is important though to identify the precise ways in which productivity growth induces an expansion of demand. The first and most obvious channel is the way in which new consumers are able to enter the market for a commodity whose production is undergoing transformational growth. As a commodity cheapens, more consumers are able to include it in their consumption bundles; the emergence of the mass market for home computers and the constant reductions in computer prices is a classic example of this process.

A second channel through which productivity growth expands demand in such a way as to induce further productivity growth is the increase in the real incomes of those people who already purchase the commodity whose relative price is declining. No longer needing to devote as much of their real income to purchasing a given commodity, these consumers redirect their demand to other commodities that they could previously not afford. This extends the division of labour in these other industries that raises the real of income of their consumers, and so on.

A third channel that is especially important in the early stages of capitalism is the way in which the cheaper (and sometimes better) goods produced in the factories destroy small-scale cottage production of similar goods. This forces more people to enter the wage labour class, who then add to the demand for industrially produced goods as they spend their money wages. The fall in the price of a commodity means that small-scale producers are competed out of the market. An example of this process is the rapid decline of domestic spinning in the face of the mechanization of the cotton industry in England in the late 1700s. 'The mechanical advantage of even the earliest jennies and water frames over handspinning was enormous: anywhere from six up to twenty-four to one for the jenny; several hundred to one for the frame. The spinning wheel, which had taken some centuries to displace the rock, became an antique in the space of a decade' (Landes, 1972, p. 85).

A fourth channel is the increase in the labour directly required to produce a commodity under mass production conditions. This follows from the sheer increase in the scale of production induced by the growth of mass markets. The employment of large pools of unskilled and semi-skilled labour, and also (in its advanced stages) the formation of a bureaucratic class of corporate managers and supervisors, buttresses mass markets for other commodities, the production of which employs large pools of labour that may, in turn, feed into the demand for the original commodity.

GROWTH THROUGH CHANGES IN THE COMPOSITION OF DEMAND

We have noted that households begin as production units, with the inputs to production consisting largely of home-grown raw materials, to which domestic labour is applied to transform these raw materials into consumption goods. As industrialization takes hold and mass production spreads from industry to industry, drawing workers into its orbit, less labour can be devoted to domestic production. The household remains a production unit (usually through a sexual division of labour), but the inputs are no longer raw; they have already been transformed in the industrial sphere, and are transformed further in the household sphere with the aid of labour-saving devices such as washing machines and microwave ovens. Eventually, very little production is undertaken in the household, which becomes almost a pure consumption unit. The history of the sewing machine illustrates this evolution. Without the raw materials or the labour time required to spin cotton and wool into yarn and then into cloth, households purchase cloth ready-made and produce clothing with the aid of sewing machines. This creates a mass market for sewing machines, the production of which requires a large labour force, which adds to overall effective demand and the growth of markets for consumption goods in general. Eventually, though, households purchase industrially produced *finished clothing*, rather than transforming semi-finished inputs through domestic labour.

The *entire* manufacture of finished clothing in the process is eventually transferred to industry.

This (albeit simplistic) story of the growth of consumer demand helps explain one of the most significant regularities in economics, the Engel curve. The Engel curve was originally developed to explain the decline in the relative importance of food in the consumption bundle of households as their incomes rise, an observation consistent with the discussion above. It has since been expanded into a statement of the gradual diversification of consumer demand as income grows, and in particular the increasing share of income spent on manufactured items, and then service items (Houthakker, 1957). The importance feature of the Engel curve is that households do not spend reasonably permanent increases in income on commodities in the same proportions as they have in the past. There is a distinct hierarchy of needs and wants (Cornwall, 1977, pp. 100–2), so that 'as per capita real income increases each increment of consumers' demand tends to concentrate on a particular group of goods and services. This group of goods and services gradually changes from one level of income to another. Hence, as income increases, the tendency is not to increase proportionately the consumption of already bought goods and services, but rather to buy new goods and services or to satisfy old needs with different (and hopefully better) goods' (Pasinetti, 1981: 77).

This clustering of goods and services, in a hierarchical fashion with respect to income, essentially revolves around the complementarities between the goods that together form a particular 'lifestyle'. As income increases there is a point where households feel that can alter their existing patterns of consumption and 'invest' in a new lifestyle (provided this income growth can be confidently projected into the future). An addition can be made to the family home that requires a new furnishing, a second TV and so on. This disproportionate growth in the bundle of commodities that dominate a household's demand is crucial to the endogenous evolution of markets, since it will allow new industries to spring up, replacing as an engine of growth those industries in which demand has reached saturation levels given their 'earlier' position along the aggregate Engle curve.

This theory of consumption, based on the evolution of demand along the Engel curve, allows for a more sociological theory of consumer behaviour. It provides a role for consumer learning in the formation of tastes and preferences through emulation and trial and error, and through the pervasive effects of advertising in 'helping' to determine the commodities that make up the lifestyles that define the points that make up the Engle curve.[2] The general point about this discussion of social structure and the growth of markets is that expansion depends on constant and far-reaching changes in the way society is organized. The ability of large groups of consumers to move into markets from which they were formerly excluded, the creation of new urban centres as more people leave traditional forms of production to engage in wage labour, the replacement of family ownership and control with managerial hierarchies populated by entirely new classes of people – such phenomena imply new lifestyles defined by an ensemble of goods and services that must be produced. As long as social stratification is fluid and new or existing markets continue to find pockets of expansion, demand will grow. But as soon as social positions begin to ossify and mobility is reduced, then stagnation sets in. This will then discourage further investment and innovation which, in turn, reduces the forces that could potentially 'churn up' the social order and cause markets to expand again. Social change, and especially social improvement on a large scale, are an essential, but not guaranteed, part of transformational growth.

THE DEVELOPMENT OF A CAPITAL GOODS SECTOR

The growth of mass markets that we have just described has implications for the other major element of demand: investment. For traditional craft firms, increases in the size of the market had normally been met by creating new production units; investment was extensive, involving a multiplication of small shops based on the optimal size of the work team. The self-reinforcing expansion of consumer demand we have just discussed places pressure on previously small-scale craft producers to alter their production methods. With the level of demand growing rapidly and its pattern shifting from discretionary expenditure to homogeneous demand, producers extend the division of labour to meet the growing mass market. With working-class families increasingly sourcing their needs through the expenditure of wage income, the craft system is pushed to its limits. Craft methods cannot meet the needs of expanding home markets, since there are diminishing returns to scale for this technology. Firms can no longer carry the fixed current costs of a skilled work team during slack periods, nor can these work teams take advantage of expansions of demand, since they usually involve rising marginal cost curves after a definable point of production. Production beyond this point is constrained by the physical limits of key personnel who can neither pass work on to the next shift, nor produce larger quantities without quality deteriorating.

Investment, therefore, becomes intensive, involving a dramatic increase in the size of the production unit and a demand for specialized capital goods. The division of labour is synonymous with the introduction of increasingly specialized equipment that is durable and capable of long production runs turning out interchangeable parts. The supply of such specialized machinery and equipment becomes the function of an emergent class of capital goods producers dedicated to the task. But how do such specialized capital goods producers emerge? A distinct capital goods sector does not lie dormant, awaiting the needs of consumer goods producers for machinery and equipment to activate its capabilities. It emerges endogenously through an evolutionary process as the growing domestic market presses against the limits to production set by craft technology, which forces small-scale producers to look for technological solutions to these limits. The key element to this is a learning process that can be described as learning-by-self-using.

Firms using craft methods of production normally create simple tools and equipment in-house for individual job lots. Under the craft system, capital goods are simple. Just as the traditional family farm produced the goods needed to satisfy its own consumption needs, traditional craft shops produced their own tools and equipment. Tools were made of non-durable materials that could be easily fashioned for specific jobs or batches of production, and then disposed of. However, the need to raise output and meet longer production runs requires tools made of more durable material and equipment increasingly specialized to an individual task. Meeting these needs forms a technological puzzle that initially engages a firm's own engineering or repair department. Thus the external demand for consumption goods becomes an internal demand for capital goods. The engineering department begins to develop the necessary equipment, which finds its way onto the shop floor. This equipment is then progressively refined and improved through trial and error (that is, learning-by-self-using). Such equipment may move through several generations, adapting to the growing demand for consumer goods for whose production it has, itself, been produced. This is often an invisible process to the outside observer because the source of demand is *endogenous to the firm itself*: the producer and consumer are one and the same.

This process of learning thereby creates within the womb of a producer of consumer goods a nascent capital goods producer. Such producers then mature into separate and distinct entities in one of two ways. The engineering or repair division of the firm takes on an increasingly independent existence as it realizes that the equipment it initially manufactures for in-house use has a commercial potential. Thus it no longer exists as an incidental service department, but becomes an autonomous unit. Alternatively, key personnel such as a foreman or master toolmaker may leave the parent firm and set up an independent operation (although often relying on a close relationship with the parent firm for continuing orders) (Argyrous, 1996). Thus vertical specialization of industry works backwards, beginning with the growth of consumer demand that feeds back as demand for machinery and equipment, which eventually induces the development of specialized producers of such machinery and equipment.[3]

For countries that develop relatively late this learning-by-self-using may take a slightly different form. In such countries, manufacturers of consumer goods can always import their needs for capital goods from countries that have already industrialized. However, the specific requirements of machinery and equipment render proximity between producer and user a distinct advantage, so that importing machinery is not always desirable. When a piece of machinery breaks down, firms often engage their engineering departments to reverse engineer the previously imported item and build anew a machine more closely suited to their own needs. Once a serviceable model is developed through the firm's own use of it, the capacity then exists for a separate firm to spin off and dedicate itself to the production of this item for sale to other firms.

The formation of a distinct layer of firms dedicated to capital goods production gives an economy new sources of endogenous demand creation. One such source is the mutual demand by capital goods producers for each other's products. Capital goods are required for the production of capital goods, and this interaction within the sector can improve the productivity of all capital goods. This then lowers costs in those consumer goods industries that purchase cheaper and better equipment, fuelling the processes we have described earlier, which then feedback as a further expansion in the demand for capital goods.

Another source of endogenous demand that arises with the development of a specialized machine building sector is the learning-by-using process discussed by Rosenberg (1982). Small capital producers sell their equipment to large mass production firms who, in using the equipment, identify methods of improvement that they make known to the producers of the equipment. Thus the demand for a particular piece of equipment today leads to a demand for an improved version of that equipment in the future. Moreover, as any given piece of equipment is adapted and improved through this process, a demand is created for complementary improvements in other pieces of equipment with which it forms a complete production system. A faster packaging machine requires a faster conveying machine, which then calls forth improvements further down the line.

LIMITATIONS ON ENDOGENOUS GROWTH

Transformational growth is a theory about the operation of two distinct systems of production; the craft system, which dominated before the First World War, and the mass production system of the post-Second World War period. The recognition that demand expands endogenously helps explain the processes by which an economy moves from one system to another. The risk for any theory of endogenous change, though, is that it may be very mechanistic, presenting industrialization as an inexorable process, resistant to limitations.

The emphasis on various learning processes in the discussion above, however, helps the TG story avoid any mechanistic overtones, and indicates why the transition from craft to mass production was so staggered and drawn out over time. While TG refers to system-wide changes in production technology, these system-wide outcomes only eventuate through incremental adaptations at the micro-level by individual firms and industries to the evolution of demand. Moreover, we can identify specific limiting factors that can undermine the endogenous forces of expansion.

One such limiting factor is the particular relationship between the capital-using and capital-producing sectors. TG does not completely eliminate craft methods of production from an economy, but rather concentrates them in the capital goods industry. As mass markets for consumer goods develop, as we have argued above, this translates into demand for specialized, often custom-made pieces of capital equipment, which encourages the adoption of craft technology in those firms making the equipment. A piece of capital such as a high-speed lathe may be used in a mass production process, but may itself have been produced under craft conditions. This means that the capital goods industry, particularly its core sector of machine tool producers, cannot easily expand production in the short run beyond its existing productive capacity. Over time, as the capital goods sector produces more equipment and raises capacity throughout the economy (including the capital goods sector itself), such limits can be overcome. But at any given point in time, an economy is constrained by the productive capacity of this core sector, and the craft-like technology it employs.

Another limiting factor on self-sustaining growth involves the hierarchy of goods in the Engle curve. In particular, manufactured commodities are not evenly spread throughout the curve's range. As income grows, consumption demand is increasingly directed to services, which are not susceptible to supply through mass production technology and division of labour. For any given household, the increasing importance of services in the consumption bundle reduces the possible feedbacks that may eventuate through the division of labour and the cumulative spread of mass production technology. Manufacturing loses its power as an engine of growth with the relative decline of manufactured goods as components of consumption. Thus the growth of markets, due to changes in the pattern of consumption over time, has an inbuilt tendency to lose its motive force.[4]

Industrialization can also slow down through changes in the way that productivity is distributed. In the competitive phase of capitalist development, productivity gains obtained through the gradual encroachment of mass production are distributed through price reductions. This spreads the benefits across a wide number of consumers, including people on fixed incomes. In the oligopoly phase of mature capitalism when economies of scale have been realized in a wide number of industries, firms increasingly use productivity gains to raise the real wages of their own workers to 'purchase' industrial peace,[5] or else to engage in oligopolistic competition – marketing, after sales service, product differentiation and so on – rather than directing them to productivity-enhancing activities *per se*. This concentrates the income (and thereby consumption) effects of productivity growth in the hands of a smaller number of individuals who are largely well-paid unionized workers, so that the potential demand effect may not be as great as when productivity growth was passed on to all consumers.

If these contractionary factors come into play, the endogenous demand relationships, which were a positive force generating cumulative expansion in the growth phase, become a negative force generating a vicious cycle of decline. Endogenous demand is a two-edged sword. Under the craft system, the level of employment, in terms of the number of workers employed, did not vary, since the integrity of work teams had to be maintained. Producers would respond to a downturn in demand by cutting prices and reducing the effort of work teams. With employment relatively stable and real wages rising, the craft system thus had an in-built mechanism for restoring demand. In the era of mass production, however, downturns are met through a decline in total employment, with work effort relatively stable and prices inflexible downwards. At the aggregate level this only exacerbates the problem of demand deficiency, leading to further reductions in employment so that downturns can lead to chronic stagnation (Nell and Phillips, 1995). This obviously provides scope for government intervention to act as a 'circuit breaker' when such a downward spiral takes hold. The automatic stabilizers built into a system with Big Government can arrest the decline and restore the conditions for self-sustaining growth (Minsky, 1986).

CONCLUSION

There has been a growing interest in theories that seek to explain capitalist expansion through recourse to internal 'engines of growth', rather than exogenous forces such as population expansion or autonomous technical change. The popularity of Romer's (1986, 1994) neoclassical endogenous growth theory is testament to this. Yet such theories have tended to concentrate on the supply side, and especially on technical change and productivity. But technologies that raise productivity are only viable if they have expanding markets in which to sell, and therefore a theory of the growth of markets needs to be developed to give a complete picture of endogenous growth. This is provided by the theory of TG, which locates the growth of markets in the dynamic interaction between household and industrial production and consumption. When this relationship is examined, we discover endogenous processes on the demand side that explain the emergence of mass markets that complement the emergence of mass production in a mutually self-reinforcing manner.

NOTES

1. A comprehensive account of TG is provided in Nell (1998a). A more schematic introduction to the theory of TG is provided by Pressman (1994).
2. Ironmonger (1972) provides an interesting model, incorporating some of these sociological features, for analysing the diffusion of new commodities based on Engel curves.
3. It would be interesting to investigate the extent to which this process also applies to the development of information technology – that is, the extent to which such technology is originally developed to service the *in-house* needs of existing firms as the demand for their products changes and grows.
4. See Cornwall and Cornwall (1994) for a growth model that incorporates these features of consumption patterns and investigates their implications for economic expansion and state policies.
5. Henry Ford's '$5 a day' was an early example of this strategy (Ford, 1922, p. 126).

REFERENCES

Andrews, J.N. and R. Michels (1937) *Economic Problems of Modern Society*, New York, Ronald Press.
Argyrous, G. (1996) 'Cumulative causation and industrial evolution: Kaldor's four stages of industrialization as an evolutionary model,' *Journal of Economic Issues*, 30, 97–119.
Bernstein, P. (1987) *The Great Depression*, Cambridge, Cambridge University Press.
Cornwall, J. (1977) *Modern Capitalism*, Oxford, Martin Robertson.
Cornwall, J. and W. Cornwall (1994) 'Growth theory and economic structure,' *Economica*, 61, 237–51.
Ford, H. (1922) *My Life and Work*, Sydney, Doubleday & Page.
Houthakker, H. (1957) 'An international comparison of household expenditure patterns commemorating the centennial of Engel's Law,' *Econometrica*, 25A, 532–51.
Ironmonger, D.S. (1972) *New Commodities and Consumer Behavior*, Cambridge, Cambridge University Press.
Kaldor, N. (1966) *Causes of the Slow Rate of Growth of the United Kingdom*, Cambridge, Cambridge University Press.
Landes, D.S. (1972) *The Unbound Prometheus*, Cambridge, Cambridge University Press.
Marx, K. (1886) *Capital* 1, translated by Ben Fowkes, London, Penguin.
Nell, E.J. (1992) *Transformational Growth and Effective Demand*, London, Macmillan.
Nell, E.J. (1998a) *The General Theory of Transformational Growth,* Cambridge, Cambridge University Press.
Nell, E.J. (ed.) (1998b) *Transformational Growth and the Business Cycle*, London, Routledge.
Nell, E.J. and T. Phillips (1995) 'Transformational growth and the business cycle,' *Eastern Economic Journal*, 21, 125–42.
Minsky, H. (1986) *Stabilizing an Unstable Economy*, New Haven, Yale University Press.

Pasinetti, L. (1981) *Structural Change and Economic Growth*, Cambridge, Cambridge University Press.
Pressman, S. (1994) 'On transformational growth,' *Review of Political Economy*, 6, 107–32.
Romer, P.M. (1986) 'Increasing returns and long-run growth,' *Journal of Political Economy*, 94, 1002–37.
Romer, P.M. (1994) 'The origins of endogenous growth,' *Journal of Economic Perspectives*, 8A, 3–22.
Rosenberg, N. (1982) *Inside the Black Box*, Cambridge, Cambridge University Press
Young, A. (1928) 'Increasing returns and economic progress,' *Economic Journal*, 38, 527–42.

14. Notes on the transformational growth of demand

Edward J. Nell

INTRODUCTION

Understanding the Growth of Demand

At present, neither conventional nor alternative approaches to economic theory provide much help in understanding the growth of demand, either in the aggregate, or for specific markets and sectors. 'Growth of demand' refers here to repeated, continuing expansion of demand (either at a steady rate or at a fluctuating rate with a persistent average), where the expansion is not offset by contraction elsewhere. Such growth of markets, and expected growth of markets, are important in making business decisions, and are an object of study by marketing divisions.

Yet explaining such growth has not been an objective of economic theorists. Indeed, from a 'real-economy' (or barter exchange) perspective, it might seem that any growth of demand has to be based on a corresponding growth of supply. For if a new demand for a certain set of goods is to be *effective* in real terms, there must be an expanded supply of some other goods with which to pay for the newly demanded set. Explaining the growth of supply has therefore seemed adequate.

But this is a way of thinking that overlooks the role of finance. Finance breaks the link between demanding one set of goods and paying for them with another; once finance is in the picture, goods can be demanded even if the other goods needed to pay for them have not yet been produced. With finance, growth of demand can be separated from the growth of supply.

For the most part, however, growth models have been held in thrall by the 'real-economy' perspective, and so have tended to focus on the supply side, assuming implicitly or explicitly that the growth will generate an equivalent growth of demand – a sort of long-run Say's Law. Both Solow and Kaldor, for example, assumed that in the long run investment would reflect the 'natural rate of growth'. Their models differed in that Solow assumed that the warranted rate would adjust to the natural rate through a process of substitution between capital and labour, whereas Kaldor assumed that the adjustment would come about through changes in income distribution resulting from variations in demand pressure. In both, however, the natural rate – a supply-side variable – determines the long-run course of investment, a Keynesian expenditure variable.

Yet this has to be considered implausible. Surely plans to spend on the expansion of productive capacity will not be developed without a prior expectation of an appropriate growth in demand? The Keynesian separation of investment from savings holds once finance is available, so that the growth of demand will not be constrained by the growth of supply and cannot be inferred from supply-side considerations. Instead, a separate account of the demand side is required.

It is often thought that, at the macroeconomic level, the growth of demand is explained by the Harrod–Domar model. The 'warranted rate of growth' is that rate at which the growth of demand just equals the growth of capacity. But in fact this model equates the current *level* of expenditure, as determined by the multiplier, with the current capacity output of the capital stock, in accordance with the productivity of capital (the inverse of the capital–output ratio). There is no necessary connection with growth.

To see this, consider an example that substitutes government spending for investment (Nell 1998, pp. 599–600). Let G be government spending, K be the capital stock, and v the capital–output ratio, K/Y. Assume that all profits, P, are saved and all wages are consumed. Then $z = 1 - wn = P/Y$, where w is the wage rate, and $n = N/Y$. $G/z = K/v$ tells us that aggregate demand equals capacity output, and this implies $G/K = z/v = r$ where r is the rate of profit.

This formula, analogous to the Harrod–Domar condition, states that the ratio of government spending to capital must equal the ratio of the profits share to the capital–output ratio in order for capacity to be fully utilized. But the latter ratio reduces to the rate of profit; the condition is analogous to the Golden Rule.

Now let the productivity of capital depend on the level of G. Suppose that higher levels of G lead to higher productivity (lower v.) Then if $G/z > K/v$, it would appear that capacity is too low, so $1/v$ should be increased. The way to do this is to increase G. Similarly, if $G/z < K/v$, it would appear that the appropriate move would be to reduce G. The Harrod–Domar 'knife-edge' results are reproduced – there is only one level of G at which there will be equilibrium, and it is unstable.[1] Any movement away from it will be reinforced. Although this model is static and makes no reference to growth, the Harrod–Domar results have been reproduced. The Harrod–Domar relationships do not, therefore, offer an account of the growth of demand.

The multiplier–accelerator model suffers from a similar problem.[2] The accelerator comes into play because output, responding to demand, is pressing on capacity. So more capacity should be built. But the multiplier only works if there is some flexibility in employment; then additional workers can be hired, and their spending will increase demand. But if there is flexibility in employment, there is unused capacity. So why should more capacity be built? The answer that is usually given is that there is a 'normal' or 'desired' level of capacity, which can be exceeded, but only at a higher cost. As it is exceeded, demand will increase, but so will costs. To keep the latter down, additional capacity will be built. But this just pushes the problem back one step – how is desired or normal capacity determined?[3] And it is still the case that when the multiplier works best, the accelerator will not be in play, and when accelerator effects are most obviously called for, the multiplier is questionable, because capacity is limited and costs are rising. In short, the multiplier–accelerator may have a role to play at points in the business cycle, but it is difficult to see how this relationships can give a reliable and long-term account of the *growth of demand.*

The problems of the Harrod–Domar account of the growth of demand surely cannot be found in the 'Cambridge' growth model in the form developed by Robinson (Robinson, 1956, 1962; also see Kaldor, 1957, 1961 and Kaldor and Mirrlees, 1962). But in fact, a related difficulty emerges. This approach determines growth by balancing the saving and investment that are induced by the rate of profits.[4] A simple version of this model (modifying the treatment in Foley and Michl, 2000, chapter 10) can be illustrated on a diagram with the growth rate on the vertical axis and the profit rate on the horizontal axis. Two functions are then defined. The first shows the growth rate made possible by the saving out of various rates of profit. This starts from the origin and rises with a slope that represents the propensity to save out of profits. The second function shows the growth rate determined by the investment called forth by the expected rate of profit. This will normally have a positive intercept, indicating that some investment (and therefore growth) would take place even if profits were expected to be zero (due to competition, especially for innovations). Higher expected profit rates stimulate investment, but not excessively, so this line will rise with a flatter slope than that of the saving function. The two lines will intersect, as shown in Figure 14.1, determining the rates of growth and profit in any period simultaneously.

The first of the relationships is based on the classical saving function. While this has well-known limitations, it provides a reasonable first approximation. But the second relationship is more problematical. Profits – business earnings – are a withdrawal from the circular flow of income.[5] But how can investment depend on a 'withdrawal' variable? This is akin to saying that saving determines investment. Put differently: why should firms build more capital for tomorrow's markets in proportion to the rate of earnings on today's capital? The current rate of profit tells us how well capital is doing today, but

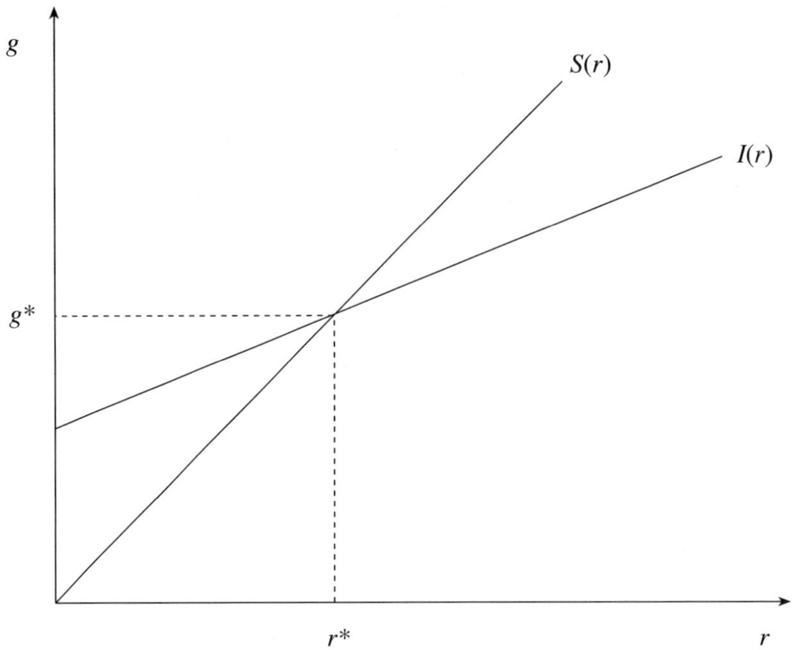

Figure 14.1 The Cambridge growth model

today's investment will not come on line until tomorrow. Today's profit helps to *finance* today's investment (as accounted for in the first equation), but it provides no *reason* to build more capacity.

Even interpreting the profit rate variable as an indicator of *expected* future profits does not help (quite apart from the fact that the profit rates in the two equations would then refer to different time periods).[6] Suppose the rate of profits is expected to rise. Why should this lead firms to build more capacity? The rate of profit on current capital will have risen without firms doing anything. On the other hand, if the rate in question is the expected rate of profit *on the newly built capacity*, after it comes into operation, then it is a *marginal* profit rate, and is not comparable to the rate which figures in the classical savings equation. If it is the expected future rate on *all* capital – present plus new investment – the question still arises, why does a higher profit rate induce more investment now (Kurdas, 1993)?

The correct answer, it will be argued here, requires first making an important distinction between investment *decisions* and investment *spending* (that is the execution of investment decisions). What induces decisions to invest is the anticipated growth of markets. If markets are growing rapidly, decisions to invest will be made readily, even if expected profitability is low. If markets are sluggish, however, even though profitable, there will be little reason to build more capacity, and decisions to invest will be few. In sum, capacity is planned to service demand. *Spending* on capacity construction, however, requires considering another variable – the cost and availability of funds. But this affects the timing of capital construction, not the decision as to whether or not the capacity should be built.[7]

Demand, Supply and Pricing

Neither equilibrium – determinateness – nor stability can be established for prices (in mass production markets) unless the growth of demand equals the growth of supply. Suppose current supply and demand are equal, but while new markets are opening up, firms are not building new capacity (for whatever reason). Future prices will start to rise, and this will lead to an increase in current demand for stockpiling, upsetting the current equilibrium. (Even if future prices were sluggish, or the futures market undeveloped, stockpiling in the light of anticipated shortages would be a good idea.) The same results follow in reverse if supply is expanding with no growth of markets in sight.[8]

By contrast, suppose current demand lies below current normal capacity, but new markets are opening up at the same rate that new capacity is being built. Current demand and supply can be brought into line by raising the scrapping or lowering the replacement rate. The same holds if current demand is above current normal capacity; scrapping can be postponed, or replacements enhanced. These are one-shot adjustments. But when current demand and supply are equal but the *growth rates* are out of line, no one-shot adjustment can restore the balance. If the growth of demand and supply are not equal, the market cannot reach equilibrium, but if growth is in balance and current levels of supply and demand are not, capacity is easily adjusted to bring them into line.

The significance for theory lies in the fact that prices are important long-term factors influencing the growth of supply, on the one hand, and the growth of demand on the other. Given unit costs, higher prices (relative to money wages) increase profit margins, and thus provide both internal finance and borrowing power, making it possible to underwrite the construction of additional capacity (Wood, 1975; Eichner, 1976; Milberg and Elmslie, 1992; Harcourt and Kenyon, 1976). On the other hand, higher prices (relative to money wages) make it harder to break into and develop new markets (Nell, 1992, 1998, chapter 10). So we can define a positive or rising relationship between long-term or 'target' prices and the planned growth of capacity, and an inverse or falling relationship between such prices and the growth of demand.[9]

However, while this approach will help in understanding the practice of modern corporations in managing their mark-ups, it sheds little light on why new markets open up in the first place. Corporations can lower their prices, and attract more business; this is simply a static demand effect. It becomes dynamic only in a limited sense, when conjoined to the income distribution. In a class society with a hierarchical income distribution, as the price of a good falls relative to the wage, new groups can progressively incorporate the good into their budgets. Such 'incorporation effects' are fully accounted for in the 'lifestyle' approach to the household, as discussed below. A function can be derived showing the expansion of markets with each lowering of the price. This is an important step. Yet it is no more than the expansion of an already existing good into new areas; innovation and social change are not involved, suggesting that more fundamental forces remain to be explored.

Demand in Mainstream Theory

Utility theory, and the principal versions of the mainstream theory of consumer behaviour, seek to determine choices in static terms. Not only are preferences given, but agents are assumed to know their preferences without having to learn or experiment. Skills and information are likewise given without regard to learning. And, of course, endowments of resources, including labour, are assumed to be known and available. The theory then determines current levels of household expenditure, but contributes nothing to explaining how this level might change or grow in a systemic way.

Household budgets do present serious choice problems, but these must be considered in a programming format, as, for example, in the work of Lancaster (1996). Here, consumers are understood not to want goods for their own sake, but for what they offer – their 'characteristics', that is, we want apples for taste, nutrition or to complement other foods. Bananas also offer taste, nutrition and (different) complementarities. We choose the bundle of *goods* (apples and bananas) that offers us the best deal for the *desired characteristics* (taste, nutrition and so) that we wish to consume – for example, the minimum cost bundle that provides a given level of the characteristics, or the highest fulfilment of desire for a given cost.

But Lancaster's 'characteristics' are, themselves, unexplained. They need to be fitted into a larger picture, in which certain 'characteristics' will be desired because they are part of a 'lifestyle', which in turn reflects class and social pressures (Nell, 1998, pp. 470–3). This will then allow for choices of goods and services to achieve the standards imposed by a lifestyle (Nell, 1998, chapter 10). Demand functions can be developed; they will show stretches of unresponsiveness to price changes alternating with large rapid responses. 'Composition' effects – changing the proportions of categories of goods in the budget – and 'incorporation' effects – including new goods, dropping others – can be distinguished and their causes studied (Nell, 1998, pp. 474–5).

Certain lifestyles will call for self-improvement, and for competition to rise in social status. Self-improvement and rising in status will also tend to increase productivity. The social pressures generating this kind of competitive career and social climbing are likely to be class-related. Responding to these pressures will lead to the setting aside of part of the household budget for investment in education, training and other efforts directed at achieving promotions and raising social status. It will also call for labour-saving innovation in household tasks, since more *time* will be needed for household members to engage in new activities. This will open the door for new products.

Setting out on such a path of self-improvement might be associated with reaching a certain level of real wages, a level associated with lifestyles in which achievement is measured in terms of income and status; that is, a certain level of real wages might be associated with investment in self-improvement, and so with increases in productivity and growth in incomes. Investment in self-improvement is likely to lead to changes in the composition of demand, while the growth of productivity and income, of course, will lead to demand growth. Let us now explore all this in greater detail.

THE EMERGENCE OF NEW MARKETS

We saw previously that a price-expansion-of-demand function could be derived on the basis of a given class structure and income distribution. But this does not take into account or explain *innovation*. It examines the growth of demand in terms of the expansion of existing (more or less mature) markets, leaving to one side the emergence and development of new ones.

New markets must first be *created*, in some process of innovation. This might result from the development of a new product, or, the route explored here, it could be part of a larger movement, the effort of a fraction of the working class to rise in the world, through a competitive process of self-improvement. Self-improvement requires the restructuring of household budgets which, in turn, requires finance.

Once they have established a foothold, new markets will develop following a more or less sigmoid-shaped path, starting slowly, then expanding at an accelerating pace, then slowing down and finally stagnating. The latter stages, of course, are the stages of expansion for mature products.

Existing markets tend to expand in line with Engel curves, so increases in the incomes of existing customers will not be spent in the same proportions. Instead, households will typically introduce new goods into the household budget, so that existing markets, depending on a set of regular customers, are likely to expand at a slower pace than the incomes of their customers, unless these markets are stimulated by some major innovation. An obvious implication is that, *ceteris paribus*, growth will slow down as markets mature; sustaining a growth rate requires the development of new markets.

But existing markets can be stimulated very simply. A cost-cutting innovation may allow a drop in price that will bring the product into the affordable region for a whole new class of potential customers. This will set off a new competitive sales drive and result in the expansion of firms in the industry. This suggests a regular relationship between prices and the expansion of a market. Similarly, a product innovation may make a product useful or more useful, or simply more attractive, thereby creating a new pool of customers.

Cost-cutting and product improvement, and specialization of product design, will continually bring new groups of consumers into the market, until all potential customers have been attracted. At this point, the market will have become mature, and will normally begin to stagnate.

The expansion of existing markets therefore largely reflects aspects of the life cycle that each market passes through, from its small-scale, early beginnings through a phase of rapid expansion, to maturity and stagnation (Penrose, 1956).

The growth of demand, then, can be broken down into two parts: the study of the emergence of new markets on the one hand, and the life cycle of their development on the other. As noted above, without the emergence of new markets, existing markets – and hence the economy as a whole – would eventually stagnate.

What has to be explained at the outset, therefore, is the emergence of new markets. New markets develop when a number of households change the composition of their budgets, add new products to their consumption patterns/lifestyles and, in particular, come to 'invest in human capital'. New markets emerge as a result of households reconfiguring their budgets. Demand grows because of a certain kind of change in its composition – a characteristic feature of TG. This may take place as follows.

First, a certain culturally or socially determined fraction of households develop the desire to rise in station. The reasons for this are complex, and grounded in the changes in culture as the social system develops from a one of tradition and 'natural order' to one of 'regular progress' (Nell, 1998, pp. 9–19). A precondition for the widespread development of a desire to rise in station is that employment in agriculture should decline, and families move from the countryside to the city. This breaks the traditional bonds that tie families to their social station. It also puts people in direct contact with opportunities and alternative ways of life and work.

A second fundamental precondition is that the workplace and home living space be separated. If they are not, then the whole family will tend to be fully involved with the family trade, and children will not be able to learn a different or better way of life. This separation of living space from working space

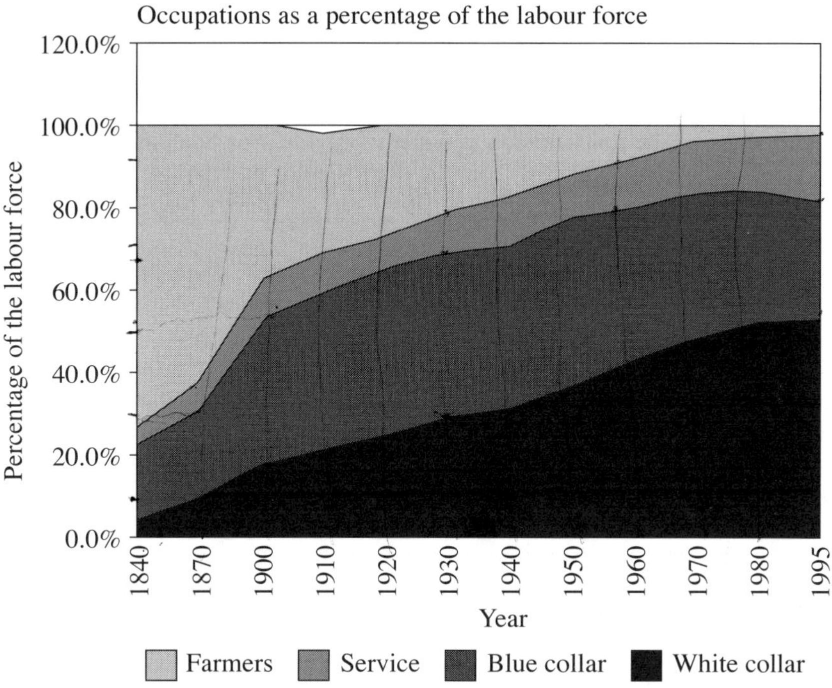

Figure 14.2 The changing composition of employment in the US, 1840–1995

will take place as energy is brought into play to drive machinery. Steam power is dirty, dangerous and loud, and children cannot be near it. Electricity is dangerous, and electric power equipment needs to be treated with circumspection. So as equipment comes to be driven by steam and electricity, the home and the workplace must be separated. These processes of de-ruralization and the separation of work and home have been characteristic of capitalist development, as illustrated by Figure 14.2.

Households seeking to rise in station will typically seek to do this by providing a better education and better opportunities for their children. These households will invest in self-improvement, more for their children than for themselves, but very often in order to provide better conditions for their children, they will have to improve themselves. (We might call this the 'Horatio Alger Effect'.) Funds formerly spent on entertainment and drink will now be used for education and self-improvement, and preparing children for a better life.

An important element in the drive for self-improvement is time-saving in the household. Households should be considered production units, producing the family lifestyle by preparing food, making and mending clothing, performing daily tasks of washing, ironing, cleaning and so on. Innovations such as detergents, improved cleaning fluids, vacuum cleaners, washers and dryers, and gas and electrical heating and lighting, cut down on the time required to run the household, and thereby provide time that can be spent on self-improvement. Looked at from the other side of the market, the drive for self-improvement opens the door to labour-saving innovations in the household.

When a household decides to rise in the world, it adopts an *investment strategy*. It begins to invest in human capital development, especially education and training, and the development of communication skills. It will come to require more flexible transportation, and it will have to rearrange its living quarters, to provide space for the new activities of learning and acquiring new skills. For any of this to happen, banks and financial companies willing to underwrite such investment must develop. The household can then commit a portion of its income to debt servicing, enabling it to borrow the capital necessary to reorient itself and develop the skills of its members.

When a sizable number of households adopts this strategy of self-improvement, they will begin to benefit from interacting with one another. Even though they are competing, they will also provide support for each other. These 'network effects' will increase the effectiveness of individual households' efforts at self-improvement.

Finally, as more and more households seek to rise in the world, new markets are created for products that contribute to self-improvement. Many of the new demands will be for education – courses, classes, night schools and so forth – and communications, such as books, newspapers, and other media. Producing these goods will, in turn, require inputs, which will be supplied by capital goods industries.[10]

Processes of Demand Growth

Here we have the development of a process, a set of linkages running from households changing their understanding of their social position and life options, to the redesign of their budgets to allow for investment in self-improvement, leading finally to the emergence of new markets. To make this effective on a large scale requires finance, so it also offers opportunities for financial institutions to develop. These changes in household spending patterns then lead to additional demand for the capital goods necessary to supply emerging markets, with the effects then feeding back to the productivity of households. So, first the composition of demand changes, leading to the emergence of a new market. This new market has to be supplied, leading to new investment. (The shift in demand, of course, also leads to a reduction in demand for some traditional products, resulting in falling prices and profits in those industries. But this frees up resources to shift capacity into production for new markets.) The new investment will embody the latest technology, so it is likely to be more productive than the old. This will provide the first increase in income, leading to increased demand, which, in turn, will lead to further increases in investment.

A direct consequence of successful self-improvement will therefore be a rise in the productivity of labour, especially of supervisory and managerial labour. Hence there will be a second increase in income, also resulting in an increase in demand, in turn calling for additional investment. (Some families who seek self-improvement and to rise in the world may fail. But this failure will not affect the development of the market in the aggregate. It merely means that their own productivity and income will not increase.)

As is evident, this develops into a *cumulative process*, each round of self-improvement expanding the new markets, leading to new investment, which raises industrial productivity, while self-improvement raises labour-productivity. Both give rise to higher incomes, which lead to further investments in self-improvement and so on.

As the new group of successful families emerges, it will become aware of itself, and increasingly develop a new *lifestyle*. This will be partly functional (that is, it will help to consolidate household productivity gains) but it will also partly be a display of class position and privilege. Either way, it will result in the further development of new markets, for products especially designed to play a role in this new lifestyle. Once again, as these further or subsidiary markets develop, there will be a need for investment, and so for new capital goods, to build up the capacity to produce for these markets.

It is important now to link this cumulative process to the economy as a whole. To do this, we combine a relationship between the real wage and the growth of demand with the well-established real wage – rate of profit tradeoff (Nell, 1998 pp. 477–8). The model contains four variables: the growth of demand, the growth of output, productivity growth and the real wage. Equilibrium requires that the growth of demand equal the growth of output. We can define three behavioural relationships.

First, there is what Joan Robinson called the 'wage-accumulation' curve, the wage–profit tradeoff adjusted by the saving ratio. This relationship is inverse, and following Nell (1998), it is likely to be linear. It will shift with changes in productivity.

Second, there is the wage rate – growth of demand relationship discussed above, which includes an effect on productivity. This will be an increasing function, with a sigmoid shape. At low levels of the wage, there will be some growth of demand, but it will be low, and increase only slowly. At higher levels, growth will accelerate, only to level off at still higher wage rates.

Finally, we adopt a Verdoorn–Kaldor relationship, relating productivity growth to output growth and real wages.

These relationships give us the following equations:

$g = g(w/p, x)$, $g'_w < 0$, $g'_x > 0$ (assumed linear)
$w/p = w(g, x)$, $w'_g > 0$, $w'_x > 0$ (assumed sigmoid in shape)
$x = x(g, w/p)$, $x'_g > 0$, $x''_g < 0$, $x'_w > 0$ up to a point, then $x'_w < 0$

where g is the growth of output, w/p is the real wage and x is productivity growth.

For a given w/*p* it is assumed that there is some level of g beyond which x will no longer increase. It is also assumed that, for a given g, at some level of the real wage, x will reach a maximum and begin to decline. These assumptions effectively bound x, and so ensure that the system of equations will have a solution. Given a few reasonable restrictions, it can be shown that these three behavioural equations have a unique, positive solution, which is stable by normal criteria. Such a solution (leaving productivity growth to one side) is illustrated in Figure 14.3.

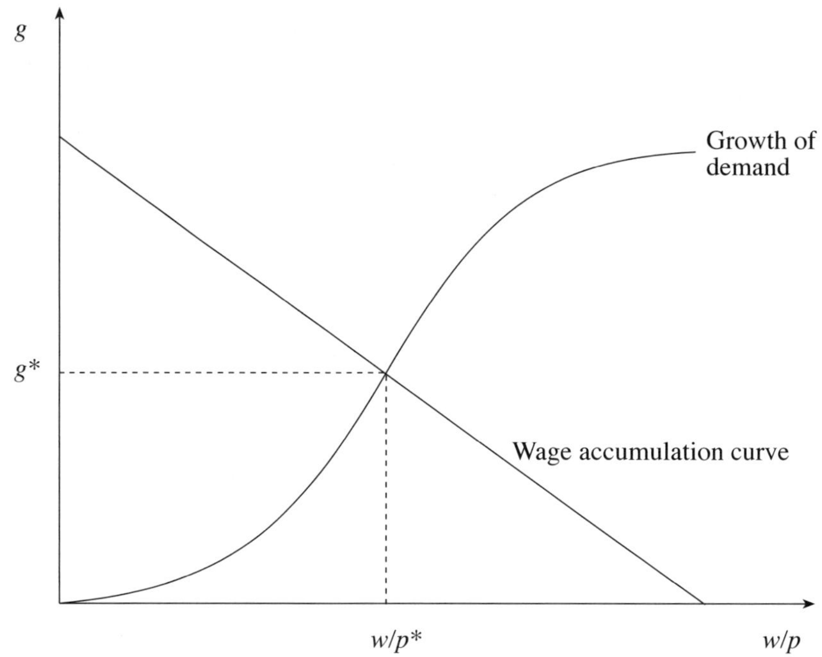

Figure 14.3 The determination of equilibrium growth and real wages

But this needs some explaining. How can a *level* of the real wage support a *growing* demand? This should not be considered so surprising. Note the analogy with businesses, where each *level* of earnings is associated with a *rate of growth* of spending on capital goods. Higher earnings mean higher profits, so resulting in a higher rate of profits, giving rise to a higher rate of growth. The same holds here. The real wage – growth of demand function tells us that for each level of the real wage there will be a corresponding level of investment in self-improvement leading to a corresponding rate of growth of demand by households. (Note that in constructing this function, we are holding capital technology constant – only improvements in worker skills are considered – so a higher wage rate will normally imply a higher wage share.) Households invest in self-improvement, and because they are doing so, they are eligible for credit and can increase their spending, particularly their spending on self-improvement. The function is economy-wide. Ultimately, then, at higher levels of the real wage there will be higher rates of growth of demand for two reasons. First, demand growth will be higher because each household may be able to sustain a larger investment in self-improvement. Second, as wages rise, more households will be drawn into the effort to rise in the world.

We must be careful about the interpretation of the model above: its solution is not a *long-period* equilibrium. Far from it; the reason that demand is growing is that families are trying to improve themselves. Innovation is taking place. On the other hand, it is not a short-run model; it covers a long enough interval for training and education to result in higher levels of productivity. So the time period to which the model corresponds might be thought of as a full business cycle.

The model developed above can be used to explore an important question in the history of growth and technology. If new innovations have been introduced simply because they reduce costs, we would expect them sometimes to be labour-saving, and sometimes to save on equipment and capital goods. Overall, there would seem to be no reason to expect any particular bias. In fact, there has been a very pronounced bias: technical change has been overwhelmingly labour-saving, but capital-using, that is, machinery and equipment has been substituted for labour. The model above can be used to suggest why.[11]

Consider Figure 14.4 below. As household investment takes place and wages rise, lifestyles will develop and the basic wage and expected standard of living will increase. So the wage growth of demand curve will shift out to the right. The wage will rise; but the effect will be to lower the growth rate. That is, when the wage rate increases, consumption increases *pari passu* and this leaves less available for investment. From the point of view of the individual firm, the rise in wages means lower profits. But this can be offset by replacing workers with machinery, if the technology is available or can be

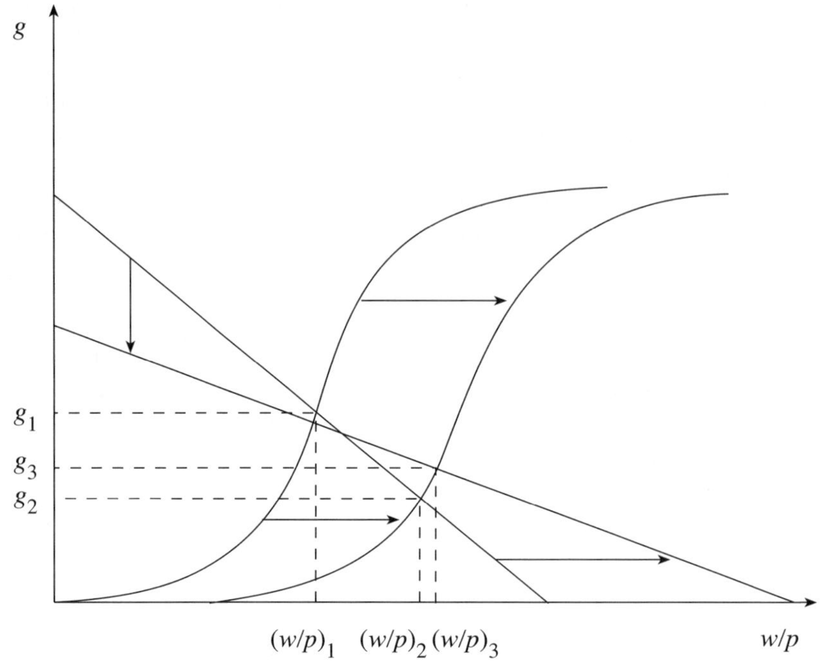

Figure 14.4 The impact of increasing real wages and labour-saving technical change

developed. If machinery is substituted for labour, the g-intercept of the wage-accumulation curve falls and the w/p-intercept rises. This will diminish the negative impact on growth of the shift in the wage growth of demand curve, and permit an even larger increase in the wage rate.

COLLECTIVE GOODS AND THE RISE OF GOVERNMENT

The desire of a set of households to rise in the world leads them to change the pattern of their consumption. More particularly, it leads to investment in education and training and to spending on communications. It will also lead to households relocating, especially to suburbs. One consequence of this is that businesses invest more. But another takes the economy in a new direction. For it means that the spending of increases in income will now be chiefly directed towards what may be called *collective* goods and *interactive* services. One person can eat a sandwich, or wear a shirt, without significantly affecting or involving anyone else, apart from the normal market processes. But for education there must be not only teachers and students, but subjects and disciplines. Indeed, there must be right and wrong answers and that implies a collectivity of minds. For a writer there have to be readers – and vice versa – but also there must be subjects and styles. No one can make a telephone call unless someone else answers. No one can travel without a destination. My health and yours are interconnected in regard to communicable diseases. Normal market processes, for these goods, involve multiple consumers acting in coordination, or even organized into networks, and there may also be networks of suppliers. As a result these goods tend to call for more intensive government regulation, and draw more intensively on government services.

Collective goods should not be confused with the familiar idea of *public goods*. The latter are defined as goods or services that are non-rivalrous, (and/or non-depletable, not quite the same thing), and non-excludable.[12] A lighthouse is a good example. If one ship uses it, this does not prevent another from doing so. Nor does it use up the lighthouse, leaving less for later ships. And once put in place and working, no ships can be excluded, that is, prevented from using the lighthouse. A bridge or a roadway is non-rivalrous (at least within limits) and non-depletable, but toll barriers can be erected, permitting exclusion.

But collective or interactive goods often do not meet these criteria. If I use the telephone line or access to the Internet, you cannot; if I use up the allotted time, others cannot. And access can easily be denied, so that fees can be charged. Education is similar: access to the class can be denied; and at a certain point the classroom is full, so that if this person is in the class, another one cannot be. (It is not true that the more one person gets from the class the less there will be for the others, however. On the contrary, the more some students get, the more the rest are likely to benefit.) One ship can use a lighthouse, whether or not any others do; one person can cross a bridge alone. But no one can make a telephone call alone, or travel without going somewhere. Commuter travel, in particular, moves people between home and work, which are socially defined places. No one can take a class or learn a subject without participating in an enterprise of many minds. No one can use money without others also doing so. No one can take out insurance unless others do so. Education, communications, transportation, FIRE[13] and entertainment – and even aspects of health – are *collective* experiences.

Collective goods, as these examples show, are often cooperative. But they can also be competitive, as with what Hirsch (1976) called 'positional goods'. Seats at a sports game, or in the theatre are positional; those with a better view are more desirable and command a higher price. The same is true of rooms in a hotel, travel packages and desirable real estate. Location is everything, and these goods are therefore rivalrous, maybe depletable – this year's World Series will never happen again – and are certainly excludable. Positional goods meet none of the criteria for being public goods, but they are clearly collective goods, and, as we shall see, like cooperative collective goods, call for more intensive government regulation, and interact strongly with other collective goods and with government services. Let us now consider some of the implications of all this.

Food, clothing and shelter, and many forms of energy are goods that can be consumed privately, by individuals or households, That is to say, the act of consuming these goods need not necessarily involve or require the cooperation of other individuals or households. (This is also true of some traditional public goods.) When per capita incomes are low, the greater part of household budgets will be devoted to these goods. But education, entertainment, communications, transportation and most forms of modern health care *do* necessarily involve or require the cooperation of others (Nell and Majewski, forthcoming, chapter 4). When per capita incomes increase, household spending will tend to shift towards these goods.

These kinds of goods often – perhaps usually – create *network externalities*, that is, the more members who join a network, the greater will be the benefits to each. A typical case is a telephone exchange. Service stations are another. Governments may need to supply or at least regulate such goods, in order to make sure that pricing for private profit does not result in an inadequate supply.

Collective goods also typically require regulation. They involve coordinated action by numbers of people, and regulation may be needed to ensure coordination. Moreover, the technology may be complicated or dangerous. Government oversight may be necessary. For all these reasons, collective goods call for more government spending.

Government economic activity in general responds to, or provides a foundation for, private economic activity. Private activity rests on public infrastructure – roads, bridges, harbors, sewers – and on basic collective services (usually with network externalities) like public health, police, justice, defence and education. The government may provide these services and infrastructure directly, or it might simply underwrite them and contract out their provision.

In either case, the amount of government *spending* required will vary in proportion to the amount and nature of private activity. Define a *coefficient of government spending* as the amount of government spending (G) called for *per unit* private economic activity. Then the general claim here is that collective goods have a higher coefficient of government spending than private goods, so that the shift from craft production to mass production has resulted in a rise in the ratio of G to income (Y) (Nell and Majewski, forthcoming, chapter 4). That is, as private businesses and households shift to collective goods and interactive services, government will not only do likewise, but it will in general be called on to spend more in a variety of ways.

There is a second feature of collective goods that contributes to the rise in G/Y. Among the major categories of government activity affected by increased demand for collective goods are education, defence, police and justice, medical services, pensions and social security and transportation. These tend to *interact* strongly with private sector collective goods and with each other. The analytical point here is that interactions increase with the *square* of the number of actors. For example, mass production leads to urban concentration. This increases interactions between people and requires increased policing and courts, and also increased attention to public health. If there are ten additional urban workers, potential interactions increase by one hundred (*actual* interactions will normally be fewer). The costs of policing and public health thus increase in proportion to the number of interactions, rather than the number of actors.

Meanwhile, more travel both requires and facilitates better communications, and both requires and contributes to better education. Better communications lead to better education and vice versa, and both stimulate the desire to travel. Better communications and better transport increases the choice of places to live and work, so that the real estate market develops.

Better education leads to higher productivity and to more rapid technical change, which, in turn, reduces the ability of the family to provide education, and so requires a further increase in public education. As people live longer and learn more, they demand better health and medical services; they also need pensions and social security, especially as they leave the land and move to the cities. All of these collective goods interact with government services. Increased transportation requires more and better traffic control, communications and education require regulation; urbanization requires public health measures and so on.

During the era of craft production, the ratio of private sector collective goods to all goods was low. As this ratio increased, interactions increased faster, but the initial impact on government was not large. As the craft economy developed into mass production, however, the ratio of collective goods increased greatly. The interactions between private sector collective goods, and between such goods and government services, increased exponentially, so that G/Y rose dramatically. This is portrayed in Figure 14.5. In the early stages of development, even a large rise in the ratio of collective goods to all goods leads to only a small increase in G/Y. But later, as the mass production era unfolds, even a modest increase in the collective goods ratio results in a large rise in G/Y.

The growth of government described above provides a significant contribution to the growth in demand.[14] As we have seen, the same process that leads to growth in household demand – competition among households to rise in the world through investment in self-improvement – leads to a shift in the

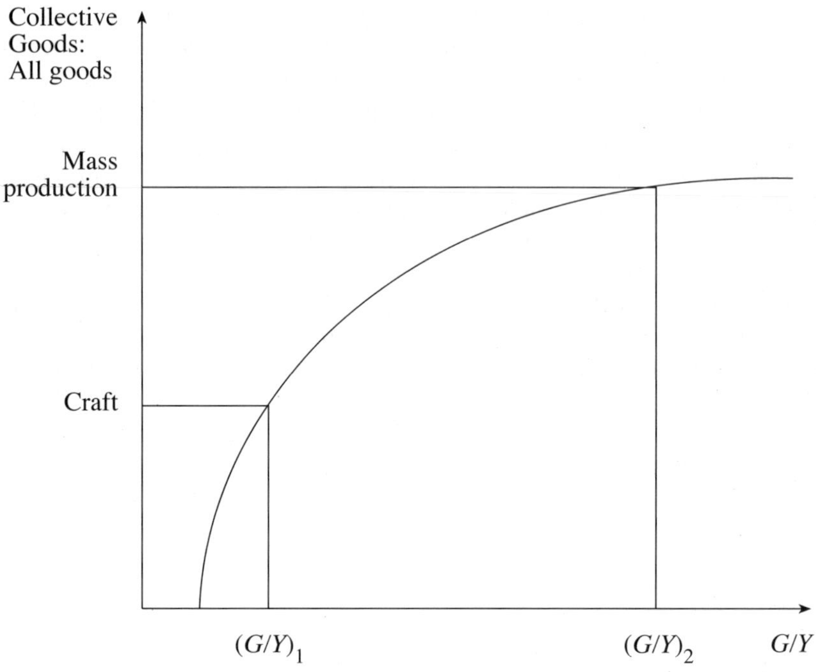

Figure 14.5 *Economic development and its impact on the ratio of government spending to income*

composition of expenditure towards collective goods. Activities requiring collective goods interact, which means that an increase in the number of such activities implies an increase in demand that is proportional to the square of the increase in activities. Also, activities requiring collective goods interact with government services, likewise implying a multiplicative increase in demand. Together, these changes require a larger size of government in relation to total output. The relative increase in government spending then raises the overall growth of demand.

CONCLUSIONS

Neither conventional nor alternative approaches offer much help in understanding the growth of demand. Indeed, most contemporary thinking does not even recognize the phenomenon or the need for an explanation. In the long run, it is held, supply determines demand. This is why growth theory has so strongly emphasized the supply side.

But when finance is available, demand can develop separately from supply. Moreover, as households identify possibilities for self-improvement, they will develop their skills and innovate. This will both change the composition of demand, and lead to the formation of new markets and to the expansion of demand generally. This growth needs explaining.

There are two parts to an explanation of the growth of demand. The easiest is the explanation of the growth of demand that follows the introduction of a new product. This follows a sigmoid path, tracing out the product cycle as the good diffuses through the income distribution. But more important is the introduction of new products, resulting from changes in the composition of demand. New products that service existing desires are easily explained, drawing on the programming approach to household budgets. Explaining changes in the composition of demand is more challenging.

Here, the clue comes from understanding changes in household budgets. the most important of these changes occur when a fraction of households tries to rise in the world. These would-be Horatio Algers invest in self-improvement and thereby change the composition of demand. Since the change in composition stimulates investment, this in itself leads to demand growth. But the effect of self-improvement is to increase productivity, and so incomes, leading to further demand growth.

As these Horatio Algers develop, they shift their demand more and more to collective goods, as these are the goods that will help them to rise in the world. Collective goods, in turn, interact; network externalities become prevalent. But these goods, in turn, require more and more government services; they have a higher government service coefficient than purely private goods. Furthermore, they interact with government services, which further intensifies the demand for government. Hence as the ratio of collective goods to private goods rises, the ratio of government spending to income (G/Y) will rise even faster. But the growth of G/Y, in turn, tends to raise the rate of growth. A higher rate of growth can be expected to increase real wages, leading to still further changes in household budgets, as households seek even greater self-improvement. This is a long-term cumulative process, leading both to perpetual demand growth, and to ongoing increases in productivity.

NOTES

1. Rather than being an account of growth, the Harrod–Domar formula might be considered a dividing line between two divergent *modes of operation* of a mass production economy (Nell, 1990; Nell, 1998). One is an excess capacity regime, in which demand always has a tendency to fall short of capacity, or rather, in which capacity is always running ahead of demand. The other is an excess demand regime, in which capacity is always running short. The first is typical of modern capitalism, the second of Soviet-style socialism.

2. The multiplier–accelerator model is very close to the Harrod–Domar, but differs in that it includes *time-lags* in formulating its investment and saving functions (Allen, 1965, Matthews, 1959).
3. Normal capacity will be built to service the expected normal level of demand; so new capacity will be added in the light of expected demand growth. It is the latter that calls for explanation. The crucially important implication of the multiplier–accelerator analysis, however, is that the aggregate demand aggregate capacity balance tends to generate an *unstable cumulative process*. That is, given the normal growth of demand to which normal capacity is adapting, a deviation from this in either direction will tend to set up a self-sustaining process that will continue moving in that direction. Expansion of capacity will generate even greater expansion of demand; contraction of investment will further contract demand. This is central to understanding macroeconomics, but it offers no help in explaining the *normal* growth of demand.
4. In the Cambridge view, short-run models of effective demand have investment-determining profits and so that the level of activity is demand-determined. But in the long run, they allow that profits may determine investment, so that supply determines demand. (New Keynesians would agree, substituting 'saving' for 'profits'.) The argument here suggests that the direction of causality assumed in the short run is also correct for the long run.
5. Strictly speaking, there can be no 'consumption out of profits'. Consumption is spending by households, whereas profits are the income of business. Business must *distribute* a portion of profits to households, for example, as dividends; then households may consume all or a fraction of that dividend income. In the case of the self-employed, a portion of the apparent profits must be designed as salary. Unusually large drawings must be considered on a par with dividend payments.
6. This would restrict the model to consideration of steady growth, in which variables were unchanged from period to period.
7. Of course the two interact, but separating them makes it possible to isolate the influence of demand growth, clearly a long-run question, while showing at the same time that interest costs are a short-run matter (Kalecki, 1939; Nell, 1988, 1998, chapters 10, 11).
8. For a related argument see Hicks (1989, pp. 10–11, *et passim*). Hicks's point is that Marshall's *flow* equilibrium for a particular period is inadequate; in most markets both suppliers and demanders may be interested in stocks, which requires admitting speculation over a sequence of periods. The point here is that the anticipated balance *over* time has to be considered in determining the best course of action at any *given* time. But the argument here concerns the growth of capacity, which is different from the holding of stocks. Current supply and demand are flows, and growth of supply and growth of demand refer to rates of change of flows. Stock-flow arguments may be superficially similar, but should be kept separate.
9. It does not follow that the long run will be characterized by steady proportional growth. On the contrary, in a class society there is good reason to think that, in general, steady proportional growth will not be attainable (Nell, 1986, 1992, 1998). A very simple argument shows this. Suppose there are only two classes, a wealthy class and a poor class, but both work and both own property. (The first group would be 'owner-operators' in early capitalism, receiving 'wages of superintendence' as well as profits; in a later era they would be professional managers owning stock. The second would be workers with pensions and savings.) The rate of interest on capital will be the same whoever owns it. But the possession of wealth will confer advantages in the earning of salaries; the wealthier will be in a better position to acquire skills and influence. So salaries will be higher than wages, in proportion to the difference in per capita wealth. The wealthy will be in a better position to save and to invest in human capital. Under these conditions the wealth of the richer class will tend to grow faster that the wealth of the poorer, thereby ensuring that the gap between the salaries of the managerial class and the workers also widens. Given that the consumption patterns of the rich and the poor will differ, the markets serving the rich will be expanding faster than those serving the poor.
10. Think of the increase in education at all levels in the early years of the twentieth century, the emergence of night schools (like the New School), the popularity of books on self-improvement, the development of guidance and vocational education in the public schools, and the

rise of new professions like personnel management. All of this was part of the emergence of a new middle class.

11. This analysis should be thought of as a study of *incentives to innovate*, not as an examination of the *choice of technique* (Nell, 1998, chapter 8). The wage-accumulation functions are assumed to be linear, in keeping with the results of input–output studies. But it would not matter were they to have some curvature, as long as it was not excessive.
12. 'Non-rivalrous' and 'non-depletable' tend to be considered the same, since both imply that the marginal cost of serving an additional customer is zero. But zero marginal cost is a supply-side criterion, whereas rivalry is a matter of demand. The neoclassical concern is that public goods lead to market failures; the exact nature of the goods is not significant. By contrast, the issue for TG is that an increase in collective goods changes the proportions and character of the economy.
13. FIRE stands for finance, insurance and real estate, all of which are collective, the latter involving 'positional goods'.
14. Government growth proceeded at a higher rate than gross national product (GNP) growth during the first half of the post-war period, tending to boost the economy. All government purchases of goods and services grew at 4.24 per cent from 1948–73, compared to GNP growth of 3.67 per cent, and all government employment grew at 3.62 per cent, compared to civilian labour force growth of 1.57 per cent. This was the 'golden age' of the modern economy. By contrast, in the second half of the post-war era, up until the Clinton boom, government growth was slower than that of GNP, measuring 1.80 per cent from 1973–93, compared to GNP growth of 2.36 per cent. The government labour force grew at 1.8 per cent during this period, slower than the approximately 2 per cent growth of the civilian labour force. So after 1973, the government tended to act as a drag on the economy's growth (Walker and Vetter, 1997, pp. 80–1, table, p. 170).

REFERENCES

Allen, R.G.D. (1965) *Macroeconomic Theory*, London, Macmillan.

Eichner, A. (1976) *The Mega-corp and Oligopoly*, Cambridge, Cambridge University Press.

Foley, D. and T. Michl (2000) *Theory of Economic Growth*, Cambridge, MA, Harvard University Press.

Halevi, J., D. Laibman and E.J. Nell (eds) (1992) *Beyond the Steady State*, London, Macmillan.

Harcourt, G.C. and P. Kenyon (1976), 'Pricing and the investment decision,' *Kyklos*, 29, 449–77.

Hicks, J. (1989) *A Market Theory of Money*, Oxford, Clarendon Press.

Hirsch, F. (1976) *Social Limits to Growth*, New York, Pantheon.

Kaldor, N. (1957) 'A model of economic growth,' *Economic Journal*, 67, 591–624.

Kaldor, N. (1961) 'Capital accumulation and economic growth,' in F. Lutz (ed.) *The Theory of Capital*, London, Macmillan, 177–222.

Kaldor, N. and J. Mirrlees (1962) 'A new model of economic growth,' *Review of Economic Studies*, 29, 174–92.

Kalecki, M. (1939) *Essays in the Theory of Economic Fluctuations*, London, Allen and Unwin.

Kurdas, C. (1993) 'A classical perspective on investment: exegesis of behavioral assumptions,' in R. Blackwell, J. Chatha and E.J. Nell (eds) *Economics as Worldly Philosophy*, London, Macmillan, 335–55.

Lancaster, K. (1966) 'A new approach to consumer theory,' *Journal of Political Economy*, 74, 132–57.

Matthews, R.C.O. (1959) *The Trade Cycle*, Cambridge, Cambridge University Press.
Milberg, W. and B. Elmslie (1992) 'Technical change in the corporate economy: a vertically integrated approach,' in W. Milberg (ed.) *The Megacorp and Macrodynamics: Essays in Memory of Alfred Eichner*, Armonk, N.Y., M.E. Sharpe.
Nell, E.J. (1988) *Prosperity and Public Spending*, London and New York, Unwin Hyman.
Nell, G.J. (1992) *Transformational Growth and Effective Demand*, New York, New York University Press.
Nell, E.J. (1998) *The General Theory of Transformational Growth*, Cambridge, Cambridge University Press.
Nell, E.J. and R. Majewski (forthcoming) *Leviathan's Wallet: Prosperity, Public Spending and Transformational Growth.*
Penrose, E. (1956) *The Theory of the Growth of the Firm*, Oxford, Basil Blackwell.
Robinson, J. (1956) *The Accumulation of Capital*, London, Macmillan.
Robinson, J. (1962) *Essays in the Theory of Economic Growth*, London, Macmillan.
Walker, H. and J.G. Vetter (1997) *The Rise of Big Government in the United States*, Armonk, N.Y., M.E. Sharpe.
Wood, A. (1975) a *Theory of Profits*, Cambridge, Cambridge University Press.

15. Is a biased technological change fuelling dualism?[1]

Pascal Petit and Luc Soete

A PERIOD OF 'TRANSITION' WITH LASTING EFFECTS?

Over the past two decades, major structural changes have affected the growth process in developed economies. A cluster of radically new information and communication technologies (ICTs) has emerged, accompanied by the internationalization of markets, financial capital and production processes, and the transformation of work in general and the structure of the labour force in particular. Such changes have both transitory and longer-lasting effects, and only through experience and learning will economic agents ultimately adjust their behaviours to the demands of the new environment.

Learning processes exist at various levels: within the technology-adopting firm, where efficient use of new technologies is heavily dependent on other users (subcontractors, customers or other firms and partners); among technology producers, who must adjust equipment to meet different user needs and confront different national technical standards; and among consumers, where cultural barriers slow the diffusion of new 'practices' in some cases, and erect barriers to access in others. This nexus of only loosely related learning processes lends credence to the assumption made by Freeman and Soete (1987) and David (1991) that transitions from one technological system to another may be long drawn out.[2]

But we should also be aware that all transitional periods have historically specific features that can condition final outcomes (Amendola and Gaffard, 1988). Schumpeterian evolutionary theory (Nelson and Winter, 1982, Dosi et al., 1988; Arthur, 1989) stresses that adjustment paths may be irreversible, and that the evolutionary nature of long-run development can completely transform choice sets and policy options following a so-called 'period of transition', This path dependency is all the more important if there exists some interplay between the various learning processes described above that results in a self-reinforcing growth process of the sort identified (in other contexts) by Myrdal (1957) and Kaldor (1972).[3] Three stylized facts suggest that such a growth process currently exists – one that could further divide societies and limit their ability to offer fair conditions of personal and collective development to their citizens in the future.

Growing Income Inequalities

Inequality has increased in nearly all Organization for Economic Cooperation and Development (OECD) economies over the last two decades. While the situation differs among countries and the type of income one considers (family or personal, before or after taxes and specific allowances and so on), there is a clear general trend within the industrialized world towards increased dispersion in wage incomes.[4] As economic growth has slowed down, some post-war trends in income distribution have been maintained (such as the life-cycle earning patterns of salaried professionals), some have been dampened (such as income growth among middle-income groups) and others have been reversed (such as income growth among low-wage earners and people on welfare).

These developments reveal differences in the tactical and strategic abilities of public and private agents. Some private agents have taken advantage of the new labour market, accessing new jobs and new sources of income, while others have struggled to follow suit for both economic and cultural reasons. Meanwhile, governments in most countries have been forced to reduce the magnitude and scope of income redistribution by a fiscal revolt, examples of which include the California balanced budget amendment and the fiscal crisis of the Swedish welfare model.

Skill-Biased Technological Change

Technological change, which has a broad systemic dimension and involves the reorganization of many tasks and activities, appears to display a strong skill bias. This bias will tend to cumulatively reduce the share of unskilled jobs, decrease the relative wages of unskilled workers and downgrade the working conditions of the unskilled.[5]

There may be numerous reasons for skill bias that are not technologically determined. Employment of skilled workers can help firms to face increased uncertainty, for example. Furthermore, innovators are increasingly prepared to pay for skilled workers as the costs associated with tangible investments (for example, in machinery) fall. The development of trade with low-wage countries also contributes to skill bias, by increasing the specialization of developed economies in production activities that require more skilled labour and/or advanced technologies. Finally, the growing supply of more educated workers may also promote increases in skilled work. It should also be noted that there are counter-trends at work. Shifts in the composition of demand that have increased the size of the service sector, for example, have enlarged the overall number of unqualified jobs.

A Biased Intangible Consumer Surplus

Products and services have undergone large and interrelated quality changes in terms of their content and conditions of use. Not all consumers are positioned to fully appreciate and benefit from these changes, especially when they are intangible. The debate over the mismeasurement of price indices demonstrates the magnitude of this phenomenon (see, for example, Boskin, 1996). While there are good reasons to doubt whether all of the biases in US consumer price index (CPI) measurement are important in other countries,[6] there is little doubt that the omission of quality improvements and poor measurement of new products and services is a world-wide phenomenon.

Quality improvements may be perceived in different ways by different consumers. This claim is consistent with analyses of consumption that stress the importance of social differences in attitudes towards new technologies. Consumers are in very different positions to organize their time and consumption when this requires specific competencies and information. Moreover, quality changes require users to spend time in learning processes before adjusting their choices. Finally, different capacities for interaction will affect the design and provision of 'networked' goods and services, in the development of which user-producer relationships are decisive.

Transitory or Lasting Cumulative Processes of Segmentation . . . and Slow Growth?

Our contention is that the dynamics of the three trends discussed above are linked in ways that are mutually reinforcing. Technologically driven skill bias puts downward pressure on the wages of the less qualified, limits the scope of their on-the-job training and hence reinforces rising income (wage) inequality. This, in turn, limits the capacities of these groups to develop new patterns of consumption, and induces producers to design their products and services in accordance with this market segmentation (even if such adjustment reduces the mass-market potential of their innovations). This process fuels dualism and specialization in consumption patterns. At the same time, differences in consumption patterns influence the structure of the labour forces' qualifications. Hence learning takes place through consumption patterns and lifestyles, so much so that some processes (such as information and communication technology (ICT) use) can be considered a form of training. Meanwhile, work practices influence lifestyles and consumption choices. These interrelated learning processes increase inequality by allowing those already well positioned in the labour market to reap the advantages of technology-intensive consumption goods.

An important question is whether these developments are transitory or lasting. They may represent a transitory phase during which the diffusion of new lifestyles and new work practices necessarily begins among those who are initially best able to adopt them. Increases in inequality will thus be confined to a temporary phase of innovation diffusion that will ultimately benefit all members of society. However, increased inequality may represent a durable characteristic of a new growth regime, in which the segmented development of production and consumption hinder the growth potential of the new technological system and lock economies into slow growth paths. There are reasons to believe that actual growth trajectories will fall somewhere between these extremes. For example, the diversity of individual learning trajectories may create a new form of social mobility that refashions the boundaries between traditional social groups. How large this effect is likely to be in practice remains, of course, an important and open question.

These complex issues cannot be resolved within the confines of this chapter. They can be clarified, however, by drawing attention to some ongoing debates and empirical findings that reflect on the workings of certain relationships and the magnitudes of some of the effects discussed above. In section 2, then, we begin by showing how the learning processes inherent in both production and consumption activities are linked and interact cumulatively. We then investigate in more detail the complex nature of these learning processes, and their relationship to skill-biased technical change on one hand (in section 3); the underestimation of the consumer surplus on the other (in section 4); and section 5 concludes.

INTERRELATED LEARNING PROCESSES AND ECONOMIC GROWTH

When studying the effects of a change in the technological system, analysts often invoke organizational problems in order to account for unexpected outcomes. The debate surrounding the productivity paradox in the 1980s and 1990s (a large-scale technological change, manifest in the omnipresence of computers, which had relatively little impact on productivity growth) provides a good example of this. For most analysts, the productivity paradox resulted from problems of organization on the supply side. We believe that this explanation has merit, but that it would be more comprehensive (and less of a black box) if it referred explicitly to the role of 'broad' learning processes operating simultaneously and interdependently in production and on the demand side. We suggest, moreover, that these learning processes are linked (much as learning-by-doing and learning-by-using are linked in some activities) and have a strong sectoral dimension. As much is obvious, if only in the fact that the productivity slowdown is more marked in certain service sector activities where productivity is difficult to measure.[7]

We take a broad approach to what we call the learning processes in production and on the demand side.[8] Numerous studies have looked at the dynamics of production. One could begin with Adam Smith's claim that the division of labour responds to the extension of markets. Some Marshallian notions of the industrial district are also good illustrations of 'meso' learning processes, as is Allyn Young's (1928) notion that the extension of markets promotes a division of labour stimulated by the dynamics of product and process innovations. Solow's (1957) work constitutes an explicit step towards accounting for increasing efficiency in production, even though his schematizaton of technical change is an entirely exogenous 'learning process'. Contemporary endogenous growth theory overcomes this, by combining the insights above. It centres its approach on the learning process taking place in production through the creation of externalities, whereby an activity, internal or external to the firm, has an impact on the dynamics of all firms. Many factors have been cited as generating these externalities. The accumulation of various forms of human capital (or research) is the factor referred to most frequently. It underlies the accumulation of on-the-job experience (which varies directly with the net capital stock, as in Romer, 1986), efforts to develop research activities (as in Romer, 1990) and the positive effects on labour efficiency of the general level of training (identified by Lucas, 1988).

Another related aspect of the literature on endogenous growth focuses on the positive externalities brought about by the successful development of certain activities, such as intermediary services (for example, baking, transportation, telecommunication and distribution). Ashauer (1989, 1994) and Barro (1990) study the positive impact on growth of public expenditures, Berndt and Hanson (1992), Munell (1992) and Morrison and Schwartz (1996) that of public infrastructure, Röller and Waverman (1996) that of telecommunications, and Amable et al. (1997) that of the financial system. Theories of endogenous growth focusing on the role of equipment investment (as in De Long and Summers, 1991) should also be included in this group.

These two branches of development in endogenous growth theory present a two-sided view of the global learning process in production. One focuses on the role of human capital, while the other focuses on the benefits of various types of infrastructure (including public infrastructures and intermediation services) that support productive activities. Notice also that the first branch tends to look at characteristics incorporated in individuals, while the other focuses more on organizational issues (if only because large public and private network services are central to this last approach). This distinction is not clear cut, however, since the first branch includes discussion of research and development (R&D) (an organizational issue) while the second discusses the effects of general equipment investment (a decision of individual firms).

Similar schemas exist on the demand side, although they are treated less frequently in terms of learning or adjustment processes. But to describe consumption in terms of levels of experience, income or capital is similar to describing it in terms of learning processes. Analytical studies of the diffusion process of new products present just such a perspective, whether they invoke imitation effects in the epidemiologic model, or changes in purchasing power as in the probit model of diffusion. More generally, analyses that show how the consumption patterns of particular social groups either imitate or become more differentiated from the consumption patterns of other social groups over time as prices and/or the distribution of wealth change) invoke precisely the sort of 'broad learning processes' on the demand side that were alluded to earlier in the case of production. Again, one may distinguish the process of individuals learning from reference groups (an individualistic process) from learning processes in which consumers respond to changes in the structure of market intermediation (an organizational issue).

Let us now consider the interdependence between the learning processes in production and on the demand side as discussed above. Both dynamics are bound to be functionally linked, if only because of the Smithian observation that the extent of the market influences the organization of production. But conversely, institutions (including those at the point of production) condition distribution in ways that determine the growth of various components of demand. This two-way interaction, which can be thought of as a process of cumulative causation *à la* Kaldor, is at the core of the interdependence between the two broad learning schemes that we wish to emphasize. The relationships linking these learning processes can be understood to operate at three levels: functional, institutional and ethical.

Functional links follow directly from the very structure of the production and consumption processes, as exemplified by the development of mass production and mass consumption in the past. This implied that patterns of consumption of final durable goods developed in lagged but similar ways among social groups with different incomes. Part of this development of consumption patterns relied on the fact that consumer durables freed some labour time from domestic activities, so that this labour time could then contribute to the development of organized lines of mass production and generate new sources of income. These linkages also had a strong institutional dimension, as evidenced by the wage-setting and welfare institutions that helped to stabilize demand. One could add an ethical value dimension, meaning that attitudes towards work, family and consumption all contributed to the overall interdependence of consumption and production.

A variety of linkages accounted for the self-reinforcing development of mass consumption and mass production, then. But this model of mass production and mass consumption is largely *passé*, and we now need to describe the equivalent features of the 'new economy'. Our understanding is that learning processes in production and consumption (intermediate or final) are now interacting on a new scale (and in ways that may either reinforce or hinder one another), at two levels: that of personal qualifications (individual human capital) and that of intermediation infrastructures (physical capital at the level of large organizations). In other words, the two perspectives on endogenous growth described earlier can help us to assess the specific linkages at work in the present mode of development. We shall try to clarify these linkages by reviewing the debates on skill-biased technology and on the intangible consumer surplus.

It may also help to present a preliminary model of the various relations we have so far described. Part of the complexity of this exercise stems from the fact that we must deal with at least two productive sectors, two types of workers and two types of consumers.

Let $i = 1, 2$ be the two sectors of the economy, where sector 1 broadly corresponds to manufacturing, and sector 2 to intermediation services broadly defined to include most business services and social services. Sector 2 thus comprises activities with strong external effects.

Following the Smithian tradition as elaborated by Kaldor, wherein productivity gains are stimulated by the expansion of markets, and adding some of the insights developed in endogenous growth theory, we begin with the following general expression for productivity gains in each sector:

$$z_i = f_i(x_i, Ip_j, Ih_i) \qquad [15.1]$$

where z_i and x_i represent, respectively, the growth rates of productivity and production in sector i over the medium run, and Ip_j is an indicator of the external effects of production in sector j on productivity in sector i. We postulate that $Ip_2 >> Ip_1 = 0$, since sector 2 encompasses large network services that are more likely to influence growth in sector 1 (according to the second line of thought in endogenous growth theory). Finally, Ih_i is an indicator of the quality of the human resources employed in sector i. This indicator of human capital formation (which corresponds to the first line of thought in endogenous growth theory) could be proxied by the ratio of qualified to unqualified labour in each sector.[9] Ih would thus reflect the rise in the demand for qualified labour that has been observed during the last decade. Conversely, this effect seems to have been more important in sector 1 (manufacturing) than in sector 2 (services).

Assumptions about the dynamics of demand must now be added to the preceding description of the dynamics of productivity gains. In accordance with our previous discussion, we suggest that the growth of demand in each sector depends not only on the usual price and income effects (subsumed here in the effects of productivity on demand), but also on two indicators, one measuring the 'qualifications' of consumers, *Il*, and the second capturing the external effects of the organizational quality of a sector ('provisionability'). For the sake of simplicity, we assume that provisionability is approximated by Ip_2 (our measure of the external effects of service infrastructures).

The growth of sectoral demand (q_i) can thus be described as follows:

$$q_i = g_i(z_i, z_j, Ip_2, Il) \qquad [15.2]$$

where z_i is productivity growth in sector *i*.

It seems reasonable to believe that Ip_2 (the organizational and provisional quality of sector 2) can be linked with the qualifications of users (*Il* for consumers and Ih_1 for firms) and the qualifications of the workers in sector 2, Ih_2. These linkages – together with those in equations [15.1] and [15.2] – are illustrated in Figure 15.1, which shows how interdependent learning processes

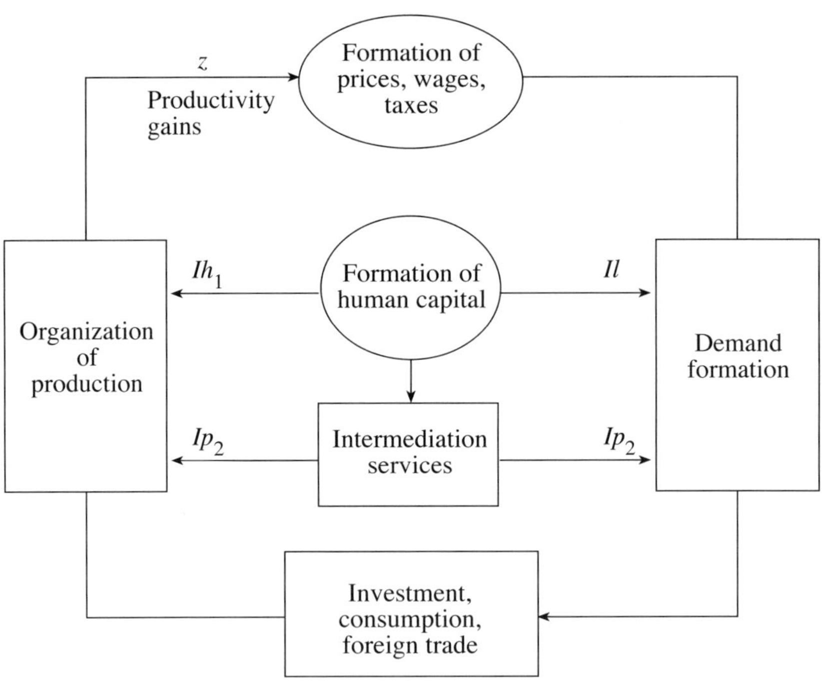

Figure 15.1 Dualism

on the demand side (distribution and demand formation) and in production (the generation of productivity gains) are influenced by human capital formation and the organization of intermediation (where services play the main role). These latter two, broadly interdependent features of endogenous growth, thus strongly condition the dynamics of an economy.

The effects on demand and production that are captured in equations [15.1] and [15.2] are somewhat crude and are based on the general assumptions presented in the introduction. However, it is possible to take advantage of two contemporary debates linked to the impact of new technologies on production and consumption to demonstrate the relative importance of what are postulated above as being the main traits of the growth process in contemporary developed economies. The first debate concerns the skill-biased nature of technological change, and tells us about changes at the point of production. The second debate concerns the measurement of the CPI, and reflects changes in consumption. Both debates are unresolved, something which is, itself, a reflection of the as yet hazy features of this period of transition in capitalist economies.

ON THE SKILL-BIASED NATURE OF TECHNOLOGICAL CHANGE

During the 1980s, when investment in new ICTs was growing, a marked change in the structure of manufacturing employment occurred, in favour of skilled labour (Howell and Wolff, 1992; Berman et al., 1994; Machin and Van Reenen, 1998; Berman et al., 1998). This skill bias seems to represent a major characteristic of the impact of ICTs on the labour market, and has even been coincident with a reduction in the demand for low-skilled labour in most countries (see Table 15.1). The impact of ICTs on service employment is much less clear cut, however, the situation varying from one country to another.

These observations suggest a new, *complementary* relationship between capital and skills (both being a substitute for unskilled labour), which contrasts with the fact that during the 'Fordist' era, capital was more often a *substitute* for skilled labour. Griliches (1969) explains this complementarity in terms of a decline in the relative price of capital,[10] whereas Denny and Fuss (1983) attribute the phenomena to specific effects of technical change. The questions arise as to how new technologies have had such an impact on work organization, and whether this impact is transitory, or a lasting departure from the old Fordist model. Moreover, if the new technologies possess such strong characteristics, why is their impact so different from one firm to another, from one country to another, and most markedly, from one sector to another (especially from manufacturing to services)?

Table 15.1 *Employment growth by skill level in manufacturing and services (annual percentage growth rates)*

	Blue-collar low-skilled		Blue-collar high-skilled		White-collar low-skilled		White-collar high-skilled	
	Manufacturing industries	Market services	Manufacturing industries	Market services	Manufacturing industries	Market services	Manufacturing industries	Market services
USA 1983–93	–0.2	0.2	–0.1	0.2	–0.1	1.4	0.2	0.9
Canada 1981–91	–0.7	0.1	–0.2	–	0.1	0.8	0.4	1
Japan 1980–90	0.1	0.3	–0.2	–0.1	0.5	1.3	0.4	0.9
Germany 1980–90	–0.8	–0.2	0.2	0.3	0.2	1	0.3	0.6
France 1982–90	–1.4	0.2	–0.3	–	–0.2	0.5	0.4	1.2
Italy 1981–91	–0.5	0.6	–1.0	0.1	–0.1	1.2	0.2	1.0
Australia 1986–91	–0.6	0.5	–0.3	0.1	–	1.2	0.4	1.8
New Zealand 1976–91	–0.5	–1	–1.3	0.3	–0.1	0.8	–0.1	2.3

Source: From Graph 4.3 in OECD (1996a, p. 88).

Before investigating these questions further, we first examine whether changes in the composition of employment may not have resulted from factors other than technological change, such as increased competition from low-wage countries (the trade effect) or an excess supply of qualified labour (resulting from a rise in the average level of education).

A Trade Effect?

Skill-biased technological change (SBTC) may be an indirect effect of trade specialization, whereby developed countries with high wages are forced to specialize in activities that are more skill-intensive. Although trade effects certainly explain part of the changing composition of employment, however, they cannot account entirely for the phenomenon. Most sectors are affected by technological change regardless of their exposure to trade (Berman et al., 1994; Machin, 1996). Berman et al. (1998) estimate that SBTC accounts for 70 per cent of the bias in labour demand by skill, whereas trade accounts for just 9 per cent.

Moreover, the trade effect argument can be broadened to include any change in demand, be it internal or external. Some studies insist that changes in competition, which have given more weight to non-price factors (such as product innovations, delivery and after sales servicing improvements and so on), have upgraded production processes towards more sophisticated products that make more use of qualified labour (see, for example, Goux and Maurin, 1995). At this stage, it is difficult to distinguish between labour market changes due specifically to technology and those due to a general change in product demand.[11] However, the narrow view that a mainly external trade effect accounts for the changing composition of employment can be discarded, because skill bias impacts across *all* sectors, including non-tradables.

The Effect of an Excess Supply of Skilled Labour?

Part of the skill bias may be the result of an increase in the demand for education in developed economies. This increased demand could be stimulated by slack in labour markets, which induces longer stays in initial formal education designed to delay entry into the labour market, and by individuals trying to improve their chances of finding employment. Such an effect has been underlined by, among others, Howell and Wolff (1992) for the USA and by Goux and Maurin (1995) for France. The increased demand for education, which has led to an increase in the average level of education in the labour force, is certainly part of the explanation for the skill bias in contemporary labour markets. Acemoglu (1998) suggests that skill bias can result from a large supply of skilled labour which, in turn, influences the organization of the work process and the choice of equipment (an endogenous change from this perspective).

Such effects should not, however, be exaggerated. In Europe, the unemployment rates of those with diplomas have increased along with those of other groups, so that schooling – even at high levels – does not provide full protection against unemployment or poor jobs. Conversely, the average yield on educational investments for college graduates has risen in the USA and the UK (Mishel et al., 1997). If the supply effect described above had been the main cause of skill bias, one would expect the yields on educational investment to have fallen.

The discussion above suggests that the effect of the large supply of skilled labour on labour demand was mixed with other changes in the functioning of labour markets, particularly with regard to wage formation. Analyses of the impact of investment in and the use of new technologies on wages have been carried out at firm and sectoral levels, both for specific types of workers and for the work force as a whole. This last distinction is crucial for the skill bias issue. In the first case we are examining the premium to users of new technologies, and in the second, the shared benefits of new technologies among all workers. We can expect that investment in new technologies, when it substitutes capital for labour, will increase the average wage rate. At the individual level, however, the expected effects are less clear.

Krueger (1993) shows that in the USA, the use of computers bestows upon workers a wage premium of some 15 per cent. This premium could be attributed either to an increase in productivity, or to the personal characteristics of computer users, which would have led to them receiving higher wages regardless. Recent studies tend to counter Krueger's view (which favoured the first explanation). In France, for example, Entorf and Kramarz (1994, 1996a, 1996b) show that workers using computers are paid more, but that they were also paid more before the introduction of the new technologies.[12]

For the most part, these empirical findings suggest that the use of a computer does not necessarily lead to an 'extraordinary' increase in personal wages. Individuals mainly receive a higher wage based on their personal characteristics. New technologies appear to be used by workers who already possess the personal characteristics that, according to conventional criteria, would result in their receiving higher wages.

But the introduction of computers is not the only change that occurred in labour markets at about the same time as the supply of educated labour increased. Changes in the economic environment coupled with adjustment to new technology and freer trade weakened the bargaining power of workers, as evidenced by the decline of unions and the reduction in minimum wages during the 1980s. This certainly helps to account for the relative decline in the wages of unskilled workers in the Anglo-Saxon countries at a time when those of skilled labour seemed to remain more or less constant in real terms. More precisely, as stressed by Storper (1999), the real wages of a small group of highly skilled professionals have increased on average, while the wages of the semi-skilled were losing ground and those of low-skilled workers declined significantly.

SBTC is therefore part of a large-scale reorganization of work and labour markets, in which the supply of educated workers, trade technology and the dynamics of work organization (within firms and intra-firms) and labour market relations all play a role. Examining the content of skills and their sectoral dimensions assists further investigation of these transformations.

What is the Content of Skills?

The empirical findings reported above show that firms tend to select potential users of ICTs based on individual criteria that pre-date the introduction of the new technologies. Preferences for skilled workers *per se* (as opposed to those with job or firm specific skills) characterize a technological environment that requires more general knowledge and competencies that can be applied in various contexts. The content of these skills seems to be, to a greater extent than before, knowledge geared towards transversal problem solving (Gibbons, 1994) and personal experiences that demonstrate awareness and responsiveness. Firms do not seem to pay specifically for a skill bias (since they do not upgrade the jobs of those using ICTs) but do seem to attach importance to certain personal characteristics and to ensure that ICT users possess specific individual competencies. This focus on the abilities of individuals seems to be more important than any collective reorganization of work designed to service the new technologies.

The notion of skill used in many of the studies referred to above makes only a crude distinction between production and non-production workers.[13] Moreover, jobs require a multitude of different skills. By considering three major dimensions of skill – cognitive (analytic and synthetic reasoning, numerical and verbal facilities), motor (physical abilities, coordination, dexterity) and interpersonal skills (supervisory skills, leadership) – Howell and Wolff (1992) and Wolff (1995) construct three skill scales on which basis they grade occupations by sector, and document changes in these grades during the 1980s. The more sophisticated picture given by these studies confirms the general decline in the demand for unskilled labour, but associates it with a drop in the demand for motor skills.[14] Meanwhile, the demand for higher cognitive and interactive skills is shown to increase. These studies also suggest that the effects of investment on the skill structure may differ depending on whether investment is in general equipment or ICTs. As the latter represents only a small fraction of total investment (Oliner and Sichel, 1994; Sichel,

1997), the specific effects of ICTs on skills may sometimes be obscured by conventional capital–labour substitution effects.

Are there Sector-specific Biases in Skill-bias Trends?

Most of the studies referred to above concentrate on manufacturing industries. But as two-thirds of employment and ICTs are found in service industries, it is not appropriate to draw conclusions about skill bias without verifying that most of the arguments apply to services.

The evolution of low-skilled employment in Table 15.1 shows just how different the experiences of the manufacturing and service sectors have been. Looking in more detail at the evolution of employment by skill level in French service industries from 1982 to 1991, we observe that in activities like social services, public administration and household services, the growth of unskilled employment outpaced the growth of skilled employment (OECD, 1994).[15] In most services, the number of unskilled workers continually rose, though at a lower rate than for skilled workers. Only in finance and communication do we observe a net decrease of the unskilled labour force as observed in all manufacturing industries (as well as in agriculture, mining and construction). As these industries have also invested more in ICT equipment than the others, this observation provides some support for the SBTC thesis. The diffusion of ICTs may also increase the relative demand for skilled labour in other service industries, but the demand for unskilled labour in absolute terms is likely to remain important as these activities continue to grow. And because of the absolute amount of employment in these activities, the way in which they use the new technologies is a crucial issue.

A Reorganisation of the Supply Side

Most of the studies discussed so far analyse the skill bias of new technology as if it were an individual issue, disregading the fact that the primary concern of a firm is with work organization as a whole. These organizational issues are certainly difficult to typify in times of structural change, where diverse reactions by firms are frequently observed (Attewell, 1994). This explains the lack of statistics on organizational structures in general and, in particular, the lack of studies exploring skill bias and the productivity paradox as extensively as these issues have been examined in the context of more individual aspects of employment.

Questions about work organization can be addressed by referring to Aoki's (1988) distinction between the information structures embodied in the different forms of work organization in Japan (horizontal structure of decentralized decision-making processes) and the USA (vertical structure of centralized decision processes).[16] Hence Piore (1988) suggests that the US model has used the new technological context to change towards more horizontal channels of communication, with less hierarchy and reduced specialization (thus moving closer to Aoki's Japanese model of organization). However, even if this is true, the 'tacit' channels of horizontal communication typical in Japan cannot be perfectly replicated by communication based on information technologies, which is bound to be more codified. In the new systems created by these latter organizational changes, there may be more communication between units, but fewer ways to control the instability at lower levels of the organization that this creates. The factors that inhibit the strengthening of linkages between individual and organizational productivities, as discussed by Goodman et al. (1994), are effectively universal: the permanence of slack, the hierarchy between core and peripheral activities, compatibility between problem-solving methods and so forth. The question, then, is why are ICTs diffusing in all sectors and countries if their uses are so problematic?

The most fundamental reason concerns firms' need to respond to market pressures, to differentiate and enrich products and to provide commodities in new ways. Such responsiveness to product market forces necessitates greater interdependency within productive systems. A second reason is that 'codified' horizontal communication is much more open to central control that the tacit horizontal coordination of information, and therefore permits greater responsiveness to radical process or product innovations. This is vital for firms operating in global markets and organizing their production on an international basis as well. Both of these reasons are compatible with the increased demand for cognitive skills and interactive/supervisory skills noted earlier.

These comments on qualifications of organizational change remain highly tentative, but their spirit is broadly in accordance with studies that insist on the diversity of work organization responses to technical change. These studies confront us with two hypotheses. First, that firms undergo a standard process of trial and error before one best practice of work organization imposes itself and diffuses to a majority of firms.[17] And second, that the new technological environment of the firm is such that there is no dominant model, only specific applications that are relevant in particular competitive/cooperative contexts. It follows that the work reorganization process becomes chronic (Attewell, 1994). In such a rapidly changing work organization environment, skills are bound to become obsolete more quickly than before. The relative instability of this environment, which leads firms to opt for organizations that can be continuously transformed and adapted, is also related to the increasing number of linkages that have developed between firms (see the contributions to Harris, 1994).

If a significant change in firms' perspectives on work organization has, in fact, occurred, and if work reorganization has become a chronic issue with diverse solutions (as illustrated by the continuous spread of new organizational forms, such as re-engineering, merging, networking, externalizing, work-flow processes, groupware and so on), then it is likely that the relationship between the spheres of work activities and household activities will be transformed as well. The fact that skills are becoming obsolete more quickly will be an important factor in the evolution of this relationship. The conclusions drawn from this brief survey of the skill-bias issue lead us now to review how the new technical system can be viewed from the 'other' sphere, that is, from the perspective of the consumer and worker.

NEW CONSUMERS AND THE DISTRIBUTION OF THE CONSUMER SURPLUS

Our main claim here is that the divisions occurring in society in terms of the desire and ability of individuals or families to use new technologies are closely related to what is happening within work organizations. This broad learning process occurring outside the firm concerns not only the composition of the baskets of consumption goods and services that consumers buy, but also the way in which the provision of these commodities, together with the processes through which they are consumed, incorporate new technologies and the know-how associated with them. This is especially relevant for those services organized in networks. Linkages between the two broad learning processes (within and outside the workplace) may be transitory, and may correspond to a classic sequencing in the access to new lifestyles, as a result of which everyone will eventually converge to some general standard. But they may involve a more lasting and structural drift with detrimental long-term effects on social cohesion that could, in turn, hinder the process of economic growth. We return to this possibility below, but begin by discussing some of the stylized facts about changes in consumption patterns that have been highlighted by the debate about the 'consumer surplus'.[18]

Lessons from the Debate over the CPI

The current debate over the CPI helps illustrate some of our concerns. Questioning the accuracy of the CPI raises questions about measurement techniques and about how well consumers are able to appreciate changes in the content of goods and services and in the way they are provided. In what follows, we do not discuss the techniques of CPI measurement employed by national statistical agencies. This issue is important, due to the role that price indexing plays in fixing wages, public transfers and contracts in most countries, but it is not directly linked to our topic. However, those aspects of the CPI measurement debate, which are concerned with the difficulties involved in comparing the real values of two baskets of goods and services at different points in time when a large, systemic technological change has occurred, are central to our topic.

The debate over the CPI has drawn attention to those areas where diverse technological changes are most difficult to appreciate, and attempted to attach an order of magnitude to the underassessment of quality change. In the USA, the Boskin report (Boskin, 1996) provides a detailed account of the 'guesstimations' that the commission arrived at for measuring various components of CPI mismeasurement, on the basis of a large body of pre-existing econometric work. The report concludes that the underestimation of quality change may have led to an upwards bias in the CPI of 0.6 per cent per year. The impact of an increasing ability to substitute one type of retail outlet accounts for a further 0.1 per cent upward bias.[19] Overall, the unmeasured consumer surplus, net of the technical drawbacks due to measurement procedures, amounts to 0.7 per cent a year.[20] This net bias is quite sizeable if one compares it with the average growth rate of large OECD economies (1.6 per cent per annum from 1989–93).

Most critics of the Boskin report have emphasized two points: the inevitability of delays when taking account of innovations, and the report's biases in selecting information on quality changes.

Delays when taking into account innovations present a dilemma for national institutions measuring the CPI. If, in order to keep pace with the behaviour of the average consumer, they wait until a sizeable share of consumers have adopted a new product, then its price will already have fallen significantly and the quality improvement may go unnoticed. If, however, they include the product in the CPI at too early a stage, it concerns too few consumers and carries little weight. The introduction of new product or service thus necessitates a careful choice as to when to include the product in the CPI basket, and an appreciation of the quality improvement it involves. Neither is easy. It seems that institutions measuring the CPI tend to include new products with some sight delay.[21] Meanwhile, estimates of quality improvements require detailed information and are all the more open to criticism of whether the innovation in question is radical.

The second line of criticism also bears on the quality of information on innovation. The Boskin report has been criticized for relying on limited sources of pre-existing information (specifically, the hedonic pricing of innovations) that are biased towards suggesting that price inflation is overestimated. Indeed, the argument that, in some instances, price inflation may have been underestimated is hard to deny. But even if the overestimation of price inflation suggested by the Boskin report is, itself, overestimated, the CPI measurement debate has drawn attention to important sources of uncertainty surrounding the quantification of goods and services, and the increased importance of product innovation.

At this point, it must be acknowledged that, when changes are as far reaching as those induced by ICTs, the very meaning of a cost of living index is transformed. Moreover, many of these changes are taking place in domains where change has always been difficult to measure. The housing category, for instance, encompasses various issues that are not given much weight in the correction of the CPI in the Boskin report, such as housekeeping services (where an ever-increasing variety of services is on offer). Medical care is accorded a relatively high unmeasured rate of technical change, but entertainment and educational services are not, despite the profound structural changes in these activities brought about by ICTs.

In sum, those areas where the magnitude of unmeasured technical change is uncertain remain important. These are mainly service activities. Nakamura (1995), who performed an exercise similar to that of the Boskin Commission on the Bureau of Economic Analysis (BEA) national accounts, estimates that the net unmeasured technical change in personal consumption is as high as 2.5 per cent per year over the period 1984–93. The differences between Nakamura's and the Boskin report's findings arise from the recreation services, education and housing industries.

This leads us to stress that, in addition to the way in which products and services are provided, the *context* in which consumption occurs matters. If products are more differentiated, then it follows that their utility is more context-specific. It becomes ever more difficult to appreciate a consumption basket as a collection of separate items. The welfare effects of the consumption of these products are more interdependent, because the temporal and personal dimensions are becoming more closely tied to consumption. The facts that people are faced with a time budget constraint and that consumption is becoming more time consuming (if only because of its increasing service content) implies, when technologies are transforming these time constraints, that changes in the management of time constraints will take place. The fact that products are becoming ever more customized also implies changes in consumer behaviour. These transformations, which are bound to be highly dependent on individual characteristics, generate a consumer surplus that is largely hidden and very likely unevenly distributed.

The next step is to consider how this hidden consumer surplus affects different social groups, and what it tells us about the dynamics of consumption and the learning process that is shaping consumer behaviour.

The Distribution of the Consumer Surplus: the Role of Large Service Networks

The debate over the unmeasured consumer surplus is motivated by two issues. One is a fiscal issue; many public transfers, pensions and revenues are indexed on the basis of a CPI, and overestimation of this index has a sizeable effect on the public budget deficit. The second issue relates to the distribution of income; income inequalities have been growing in most developed countries over the last two decades.

It is relatively easy to get a rough estimate of the impact of mismeasurement of the consumer surplus on the budget deficit or on the balance of taxes and transfers to various social groups. It is much harder to get an idea of its effect on the distribution of welfare, however. One can argue that gains and losses to different groups balance out. Groups with less income, education and culture will certainly miss out on some of the advantages of unmeasured quality changes, but will gain by having improved access to, and facing lower prices for, goods and services. But this hypothesis underestimates the facts that we begin with very unequal distributions of income and education, and that the existence of an unmeasured quality change underscores the opacity and inequality that exists in access to and the diffusion of new commodities. People will differ as to how they access new goods and services, and with regard to what they get out of them.

The large variety of goods (see Gordon, 1990), together with the increase in the range of services at our disposal, has been accompanied by proliferation of the ways these goods and services are bought and sold, and financed. Consumption in this environment has become more complex, and has broadened the opportunities for 'smart' consumer behaviour. Indeed, the pressure of smart consumers (either individually or organized in associations and through the media) is playing a major role in increasing competition and shaping more demand-oriented market economies – although conversely, large numbers of people in the lower reaches of the income distribution find it hard to escape quality changes they cannot avoid, varieties they cannot afford or improvements that are of no use.

We have chosen to analyse two dimensions of consumer 'skills': those linked with appropriate and efficient use of intermediation services, and those embodied in personal skills. We begin by focusing on the intermediation provided by large (public or private) services.

The provision of services via large network systems is one area in which social discrimination is both effective and structuring. Particularly important in this respect are financial services, which have greatly increased in variety and have led to a wide spectrum of results, from rapid fortunes built on speculation to the unbearable indebtedness of some low-income households. Similar increases in the range of consumers' capabilities to use new services efficiently can be observed in education, health, communication, transport and public services. This social differentiation in patterns of use can originate from two factors: the differing abilities of users to take advantage of modern intermediation systems, and the tendencies for large systems to develop their organizations while taking this differentiation for granted.

Education is a classic case, even if it has not yet been thoroughly transformed by ICTs. The fact that an increase in the average number of years of schooling years has been accompanied by rising illiteracy and other poor results (such as the increasing incidence of dropouts, of unqualified school-leavers, of poor scores on general and specialized tests – see OECD, 1998) suffices to illustrate the widening of the range of achievements.

The development of telecommunications between the various agents and phases of treatment in health systems is still at an early stage, but already raises some of the main issues regarding the path of contemporary technological change. These developments imply an active interface between health system professionals and their patients. The design of this interface presents a standard trade-off: the larger its scope, the more useful and beneficial will be its operation in terms of the range of interventions covered. Conversely, the more complex the interface, the higher will be the barriers to access, depending on the general 'skill level' of the population. Modern treatment systems – such as HMOs – have improved the quality of care, but have also been accompanied by some ordering of access which, in the context of large inequalities in education or income, may result in the exclusion of some patients from care (see Boulier, 1994).

Financial services, and especially retail banking, have already experienced various phases of computerization of their network facilities. Increased competition and improvements in the quality of equipment fuelled the reorganization of financial networks and organizations, which has, in turn, resulted in some exclusion of access to services. For example, banks in the USA and the UK have closed local branches, replacing them with the limited services of automated tellers (see Pratt et al., 1996 for the UK and Dymski and Veitch, 1993 for the USA). This has had detrimental effects on local communities.

When examining these developments, we must distinguish between personal services (such as education and health) and intermediation services, which are offered to both firms and individuals and where technological and/or organizational transformations are interdependent. While in the first case the potential created by ICTs is being realized only slowly, and depends extensively on public policy interventions, the dynamics of market competition have resulted in a rapid transformation of the ways in which most intermediation services (distribution, transportation, communication, banking and so on) operate. This pressure to restructure has been both a cause and consequence of recent deregulation and re-regulation initiatives, an institutional context that is crucial to the provision of these intermediation services.

The development of large network services, as stimulated by the new technologies, can thus perpetuate segregation in the provision of the sort of consumer services that are crucially important in the new economy. Moreover, these developments possess a strong path-dependent dimension that may hinder the development of new personal skills. In this respect, universal access to such services does not guarantee that there exists equal opportunity to use service networks with the same efficacy.

The Distribution of the Consumer Surplus: the Role of Personal Skills

Consumer behaviour is supposed to be determined by income, education and social background. These social roots have been very important in shaping the preferences of consumers in the post-war period, making all consumption projects in a given society more or less commensurable (see, for example, Galbraith, 1958 or Packard, 1957). A characteristic of the current period may be a loosening of these social ties, transforming societies of classes into societies of individuals or transient small groups.[22] In these more atomistic societies, what do 'consumer skills' consist of? Their generation is more evolutionary, meaning that they are more dependent on individual experience within the universes of markets, law and public (welfare) interventions (universes that are, themselves, evolutionary). The use of ICTs, at work or at home, contributes to these interfactes. It is in this sense that we can speak of a broad learning process for the building-up of consumer skills. Beyond some common hedonic principle, social links have become more uncertain or differentiated and casual personal networks more important. Paradoxically, this lack of social cohesion, because it means the absence of centripetal forces, leads to more risky dynamics, where failures will be more difficult to overcome and will tend to cumulate over one's lifetime.

Atomistic societies may therefore lead not to more egalitarian societies but to more divided societies. Such will be the case if the level of individual risk has increased. Such may be the case if one considers the relative erosion of the means of social promotion or of self-achievement brought about by education and work. We have already discussed this development, which may be due to excess supply of educated people as well as to rapidly changing markets and production processes. If ICTs play a role in this evolution of the labour market, however, then they can also confer new abilities on individuals, helping them to overcome some of the drawbacks of labour market developments.

But the private use of ICTs has its limits. It may be complex and require much coordination, while opportunities for misuse proliferate (see Landauer, 1995). Personal ITC use may also be too specific and hence ultimately irrelevant in terms of skill development and personal autonomy, while the overlap between cognitive skills developed at work and in the home may vary considerably. And yet, the development of skills in the home, where the learning process may last longer, is especially important when the learning process at work is limited or constrained. Ultimately, the interplay of skill development at home and at work is bound to be very different across groups with different experiences and backgrounds. Cultural and financial barriers to the access to new facilities or the use of new equipment has led experts to express fears that a two-tier Information Society could develop. Policy statements have emphasized the important role that domestic ICT use can play in curtailing this development (see, among others, the Group of Prominent Persons, 1994 and the EU's High Level Expert Group on the Social Aspects of the Information Society, 1996.

Elites and professional classes will have more opportunities to benefit from what ICTs can offer, while those at the margins, with low income, little education and limited social connections, will find it increasingly difficult to keep 'in touch' with the capabilities bestowed on consumers by ICTs. The shift towards services in consumption patterns is increasing the challenges this dilemma presents. Time becomes a binding constraint in producing one's own welfare (Petit and Soete, 1996), a problem that consumers can solve with differing efficiencies depending on their ability to use ICTs.[23]

Parallels can be drawn between the personal requirements for a skilled consumer and the requirements for a skilled worker. In both cases, a skilled person will be expected to respond positively to external challenges induced by ongoing structural changes, and to constantly find ways to improve the internal efficiency of their actions (the ability to develop a learning-by-doing process). In a world of bounded rationality and limited information, one way to balance these internal and external learning processes is to have access to various groups or networks (either more or less formal) from which information and support can be obtained. Two illustrations of this are instructive. Gollac (1996), looking at how computer users at work manage their work, finds that those using their computers in the most innovative ways (programming or using several software programs) typically form a reference group based on relations outside the firm. Referring to colleagues in remote positions within their own firm is listed second in importance, and close colleagues third. By contrast, for people using computers in limited ways (for example, always using the same software for definite operations), the order of importance was the opposite.

Similar signs emerge from investigations of the best means of protecting individuals against unemployment: those with a large range of diverse connections enjoy the most effective protection. It follows that having strong links within a particular network or community may not be as valuable as a portfolio of connections.[24] Having numerous weak ties (in the sense of Granovetter, 1995) markedly increases an individual's reach, the scope of their action and their ability to respond rapidly to changes in the labour market.

The similarity between the abilities and skills required of individuals at work and in the home seems to be a key feature of the new environment. Similar capacities to learn and to adapt to new contexts are required in production and consumption. Learning processes at work and home are therefore broadly complementary at an individual level. Nevertheless, these processes are affected by the intermediation structures that provide education and the various logistics of services that we discussed earlier. Moreover, it does not follow that the two processes are spontaneously self-reinforcing. There are many reasons to believe that this cumulative interaction involves risks, and that part of the learning process concerns how best to monitor these risks. For instance, the fabric of weak ties and the logistic support systems mentioned above have a high rate of obsolescence. Individuals may then be exposed to hazards that result in lasting or irreversible consequences ('accidental' poverty and unemployment can act as traps in some cases). There is also uncertainty as to the best portfolio of connections. Moreover, as Attewell (1994) suggests, the use of ICTs may have considerably increased risks by multiplying the number of cases that involve asymmetric information, as schematized in principal-agents problems. Finally, it is a general property of systems to become more unstable when the number of internal linkages they involve increases.

CONCLUSIONS: ON UNBALANCED AND UNEQUAL GROWTH

Both the productivity paradox and the difficulties most economies have encountered when trying to turn the diffusion of contemporary technological change into steady and evenly distributed rates of economic growth have largely been attributed to the length of the learning processes involved. On the production side, these learning processes seem to require intricate coordination, which is largely decentralized and therefore difficult to implement (Freeman and Soete, 1994; David, 1991). Our survey of the 'skill-bias' issue stressed some of the characteristics of this learning process. It conveyed the impression of a rather atomistic approach to the reorganization of work, which puts a new emphasis on personal characteristics. From this perspective, the changes occurring in the workplace and in consumption activities appear similar: 'smart' consumers seem capable of improving their share of a 'reconstructed total welfare', while many others find that their situation has deteriorated.[25] A review of the debate over the unmeasured consumer surplus lent support to this view, and emphasized the fact that consumer learning processes now appear more casual and less dependent on a pre-existing class structure, even if both education and the infrastructure of service provision play a major structuring role. Moreover the development of a sizeable set of skilled or 'smart' consumers, which, together with globalization, accounts for the more competitive nature of markets, is related to the development of a group of skilled workers who suceed in tying together the learning processes in which they are engaged at work and in the home. Meanwhile, no sign was found of any significant catch-up mechanisms, which would ensure that those currently lagging behind will do so only temporarily. On the contrary, the system seems to have generated new risks and instabilities which, thus far, policies have not learned to cope with.

The prospects for economic growth are thus related to two interdependent 'macro'-learning processes, which, in turn, provide an important perspective on the relationship between inequality and growth. Inequality of access to education and service infrastructures hinders developments that utilize ICTs to best advantage, as they limit the positive network externalities that would otherwise occur. That some groups are able to take increasing advantage of networks and even adjust them in order to do so does not seem to counterbalance the negative effects of exclusivity.

Mechanisms capable of countering this dualist trend are few in number. Income redistribution can help, but cannot by itself fill an access gap that includes non-monetary barriers. Education and the services, which provide the intermediation necessary to reduce access inequalities, certainly contain the solutions, but effecting these solutions, in turn, poses a variety of quantitative and qualitative problems. In particular, it is difficult to set up the idiosyncratic formulae that will help countries to take advantage of their specificities, design the proper learning schemes that will develop the mechanisms enabling them to strengthen social cohesion, and thereby make the best use of contemporary technological change.

The aim of this chapter has been to summarize the architecture of the linkages between technical change, inequality and growth. In short, we have stressed that inequalities in welfare hinder growth prospects as never before. They impede economic growth without developing any self-correcting mechanisms, while simultaneously limiting the efficacy of old remedies, such as income redistribution. The sooner these issues are understood and rendered manageable, the better able society will be to benefit from the current historical turn.

NOTES

1. Earlier versions of this chapter were presented at the meetings of the AEA, Chicago, January 1998, and at the conference on the Service Sector, Productivity and the Productivity Paradox organized by the Centre for the Study of Living Standards in Ottawa in April 1997. We are grateful to Ellen Dulberger, Mike McCracken and Andrew Sharpe for helpful comments and suggestions.
2. The diffusion of electrical power and the dynamo, for example, took 50 years.
3. Neoclassical endogenous growth theory, stressing the external effects of increasing returns, has been inspired by this tradition.
4. See Atkinson et al. (1995), Gottshalk (1993), Freeman and Katz (1993), Sharpe and Zyblock (1997) and Mishel et al. (1997).

5. See Howell and Wolff (1992), Berman et al. (1994), Card et al. (1995), Machin (1996) and Nickel (1996).
6. See Lequillier (1997), Fenwick (1997) and the OECD survey of the measurement of CPIs presented at the Economic Policy Committee meeting, December 1997. The Boskin Report is, itself, much debated of course (see Moulton et al. 1997).
7. According to Griliches (1994), three-quarters of the output of the computer industry goes to activities where real output cannot be measured.
8. The use of the term 'learning process' is somewhat metaphorical, as it combines various time-dependent processes, only some of which constitute real microeconomic learning processes. This 'global' use of the term 'learning process' will become clearer as we proceed.
9. Note that this is a restrictive measure given the assumption in endogenous growth theory that the *entire* stock of human capital impacts the efficiency of production.
10. The sharp reduction in the price of microprocessors is an important feature of ICTs.
11. See Nickel (1996) and Cotis et al. (1995).
12. Similarly for Germany, Di Nardo and Pischke (1997) show that the use of computers results in positive returns for individuals . . . but so does the use of pencils. Only Bell (1996), using a sample of 1000 individuals, born in 1958 and surveyed in 1981 and 1991, found a net increasing effect on wages for those using computers at work in 1991, thus supporting Krueger's view (assuming that no one used computers in 1981).
13. This distinction is correlated with a number of alternative distinctions based on broad characteristics of educational attainment or occupational category, as Berman et al. (1995) have shown for the USA.
14. The shift towards service activities is a major cause of the decrease in demand for motor skills.
15. A similar result is observed in most large OECD countries (see OECD 1996b).
16. These structures display different capacities for facing and organizing technological change, with the Japanese horizontal structure of information (in its work organization) being more fit to diffuse and implement incremental innovations in products or processes, whereas US firms, with their more vertical structures of information (as characterized by their hierarchical work organization) would be better at facing radical technical changes.
17. This hypothesis would explain the current period as a standard period of transition.
18. This debate seems more active in other social science disciplines, such as sociology, political science, geography or business and management sciences. Most economic studies of the consumer surplus deal with very narrowly defined products (see, for example, Fischer and Griliches' (1995) study of two prescription drugs, Trajtenberg's (1990) discussion of CAT scanners or Hausman's (1994) analysis of a new breakfast cereal.
19. This is based on Reinsdorf (1993).
20. The total bias in CPI measurement in the USA amounts to 1.10 per cent a year when all of the technical improvements in measurement made by the BLS (Bureau of Labor Statistics) since 1996 are taken into account.
21. The Boskin report gives some examples of this delayed inclusion (p. 39), mentioning that cellular phones (with over 36 million users in the USA) were not included in the CPI basket at the time of the report's writing, despite being used by over 36 million people.
22. Forse (1998), for instance, stresses this weakening of class ties.
23. These problems are compounded by the fact that low-skilled workers are subject to rigid work schedules, while skilled workers and professionals have more flexible working arrangements, even if their hours are longer (see Schor, 1999).
24. We are the word 'portfolio' in reference to studies in industrial organization that stress that new large firms are engaging in a series of alliances, joint ventures and the like, which they attempt to manage in an optimal fashion so as to deal with rapid changes in competition and technologies in various markets.
25. There are absolute and relative dimensions to this dissatisfaction. Some have increasing difficulty coping with the contemporary challenges of more demanding labour markets and consumer know-how (a euphemism for those with low incomes), while others (as stressed by Storper, 1999) resent the growing range of consumer outcomes, based on the fact that individual satisfaction may depend on the position of others as well as oneself.

REFERENCES

Acemoglu, D. (1998), 'Why do new technologies complement skills? Directed technical change and wage inequality,' *Quarterly Journal of Economics*, 113, 1055–89.

Amable, B., J.B. Chatelain and O. De Bandt (1997) 'Stability and efficiency of the banking sector and economic growth,' paper presented at the Royal Economic Society Meeting, University of Stoke on Trent, UK, March.

Amendola, M. and J.L. Gaffard (1988) *The Innovative Choice. An Economic Analysis of the Dynamics of Technology*, Oxford, Basil Blackwell.

Aoki, M. (1988) *Information, Incentives and Bargaining in the Japanese Economy*, Cambridge, Cambridge University Press.

Arthur, B.W. (1989) 'Competing technologies, increasing returns and locks-in by historical events,' *Economic Journal*, 99, 116–131.

Ashauer, D.A. (1989) 'Is public expenditure productive?' *Journal of Monetary Economics*, 23, 177–200.

Ashauer, D.A. (1994) 'Public capital, productivity, and macroeconomic performance: a literature review in infrastructure in the 21st century economy,' Federal Infrastructure Strategy Program, Washington DC.

Atkinson, A., L. Rainwater and T. Smeeding (1995) 'La distribution des revenus dans les pays de l'OCDE: documentation tirée du Luxembourg Income Study' in La distribution des revenus dans les pays de l'OCDE, *Etudes de Politique Sociale*, 18, 32–65.

Attewell, P. (1994) 'Information technology and the productivity paradox,' in D. Harris (ed.) *Organizational Linkages: Understanding the Productivity Paradox*, Washington, National Research Council, National Academy Press, 13–53.

Barro, R. (1990) 'Government spending in a simple model of endogenous growth,' *Journal of Political Economy*, 23, 103–25.

Bell, B.D. (1996) 'Skill biased technical change and wages: evidence from a longitudinal data set,' mimeo, Institute of Economics and Statistics, University of Oxford.

Berman, E., J. Bound and Z. Griliches (1994) 'Changes in the demand for skilled labor within US manufacturing: evidence from the annual survey of manufactures,' *Quarterly Journal of Economics*, 109, 367–97.

Berman, E., J. Bound and S. Machin (1995) 'Implications of skill biased technological change: international evidence,' paper presented at the Expert Workshop on Technology, Productivity and Employment: Macroeconomic and Sectoral Evidence', OECD, Paris, 19–20 June.

Berman, E., J. Bound and S. Machin (1998) 'Implications of skill-biased technological change: international evidence,' *The Quarterly Journal of Economics*.

Berndt, E.R. and B. Hanson (1992) 'Measuring the contribution of public infrastructure capital in Sweden,' *Scandinavian Journal of Economics*, Supplement, 94, S151–72.

Boskin, M. (ed.) (1966) *Towards a More Accurate Measure of the Cost of Living*, Final Report to the Senate Finance Committee, December.

Boulier, D. (1994) 'L'accès aux soins' in P. Musso (ed.), *Communiquer Demain*, Paris, Datar/Editions de l'Aube.

Card, D., F. Kramarz and T. Lemieux (1995) 'Changes in the relative structure of wages and employment: a comparison of the US, Canada and France,' Working Paper, Princeton University.

Cotis, J.P., J.M. Germain and A. Quinet (1995) 'Progrès technique, commerce international et travail peu qualifié,' mimeo, Direction de la Prévision, Paris.

David, P. (1991) *Computer and Dynamo: The Modern Productivity Paradox in a Not Too Distant Mirror*, Paris, OECD.

De Long, B. and L. Summers (1991) 'Equipment investment and economic growth,' *Quarterly Journal of Economics*, 106.

Denny, M. and M. Fuss (1983) 'The effects of factor prices and technological change on the occupational demand for labour: evidence from Canadian telecommunications,' *Journal of Human Resources*, 18, 161–76.

Di Nardo, J.E. and J.S. Pischke (1997) 'The returns to computer use revisited: have pencils changed the wage structure too?' *The Quarterly Journal of Economics*, 112, 291–303.

Dosi, G., C. Freeman, R. Nelson, G. Silverberg and L. Soete (eds) (1988) *Technical Change and Economic Theory*, London, Pinter Publishers.

Dymski, G. and J. Veitch (1993) 'Race and the financial dynamics of urban growth: LA as Fay Wray,' Working Paper 92–21, Dept. of Economics, University of California, Riverside.

Entorf, H. and F. Kramarz (1997) 'Does unmeasured ability explain the higher wages of new technology workers?' *European Economic Review*, 41, 1489–1510.

Entorf, H. and F. Kramarz (1998) 'The impact of new technologies on wages: lessons from matching panels of firms and individuals,' *Economics of Innovation and New Technology*, 5, 165–97.

Entorf, H., M. Gollac and F. Kramarz (1996) 'New technologies, wages and worker selection,' *Journal of Labour Economics*.

Fenwick, D. (1997) 'Does the UK retail prices index exaggerate inflation?' mimeo., Congrès AFSE, Paris.

Fischer, F.M. and Z. Griliches (1995) 'Aggregate price indices, new goods and generics,' *Quarterly Journal of Economics*, 110, 229–44.

Forsé, M. (1998) 'Diminution de la conscience de classe,' in L. Dirn (ed.) *La société française en tendances 1975–1995*, Paris, coll. Sociologie d'aujourd'hui, PUF.

Freeman, C. and L. Soete (1987) 'Information, technology and change in techno-economic paradigm,' in C. Freeman and L. Soete (eds) *op. cit.*, 49–69.

Freeman, C. and L. Soete (eds) (1987) *Technical Change and Full Employment*, New York, Basil Blackwell.

Freeman, C. and L. Soete (1994) *Work for All or Mass Unemployment*, London, Pinter Publishers.

Freeman, R. and L. Katz (1993) 'Rising wage inequality: the United States vs other advanced countries,' in R. Freeman (ed.) *Working Under Different Rules*, New York, Russell Sage Foundation, 29–62.

Galbraith, J.K. (1958) *The Affluent Society*, Boston, Houghton Mifflin.

Gibbons, M. et al. (1994) *The New Production of Knowledge*, Sage, London.

Gollac, M. (1996) 'Le capital est dans le réseau: la cooperation dans l'usage de l'informatique,' *Travail et Emploi*, 68, 39–60.

Goodman, P., J. Lerch and T. Mukhopakhyay (1994) 'Individual and organizational productivity: linkages and processes,' in D. Harris (ed.) *Organizational Linkages: Understanding the Productivity Paradox*, Washington, National Research Council, National Academy Press, 54–80.

Gordon, R. (1990) 'The measurement of durable goods prices,' *NBER Studies in Income and Wealth*, Chicago, University of Chicago Press.

Gottschalk, P. (1993) 'Changes in inequality of family income in seven industrialized countries,' *American Economic Review*, 83, 132–42.

Goux, D. and E. Maurin (1995) 'Les transformations de la demande de travail en

France. Une étude sur la période 1970–1993,' Document de travail INSEE. Translated as 'Changes in the demand for labour in France: a study for the period 1970–93,' paper presented at the Expert Workshop on Technology, Productivity and Employment: Macroeconomic and Sectoral Evidence', OECD, Paris, 19–20 June.

Granovetter, M. (1995) 'Economic action and social structure: the problem of embeddedness,' *American Journal of Sociology*, 91, 481–510.

Griliches, Z. (1969) 'Capital-skill complementary,' *Review of Economics and Statistics*, 51, 465–468.

Griliches, Z. (1994) 'Productivity, R&D, and the data constraint,' *American Economic Review* 84, 1–23.

Group of Prominent Persons (1994) 'Europe and the Global Information Society: Recommendations to the European Council,' Industrial Group of Prominent Persons, Brussels, European Community.

Harris, D. (1994) *Organizational Linkages: Understanding the Productivity Paradox*, Washington, National Research Council, National Academy Press.

Hausman, J. (1994) 'Valuation of new goods under perfect and imperfect competition,' NBER Working Paper no. 4970, December.

High Level Expert Group (1996) *Building the European Information Society for Us All*, Report by the High Level Expert Group for the European Commission, January.

Howell, D. and E. Wolff (1992) 'Technical change and the demand for skills by US industries,' *Cambridge Journal of Economics*, 16, 128–46.

Kaldor, N. (1972) 'The irrelevance of equilibrium economics,' *Economic Journal*, 82, 1237–55.

Kremer, M. and E. Maskin (1996) 'Wage inequality and segregation by skill,' NBER Working Paper no. 5718.

Krueger, A. (1993) 'How computers have changed the wage structure: evidence from micro data 1984–1989,' *Quarterly Journal of Economics*, 108, 33–60.

Landauer, T.K. (1995) *The Trouble with Computers: Usefulness, Usability and Productivity*, Cambridge, MA, The MIT Press.

Lequillier, F. (1997) 'Does the French consumer price index overstate inflation?' Working paper no. G9714, Direction des Etudes et Synthèses Economiques, INSEE, Paris.

Lucas, R. (1988) 'On the mechanics of economic development,' *Journal of Monetary Economics*, 22, 3–42.

Lundvall, B.A. (1988) 'Innovation as an interactive process: from user-producer interaction to the national system of innovation,' in G. Dosi et al., *op. cit.*, 3–42.

Machin, S. (1996) 'Changes in the relative demand for skill in the UK,' in A. Booth and D. Snower (eds) *Acquiring Skills*, Cambridge, Cambridge University Press, 127–46.

Machin, S. and J. Van Reenen (1998) 'Technology and changes in skill structure: evidence from seven OECD countries,' *Quarterly Journal of Economics*, 113, 1215–44.

Mishel, L., J. Bernstein and J. Schmitt (1997) *The State of Working America 1996–1997*, Washington, Economic Policy Institute.

Morrison, C.J. and A.E. Schwartz (1996) 'State infrastructure and productive performance,' *American Economic Review*, 86, 1095–111.

Moulton, B. and K. Moses (1997) 'Addressing the quality change issue in the consumer price index,' *Brookings Papers on Economic Activity*, 1.

Munell, A. (1992) 'Infrastructure investment and economic growth,' *Journal of Economic Perspectives*, 6, 189–98.

Myrdal, G. (1957) *Economic Theory and Underdeveloped Regions*, London, Duckworth.

Nakamura, L. (1995) 'Is US performance really that bad?' Working paper, Federal Reserve Bank of Philadelphia, October.
Nelson, R. and S. Winter (1982) *An Evolutionary Theory of Economic Change*, Cambridge, MA, Harvard University Press.
Nickel, S. (1996) 'Unemployment and wages in Europe and North America,' mimeo, Institute of Economics and Statistics, University of Oxford.
OECD (1994) *The OECD Jobs Study: Evidence and Explanations; Part 1: Labour Market Trends and Underlying Forces of Change*, Paris, OECD.
OECD (1996a) *Technology, Productivity and Job Creation, vol. 2*, Paris, OECD.
OECD (1996b) *Technology and Industrial Performance*, Paris, OECD.
OECD (1998) *Science, Technology and Industry Outlook*, Paris, OECD.
Oliner, S. and D. Sichel (1994) 'Computers and output growth revisited: how big is the puzzle?' *Brookings Papers on Economic Activity*, 2, 273–317.
Packard, V. (1957) *The Hidden Persuaders*, London, Longman.
Petit, P. and L. Soete (1996) 'Technical change and employment growth in services: analytical and policy challenges,' paper presented at the conference on Technology, Employment and Labour Markets, Athens University of Economics and Business, 16–18 May.
Piore, M. (1988) 'Corporate reform in American manufacturing and the challenge to economic theory,' MIT Working Paper no. 533.
Pratt, J., A. Leyshon and N. Thrift (1996) 'Financial exclusion in the 1990s: the changing geography of UK retail financial services,' Working Paper no. 34, Department of Geography, University of Bristol.
Reinsdorf, M. (1993) 'The effect of outlet price differentials on the U.S. consumer price index,' in M.F. Foss et al. (eds) *Price Measurements and their Uses: NBER Studies in Income and Wealth*, no. 57, Chicago, University of Chicago, 227–54.
Röller, L. and L. Waverman (1996) 'Les répercussions de l'infrastructure des télécommunications sur le développement économique,' in P. Howit (ed.) (1996), 425–45.
Romer, P. (1986) 'Increasing returns and long-run growth,' *Journal of Political Economy*, 94, 1002–37.
Romer, P. (1990) 'Endogenous technical change,' *Journal of Political Economy*, 98, 71–102.
Schor, J. (1999) *The Overspent American: Upscaling, Downshifting and the New Consumer*, New York, Harper Collins.
Sharpe, A. and M. Zyblock (1997) 'Macroeconomic performance and income distribution in Canada,' paper presented at the meetings of the American Economics and Finance Association, New Orleans, Louisiana, January.
Sichel, D. (1997) *The Computer Revolution: An Economic Perspective*, Washington, Brookings Institution Press.
Solow, R. (1957) 'Technical change and the aggregate production function,' *Review of Economics and Statistics*, 39, 312–20.
Storper, M. (1999) 'Lived effects of the contemporary economy: globalization, inequality, and consumer society,' *Public Culture*, forthcoming.
Trajtenberg, M. (1990) *Economic Analysis of Product Innovation: The Case of CT Scanners*, Cambridge, MA, Harvard University Press.
Wolff, E. (1995) 'Technology and the demand for skills,' paper presented at the Expert Workshop on Technology, Productivity and Employment: Macroeconomic and Sectoral Evidence,' OECD, Paris, 19–20 June.
Young, A. (1928) 'Increasing returns and technical progress,' *Economic Journal*, 38, 527–42.

Table 15.2 Productivity growth by sector for the USA, Canada, Japan, Germany and France, 1960–73 (period 1)) and 1984–93 (period (2))

		USA			Canada			Japan			Germany			France		
		w	Z	P	w	Z	P	w	Z	P	w	Z	P	w	Z	P
Agriculture	(1)	3.1	2.4	–0.1	3.1	0.2	–0.1	3.1	1.7	–0.1	2.7	7.0	0.0	7.8	8.4	0.1
	(2)	1.9	3.6	0.0	3.3	0.7	0.0	3.2	0.7	–0.1	2.0	1.8	0.0	4.1	2.0	0.0
Mining	(1)	5.0	3.5	0.0	5.0	13.1	0.0	5.0	11.2	0.0	4.0	3.3	–0.1	2.9	–0.6	–0.1
	(2)	3.3	5.8	0.0	6.3	4.1	0.1	0.3	4.0	0.0	0.9	1.4	0.0	0.9	6.3	0.0
Manufacturing	(1)	19.9	3.3	0.5	19.9	5.0	0.5	19.9	7.3	0.5	33.3	4.5	1.3	20.3	4.7	1.0
	(2)	19.6	3.2	0.2	18.8	2.2	0.0	27.9	2.9	0.6	32.2	0.9	–0.1	23.6	2.4	0.0
Utilities	(1)	2.8	4.7	0.1	2.8	5.9	0.1	2.8	0.8	0.1	1.6	5.5	0.1	1.2	8.9	0.1
	(2)	3.1	2.7	0.1	3.3	0.0	0.0	3.0	3.6	0.1	2.8	2.5	0.0	2.5	3.7	0.1
Construction	(1)	8.5	–2.4	–0.2	8.5	–1.1	–0.2	8.5	1.3	–0.2	8.6	2.5	0.2	7.8	2.8	0.1
	(2)	4.1	0.2	0.0	5.9	–1.0	0.0	7.8	2.2	0.2	5.8	0.6	0.0	5.6	1.9	0.0
Distribution	(1)	13.2	1.7	0.3	13.2	2.7	0.3	13.2	2.7	0.3	11.5	2.3	0.3	n.a.	n.a.	n.a.
	(2)	16.5	1.2	0.2	13.1	1.2	0.2	14.3	1.2	0.2	10.3	1.3	0.2	15.3	0.7	0.1
Transport and	(1)	4.8	3.7	0.1	4.8	3.1	0.1	4.8	1.1	0.1	5.0	4.0	0.2	n.a.	n.a.	n.a.
Communication	(2)	6.3	2.5	0.1	7.0	2.7	0.1	6.3	1.7	0.1	5.8	3.1	0.2	6.3	4.2	0.3
Financial and	(1)	17.2	0.1	0.4	17.2	2.8	0.4	17.2	7.8	0.4	9.3	7.8	0.4	13.3	1.8	0.7
Business Services	(2)	23.1	–1.0	0.2	18.0	0.8	0.4	14.6	1.8	0.3	12.9	1.8	0.3	18.8	–0.5	0.5
Social Services	(1)	8.2	1.1	0.1	8.2	–4.8	0.1	8.2	1.2	0.1	9.8	1.2	0.3	n.a.	n.a.	n.a.
	(2)	8.9	–0.9	0.1	5.4	1.3	0.1	13.5	1.2	0.2	13.0	2.1	0.7	5.1	1.1	0.2
Total Industry	(1)	85.5	1.7	1.4	85.5	3.0	1.4	85.5	4.8	1.4	85.9	3.7	2.9	77.6	4.3	3.3
	(2)	88.2	1.0	0.9	81.2	1.3	0.9	90.0	1.5	1.5	85.8	1.7	1.4	82.2	1.9	1.2
Total all sectors	(1)	100.0	1.5	1.5	100.0	2.2	2.2	100.0	4.4	4.4	100.0	3.3	3.3	100.0	3.6	3.6
	(2)	100.0	0.9	0.9	100.0	0.9	0.9	100.0	1.5	1.5	100.0	1.5	1.5	100.0	1.4	1.4

Notes: w denotes share in value added, Z is labour productivity growth (annual percentage rate) and P denotes contribution to total productivity growth.
Source: OECD ISDB.

Index